Discovering Music

DISCOVERING

MUSIC Where to
Start on Records and Tapes,
The Great Composers and
Their Works, Today's Major
Recording Artists.

BY ROY HEMMING

FOUR WINDS PRESS · NEW YORK

LIBRARY OF CONGRESS CATALOGING IN PUBLICATION DATA

Hemming, Roy.
  Discovering music.

  1. Phonorecord collecting. 2. Phonorecords—Reviews.
3. Music—Discography. 4. Music—Biobibliography.
I. Title.

ML111.5.H44   789.9′131   72–87086

  Published by Four Winds Press
A Division of Scholastic Magazines, Inc. New York, N.Y.
Copyright © 1974 by Roy Hemming
All rights reserved
Printed in the United States of America
Library of Congress Catalogue Card Number: 72–87086

Designed by Sophie Adler

1 2 3 4 5 78 77 76 75 74

This book is dedicated to the memory of my father,
who, to my knowledge, attended only one concert
in his life, but who encouraged me
in thousands of ways to discover things he never knew.

PHOTO CREDITS

ACKNOWLEDGMENTS

The author wishes to thank the following persons who assisted in arranging the interviews for Section One of this book: Christie Barter, Lloyd Gelassen, Herb Helman, Robert Holton, David Kleger, David Levenson, Joe McKaughan, M. Scott Mampe, Audrey Michaels, Frank Milburn, Carlos Moseley, Sim Myers, Cynthia Robbins, Marvin Schofer, Wayne Shilkret, Mary H. Smith, Edgar Vincent, and Elizabeth Winston.

Thanks also to the following persons for providing various kinds of assistance with other sections of the book, including the verification of record release dates and miscellaneous data: Robert Altshuler, Alison Ames, Jody Breslau, Gustl Breuer, Dick Bungay, Sedgwick Clark, B. Claudian, John Coveney, Dinah Daniels, Brad Engel, Johanna Fiedler, Don Foster, Lloyd Gelassen, Louis Hood, John Hurd, Alfred Kaine, Leonard Meyers, M. Scott Mampe, Pali Meller-Marcovicz, Sim Myers, Dona Murphy, Marilyn Posnick, Earl Price, Marvin Schofer, Steve Simon, Sheldon Soffer, George Sponhaltz, Teresa Sterne, Peter Tracton, Donna Walcovy, and Herbert Weissenstein.

Special appreciation goes to Josephine Lovaglio and Rose Guardino for their assistance in coordinating material originally prepared for use in Scholastic Magazines, and for transcribing most of the interview tapes. And to Margaret Hauser and Eric Berger, special gratitude for providing my first opportunities to write about records for national publications.

Last, but far from least, special thanks to Judith Whipple and Linda Zuckerman for their counsel in shaping the various sections of the final manuscript.

Contents

x • *Contents*

Contents • xiii

Introduction

This book is *not* written for musicians or music students. It is written in simple, nontechnical language for general listeners who like good music and who want a guide to some of the best works now on records and tapes.

Never before has the opportunity for enjoying good music been available to so many. The growth of FM stations has been one factor. The use of classical music in film scores has been another. But most significant has been the development of high-fidelity records, cassettes, and cartridges. The record catalogs today are filled with hundreds of thousands of listings—offering a tremendous feast to anyone who wants to indulge. But *where* does the average listener begin?

This book is designed as a guide for those who want to get started building their own record collections, according to their own tastes.

It is divided into three basic sections:

First, a section in which fifty prominent musicians tell what works they would advise a newcomer to start with—and why. The musicians were chosen for interview by the author to represent a wide variety of musical experience (conductors, instrumentalists, singers, teachers).

Second, a section on composers from the Baroque period to today's avant-garde, with capsule reviews of their major works as available on long-playing stereo and quadrasonic records, tape cassettes, and tape cartridges.

Third, a "who's who" section providing basic background information on the leading performers whose work is available on records and tapes today.

"Nothing is, in a way, more exciting than a first discovery in music through listening."

—ALEXIS WEISSENBERG

PART ONE

Where to Start

Where to Start

> If a high school or college student should come up to you and say,
> "I don't know very much about classical (or serious) music, but I'd like to learn more, and I've got enough money to go out and buy five or six recordings—"
> Which would you recommend? What composers? What specific works? And why?

I asked this question of fifty musicians in a series of interviews. The musicians, all presently active as performers and/or teachers, represent a cross section of types, background, age, and experience.

• *VLADIMIR ASHKENAZY*

Russian pianist, now living in London and Reykjavik.

V.A.   I would begin with either the Fifth or Seventh Symphony of Beethoven, as conducted by Furtwängler. Then I would suggest a record with some Mozart symphonies as conducted by Barenboim. Actually, I think I should put these two records near the end of the list, and suggest starting with program music—something like Mussorgsky's *Pictures at an Exhibition*. The orchestral version would be better for a beginner, although I prefer the piano version myself.

R.H.   There's a recording that has your piano version on one side and the orchestral version, played by Zubin Mehta and the Los Angeles Philharmonic, on the other.

V.A.   Yes, but that would be advertising my own record and I cannot do that. I feel it would be better to find a version that has something different on the other side—something also programmatic. Now, we need something on the Romantic side: A record of Wagner overtures would be a good one, but an orchestral record, *not* a vocal one. The overtures to *Lohengrin* or *Meistersinger*, or *Siegfried's Rhine Journey*, things like that. There are some very beautiful Toscanini recordings of these works. And, for the last choice, I would say Tchaikovsky's Fourth Symphony. There again, I would recommend Furtwängler conducting, if it is available in this country. I would hesitate to recommend any solo instrumental or chamber pieces, because they can be difficult for a beginner.

R.H.   And opera?

3

David Bean

1

Vladimir Ashkenazy

6

John Browning

2

Daniel Barenboim

4

Karl Böhm

7

Mark Bucci

5

Pierre Boulez

V.A.   No. I'm afraid that opera could lead a person down the wrong path. If one ever expects to achieve a reasonable appreciation of classical music, I don't think one should start with opera—except, maybe, for Mozart's operas. But the operas of Wagner or some of the Russians can be a little too complicated to start with.

R.H.   You're a pianist, yet you haven't mentioned any piano concertos or a solo piano record.

V.A.   I wouldn't recommend a solo piano record—not to start with. But a piano concerto, certainly: the "Emperor" by Beethoven. His First and Second Piano Concertos are beautiful, but if I had to choose only one, I would choose the Fifth, the "Emperor." It's such a mature work. Therefore, I think it's along the right path. For me, Beethoven is like Shakespeare. There is no word to describe his greatness. He's just great! At the same time, in most cases, he is easily accessible, easily understood. Perhaps this is part of his greatness.

R.H.   You didn't indicate a specific Mozart symphony. Can you?

V.A.   The G minor (No. 40) would be one of them. I think that the minor key and Mozart are very special. There are so few great pieces composed in minor—they always have special meaning. At the same time, Mozart's G minor Symphony is not complicated for a beginner, although he might not understand everything. Another symphony, if a coupling permits it, would be Mozart's Symphony in A major (No. 29).

• DANIEL BARENBOIM

Argentine-born Israeli pianist and conductor.

D.B.   Before answering the question directly, I would like to stress that it really isn't necessary to know a great deal about music and the way it's constructed in order to appreciate it. What makes music so universal, and gives it so powerful an impact, is that it is one of the most direct forms of human expression. It addresses itself to different people in different ways. Music can be appreciated intellectually or it can be appreciated emotionally, as when the listener gets carried away by the climaxes of a big symphony. Or perhaps it just grows on you.
This is the marvelous thing about music. But I feel a lot of people avoid concerts or classical records because they hear musicians talking about "the dominant chord" or something else that sounds complicated, and they become frightened. It's a pity, because we *need* people to appreciate music in different ways, so that music can have its full impact. Once you understand that, the choice of the records you buy or the music you listen to in the beginning is relatively unimportant. In other words, it doesn't make much difference whether your first record is a Mozart symphony, a Beethoven string quartet, a Tchaikovsky concerto, or something by Stravinsky or Schoenberg.

But to answer your question directly, I would say the best way to start is with pieces that have become pillars of our musical culture—by musicians such as Mozart, Bach, Beethoven, Brahms.

R.H.   Would you recommend any specific works by these composers?

D.B.   No. So much depends on the individual listener.

R.H.   Do you feel young people today relate more easily with a particular *type* of classical music than people of older generations do?

D.B.   Obviously young people today grow up hearing much more music than they would have one or two generations ago. Still, the repertory that's regularly played can practically be counted on your fingers—plus perhaps some of your toes. And you can count almost on one hand the number of works that have been written in the last fifty years that have become accepted classics. Yet, the number of concerts given by orchestras is about five thousand per cent greater than it used to be! Therefore, young people today are able to *hear* more music—and a lot of it through recordings, of course.

R.H.   Because of the wide popularity of rock, do you feel that young people today respond more immediately to music with a strong rhythmic drive?

D.B.   I don't know. Yet I must admit that basically rhythmic works, modern works, generally do receive better performances now than older works do. There's a great tendency to achieve what's called faithfulness to the text, purity in music, and all that with the classics. It sounds very right, very moral. Yet although we often hear a classical work played correctly and very precisely, a lot of musicians *do* feel they give more of themselves, or that they let go more in Bartók or Stravinsky—whereas they wouldn't dare do that in Beethoven or Brahms.
The way we play a piece of music, or react to it, reflects our inner life—what we really are. I believe very strongly that every great work of art has two faces. First, it faces toward its own time—and that's something we cannot always really grasp. For example, the shock of a work like Stravinsky's *Rite of Spring* or of certain works of Beethoven when they were played in their own time. Then there's the other face—its more universal value, its contribution not only to musical culture but to civilization itself. I think that the great works of music, like the other arts, are really contributions to our civilization. This is what makes us human beings, not just organisms.

• *DAVID BEAN*

American pianist. Artist-in-residence at Miami University at Oxford, Ohio.

D.B.   Within limits, I would suggest starting with the best-selling pieces. In other words, go through the Schwann catalog [which lists currently available recordings] and pick out five or six pieces that have the longest list of recordings—because chances are they'll be the most accessible pieces, the pieces that people love the most, and like to hear the most.

R.H.   Are you saying that the most frequently played works are the best?

D.B.   Not at all. But there must be something in them that makes them accessible. A Tchaikovsky symphony comes out ahead in popular appeal for one reason or another—at least for the average listener, and that's what we're talking about, isn't it? Now, if you start out with a more esoteric piece, you have nowhere to go as a follow-up—and you may risk being turned off altogether. The "Appassionata" Sonata of Beethoven, for example, is apparently much easier for the general public than his "Hammerklavier" Sonata. And this is true for musicians, too. Therefore, if I were going to give someone a choice of which one to listen to first, I'd begin with the "Appassionata." He can stimulate his own interests further after he feels he comes to understand the more accessible pieces.

R.H.   Any other works you would single out?

D.B.   Well, I can remember the things that knocked me out when I was in my teens. Tchaikovsky's *Romeo and Juliet* was one. I'd already heard a lot of music by that time, but I really *loved* that. I also remember an old recording of Emanuel Feuermann and the Philadelphia Orchestra of Bloch's *Schelomo* (Solomon) which I thought was out of this world. It had a tremendous amount of fire and brimstone. Then I remember first hearing the Budapest Quartet playing the Debussy String Quartet. That was a real shock—that four people could get that much sound out of a string quartet. I'm not sure that that's the same reaction a person who's not heard much music would have, because I had been going to chamber music concerts in Washington since I was six or seven. But it was those kinds of pieces that knocked *me* out. Still do.

● *KARL BÖHM*

Austrian conductor. Former music director of the Vienna State Opera.

K.B.   Certainly a symphony by Beethoven. And then a symphony by Mozart. Those, I think, would be the best to start.

R.H.   Which specific Beethoven symphony?

K.B.   I would say either the First or the Second. The early ones.

R.H.   And of Mozart?

K.B.   Any of them. They are all the same for me—*all* great.

R.H.   I know you've recorded all of them, or soon will complete doing so. But which one would you feel is the best to start someone with?

K.B. It's so very difficult to say. Why not the First Symphony? It's very interesting. He wrote it when he was only about eight years old in London, and already it's completely Mozartian.

R.H. Did he ever revise it later when he was older?

K.B. No, no. It is the original. This man was a genius from the very beginning. For me he is the *only* genius in all music.

R.H. And after Mozart and Beethoven?

K.B. I would recommend Schubert, either his "Unfinished" (Eighth) Symphony or his Fifth Symphony. Then Schumann, either his First or Fourth Symphony.

R.H. For a long time you've been identified with the music of Richard Strauss. Which Strauss piece would you start someone with?

K.B. Either *Don Juan* or *Till Eulenspiegel.*

R.H. And what about an opera?

K.B. Certainly something by Puccini. He is so popular and sweet and easy to like. And certainly an opera by Mozart, perhaps *The Marriage of Figaro* or *Don Giovanni.* In Mozart operas, *everything* is in the music. He was funny, he was tragic, he was romantic, but never sentimental.

R.H. Whom do you consider the most significant composers to have come up since World War II?

K.B. I would say Orff, Egk, and Henze. And Alban Berg—even though he was dead before the war, his music has come to be appreciated since then. Berg's *Wozzeck* is such a great work. I like some of Henze's operas: *König Hirsch,** for instance, is very good. Henze has colors in his music and he has inspiration. He writes with his heart. If a composer has no inspiration from his heart, his construction is like a bare house.

R.H. What about contemporary American composers? Do any impress you specially?

K.B. Samuel Barber. And for the stage, Menotti.

• *PIERRE BOULEZ*

French composer and conductor. Music director of the New York Philharmonic Orchestra and principal conductor of the BBC Symphony in London.

P.B. I cannot tell you exactly what works, because there are so many works which are very important. But I could recommend, say, a succession of works which would show someone the evolution of music. That way he or she could compare, for

---

* Not recorded as of 1974.

example, some twentieth-century work with, let's say, a sixteenth-century work. I would not concentrate on one period of music. Ideally I would try to pick something that's important in each period. I would begin, perhaps, with the Monteverdi *Vespers*. And I would finish with Berg's *Wozzeck* or something like that. In the middle I would include something by Beethoven. And a Mozart opera—because Mozart is at his best, for me, in the theatre.

R.H. A whole Mozart opera, or just highlights?

P.B. No, the whole works. The listener can stop when he wants to, if he feels he's got too much.

R.H. Any specific Mozart opera?

P.B. I would choose *Don Giovanni*, which I find the best document of Mozart himself.

• JOHN BROWNING

American pianist.

J.B. I would say a Tchaikovsky symphony to start with—the Fifth. Then I might work backward and recommend something by Chopin. Then a Brahms symphony, the Second. Then I'd say, surprisingly enough, the Bach B minor Mass. Big things first. Then maybe an early Beethoven quartet, and a Mozart piano concerto.

R.H. Why these specific works?

J.B. I think the Tchaikovsky symphonies are the most available and the most obvious for people who are not well educated in music. German music takes a little longer.

R.H. Which particular Chopin work or works?

J.B. Almost any solo work.

R.H. Any contemporary composers?

J.B. Yes, Bartók. I definitely think today's younger generation would get something out of Bartók's *Music for Strings, Percussion and Celesta*, or his *Concerto for Orchestra*. It's a psychedelic generation, and Bartók in a way is psychedelic.

R.H. Why did you say "surprisingly enough" for the Bach B minor Mass?

J.B. When I was in the Army, we were all in the barracks one day, cleaning weapons and getting ready for inspection. Usually everybody listened only to Elvis Presley on the radio, but suddenly that day the B minor Mass came on. Everybody in the barracks was as quiet as a mouse. And one guy, who had obviously never listened to anything but Elvis Presley in his life, came up to me and said, "You know, that's not bad. I like that."

R.H.   You believe, then, that it's an accessible work for anyone.

J.B.   Yes, and it's also religious. Most Americans are used to going to church and hearing a little bit of something like that. I think it has a great effect.

• MARK BUCCI

American composer.

M.B.   If this newcomer is in his teens or early 20's, I would say the Beatles and then *Switched-On Bach*.

R.H.   Why do you think young people should start out this way?

M.B.   Because there is a subtle connection between classical music and the stuff that's going on today with some of the pop groups. They share a very far-out quality, and it is quite possible for young people to relate to it. Also, it isn't too obviously structured.
   For the third selection, I would choose Bartók's *Music for Strings, Percussion, and Celesta*, because it is one of the most classically structured pieces in the world, and yet it has fantastic vitality. Then, I think Berg should be included, because he's really one of the greats. He has a prismatically distorted view of the Establishment that is apparent in *Wozzeck*, and it's also strongly anti-war. Now, this next one may seem a bit strange, but it just happens to be a favorite of mine: William Walton's *Violin Concerto*. It probably has no business being on this list, but I think everyone should hear a melodic work too.

R.H.   Why this one for a melodic work?

M.B.   Just because I like it, and it isn't played enough. I have the old Heifetz recording. It's a spotty work, but it has some really marvelous stuff in it.
   Then I'd suggest an opera, but I would qualify it by saying the listener should follow the libretto word for word.

R.H.   Should someone starting out begin with excerpts from an opera or should he try an *entire* opera?

M.B.   The entire opera, with the libretto. Arias by themselves have little meaning. I was about to suggest starting with Puccini's *Madame Butterfly*—but actually, for the philosophical needs of a young person today, his *Turandot* might be better. It's a great philosophical work, really very symbolic. *Turandot* is a little bit like the film *2001: A Space Odyssey*—about a big breakthrough and change in someone's whole being.

R.H.   How do you, as a composer, feel about the parts of *Turandot* that were completed by Alfano after Puccini's death?

M.B.   I think Alfano did a marvelous job working from Puccini's sketches. "*You* just try and do that" is what I'd like to tell all those people who keep criticizing his work.

R.H.   You mentioned *Switched-On Bach*. Apparently you, as a composer, don't feel as some critics do that a composer's original version shouldn't be tampered with.

M.B.   I think all those people wrote music to be played. And all the Moog does, in my opinion, is sound like a more powerful organ. The important thing is that it's a best seller and that kids hear it. They become very aware of linear writing—and apparently love it. Also, we mustn't forget the Swingle Singers and their albums. I think young people have become tremendously aware of this kind of music without having to be "taught" how to like it.

R.H.   You've mentioned Bach, but you've left out two other composers that are generally regarded as musical cornerstones: Beethoven and Mozart.

M.B.   I know. As I was speaking, I thought to myself that I should include some Mozart and Beethoven. But if you're trying to reach someone with no experience in classical music—well, we're not experiencing World War II anymore with that Beethoven Fifth Symphony "logo."

R.H.   In other words, you reject the idea that the way to learn about music is to progress chronologically, the way music itself developed.

M.B.   Not necessarily. It's just that I believe that the way to get non-musicians interested in music is through an emotional approach, not an intellectual one.

● *VAN CLIBURN*

American pianist.

V.C.   I believe a beginner can get a great deal of pleasure, and learn a lot about musical form and different rhythmic patterns, from the Sixth Symphony of Tchaikovsky. It has a great deal of melody. It has rhythmic variation. And it has something that, when you get through listening to it, you'll want desperately to hear again. To me, that is the first thing to learn about classical music: That when something is classic, it is enduring; it stands endless rehearing. There is no such thing as being bored with a great piece of music.
   Now, we're talking about recordings as a springboard—to get people into the habit of *listening* to music. So I would say let's go to another man who was also born on May 7th: Brahms. And let's make up a special composite Brahms symphony. I'd recommend the last movement of his First Symphony, the first two movements of his Fourth Symphony, and the third movement of his Third Symphony.

R.H.   Leaving out the Second Symphony altogether?

V.C. I adore the Second Symphony, but it is harder for a newcomer. I think it can come later.

R.H. You don't feel it's necessary to listen to an entire symphony as an entity?

V.C. No, because you cannot deny that certain parts of great symphonies or concertos are jewels in themselves. The third movement of Brahms' Third Symphony is a jewel standing alone in the sunset. While *all* of the Brahms First Symphony, *all* of the Third Symphony, and *all* of the Fourth Symphony are tremendously thrilling to listen to, I'd suggest taking just highlights for a moment. Then, if he or she liked that, I'd say listen to the rest. You can always go back to listen to more.
Next, I would suggest the *Water Music* of Handel. It has a festive, almost modern quality which should appeal to young people.

R.H. How do you mean "modern"?

V.C. Because of the fanfares and brass sounds, which I think a lot of people associate with some modern music. And then, as a pianist I naturally think of music written for the piano—and Chopin. You can pick almost anything of his and get an idea of piano music, because he was such a master of writing for the piano.

R.H. But if you had to pick just one piece for a person to start with?

V.C. I would probably choose the Scherzo No. 2 in B-flat Minor. It embodies beauty, melodic content, varying moods, that sort of thing.
Next on my list would be the Fifth Symphony of Beethoven. And I certainly would not want to forget an opera—because I think the human voice, since it was the first instrument, can *never* be forgotten. Depending on the personality of the young person to whom I was speaking, I would suggest either *La Bohème* or *Turandot* by Puccini.

R.H. Would you recommend the entire opera, or just an album of highlights?

V.C. Some young people today certainly have the capacity, the interest, and the sustaining powers of concentration to be able to listen to *all* of it. But I would probably suggest listening at first to part of Act Two of *La Bohème*—if only because it is my own favorite portion—and then to *all* of Act Three. As far as form and composition go, *La Bohème* is one of the most nearly perfect of all operas. It has great freedom, yet within all of this freedom there is a distinct form. It has a wealth of melodic content. It has great characterization. It has a very good story too—very contemporary. You can relate to *every* character—it's so universal. It's not for any special group.

R.H. And *Turandot*?

V.C. I happen to adore *Turandot* very much. It's a magnificent work—and can be one of the most thrilling and memorable experiences to *see*. From the standpoint of melodic content, there again, it's very rich. I think one of the most beautiful scenes

8

Van Cliburn

11

Misha Dichter

13

Dean Dixon

9

Phyllis Curtin

12

Harry Ellis Dickson

14

Stanley Drucker

10

Colin Davis

15

Christoph Eschenbach

in the whole opera—one that's usually left out of highlights albums—is the beginning of Act Two, Scene One, with Ping, Pang, and Pong.

R.H.   Most of your answers have involved 19th-century works. Some other musicians I've interviewed have said they feel young people today relate more quickly to 20th-century music than to the music of the 18th and 19th centuries.

V.C.   I don't think that's entirely true. That applies to only a very small percentage. The 19th century was a focal point for music. Most of the music of the 18th century lacked the luster and the splendor that came to be realized in the 19th century. I think the 19th century was an apex of not only Classic beauty but of great statements in music.

• *PHYLLIS CURTIN*

American soprano of the Metropolitan Opera.

P.C.   I would say, first, that he or she ought to take some of that money and go to a few live concerts—if he or she lives where there's a good symphony orchestra. Live music still has the most excitement, I think. If he lives in Cleveland or anywhere near it, for example, he has a chance to hear the greatest symphony orchestra in the world. So why not spend half the money picking out several concerts and spend the rest on records? If he doesn't live anywhere near an opportunity like that, and has to rely altogether on records, maybe there's a college nearby with a live concert series. He should try, first of all, to involve himself in whatever is going on *live*. Because marvelous and divine as it is for us to have recorded music as a library and as a stimulus, it is nonetheless a mechanical art—and in some respects it's becoming more so all the time. In other words, it's getting to be the art of the engineer rather than the art of the musician. Therefore, I should like to recommend looking first for a source that is alive and breathing.

Then, as to records: If he's a young person who likes electric guitar or electronic pop, then he certainly ought to look into Varese, or Stockhausen, or Boulez—to become aware of the fact that there's a tremendous, wild, gorgeous electronic field in serious classical music, too.

R.H.   Do you think young people today relate more easily to that than to other kinds of music?

P.C.   Absolutely. I think it's a great mistake to say that everybody should go back and begin with Monteverdi. They should begin with what's relative and fascinating to them in their own time. And young people today are much more equipped to cope with music by Stockhausen, Henze, Boulez, or Varese than my generation is. At the same time, I think they ought to balance this with similar works from different periods—for example, the Bach *St. Matthew Passion* and the Benjamin Britten *War Requiem*. They both deal very powerfully with man and his relation to religion and his fellow man. This is an aspect of music we tend to forget about. Music is vital to man's behavior in life. A man like Benjamin Britten has written a very serious message—probably the strongest, most artistic anti-war message of the twentieth century. It is a glorious example of music and poetry on a terribly moving level. The *St. Matthew Passion* is not the same message, but it's a very human concern from another period of music. And it almost leads, musically, into the whole Romantic era. For Romantic music, oh, there's so much—Brahms, Berlioz, Strauss, and so on.

R.H.   How about opera?

P.C.   I think I'd start with *La Bohème* or *Carmen.*

R.H.   Do you believe in starting out with the whole opera or just a highlights album?

P.C.   I'm not a believer in highlights. If you just listen to highlights, you're never going to know what an opera is. An opera is living, honest-to-God, hot, breathing theatre—which is a point so many Americans forget. They want to listen only to arias, and they forget that opera is connected to real life. A work like *La Bohème,* particularly if a young person is interested in learning Italian, has all the basic Italian words for eating, going to a restaurant, making love—it's a very basic opera. There again, it's about people who are not unlike today's younger generation—people who are looking for something, young people beginning life and finding out about its beauties, its futilities, its terrible agonies. It's an opera for young people. And they should listen to the whole opera, not just excerpts—and *with* a libretto. They must know the words, not just listen to the pretty music.

• *COLIN DAVIS*

English conductor. Music director of the Royal Opera at Covent Garden, London.

C.D.   I'd start with Stravinsky's *Symphony in Three Movements,* Webern's *Six Pieces for Orchestra* (Op. 6), Bartók's *Music for Strings, Percussion and Celesta,* Beethoven's *Eroica* Symphony, Berlioz's *Symphonie Fantastique,* and probably the Monteverdi *Vespers.* Now then, if he finds he doesn't like any of that, then I'd say forget it!

R.H.   Since you started your list with three twentieth-century composers, do you feel that young people today respond better to contemporary music than people of your own generation did?

C.D.   That depends on their background. You see, if young people are not told anything, if they don't have standards imposed on them, they will respond to nearly anything—especially if it's good. I find kids today love the music of Stravinsky because it's so exciting, so energetic, so explosive. I think they do not take as naturally to Brahms. But anything that's got a kind of wildness or vitality about it—like Berlioz or Beethoven—I'm sure would appeal to them. It's because they've all got imagination. I haven't met a kid who hasn't.

• *MISHA DICHTER*

American pianist.

M.D.   My basis for selection would be: What works, from all periods, historically, still retain a meaning for our times—what works can continue to speak to us freshly about human experience? The works that I'd begin with, then, are Stravinsky's *Firebird* or *Rite of Spring*, Beethoven's Ninth Symphony, Mahler's *Songs of a Wayfarer*, Bartók's *Concerto for Orchestra* or his *Music for Strings, Percussion and Celesta*, and Bach's *St. Matthew Passion*.

R.H.   Since the first work on your list was by Stravinsky, do you believe in starting someone out with music of the twentieth century?

M.D.   I don't see why not. And if you do, one of the first works, I would say, should be *Rite of Spring*. It really ushers in the twentieth century, and it's certainly a basis for any further study of twentieth-century music.

R.H.   Do you feel young people today relate more to twentieth-century music?

M.D.   Judging from the remarks of young people who come backstage after my concerts, it seems that they usually single out the twentieth-century piece of the program, saying, "I particularly liked the Stravinsky this or the Bartók that." So I feel that they *do* relate more to the twentieth century.

R.H.   The second piece you mentioned was Beethoven's Ninth.

M.D.   That for me is the end-all. It never ceases to amaze me. I really think it's timeless. From beginning to end it's a remarkable piece. I would even say that the choral last movement really doesn't stand out in my mind as being, necessarily, the focal point of the piece. The Ninth, overall, is the culmination of all of Beethoven's work.

R.H.   And then Mahler's *Songs of a Wayfarer*—your reason for that?

M.D.   That's just a sentimental choice. It is one of my favorites. It's truly Romantic, embodying all the beauties of the nineteenth century.

R.H.   Then the two Bartók works?

M.D.   I tend to be closer to the *Music for Strings, Percussion, and Celesta*. The *Concerto for Orchestra* is a more superficial work, but still a fine one. Then I would say, if somebody really got into Bartók, to go on to his string quartets, because I think they're the best thing since Beethoven's quartets.

R.H.   You don't feel they're too difficult for somebody just starting out?

M.D.   I think the jagged rhythms and the interesting harmonies and, if nothing else, the virtuosity of the pieces would make any listener perk up. They're not the most accessible pieces in the world, but I don't think they're forbidding. I think they've got beautiful Hungarian folkloric elements.

R.H.   Your final selection was Bach's *St. Matthew Passion.*

M.D.   That's just so beautiful. Actually, it's silly just to try to pick out one Bach piece. But to me that one—with perhaps also the B minor Mass—well, there's nothing like them just for meditative, beautiful listening.

R.H.   Although you're a pianist, you've listed no solo piano piece, or even a piano concerto.

M.D.   I don't know if other pianists feel this way, but I find that when I listen to piano music—maybe it's the unfortunate result of playing the piano—but I become too aware of piano *playing.* So it's difficult for me to detach myself and listen to the music only. If the playing is really fantastic, then my first reaction is, "How is that done?" And if it's less than wonderful piano playing, then it's very difficult for me to listen. But I would say that I still regard very highly many old Schnabel recordings, even though they were not always the most perfect piano playing.

R.H.   But if somebody were to say to you, "I don't know very much about piano music, could you direct me to what you think would be a good piece to start with?" Would you have an answer?

M.D.   I would go to my favorite pieces and hope they would become that person's. I think Schumann's music is just an endless world of beauty, although most people might say that's getting pretty obscure for a start. But I believe Schumann's *Kreisleriana* or *Carnaval* are beautiful pieces. *Carnaval* may be a little more accessible to a new listener. I'd also suggest Mozart concerti.

R.H.   Would you specify one?

M.D.   Numbers 1 through 27! Also, for me, the greatest piano piece ever written is Brahms' First Piano Concerto, in D minor. I think anybody who would like the Beethoven Ninth Symphony would also love that—it's straight out of that realm. You know, it just occurred to me that I didn't mention Mozart operas. I think there's nothing greater than *Don Giovanni* or *The Marriage of Figaro.* Yes, those two would be among my "desert island" records.

R.H.   Would you start a young person with the complete opera or just the highlights?

M.D.   Highlights, mainly because of the sections where there are long spoken passages or recitatives that might sidetrack a newcomer or cause him to lose interest. With highlights, at least the principal themes can be learned—and loved. After that, he or she can look beyond the highlights and try the whole work.

• *HARRY ELLIS DICKSON*

> Associate conductor of the Boston Pops Orchestra, a violinist in the Boston Symphony Orchestra, a director of Youth Concerts at Symphony Hall (Boston).

H.E.D. The obvious one to start with, of course, is the Beethoven Fifth Symphony, probably the most popular piece of music of all the symphonic literature. Then I would choose something from the Classical period—Mozart or Haydn. Then, from the Baroque period, a recording of something by Bach, and perhaps Handel. Now the Romantic period: how can you *not* include Tchaikovsky? Then, coming up to the twentieth century: Stravinsky—perhaps his *Rite of Spring*, a turning point in music. Then Bartók. And if the person is an American, you should include Aaron Copland.

R.H. Can you suggest specific works by these composers?

H.E.D. For Mozart: the "Jupiter" Symphony. It is the symphony that has the greatest, the most marvelous form. There's a grandeur about the style that foretells what Beethoven is going to do. For Bach, I think the Fifth *Brandenburg Concerto* is a great one. For Tchaikovsky, the *Pathétique* Symphony (No. 6). For Bartók, the Concerto for Orchestra which, incidentally, was written for the Boston Symphony.
I played in its very first performance, under Serge Koussevitsky, in December, 1944, in Boston's Symphony Hall. There are a number of us in the orchestra who remember the rehearsals, with Bartók there in the balcony. This very meek, white-haired, frail, sickly man wouldn't let anything go by that he didn't approve of in the rehearsal. And he would scream every few minutes and make Koussevitsky rather embarrassed. But it was a great, wonderful occasion when we played that first performance. Today it's a classic.
Now, what should I suggest of Copland's? I remember the first performance of *Appalachian Spring*. But I think I'd choose his *Lincoln Portrait*, which embodies a great deal of both Copland and Americana—and it's a great example of what a composer can do with words. We've forgotten Schoenberg and his *Chamber Symphony* and the *Six Pieces for Orchestra* of Webern. And even the Berg Violin Concerto! These were the beginnings of the twelve-tone system.

R.H. From your own experience as a conductor of young people's concerts, have you found that young people respond more immediately to any specific type of music?

H.E.D. I don't believe that there's such a thing as special music for young people. I think that they're less likely to be shocked by things than their parents. I've played Webern for them and talked to them afterwards about it, and they don't seem to find it shocking at all. The only concession that I make to young people has to do with their span of attention. I don't think young people can sit and listen to a complicated piece for a long time. That's why they like Webern's *Six Pieces*—they're so short. They're not shocked by what *we* think of as strange harmonies, not at all! But they can *love* Tchaikovsky and Beethoven, too. I think young people today have a greater range of musical interests and tastes than adults do.

• *DEAN DIXON*

American conductor. Director of the Hessian State Radio Orchestra in Frankfurt, West Germany, and former director of the American Youth Orchestra, New York.

D.D. Based on my own early exposure and my philosophy of learning, I would suggest the Beethoven Fifth Symphony, the big G minor Symphony of Mozart (No. 40), the Haydn "Clock" Symphony (No. 101), the Brahms First Symphony, and the Mahler First Symphony. I feel they represent high points in these composers' outputs, and the listener can achieve a level of understanding of these composers from exposure to these particular works. Then, if he's conversant with these, he won't have much trouble spreading out to Brahms' Second, Third, or Fourth Symphonies, or to Beethoven's Sixth, Seventh, Eighth, or Ninth, and so on. He will have a feeling for the "dialect" of the language, even though he doesn't understand the language very well yet. It's something like having a feeling for the Cockney accent even though you don't understand the exact meaning of each word.

R.H. In other words, you believe these works represent the most significant peaks in music, rather than that they are works a newcomer will relate to quickly.

D.D. Yes. Now, there are a lot of composers I love but that I wouldn't place in the same category with the five I named. I've limited my list to the five composers that I believe mean the most. I am a very great admirer of Tchaikovsky, but he wouldn't be in that class. The same with Prokofiev, with some Shostakovich, some Stravinsky.

R.H. You believe, then, that a young person should begin with the best?

D.D. Definitely. Anybody should. I don't make a distinction between what a young person should listen to and what anyone else should listen to. It would be the same for a three-month-old baby, too. If you asked me what a mother should put on as background in her baby's room, I'd give the same answers. I don't believe that "children's music" or that "light classics" are helpful for *anyone's* cultural education. I would suggest, however, that a young student listen the first hundred times without necessarily concentrating. He should listen while he's eating with his family, or doing work around the house. Just have it loud enough to be there—not like soft dinner music—loud enough to make him aware of it, so that it's as if he's been working in Philharmonic Hall while the Philharmonic's been rehearsing. From that type of subconscious listening, he can then go on to more serious listening.

• *STANLEY DRUCKER*

Principal clarinetist of the New York Philharmonic.

S.D. One work that I think is very beautiful is Mozart's Quintet for Clarinet and

Strings. I'm not thinking of any particular recording of it, but the work itself. It's one of the great pieces in the chamber music literature—one of the very greatest, and we clarinetists are fortunate to have it. Next, since I think a lot of young people, especially, are interested in very modern sounds, one work I would recommend in that vein—even though it was written quite a while ago—would be Stravinsky's *Rite of Spring*.

R.H.　Do you think young people today relate more quickly to a work like that because of their feeling for rhythm and rock beats?

S.D.　Yes, and because of the excitement of the work. I also think Ravel's *Bolero* is very good, for the same reason. It's got a very vital rhythm, it has motion and excitement—like the *Rite of Spring*, but in a different way. Another work I'd recommend is Tchaikovsky's Symphony No. 5, for just beautiful melody and the song that it contains. It just "sings" from beginning to end. I think every basic library should contain a Beethoven symphony, and I would start with No. 7—what some people call his "Dance Symphony." Then, there's such a lot of good contemporary music—by Bartók, Prokofiev, Shostakovich, Barber, Copland. One work that would be very good is Copland's *El Salon Mexico*, or his *Appalachian Spring*. Both are interesting, beautiful works.

R.H.　As a member of the Philharmonic you have played in many Young People's Concerts under Bernstein and others. Have you noted any particular audience reactions as to the type of music young people seem to respond to most?

S.D.　The degree of sophistication in young audiences today is amazing. They really equal the adults in many ways. You can play just about any style of music and get a good reaction. I think the Philharmonic's concerts over the years have been at a very high musical level. There were some concerts that included very modern music, things I wouldn't have thought would be for every audience—and yet the response was *very* good.

• CHRISTOPH ESCHENBACH

German pianist.

C.E.　I would start with some bright, very colorful Baroque work, such as the *Water Music* or the *Royal Fireworks Music* by Handel. Then I'd say something by Bartók: the Second or Third Piano Concerto, or the *Concerto for Orchestra*—because they're so exciting rhythmically. Next, the *Concerto for Piano and Wind Instruments* by Stravinsky. And then a piece by Mozart, either a symphony or a piano concerto. The Mozart concertos are very beautiful, and make an excellent introduction, I think, to all classical music. I'd also suggest an excerpt from Mozart's opera *Don Giovanni*.

R.H.　You feel an excerpt is preferable to the whole opera to start?

C.E.   That depends on whether a newcomer is willing to sit still for two or three hours to hear a whole opera. Personally, I think it would be better if he tried. But I don't think many young people today would, so perhaps the highlights would be better after all.

R.H.   Is it important that an opera be in a language the listener knows?

C.E.   No, that has little importance. With a song or *lied,* perhaps. But not with an opera.

R.H.   Any other non-operatic recommendations?

C.E.   Yes, some Romantic music—Chopin, of course. Maybe the Chopin *Nocturnes.* Finally, I'd say something modern: Stockhausen—why not?!—perhaps some excerpts from his electronic national anthems of the world, called *Hymnen.*

• *ARTHUR FIEDLER*

Conductor of the Boston Pops Orchestra.

A.F.   There is such a vast supply of music to start with that I almost don't dare say. But I think most young people today have had a chance to hear at least one or two youth concerts, and from them they get a smattering of what's important in the classical literature. From there they can branch out themselves and see what they like. As for recommending five or six specific recordings, I think, certainly, they should try something by Mozart. And one of the Beethoven symphonies. And some Ravel, which is very colorful. Also some Rimsky-Korsakov. And I think they'd find Sibelius interesting. In the meantime I'm not one of those who object to their listening to a lot of rock'n'roll. Eventually their curiosity about other kinds of music will get the best of them, and they will branch out on their own.

R.H.   Since so many of your own recordings combine pop arrangements with classics, is there any one you feel would be appropriate for this kind of a beginner?

A.F.   I don't know how to answer that objectively. Actually, some of our albums might be rather helpful for this type of thing. There was one that was a best-seller a few years ago, called *Up Up and Away.* It included several of the very fine Beatle tunes and the theme from the Mozart 21st Piano Concerto, used in the film *Elvira Madigan.* This kind of album, I think, might lead young people in the right direction.

• *MALCOLM FRAGER*

American pianist.

M.F.   This is one of the hardest questions I've ever been asked. I cannot come up with any five or six LPs that I would be able to recommend to just anybody. There are

18

Saul Goodman

16

Arthur Fiedler

19

Bernard Haitink

21

Byron Janis

17

Malcolm Frager

22

Milton Katims

Hans Werner Henze

20

The Guarneri String Quartet

lots of kids today who study piano, and many of them live in towns where they don't get a chance to hear a live orchestra—so let me recommend six piano concertos.

I'd start with the Mozart Piano Concerto No. 23. That's a piece I played myself when I was six, and I think it's very accessible in mood and in spirit. If a person can't start off with Mozart and feel *that* as music, he's almost hopeless. I've read that headhunters in the Brazilian jungle were not able to listen to Stravinsky but could listen to the Mozart Clarinet Quintet quite happily.

Next I'd recommend the Beethoven Piano Concerto No. 5, the "Emperor." It's emotional and therefore something young people can feel. Then the Schumann Concerto—it's my favorite concerto, really, of all the Romantic works.

R.H.   I know you yourself play two different versions or editions of the Schumann Concerto. Do you have any preference?

M.F.   No, I don't think it particularly matters. Next, Tchaikovsky's Piano Concerto No. 1. I say that because I doubt if many others you're interviewing are going to put it on their lists—yet why not? It's the kind of piece a young person is going to be able to feel. You can't say, as some do, that such Romantic music isn't any good any more.

Next, the Prokofiev Piano Concerto No. 3, because it's lots of fun and it's modern. And finally, the Bartók First Piano Concerto. This one is very tough, but they should have at least one piece that they can really get their teeth into. Now, can I recommend specific performers?

R.H.   Certainly.

M.F.   In Mozart I'd recommend something that Peter Frankl has done. I'm not sure he's done the 23rd, but I know he's done others and he's a very good Mozart player. For the Beethoven, I would say Rudolf Serkin. For the Schumann, Guiomar Novaes; hers is an old recording and may not be available any longer, but it's very good. For Tchaikovsky, I'd say Ashkenazy. For Prokofiev's Third, the composer's own recording. And for the Bartók First, Gabor Gabos, a Hungarian pianist who has recorded all of the Bartók concertos, although I'm not sure they've been released yet in the U.S.*

R.H.   How important do you think the performer is for a listener starting out?

M.F.   It's terribly important, because if the performer isn't able to re-create the mood of the music so that the listener instinctively feels it, the music is going to be dead. It's just as important to get the right performance as it is the right work.

---

* Available in the U.S. only through special import shops.

• *SAUL GOODMAN*

Timpanist with the New York Philharmonic from 1927 to 1972, and a member of the faculty of the Juilliard School of Music in New York City.

S.G.   I would say, as number one, Beethoven's Fifth Symphony. Then the "Jupiter" Symphony (No. 41) of Mozart. Then Strauss' *Till Eulenspiegel*. And finally some modern music, to give a feeling of how music changed in this century. For that, Stravinsky's *Rite of Spring*. Those four works, I think, would be rather representative. You could throw in a few others, perhaps—something by Wagner or Berlioz or Brahms. But I think those four would be the most satisfactory.

R.H.   And your reasons for choosing them?

S.G.   The Mozart Symphony No. 41 is, for me, the best example of Mozart's development. And Beethoven's Fifth is the perfect example of the symphonic form as developed from Haydn and Mozart; it's the symphony of all symphonies as we know it. Of course, I made a big jump to Richard Strauss' *Till Eulenspiegel*, but I was trying to keep the list down. If you want to put something in between, then I'd suggest Berlioz's *Symphonie Fantastique*. Then, as a further example of the nineteenth-century Romantic development, I would put in Brahms' First Symphony.

R.H.   How important is it to take these in a chronological or historical sequence?

S.G.   I think it would be very helpful. For example, if you were to expose someone immediately to the *Rite of Spring*, he might say, "My God, is that music?" Whereas, if you started with Mozart you could say, "Look, this is an early example of symphonic form." And then you could go on to Beethoven, and to Berlioz, seeing how each of them were innovators. In Berlioz you can see how orchestral color grew, and how through his imagination the orchestra itself developed—the addition of more than one pair of timpani, the two bass drums, the church bells, etc., in the *Fantastique*. And then the development of the orchestral side of opera through Wagner, particularly the *Ring* operas—although that might be a little too much for someone to take too early.

R.H.   Do you think the increased use of percussion instruments has had any significant effect on music in this century?

S.G.   Percussion has added a great deal to music—depending, of course, on who the composer is who used it—not in the melodic sense, and perhaps not as far as different tones are concerned. But in terms of rhythm, dynamics, and contrast, I think it's had a very startling influence. One composer who has really tied all that together is Varèse. What I would suggest, in the way of a recording that shows what he's done with percussion, is Varèse's *Ionization*; there used to be an excellent recording by Frederick Waldman with the Juilliard Percussion Ensemble, but I'm not sure it's still available. Of course, percussion has since gone beyond that point. There are so many composers today using percussion in a masterly fashion—among them Boulez. Boulez, I think, is a brilliant composer as well as a brilliant conductor.

• *THE GUARNERI STRING QUARTET*

American string quartet. Its members are Arnold Steinhardt (first violin), John Dalley (second violin), Michael Tree (viola), and David Soyer (cello).

SOYER   You'll probably get a different list from each of us. I'd say a Beethoven symphony to start. I think those nine symphonies probably are the greatest symphonic works. They are also very accessible, particularly the Third, Fifth, Sixth, Seventh, or Eighth. It's the most universal music.

STEINHARDT   Yes, a Beethoven symphony must be one of the five records. I would pick the Third to start.

TREE   I'd say any one from the Second through the Eighth. I think they're all equally exciting.

DALLEY   Then there would have to be a piece by Bach.

STEINHARDT   I was thinking of one of the Bach cantatas.

SOYER   I would say *any* Bach piece.

STEINHARDT   I'd say something like the *Magnificat.*

TREE   No, I wouldn't agree entirely. I would say something a little bit more accessible: one of the Bach Brandenburg Concertos.

DALLEY   That's the thing with Bach, you see. *Any* piece you pick is a great one. You couldn't pick just any piece of another composer.

TREE   The Third Brandenburg—not in terms of greatness but in terms of its immediacy. Some of Bach's work really requires a little bit more thought or preparation. Last night I heard one of the Bach sonatas played at a concert I went to, and I wouldn't recommend that to most people starting out. I barely scratched the surface listening to that piece as a musician. I should have studied the score for a couple of days before going in there. I should have read a good analysis or, better yet, attempted some sort of preparation on my own. Let's face it. Anybody runs a chance of being somewhat put off, hearing a piece like that for the first time. I would pick the Third or Fifth Brandenburg.

STEINHARDT   Or the Bach Double Violin Concerto.

DALLEY   I'm for the *Goldberg Variations.*

TREE   But that's very tough for a beginner.

DALLEY   But if he's going to be a composer or something like that, he couldn't study a better piece.

R.H.   The question was meant to apply to just an average listener.

SOYER   I'd say a work of Mozart. Maybe *Don Giovanni.*

R.H.   Do you think a newcomer should sit down with the whole opera, or just excerpts?

STEINHARDT   Maybe it's too much for a beginner to listen to a whole opera, even if it's sensational music. It involves a language he probably doesn't know and a whole new medium of expression. I'd pick Stravinsky's *Rite of Spring*, as something representing the twentieth century.

SOYER   I'd pick the Debussy *Nocturnes.*

TREE   I would say a Bartók string quartet. Any one of the late Bartók quartets.

R.H.   It's interesting that this is the first time a chamber work has been mentioned. Most of the works you've mentioned up to now have been orchestral ones.

DALLEY   I was going to mention the Mozart quintets. And I mentioned the *Goldberg Variations*, which is a solo work.

R.H.   But I'm curious as to why you, as a chamber group, have stressed works other than chamber works. Do you think people today relate better to orchestral music than they do to chamber music?

SOYER   No, I don't think they do at all.

TREE   And yet it's true—we did pick a lot of orchestral works in our choice of five records.

STEINHARDT   If you think of really typical works of specific composers, you're bound to.

TREE   I'd add one of the late Beethoven string quartets to the list.

R.H.   Which one?

TREE   That's hard to say. As a matter of fact, they may be too difficult for a person to grasp right away. But they're worth a try.

SOYER   The Ravel String Quartet.

TREE   Yes, the Ravel quartet would be a marvelous one.

R.H.   Can any of you remember the first records you went out and bought?

SOYER   I remember very well. Beethoven's A major Cello Sonata. I was about twelve years old.

TREE   I remember the first thing that really moved me deeply. I was about five years old, and I heard the Beethoven Violin Concerto. I'm amazed that I was so moved, without knowing anything about music.

DALLEY   Weber's *Oberon* Overture was the first thing I bought. I don't know why. I may have just heard it and wanted the record.

R.H. Now, as a corollary, which of your own recordings are you the proudest of, or do you feel best represents your work?

TREE I pass. I don't think I can be objective about that.

SOYER The one I like the best is the Mendelssohn Quartet No. 2.

TREE That's one I like, too.

SOYER The Mendelssohn Quartet is on one side, and Grieg on the other.

TREE But just the Mendelssohn.

SOYER I like the Grieg too.

DALLEY I think the Smetana Quartet No. 1 is probably as good as anything we've done.

TREE Our Beethoven Quartets album was certainly a very major accomplishment in our lives.

R.H. I think you're answering now so that everyone will go out and buy *all* of them!

TREE I don't like our recordings. I only buy Budapest String Quartet recordings.

STEINHARDT Michael, we're going to have to have a little talk with you.

• BERNARD HAITINK

Dutch conductor. Music director of the Amsterdam Concertgebouw Orchestra and principal conductor of the London Philharmonic Orchestra.

B.H. I would say he should try to choose an important work from each major period of music. For example, one of the works of Bach, one of Mozart, one of Beethoven, one of Mahler, one of Debussy, and one of Bartók or Stravinsky. He may not like it all at first, but he should try to see what he likes and what he doesn't like.

R.H. Why those specific composers?

B.H. Bach is, of course, Bach—and he has a special appeal for so many reasons. I think you can do with Bach what you want. You can give his music a jazz beat, or sing it the way the Swingle Singers do, but you still hear *Bach*. You can do almost anything with the poor man and he's still there. Mozart—well, because he's such a genius. What more can you say about him? Beethoven—because Beethoven has always had such appeal to the man in the street. He has so much to say to so many people. Mahler—because I think he is such a child of our time. He has no restraint in the Classical sense, the way Mozart does, for example. He's given us all his problems as a human being. He awakens you, makes you aware of the depth of music. Bartók and Stravinsky—because they're so much the language of this century. And Debussy—to hear what an Impressionist composer can do with colors.

R.H.   Would you recommend any specific works by these composers?

B.H.   No, let them listen and choose what appeals to *them*.

• *HANS WERNER HENZE*

German composer, now living in Italy.

H.W.H.   He should buy as much of the keyboard music of Bach as he can get hold of. He should have an opera—Mozart's *Don Giovanni*. Then, the Mozart string quintets. Mahler's Third Symphony. Alban Berg's *Three Pieces for Orchestra*, possibly with Schoenberg's *Five Pieces for Orchestra* on the reverse side if such a recording is available. [It isn't.]

R.H.   And your reasons for these specific works?

H.W.H.   The Bach keyboard music is, first of all, very pleasant to listen to. I'm thinking of students in their rooms, and instead of having some ear-deafening and mind-deafening rock going all the time, they would hear music that is graceful, passionate, disciplined, charming, and sexy all at once.
As for *Don Giovanni*, it is one of the most beautiful works in music, psychologically and philosophically profound. *Don Giovanni* is not about a sex hero. The sensuality is in the music. It reminds me of bodies designed by Raphael or Pontormo. It's very alive—and very *now,* I think. There's certainly more love in it than in most rock. I should emphasize that I don't dislike rock. But one cannot point out frequently enough that there is something that is wider and more beautiful. Even wilder.
The Mozart quintets are the most beautiful chamber music ever written. And the Mahler Third is the least academic [of his symphonies] in construction. It's the most daring in form, and the most unsymphonic in a new way. There's something fantastic about it, something very unorthodox and enterprising. And Berg and Schoenberg—because I think if you can understand these pieces, you can judge the rest of modern music very well. They are really the measure for everything written since.

R.H.   Which piece by Henze would you recommend to someone who has not yet heard your music?

H.W.H.   Perhaps the Double Concerto for Oboe and Harp. It is rather easy to listen to, and has melodic lines that help you to understand symphonic structures. The whole piece is built like a symphony, and people can follow easily what is meant by "doubles" and by "variations"—and that should help them very much. Also it is full of memories of when I was younger myself. That's why I like it so much.

• *BYRON JANIS*

American pianist.

B.J.   I'd suggest Brahms' First Symphony, Rachmaninoff's Second Piano Concerto, Beethoven's Third Symphony (*Eroica*), Stravinsky's *Firebird*, and Tchaikovsky's Violin Concerto. All of them are masterpieces, yet they're also easy works for the public to react to immediately. I think it's important to hear music at first that has lasted through the ages, and will continue to last.

R.H.   Although you're a pianist, the only piano work you mentioned was the Rachmaninoff Second Concerto. Do you have a special reason for that one?

B.J.   It's not the easiest, but it is one of the great concertos. You know, contrary to what a lot of people think, Rachmaninoff was delighted when he was told that some of this concerto's themes had been made into popular tunes. He was thrilled thinking of all the people who would hear them—because what we all try to do, in some way, is to make classical music become popular. But that, of course, always doesn't work. You know, Prokofiev's Third Piano Concerto would be another concerto that I would include in my list. I also think an album of various pieces by Chopin would be good. And I would pick one of the easy Italian operas—for instance, Verdi's *Aïda*.

R.H.   Would you recommend any specific performances? Or do you think that's a secondary consideration?

B.J.   It isn't secondary, but I can't think of any right at this moment. I think it's important, though, to get one of the leading performers. Some record companies come out with inexpensive things by very unknown people, and some of them are pretty dull.

R.H.   In other words, you'd recommend recordings that are done by established names on the best-known labels.

B.J.   For someone just starting out, yes. I think it would be very difficult otherwise, unless one *knew* that one of these others was a great performance.

• *MILTON KATIMS*

Conductor of the Seattle Symphony Orchestra. Former first violist of the NBC Symphony under Toscanini.

M.K.   There are so many directions I could go. So I'd say, first, that if you had enough money for only five records, go to the library and borrow the ones you can't buy. But if you're limited to just five, then pick works from different periods of music. On the basis of the reactions of young people I've met, I'd start back in the Baroque period. Or, if a young person has not had *any* contact with classical music, he might be intrigued by some of the updated versions of Bach, such as *Switched-On Bach* with the Moog Synthesizer. Then he could go on from there to the real thing. Of course, symphonies like Beethoven's Fifth must be included. The Franck D minor Symphony was one that turned me on when I was a teenager, and I would suggest that. And Tchaikovsky's *Romeo and Juliet*. Coming into our own century, there's Stravinsky's wonderful *Firebird*, and they could go from there to his *Petrushka* and *Rite of Spring*—and then on to Bartók and Prokofiev. The list is limitless once the door is opened.

R.H.   Since you mentioned *Switched-On Bach*, I take it you don't object to "impure" or popular treatments of the work of a particular composer.

M.K.   No, not at all. I usually personally prefer the original. But if it's a means of introducing someone to the original, then I don't object. As a matter of fact, I feel the same way about good rock. I think the Beatles' arrangements, their ideas, their imagination—there's no reason why they can't be an introduction to good music, too. In other words, start with things for which you have a natural affinity.

• *ISTVAN KERTESZ*

Hungarian-born conductor. Former principal conductor of the London Symphony Orchestra and music director of the Cologne Opera in West Germany at the time of his death in 1973.

I.K.   I would ask, first, what do you already know about music—and *like?* Have you heard a work by Bach, or Boulez, or Reger, and enjoyed the piece? If the answer is yes, then I would suggest that the listener go on with the type of music he's liked, and try a few more pieces from around the same period. For example, if he likes Bach, I would suggest taking something by Mozart. If the reaction to Bach and Mozart is good, then this probably indicates that the listener should try other German music, so he could go on to Haydn, to Schubert, or even further to Brahms.

R.H.   Would you recommend any specific works by these composers?

I.K.   No. It would depend, I think, on what such a person has already heard by different composers. If he were to say, "Yes, I've heard a violin concerto," then I wouldn't recommend another violin concerto. I would say he should next try to hear a piano or horn concerto. It depends on what the person comes to you with—then his experience should be widened from there.

R.H.   Since you mentioned Bach, how do you feel about what's being done with Bach on Moog Synthesizers and such?

I.K.   It's very interesting—*some* of it. It's something that may have a great future. Also, just the other day I heard the *Play Bach* jazz group, which is also interesting.

R.H.   Do you think these will help attract more people to Bach in the original, or to classical music generally?

I.K.   Possibly yes. Bach's music is very difficult, some of the most problematic in all the literature. To understand these problems helps one appreciate *Play Bach*, and vice-versa.

• *ANDRÉ KOSTELANETZ*

American conductor. Director of the New York Philharmonic's Spring Promenade concerts.

A.K.   I would suggest three orchestral pieces, then one that involves a narrator, another that involves a piano soloist, and, finally, one that involves singers. Actually, I'd start with the narrator. Certain words, sometimes, are a good bridge to music—and I couldn't think of anything more impressive than the *Lincoln Portrait* by Aaron Copland, especially when Carl Sandburg narrates.

R.H.   Isn't that a piece you commissioned from Copland?

A.K.   Yes, and I recorded it some years ago with Sandburg and the New York Philharmonic.

R.H.   You must take enormous pride in seeing how well-known this work has become, and knowing you had a role in its creation.

A.K.   It is now more than 25 years old—and, of course, it was impossible at first ever to imagine that it would have the impact it has had. It is a masterpiece, a total masterpiece—so I am, naturally, happy to have had something to do with it.
Now, for a piano concerto, I'd suggest something with recognizable themes—therefore, the Rachmaninoff Second Piano Concerto. There are many soloists who give brilliant performances of this work on records. Then we come to something with singers. For that I'd suggest excerpts from *Carmen* or *La Bohème*.

R.H.   Do you feel excerpts are more desirable to begin with than the complete opera?

A.K.   Yes. I feel the attention span is much shorter in young people. To stay with it, you have to become more familiar with opera as a form. Now, as for the strictly orchestral pieces, I'd suggest Stravinsky's *Firebird* and Ravel's *Ma Mère l'Oye* (*Mother Goose*). Short pieces. You can talk between the pieces. You can read about them. And finally, an enormous cornerstone of classical literature: Beethoven's Fifth Symphony.
Now it is impossible, of course, to say that these are *the* only six works. I don't think anybody can say that. But I think these offer a good cross-section for someone to start with.

R.H.   Could you elaborate a bit further on your reasons for *Firebird* and *Mother Goose*?

24

Istvan Kertesz

25

André Kostelanetz

26

Erich Leinsdorf

27

Ruth Laredo

28

Evelyn Lear and Thomas Stewart

29

Jaime Laredo

30

Lorin Maazel

31

Charles Mackerras

A.K.   I think that for a person who's just starting out, we have to build bridges. He will not comprehend abstract music easily at first. However, a story or a plot can be one of the things that brings the music into focus. I think that program music is very helpful in this respect.

R.H.   Do you feel that young people today relate more to any one type of classical music than to other types?

A.K.   I've noticed that I can often program very modern works for younger audiences. Not totally modern, but *very* modern. For instance, I remember doing Benjamin Britten's *Scottish Fantasy* in Toronto during an afternoon concert for young people, and they felt an enormous rapport with it. They applauded wildly. It was a big discovery. In the evening when we performed this for the usual adult audience—people more established in their likes and dislikes—the reception was not half as enthusiastic. It was a very clear example to me of what young people can understand.

R.H.   You've also been very active recording what a lot of people call "in-between music"—symphonic arrangements of show music and popular music. Is this an area young people are drawn to, or is it mostly an area of interest for older generations?

A.K.   It's difficult to say. I, myself, doubt that many young people today are particularly interested in the show music of Cole Porter and Jerome Kern, but it's very possible that they will come to appreciate it as vital American music as they grow older.

• RUTH AND JAIME LAREDO

American pianist and her husband, the Bolivian violinist.

R.L.   You have to have Bach. That's basic. And there are so many marvelous recordings of Bach. The ones I really love the most are the Brandenburg Concertos—performed, of course, by Casals and the Marlboro Festival people—and the four Suites for Orchestra. I would begin with one of those. Then some Beethoven.

J.L.   I agree with Ruth about starting with Bach. Of course, if you're limited to only five or six records, then you can't get *all* the Brandenburgs and *all* the Suites. But I would hope that you could, at least, get a set of one or the other. Then I'd say Beethoven too—either the Third, Fifth, or Ninth Symphony. Then, to get an idea of the different periods and types of music, I would recommend one of the Romantic composers: Schubert, Schumann, or Brahms—any of their symphonies. I'd include Tchaikovsky, too.

R.H.   Would you suggest any of Tchaikovsky's concertos?

J.L.   No. It's probably funny since I'm a violinist, but I'd stick with the symphonies—at least for someone starting out. Quite frankly, the Tchaikovsky Fourth, Fifth, and Sixth Symphonies are—and I hate to admit this—really greater than his Violin Concerto or Piano Concertos. Then I would recommend something by one of the French composers—Berlioz's *Symphonie Fantastique* or *Harold in Italy*, or an album of music by Debussy and Ravel. Then, I would suggest something from the twentieth century, something not yet too far out—perhaps Bartók's *Concerto for Orchestra*. Then, for my last choice, I *would* take something quite far out—maybe some electronic music or, if you don't want to get quite so drastic, something by Schoenberg or Webern. I think it is most important for someone starting out *not* to concentrate on just one type of music or one historical period.

R.H.   For Ravel, Debussy, and some of the others, you didn't mention specific works. Would you suggest orchestral works or solo works?

J.L.   I don't want to slight chamber music, but I really feel that someone starting out can relate more easily to orchestral music. Take Brahms, or any composer. I think most people can get more the first time from an orchestral work than they can from a string quartet, for example.

R.H.   What about a concerto?

R.L.   I'd say Rachmaninoff's Second Piano Concerto, which is very beautiful and so appealing.

J.L.   For me, the concerto that really *means* the violin is the Mendelssohn concerto. I think it's the most perfect violin concerto ever written.

R.L.   I'd like to mention something slightly off the beaten track—one of the albums made by Yehudi Menuhin and Ravi Shankar, a very interesting combination of Western and Eastern music which I hear young people talking about. We have one of these albums, and I think it's beautiful. I've also noticed a lot of young people taking an intense interest in Horowitz's return to the concert stage, so I think one of his solo piano albums would be good, too.

R.H.   How important is the "right" performer for someone starting out?

J.L.   I would say, at the very beginning, get the right *works*. Performers don't always make *that* much difference. When you get to be a real record connoisseur, well, that's a different story.

* * *

A week after the preceding interview, Ruth Laredo wrote:

"Since our meeting I have been thinking further about your question, and would like to revise some of my comments. First of all, the key word in building a record library for the beginner should be *enjoyment*.

"Among my favorite symphonic records are the Mendelssohn "Scotch" and "Italian" Symphonies. I would suggest the Charles Munch–Boston Symphony version of the "Scotch," and the Casals-Marlboro record of the "Italian.""

"Since I adore French music, I would say that the one record that has given me the most enjoyment is the Munch–Philadelphia Orchestra album with Ravel's *Valses Nobles et Sentimentales*, Fauré's *Pelléas et Mélisande* Suite, and excerpts from Berlioz's *Damnation of Faust*. Along with these I'd recommend the Leonard Bernstein–New York Philharmonic recording of Debussy's *La Mer* and Ravel's *Daphnis and Chloé*. Two others I would add are Stravinsky's *Firebird* and *Rite of Spring*.

"When I was a teenager I used to play a number of small concerts in and around Philadelphia to help pay my expenses as a student at the Curtis Institute of Music. After one such recital I decided to give myself a present, and I set aside some of the money I earned to buy five records. When I got to the record store, I was utterly unable to choose five records. I was, at that time, more concerned with what was 'important' or 'educational' for me to hear, rather than what records I could listen to for pleasure. My choices turned out rather badly, as I purchased a few very dull discs of what my conscience told me I *should* buy. I believe I never listened to any of them more than once or twice. So when you asked me your question, I began by mentioning Bach and Beethoven—very excellent composers, to be sure. But I was back in Philadelphia with that answer, as you can see. The records I have listed in this letter are selected for more true listening pleasure. At least *I* continue to find pleasure in hearing them, and hope that others will find pleasure in them, too."

• *EVELYN LEAR AND THOMAS STEWART*

American soprano and her husband, the American baritone. (They replied by letter from Europe.)

Our suggestions would be the following five works:

First, Bach's *Brandenburg Concerto No. 2 in F major.* This is one of the most engaging works of Bach, and it represents the Baroque period at its height.

Second, Mozart's *The Marriage of Figaro.* An opera in which we both have appeared, *Figaro* represents for us a high point in the search for musico-dramatic unity. Its characters are vivid, its plot clear, logical and funny, and ultimately very moving. Mozart, we believe, is the best choice for an introduction to opera.

Third, Beethoven's Symphony No. 9 in D minor. Arguably the greatest of all the symphonic works of Beethoven, the Ninth is the only one which employs vocal soloists and chorus along with orchestral forces.

Fourth, Prokofiev's *Classical Symphony.* This modern exercise in Classicism, an illustration of symphonic form in its purest state, provides an excellent bridge between the Classical and modern periods.

Fifth, Britten's *Young Person's Guide to the Orchestra* [also known as the *Variations on a Theme by Purcell*]. This work illustrates, by using a theme with a series of variations, all the important sections of the symphony orchestra. The theme is taken from a seventeenth-century piece by Henry Purcell.

● *ERICH LEINSDORF*

Vienna-born conductor. Former music director of the Boston Symphony Orchestra and the Cleveland Orchestra.

E.L.   You wouldn't start to learn about music with LP records. If you want to know music, you have to learn to a certain degree as an active participant. Music cannot be studied passively. You have to study rhythm, and even if you have not studied an instrument, I think you can study music as a non-instrumentalist. You must do something with your body and create rhythms, and you must do something with your voice, which means singing. So that would be my advice. I think music must be more than a spectator sport. Therefore I couldn't advise on five LPs. If somebody said which five LPs do you enjoy most, that's something else—although I wouldn't know how to answer that. But I could not honestly tell anybody to spend his money on five LPs and learn anything about music.

R.H.   Could you at least recommend their investigating five or six specific composers whose works would be available on LP?

E.L.   But only after they know something about music. You cannot learn about music just by *listening* to compositions. You can acquire a taste, you can acquire a certain amount of aesthetic sympathy and understanding. You can certainly, by listening to music enough, become very critically astute. You can develop all sorts of keen insight by merely listening, but you cannot really learn about music that way.

R.H.   You don't think someone starting out could gain an appreciation by just being able to listen to records?

E.L.   You have to study music as a discipline. My recommendation is very simply: rhythm first, pitch next, without any instrument involved; which means, in simpler words, dancing first, singing next, but with a recognition of symbols of musical notation. And if he has gone through this and is still interested, then he should apply his knowledge to the very complicated machine which is a musical instrument.

● *LORIN MAAZEL*

American conductor. Music director of the Cleveland Orchestra; former music director of the West Berlin Deutsche Opera and the Berlin Radio Symphony.

L.M.   The Second Brandenburg Concerto of Bach would be an interesting piece to start with. There seems to be some kind of affinity between our youthful years and the rhythmic impulse of a Bach work. Also, it's not Romantic, and this is very important today to the younger contemporary minds—although how contemporary the contemporary mind *is,* I've never been able to grasp—but that's another story. Next, perhaps one work of the Romantic period. There I'd suggest Strauss' *Also*

Sprach Zarathustra, if only because it's become so popular through the *2001: A Space Odyssey* film. Young people who saw the film know some of it—but probably just the introduction, so it would be good to show that there's a bottom part of that iceberg.

Next, I might suggest a little Mozart—perhaps a bassoon concerto, or the Flute Concerto in D major. Then I'd move on to Berlioz—but rather than suggesting the *Symphonie Fantastique*, I would start with the Berlioz overtures, such as the *Roman Carnival Overture, Beatrice and Benedict*, and so forth.

R.H.   Why would you choose them over the symphony?

L.M.   Because of the burden of the *Fantastique* story. It is a bit tiresome, I fear, for young people today—the continual reappearance of the image of "the loved one," the hero's desperate, romantic search for the reality of being, and all of this concept of the Witches' Sabbath that I don't think necessarily appeals to today's minds. The overtures, however, are bright and full of marvelous, attractive music. They show what an orchestra can do. Next, we need a very contemporary piece. A piece I think many would enjoy is Schoenberg's *Variations for Orchestra*, Op. 31—though that's not terribly contemporary, it's already an "old" piece. Then, something of a purely lyrical quality: the *Poem of Ecstasy* of Scriabin. Its orchestral palette is so extraordinarily rich and effective. Now, you'll note that I've mentioned no Beethoven.

R.H.   Is this deliberate because of the recent Beethoven Year and our exposure to so much that way?

L.M.   If you *give* young people their Beethoven, you have shown them Paradise. It's like the old story about the priest and the Communist official. "Why can't *we* get your public," the official asks the priest. "Well," the priest replies, "it's very simple. We *promise* our people Paradise, and you *show* them Paradise." And that's, more or less, the situation with Beethoven. If you give someone Beethoven, *whatever* Beethoven piece it is—let's say the *Pastorale* Symphony—he'll say, "Is that all it's about?" And all of Beethoven is likely to go right out the window. So I would rather that the listener discover Beethoven completely on his own.

R.H.   Some of the answers others have given have included an opera, or opera excerpts. Since so much of your own career has been devoted to opera, would you like to add one?

L.M.   Actually, I think, the best opera of all is *Carmen*.

R.H.   Would you recommend that a beginner start with a recording of the whole opera, or with an album of highlights?

L.M.   I don't believe in highlights. I'm very much against that sort of thing. I believe it doesn't make any sense if you pass only from "hit" to "hit." That's not the point of an opera.

R.H.   Which, of all of the many recordings *you* have made, are you the proudest of?

L.M. I guess I'd say I enjoyed making Ravel's *L'Enfant et les Sortilèges* (*The Child and the Sorcerers*). It's a work which isn't recorded very often, but I think it's one of *the* masterpieces of that genre. I can't imagine that many teenagers would be interested in it, though—it's very adult stuff. Not that the music is difficult to grasp; on the contrary. But it's a rediscovery of the wonders of childhood that only a more mature person can really appreciate. Colette and Ravel were both on in years—at least emotionally speaking—when they wrote it, and they were able to recapture a world which is much too close to a teenager, one from which *he's* trying to get as far away as possible. The last thing he'd want to do is sit down with a recording that makes him think about his childhood. It hasn't fallen into the proper perspective yet. But it's a marvelous work, and very close to my heart.

• CHARLES MACKERRAS

American-born conductor. Former director of the Sydney (Australia) Symphony.

C.M. I would start with some of the popular piano concertos, three symphonies, and two descriptive pieces like Debussy's *La Mer* or Stravinsky's *Petrushka.* For the symphonies I'd choose one by Tchaikovsky, one by Mozart, and one by Beethoven. Then a Beethoven piano concerto, too. All of these are easy to understand. Often they show the way music is built up in various forms. They're also easy to listen to and enjoy. If you had said ten records, I would go further and recommend starting with Monteverdi and ending up with John Cage. But if it's only five or six, then I think the range from Mozart to Stravinsky is probably enough.

R.H. Having been born in the United States and then having worked so extensively all around the world—from Australia to Europe—do you find any difference in the way people, especially the younger generation, approach music in different parts of the world?

C.M. Yes. In a way, the newer countries—if I may call the United States that, and Australia is of course still newer—seem more interested in what music has to tell them. I think that the older countries, the countries with long musical traditions like Germany and Italy, take music much too much for granted. They *think* that it's very serious and they sort of treat it as a religion. But they treat it like a religion they don't take seriously, one which they follow automatically rather than really believing in it.

• BRUNO MADERNA

Italian composer-conductor. Music director of the RAI Radio Italiana Orchestra at the time of his death in 1973.

B.M. Your question is difficult to answer, because in five or six records no one could possibly understand all that classical music is. You can only scratch the surface. But

34

Anna Moffo

32

Bruno Maderna

35

Sheldon Morgenstern

37

Garrick Ohlsson

33

Sherrill Milnes

38

Eugene Ormandy

Maralin Niska

36

I'll try to answer. I think I would first suggest something by Monteverdi—*if* you could find a good recording. With Monteverdi there's always the problem that there are so many recorded performances that aren't good. I would hope, however, that you could find a good one of the Monteverdi *Vespers*. Then I would suggest Mozart—maybe the "Jupiter" Symphony (No. 41). This is one of the greatest of all works. The "Jupiter" is so rich in itself—it could represent *all* Mozart, because there are all the different faces of Mozart in this one symphony. With Mozart, I think you come to understand something about the communication of the highest ideas in music—of man's art at its most positive. Then, from a good edition of the Monteverdi *Vespers* and a good edition of Mozart's "Jupiter," I'd go directly to more modern music—to Mahler's Ninth Symphony and Debussy's *Jeux* (*Games*). For a young person both of these works might be very difficult. But they are *so* beautiful, and I would hope he or she could come to see at least some of their beauties. After that, maybe one Stravinsky—perhaps *Les Noces* (*The Wedding*) rather than the *Rite of Spring*.

R.H. Why so?

B.M. Because the *Rite of Spring*, even though it is a marvelous work, involves only one aspect of Stravinsky—the brutal, primitive aspect, the big massive sound. *Les Noces* also has a very explosive sound, but it is a more human work, with a more beautiful body. All of these works I've mentioned seem, to me, to represent a different way of thinking about musical composition, a different way of posing a solution to a musical problem in a particular time. Each piece I've mentioned represents the composer completely, to the last degree.

R.H. At the risk of asking you to be immodest, which composition by Bruno Maderna, as a composer, would you recommend to somebody who's never heard any of your music?

B.M. That's always difficult. You know, a composer always thinks his latest work is his best. But, for someone to begin, I think maybe a very old piece of mine: a serenade, the Serenata No. 2. It dates from 1954, and the recording I made of it is very good, I think.

• *SHERRILL MILNES*

American baritone of the Metropolitan Opera.

S.M. I would ask, first of all, if the listener knows any themes from any particular works. If he's heard even one or two, I'd recommend his looking into the complete work from which those themes came. Take the theme that was turned into a pop song from Beethoven's Ninth Symphony. Well, maybe he should try *all* of

Beethoven's Ninth—perhaps in the Leinsdorf–Boston Symphony recording which just happens to have someone named Sherrill Milnes as the bass. Or maybe there's a hymn he knows from church, that can lead him toward some great choral work, like Handel's *Messiah*. Maybe there's something he recognizes from television. Or if he's seen Leonard Bernstein on television, then maybe some Bernstein recording, preferably of shorter works.

R.H. How important are performers in choosing a work to start with? For example, would you recommend *any* Bernstein recording, or a particular Beethoven symphony for which there might happen to be a Bernstein recording?

S.M. For an introduction and for a symphonic work, I don't think it makes much difference. If a conductor were sitting here with us he'd probably jump right out of his chair, objecting. But a newcomer just isn't going to hear the differences from one performer to another in a symphonic work at first, and if someone is led to the work because he at least knows the name of one performer, I think that's all right.

R.H. Does that apply to soloists, too—to singers?

S.M. In an opera there could be a difference. But even there, to start, I'm not sure it matters. It might be more important to start with American artists. I certainly would not exclude European singers, but a young American might relate more immediately to an American artist. Perhaps someone like Robert Merrill—he's probably the best-known baritone in the country because he's done a good deal of television.

R.H. Did the records of any American singer have an influence on you when you were a teenager?

S.M. Oh yes—Leonard Warren, certainly. I never saw Warren on stage. I knew his work only from records and broadcasts.

R.H. Do you think recordings "freeze" a listener's image of a singer unrealistically sometimes?

S.M. Oh yes, very much so. Someone will buy a recording, take it home, and play it as loud as he wants—with the stereophonic sound just swirling all around him. Then he'll come to the Metropolitan or some other opera house, and the same singer's voice won't be quite as big as it was in his own home. The orchestra may drown it out here, or there may be a little technical problem with the set or costumes, or something. He'll go home saying, "Gee, that wasn't so good—the recording is much better." He'll think what he saw wasn't a good performance, when in fact it was! And, speaking of stereo, I'd also suggest that our hypothetical beginner get some kind of a modern orchestral work, something by Stravinsky or Bartók, for example—a short work that shows, in the best sound, all the wonderful things modern music can do.

• *ANNA MOFFO*

American soprano of the Metropolitan Opera.

A.M.   I'd pick all easy things to start: a Tchaikovsky or Rachmaninoff piano concerto, a Puccini opera—maybe *Madame Butterfly* or *La Bohème*—the Mendelssohn Violin Concerto, Mozart's *Don Giovanni,* and Johann Strauss' *Die Fledermaus,* which is very melodic and semi-classical.

R.H.   Would you recommend starting with the complete opera or with just highlights?

A.M.   I think I'd pick the highlights albums—from *La Bohème* and *Madame Butterfly,* or from Bizet's *Carmen.* There are a lot of dead places in *Carmen* if you play the whole opera—for a beginner, that is. I also don't object to some popular arrangements of the classics. For example, Della Reese made a recording some years ago—I think it was called "Don't You Know"—based on Musetta's Waltz from *La Bohème,* and it may have helped introduce *La Bohème* itself to many people. And *Kismet,* which gets revived frequently in both its stage and film versions, has a lot of appeal—and it uses arrangements of Borodin's music, mostly from his opera *Prince Igor.* After hearing *Kismet* I imagine many have gone on later to *Prince Igor* itself. As for the Tchaikovsky and Rachmaninoff concertos, almost everyone's heard them somewhere before—in the movies or in soap operas. To start someone out, I'd suggest familiar things, easy things, rhythmic things. I'd also add something French, like Ravel's *Daphnis and Chloé,* because to me it's such great mood music—and very sexy.

• *SHELDON MORGENSTERN*

American conductor of the Greensboro (N.C.) Symphony Orchestra. Founder and music director of the Eastern Music Festival and Music Camp in North Carolina.

S.M.   First, Bach—any one of the keyboard albums, such as the preludes and fugues, or the *Goldberg Variations.* Then a Beethoven symphony—the Seventh. Next, a Romantic symphony—perhaps Tchaikovsky's Fifth. Then something by a twentieth-century American composer—either Copland's *Appalachian Spring* or his Third Symphony. Then a twentieth-century standard, maybe Prokofiev's Violin Concerto No. 2 in G minor. And finally the Stockhausen *Gruppen* for three orchestras.

R.H.   And your reasons?

S.M.   I would think that a young person would find that some of the things he associates with rock are inherent in Baroque music—thus, the Bach. I also think that the youth movements of the past few years have involved youth in a way that they feel they can fight for a cause, that they can show themselves to have personal strength, and yet at the same time they're involved in a sort of Romanticism. Thus, I think the Beethoven and Tchaikovsky symphonies would be appealing on all these levels. I believe many would find the Copland work agreeable, because it's folksy in a sense, and it's different from the kind of music they associate with the classical tradition. The Prokofiev Violin Concerto is a good example of a modern fusion of styles. And the Stockhausen *Gruppen* would make them aware of some of the fascinating directions music is taking today.

• MARALIN NISKA

American soprano of the New York City Opera and Metropolitan Opera.

M.N.   I think he or she should buy Mozart's *The Marriage of Figaro*, Beethoven's Ninth Symphony, and Stravinsky's *Firebird*. And I think he or she should also buy some kind of recording of very early church music, Renaissance or even earlier if possible—maybe a recording that has several different things on it. Then I would suggest a recording that has two or three very modern things—a piece by Penderecki, Nono, or Berio. In other words, what I'm saying in essence is: Get a capsule history of music.

R.H.   Why would you approach it in a historical way?

M.N.   Because if this is a person who has not heard much of anything, it would be unfair for him to hear just one kind of music. He should, first of all, hear where Western music came from. He should hear something from the giants: Mozart and Beethoven. There's nothing like Beethoven's Ninth anywhere! It's a great symphony, with chorus and soloists as well as orchestra. As far as Mozart is concerned, you might quibble whether it should be *Don Giovanni* or *The Marriage of Figaro*.

R.H.   Why did you pick *Figaro*?

M.N.   Because if you take *Don Giovanni*, you have to wade through Donna Elvira's screaming around, and a newcomer could find some of that tiresome. Whereas, if you pick *The Marriage of Figaro*, it's all easier to assimilate.

R.H.   Would you suggest that a newcomer start with the complete opera or an album of highlights?

M.N.   When I was a little girl, if somebody suggested a song I should learn, I always tried to get it in a book, because there'd be a lot of other songs in it. You'd pay a dollar for the song, but if you paid three dollars you had ten songs. It's just like that with opera, I think. I believe in buying the whole thing.

R.H.   I notice, you haven't mentioned any of the 19th-century composers we normally associate with opera.

M.N.   For that, I'd certainly pick Puccini, even though he extends into our century.

You'll also notice I skipped over Tchaikovsky and Brahms, and other Romantic composers we hear all the time. They're with us every minute, all around us. I don't think you need records to get to know *them* anymore.

• GARRICK OHLSSON

American pianist.

G.O.   First of all, I would like to talk to this person about music for about an hour, if I could. I would talk about *listening* to music, about what music means, and what it does. I don't mean things like snowflakes or tigers dancing, but what music *is*, in very concrete terms. Lacking that opportunity, I would suggest—boy, this is a tough question!
Right now, the Stokowski recording of Beethoven's Ninth Symphony stands out in my mind because it's a recent acquaintance—and one of the most joyful performances of *anything* I've ever heard. So I think a piece by Beethoven wouldn't be a bad idea. But maybe not the Ninth to begin. But something terribly visceral and gripping, like the Fifth Symphony.

R.H.   You're a pianist, yet you immediately named a symphony. Why?

G.O.   I don't know, frankly. Maybe it's just that I would have a tougher time choosing piano recordings of anything, because my taste is so fussy. But something like the Beethoven Fifth Symphony is a good place to start, because the sound of a lot of musicians doing something so forceful together has its own excitement, it's own impact. The *Bolero* of Ravel should make a big impression too, because of its insane rhythmic drive and cumulative tension. It's much closer to hard rock or some of the exciting contemporary things kids grow up with today. It's just physically overwhelming. For me, that's one of the most important things about music. I think music is a physical force as well as an intellectual or emotional exercise. It can actually *overwhelm* you. You know, one of the reasons that young people have a tougher time getting into classical music these days is that the noise level of our society has risen so high that our sensibilities have become dulled. As a result, the sound of a symphony orchestra playing *fortissimo* in a concert hall simply isn't loud enough to shock anyone anymore.

R.H.   The way it did for other generations?

G.O.   Right. I think part of the nature of music is that it intends to be overwhelming—literally. Then, of course, you go on to develop more refined sensibilities. But I think you should start with the biggest, broadest gestures possible, and then refine them. OK, now we have a Beethoven symphony and Ravel's *Bolero*.
Then I'd suggest some Chopin. If you could get a recording of a piano collection with the Polonaise in A flat on it, that would say quite a lot about the piano, and what a certain great composer is about. I've found Chopin is the most incredibly

popular composer among general listeners. His music is appealing and immediate, and communicates directly. You don't have to listen intensely for form. It's pleasing to all the senses. It's very noble music. And it's full of love. It may sound corny to say that, but it *is* full of some of the most beautifully personal qualities in all music. I love Chopin! Then I'd suggest the Bach *Magnificat*, or a similarly big choral work. Or maybe the Beecham recording of Handel's *Messiah* would be better. You'll notice I'm not a purist about Handel by suggesting the Beecham version.

R.H.   There's much division about Beecham's version these days. The younger conductors seem to stress less grandiose approaches.

G.O.   I know, but I think the Beecham recording of *Messiah* has a fantastic orchestration. Sure it's late Romantic in style, but the playing itself is so incredibly beautiful! I'm speaking from a musician's standpoint now. You know when they begin, "Every valley shall be exalted," with the high trumpets screeching away, the percussion, and all that—I mean you *really* have a spacious feeling! It really feels exalted. I've gotten so sick of Baroque performances where you don't hear things full voice when they're supposed to be. Beecham's recording has such buoyancy, such spring, such a natural joy to it. I think beginners respond well to choral music if it's very strong. I don't mean some obscure Schütz pieces, but something that really has an impact.

The thing that I think is most important in listening to music is that, while it lasts, it should involve you totally. For me, the greatest music is that which is so good that comparisons become irrelevant. People who say this is greater, or this is not as great—well, that's not for me. I think music must be an experience for each individual on his own terms.

• EUGENE ORMANDY

Conductor of the Philadelphia Orchestra.

E.O.   I would start with the most accepted classics—Beethoven, Mozart, Haydn—and then go gradually to Wagner. And then Tchaikovsky, of course; he's such a favorite of all young people.

R.H.   Any particular works of these composers?

E.O.   I would take those which are the most famous compositions, because they are the ones everybody knows, the ones you will hear all the time and want to know.

R.H.   Do you feel young people today might relate more to contemporary composers than to the more established classics?

E.O.   Yes, but afterwards. They should *start* with the classics.

R.H.   What about an Ormandy recording? You've probably made more famous ones over the years than any other conductor.

E.O.   [*Chuckling*] Oh, I'm not particularly fond of Ormandy recordings.

R.H.   I'm sure that's not true.

E.O.   No, it's not exactly true, but—well, if people like them, I'm very pleased. If they don't, well, I can understand it. I'd say listen to as many good recordings as you possibly can—and there are *many* good recordings. Then, once you are acquainted with certain works, get other recordings of the same works, with other interpretations, so you can compare the one you already know with the one you are about to hear or have just heard. Then you'll be in a position to decide which one *you* like best.

• *SEIJI OZAWA*

Japanese conductor. Music director of both the Boston Symphony and San Francisco Symphony Orchestras.

S.O.   If he lives near or in a city which has an orchestra, I would suggest spending some of the money to buy a concert ticket. If the orchestra has an open rehearsal, I would suggest that he go to that first, and then to a concert. Then, for records, I would suggest he buy the record by Dinu Lipatti of Bach's "Jesu, Joy of Man's Desiring," from the Cantata No. 147. To me, it's one of the most beautiful and simplest works in all music. You don't have to know anything about classical music. You just listen a few times—alone, I suggest, because I believe music is really "one-to-one." Bach should be ranked alone among composers, too. Sometimes people think Bach is antique or square. He's really not. Bach lived only two hundred years ago. His music is not square at all.

R.H.   Any other composers or recordings?

S.O.   No. In the beginning, that's enough. After hearing Lipatti's recording about five times, you should have your taste tempted—or else just give up music. I think that is enough.

R.H.   Why do you, an orchestra conductor, pick a piano recording? Do you think it's best to begin with the piano?

S.O.   No, I just happened to choose that because the music—line, melody, harmony— is so simple and so beautiful. Bach wrote for the orchestra, too, and for chorus. But I believe it's easier to start with this piano record. Dinu Lipatti played it so beautifully, so simply, so cleanly. And so warmly. It's really deep and human.

• KRZYSZTOF PENDERECKI

Polish composer.

K.P.   Bach and the Beatles. Beyond that, I don't know what to answer. There's so much in between.

R.H.   Any particular work of Bach?

K.P.   He's so extraordinary that just about *everything* is good.

R.H.   Aren't there any other composers you'd recommend?

K.P.   You'd have to mention so many. It's like choosing Shakespeare and the Bible, and then trying to say what other books.

R.H.   What piece by Penderecki do you think should be the first that someone who doesn't know your music should listen to?

K.P.   Possibly *Polymorphia*, which I wrote in 1962.

R.H.   Your *St. Luke Passion* has become one of the most talked-about works in many years. Do you consider it your most significant work to date?

K.P.   Actually it's one of my least characteristic. My quartet or the *Hiroshima Threnody* are perhaps more representative, although I'm not sure they're necessarily better works. Composers and the public rarely agree on what are their best works. Look at Schubert, who is best known for his *lieder*, his songs; and yet his symphonies were probably closer to *him*.

R.H.   There's a tendency these days for composers to record their own music—Stravinsky, Copland, Henze, Boulez, and others have done this. Have you plans to similarly conduct any of your own works too?

K.P.   Yes, I started recently and it gives me great satisfaction, although earlier I had grave misgivings about composers conducting.

R.H.   Stravinsky took great exception to the way some conductors performed his works, and said that was why he started recording most of them himself.

K.P.   I would much rather hear Ansermet conduct Stravinsky than Stravinsky himself.

R.H.   What conductors do you prefer to hear conduct *your* music?

K.P.   There are quite a lot. But I particularly admire Skrowaczewski.

• LEONTYNE PRICE

American soprano of the Metropolitan Opera.

L.P.   I think one of the first should be something by Mozart; one of the early symphonies perhaps. Mozart is so wonderfully easy to listen to, and so uncompli-

41

Leontyne Price

39

Seiji Ozawa

42

Warren Rich

44

Joseph Silverstein

40

Krzysztof Penderecki

43

Gunther Schuller

45

Stanislaw Skrowaczewski

cated. Then, to broaden his horizon and point him toward opera, I might pick something by Verdi. And you just can't beat *Aïda*. Even if someone can't *see* an opera, I think *Aïda* is one of the two operas that are easy to hear on records. *Carmen* is the other. But I think *Aïda* would have a more interesting dramatic intensity for a beginner. You can always hum Verdi's tunes, and that's a good start.

Then I'd suggest something by Beethoven. His is a pure, Classical line—something like Mozart yet with a little more drama to it. I remember very vividly the first time I heard Beethoven's Ninth as a youngster, particularly the choral part—so I would include the Beethoven Ninth.

Then, something Romantic. I'll stick with my favorite, and that's the Tchaikovsky First Piano Concerto. It's not only listenable, but also rather poetic—a lovely, lovely work. After that, well, I like Bach very much—but I think Bach might be a little complicated for a newcomer, especially a young one. I would rather suggest works that not only would make a lasting impression, but would leave a *desire* to hear more. Therefore I can't leave out Puccini. I really think *Madame Butterfly* should be in there. For someone who's been exposed to very little opera, it's the sort of thing that can whet the appetite. At least it definitely did for me when I was young. Puccini is so beautiful and so very exciting.

R.H.   What do you see as the big difference for a newcomer in approaching Verdi and approaching Puccini?

L.P.   Both of them are theatrical, but they paint scenes in very different ways. Verdi is so much more noble and majestic. Puccini is not quite so removed. He's a Romantic, and more real in some ways.

R.H.   Should a newcomer start with an album of highlights from *Aïda* or *Butterfly*, or with the complete work?

L.P.   If he hasn't been exposed to anything before, I think highlights will suffice. They provide the main background, and perhaps whet the appetite for more.

• WARREN RICH

American pianist. Head of the piano department of the School of Musical Education, New York.

W.R.   My first choice would be one of the Bach Brandenburg Concertos—the Fifth. I think it is one of the most individualistic of the six he wrote, and certainly something a young person could like and appreciate. Next, the Beethoven Third Symphony, the *Eroica*. I feel this is one of Beethoven's most powerful works and, next to the Fifth, the most popular. Then, I would go along with something else in the Classical vein, the Mozart "Jupiter" Symphony, in C major. Melodically, it's one of the most beautiful symphonies Mozart wrote. I find it almost an operatic symphony and extremely appealing. Next would be Stravinsky's *Petrushka*—one of the most ingenious of all of his works and very, very appealing to most listeners. Finally, I'd choose Gershwin's *Rhapsody in Blue*, a piece which has enormous appeal and which is a bridge, in a sense, between classical and contemporary music.

R.H.   You have considerable experience as a teacher as well as a performer. In your view, is there any particular aspect of music—the rhythm, the melody—that has special appeal for young people?

W.R.   The greatest, I'd say, is the rhythmic drive of a piece. And all the pieces I listed, I feel, have an enormous amount of drive rhythmically. This in itself is important— besides the fact that they are beautiful pieces of music. I've also found considerable identification among young people today with music of the Baroque period. Baroque music, you know, is very orderly music. Everything seems to fall into place. You know more or less instantly where it's going to end. There are no extraordinary surprises. In the turmoil of today, this is a wonderful feeling—a very comforting feeling.

R.H.   What about opera? Would you try to start young people in this area?

W.R.   Yes, but you asked me for only five selections. I'd certainly add a Mozart opera—*The Marriage of Figaro*.

R.H.   Should they start with the complete recording or just a highlights version?

W.R.   I think a highlights version. First of all, this opera is long and involved, although it's a very beautiful, happy, and gay opera. It would be a bit too much, perhaps, to try it all at once. I think highlights would be preferable for most people starting out.

R.H.   And in what language? The original language or in English?

W.R.   That question always puts someone on the spot. I think Mozart lends himself very well to English, and newcomers to the opera would get more out of it in their native language. Yet, in the final analysis, I always feel opera is best in the original language. The singers usually "feel" the work more naturally. It's a little more work for Americans to follow if they don't know Italian or German or French, but there are translated librettos provided with almost every opera album today.

• GUNTHER SCHULLER

American composer, conductor, and teacher. President of the New England Conservatory of Music, Boston.

G.S.   I think I'd have to backtrack a little first, and ask the questioner a couple of questions. For instance, what music has he heard before? Everybody, presumably, has heard *some* music by the time he's a teenager. But let's say, for example, that he's a black teenager who's heard only soul music. I wouldn't tell him to listen to the Beethoven Fifth Symphony. I wouldn't even tell him to listen to Stravinsky's *Rite of*

Spring. But if he's a kid who has heard some of the more advanced rock music, and then maybe he has also heard snatches of symphonic music on the radio—even though he hasn't liked it or understood it—then I *could* start him with something like Stravinsky's *Firebird Suite.* That would have the beginnings of some kind of meaning for him. I have thought a lot about this, being involved in education. It's not just because of my own kids—I have a whole school full of kids, and they come to us with varying backgrounds.

Just how *do* we bring more people into the so-called serious musical culture? I include in "serious" even the serious endeavors of rock or jazz musicians, naturally. But even though I have thought a lot about this, I'm afraid I can't give a general answer—because the particular environment out of which someone comes and that he brings with him will determine the point at which he can plug into the tradition. Now, that's going to have to be different for each person—and there's nothing wrong with that. I think any teacher, any school, or any educational system ought to be ready to take that "plugging in" at any point along the line. That's one of the problems today—that by and large most educational systems—not just music ones—are so inflexible. They teach a certain curriculum, and if the student doesn't fit into that, well, it's too bad for *him.* That's got to change.

R.H.   How much difference do you find among young people today in their musical instincts because of the environment they grew up in? For example, someone raised in a black ghetto in relation to a white suburbanite? Are their musical tastes so completely different that neither would be able to appreciate something like the *Firebird* or the Beethoven Fifth?

G.S.   Yes. There *are* such pockets of—what shall we call it?—complete negligence of one aspect of our musical culture. In other words, with a black ghetto student, what I'd have to do first is take the music that he knows. Then I'd show him the links. But I have to know *his* music well enough—his soul music or his gospel music—to find things in it which I can relate to other music, and expand from there. I can say to him, "Look, I know you like this sound right here. Now, I can show you that same chord here in Stravinsky."

The minute I am able to make that kind of connection, unless he's really dense or obstinate—which is rarely the case—a door has been opened to another world. So, in answer to your question, yes, there *is* such a divergence. Even within, let's say, a certain urban or suburban culture, you'll find people who come out of homes where serious music—even in the sense of Kostelanetz or Mantovani—just isn't known.

R.H.   Even if you can't name specific works for some unknown "average person" to start with, why do you believe young people should make the effort to try to learn something about serious music?

G.S.   Someone like me can never answer such a question in a simple way—because, to me, classical music is not what it is to most people, namely Beethoven or Mozart. To me classical music is a long tradition of seven hundred years of music, a tradition that's still going on. Now, if you mean contemporary classical music, there are some obvious answers to why one should relate to that—because that's the music of our time. And there are young people—nineteen- and twenty-year-old composers—who are writing this music. It's not involved with soul music or rock, and they're putting their all into it. I think—as a basic rule of thumb—that if we are going to involve young people in music other than rock music, then we have to try and start with these more contemporary manifestations, and then work our way *back* through Tchaikovsky and Brahms to Beethoven.

• JOSEPH SILVERSTEIN

American violinist. Concertmaster (first violinist) of the Boston Symphony Orchestra since 1961 and assistant conductor since 1972.

J.S.   I would suggest, first of all, that he take half the money and spend it to go to hear a concert. There is something about the immediacy of a concert that just can't be duplicated by a record. Then, if he hears a piece that he likes in the concert, he should buy a record of it. Once he has the frame of reference of having personally heard it "live," there's a certain kind of excitement about going back to hear the piece again at home. I regard records highly, and I listen to records a great deal, but I consider them a supplement to a concert—something that can heighten your enjoyment of a piece in a concert hall. Your response to a given piece of music gets much more complicated each time you hear it.

R.H.   But suppose someone does not have "live" music easily accessible to him?

J.S.   OK. Five records? I would say Beethoven's Fifth Symphony, Rachmaninoff's Second Piano Concerto, Tchaikovsky's Violin Concerto, a recording of Wagner overtures or some orchestral excerpts from Wagner operas. And, for the fifth record, I would suggest that he get a record of highlights from one of the Verdi operas, either *La Traviata* or *Rigoletto.*

R.H.   Why highlights rather than the complete opera?

J.S.   Well, I'm assuming, I guess, that he doesn't have the money to buy the whole opera, and I think beginners ought to hear some singing, just as they ought to hear some piano playing, some violin playing, and several of the big orchestral kind of pieces.

R.H.   As a violinist, why did you pick the Tchaikovsky concerto?

J.S.   I think it's the most readily accessible piece for a novice listener. It's got things in it that he can grab hold of right away, on first hearing.

R.H.   And why the Rachmaninoff Second Piano Concerto?

J.S.   Because it's a piece a person can relate to very quickly. It's not that I feel it's such an enduring masterpiece. But if someone doesn't know anything about classical music, he should start with pieces that he's going to feel an immediate attraction for. Take the example of my wife. When she was a teenager, she thought that the Sibelius Second Symphony was the greatest piece of music ever written. She loved it and really enjoyed it. Today, she's not as fascinated with it as she was then. But the piece paved the way for her appreciation of other works—and that's what's important.

R.H.   Why the Beethoven Fifth?

J.S.   When you go out and buy prints to decorate the walls of a house and don't have enough money to buy original paintings, you buy prints of masterpieces. And the Beethoven Fifth is one of the great masterpieces of all time. I have played the Beethoven Fifth hundreds of times. I have heard it hundreds more times. And it is no less exciting to me today than it was the first time I heard it. If anything, it's even more remarkable. It's amazing when one thinks that the first movement of Beethoven's Fifth Symphony is barely seven minutes long. It's incredible how short it is and how much there is in it.

• STANISLAW SKROWACZEWSKI

Polish-born conductor of the Minnesota Orchestra.

S.S.   I would say, first of all, try to get recordings with historical significance—and in historical sequence. That way he or she can see the style of certain periods, how long it was maintained, and what happened when someone else went beyond this style. And, finally, it comes down to our own times, where no style is more important than any other. So I would recommend trying to get this historic point of view, in a chronological sequence.

R.H.   Could you be specific as to composers?

S.S.   With Renaissance music, the specific composer may not be so important. But it *is* later, when you consider someone like Bach or Vivaldi or Haydn. And within Haydn's lifetime, you also have Mozart—and there's such a big change between Mozart's first and last works. Then you have, similarly, important changes between the first and last works of Beethoven.

R.H.   If somebody did not know any Mozart or Beethoven works could you recommend something specific to start with?

S.S.   With Mozart it is easier. I would recommend the Symphony No. 35, the *Haffner.* It has an enormous variety of tempos and moods, and can be easily assimilated. Then, any symphony of Haydn—maybe one of the better-known, later ones which have much spirit and wit. With Beethoven, I would say listen first to his First or

Second Symphony, and then go to his Fifth or Seventh or Ninth—just to see the great difference. I would also suggest trying one of his last piano sonatas and the last string quartet. Then, maybe one of the Schumann symphonies—either the First or the Fourth; it's not so important which one, because he didn't change as much within his lifetime as Beethoven did. Then I would certainly put Wagner in—and, again, I'd try to compare early Wagner, such as *The Flying Dutchman*, with his later *Tristan and Isolde*.

R.H.   Do you feel that people starting out should listen to excerpts before they try to listen to the whole opera? Or should they try the whole opera first?

S.S.   I would start with excerpts, just the highlights. And with Wagner, there are also some splendid orchestral excerpts. From Wagner I would go straight to Schoenberg and Webern. Since Schoenberg started from Wagner, I would say *Transfigured Night* (*Verklärte Nacht*) to start, and then on to something like Schoenberg's *Five Orchestral Pieces*. Then, next, Webern and Berg to see how the three composers were connected by more or less the same ideas yet were very different.

Then I would try to see what happened with Debussy and Stravinsky—to see different roads composers took in our own century. Speaking of Stravinsky, here again there is so much change between his early and later works—how different they are! We find, for example, Stravinsky going back to the old Classicism after the first wave of shocking works that broke with the past. And then, still later, he finally came very close to Schoenberg and Webern; I think this is so very interesting. As for Debussy, he's one of the big fathers of music in our century, because of his breaks from tonal harmony and so forth. From him, some might find it interesting to investigate Messiaen or Boulez because they've taken certain elements from Debussy.

Of course, composers like Bartók and Richard Strauss should also be mentioned. There are marvelous works by both of them. The Strauss symphonic poems are really the core of music after Wagner, I would say.

R.H.   Do you feel that young people today relate more to contemporary music than their parents and grandparents did? We think of most people in their 40's to 60's today—even though they've been raised in the twentieth century—as still being basically oriented to nineteenth-century Romantic music. Do you feel this is true of younger people?

S.S.   Well, young people are not as shocked, maybe, as some of the older generation—who were unprepared. But I don't think, really, that young people today relate to contemporary music directly. I still believe that the only true way to understand music is through knowing the past. This is my deep belief. I think contemporary music is fascinating, but the only way to really appreciate what is being done now is to know what went before.

• *HILDE SOMER*

Vienna-born pianist, now living in the U.S.

H.S.   I would start off with modern music—because I think that music that has a beat, or dissonance or folk roots will be easier for today's young people to relate to. They've been weaned on rock and folk and country music. My first suggestion therefore would be a recording by Copland, the dean of American composers— either his *El Salon Mexico* or his *Lincoln Portrait*. I think it's marvelous to hear Lincoln's words as spoken by someone like Adlai Stevenson, with Ormandy conducting Copland's beautiful music. People who don't know too much about music may relate better if there is something else that involves them—like the words in the *Lincoln Portrait* or the Mexican folk tune of *El Salon Mexico*.

Next, I would recommend Stravinsky's *Rite of Spring*—for the rhythm. I would suggest the Boulez recording of this work. For a third modern recording I would suggest Villa-Lobos' *Bachianas Brasileiras No. 5*, for soprano and celli—preferably the Victoria de los Angeles recording with Villa-Lobos conducting, and which also includes the Bachianas No. 2, 6, and 9 on the same recording. They are all very folklike and very interesting. Then I'd suggest the recording called *The Well-Tempered Synthesizer*.

R.H.   With the Moog Synthesizer?

H.S.   Yes. It's a take-off on Bach's *Well-Tempered Clavier*, and includes works by Bach, Handel, Monteverdi, and others. I think it's fascinating to hear a modern electronic instrument with man-made sound *combined* with such music. It will introduce young people to some great old music in an interesting, contemporary way—and certainly give them something to think about. Of course, it's a thrilling recording on its own, and the sound is extraordinary.

Then, I think we should include a basic Beethoven Symphony—the Fifth, as recorded by Bernstein and the New York Philharmonic, since it also includes a most marvelous lecture by Bernstein called "How a Great Symphony Was Written."

Lastly, I think Scriabin is a good choice for young people today. He's all rainbows. He was for brotherhood and eternal peace long ago. He saw lights with his music and *wanted* lights with his music, but seventy years ago technology was not advanced enough to fulfill his dream. If he lived today he'd be one of the heroes of the young generation. I am particularly fond of his Fourth Piano Sonata. He wrote a poem for that sonata, and it says: "There's a star beckoning from far away. . . ." This star, in the course of the sonata, is transformed into the blazing sun. It's one of his most beautiful pieces—and, I would say, a bridge between Romantic and modern music.

R.H.   Your recording of it was the first, I believe.

H.S.   Yes. I hope you don't think me too immodest for including it on my list. But I really would like every young listener to hear some Scriabin, and I think that's a good piece to begin with.

48

Michael Tilson Thomas

46

Hilde Somer

49

Tamas Vasary

50

Roger Voisin

47

Christian Steiner

51

Alexis Weissenberg

R.H.   When you play Scriabin in concert, you sometimes do so with a light show. You're not packaging any light shows with your records yet, are you? Do you think it might happen some day?

H.S.   Oh, yes! As a matter of fact, a number of companies are working on a compatible system by which you can put a tape into your television set and see a picture simultaneously with a recording. So that may be the thing of the *near* future!

R.H.   You indicated earlier that you liked electronic music.

H.S.   I didn't say electronic *music*—I said instruments. I think some electronic music is interesting, but to me it's not really music—it's just sounds. But instruments like the Moog—well, *that* might well be something for the future. Strings and all these very perishable and fragile components which we use today might be supplemented by things which could be much sturdier. Look, the piano tuner is a dying breed. An electronic instrument needs no piano tuner. You just turn a lever and it's tuned. So I think modernization of a lot of old equipment will take place.

R.H.   You're not implying that the pianist is a dying breed too?

H.S.   I hope not! I think machines are marvelous, but even for landing on the moon we needed the human brain and human beings to supplement the computer.

R.H.   But do you think pianists will be less involved in the future with the piano as a pure instrument, and may use it in a different form from that which we now know?

H.S.   I wouldn't be surprised. I think there's a lot of mind expansion, and old barriers are falling. I think there's an evolution all around. But music will always *be*.

• CHRISTIAN STEINER

Berlin-born pianist and photographer, now living in New York.

C.S.   I am in violent disagreement with those people who think you should have one piece from the Baroque period, one piece from the Classical, one from the Romantic, and so forth. The person may get a good view of music overall, but I don't believe that's the way to start to *love* music. And loving music is, actually, what the result should be.

R.H.   Then how would you start?

C.S.   You start the same as when you learn anything—and that's very simply. You start with music that is the easiest to understand, easiest to listen to, and easiest—immediately—to like. It should be music that will stimulate you to listen to more music, that is so compelling that someone who has not listened to classical music before has the urge to go on. I know that, as a child, one of the easiest pieces I found to listen to was the Tchaikovsky Piano Concerto No. 1. I loved it. I wanted to play it. And I learned it.

R.H.   Was this before or after you started taking piano lessons?

C.S.   I heard it, probably, about the age of nine. I started studying piano at five. It was also the first piece I ever performed, when I was fifteen, and that was because I had fallen in love with it right from the start.

R.H.   Do you think it is a good introduction for others?

C.S.   Definitely. Its popularity proves that it is easy to listen to. Also, take the second movement of the Mozart 21st piano concerto, which was used in the film *Elvira Madigan*—this, too, is easy to listen to. I've read somewhere that when explorers went to Africa and tried music on primitive tribes, Mozart seemed to have the most impact. So maybe Mozart would be a good idea for anyone to start; I'm afraid I'm too involved with music myself to be able to judge that. But the fact that the *Elvira Madigan* theme was such a hit would seem to prove that it is easy to like.
Another piece that I believe would immediately stick is Orff's *Carmina Burana*. It's primitive. It's powerful. It's rhythmic. A listener might say, "Oh, so that belongs to that so-called highbrow music? I'm going to listen to more." The incentive has to be there. The work has to be appealing. Even if later on you decide you can't stand it anymore after the tenth hearing—it's still a good work to start with. Also, maybe some French Impressionistic music might be easy to listen to at first.

R.H.   Like Debussy or Ravel?

C.S.   Debussy more than Ravel, I think.

R.H.   Why do you single out Impressionism? Didn't you say you disliked the idea of somebody taking a representative piece from each period?

C.S.   Yes, unless you can find a piece that is really easy to understand. And that's not likely in each period. I tend to feel that Baroque music would be—to the non-experienced listener—fairly boring, run-of-the-mill. There are exceptions to that, of course. My point is simply to choose works that are as palatable as possible. Avoid scholarly works at the beginning.

R.H.   In other words, each person should decide what *type* of music he or she likes most and then stick to that, rather than what a teacher or someone else says he *should* listen to?

C.S.   Young people should expand their interests gradually. Since you are asking for records which someone will listen to by himself, then I'd say start with something that will sustain the listener's interest—so that he will *want* to go out and buy the sixth, seventh, and eighth record, and much more. Gradually he can get into the more difficult things. But start out light. When you learn *anything*, you have to start out light.

• *MICHAEL TILSON THOMAS*

American conductor and pianist. Conductor of the Buffalo Philharmonic, and director of the New York Philharmonic's Young People's Concerts.

M.T.T.   The pieces I'd recommend would be ones which would involve the listener in the *experience* of music, rather than necessarily pieces which I consider to be the most important masterworks. Hopefully, one could find a combination of both of those. But I'd start out by recommending a recording of *The Play of Daniel* [Decca, 79402], as an example of the most important, germinal phase of all our music. I would then suggest a stylistic recording, if such exists, of harpsichord music—perhaps some harpsichord concerti of Bach. This has interest in terms of performance practice, instruments and virtuosity, as well as being sublime music.

Then I'd skip a little bit and recommend a recording of Stravinsky's *The Rite of Spring*. Also, perhaps some pieces like the Davidovsky *Synchronisms for Electronic and Live Instruments* or one of Stockhausen's electronic pieces. I would also certainly have to recommend that he get *some* record of a major Asian musical discipline or some non-Western musical discipline—without which, I think, it's almost impossible to understand the uniqueness of *our* music.

R.H.   Would you skip all between Bach and Stravinsky?

M.T.T.   Not at all. But when we get to the nineteenth century, I have a feeling that young people today simply do not connect with certain aspects of late nineteenth-century music. But a piece like the Brahms *Variations on a Theme by Haydn* might be very good. Or maybe some big, sweeping Russian work like the Tchaikovsky Fourth Symphony. I would also certainly suggest they get a Victoria de los Angeles record—such as the *Centuries of Spanish Song* record—just for the sheer appreciation of the possibilities of vocal expression.

R.H.   Any particular piano pieces, since you've also recorded as a pianist?

M.T.T.   Some Liszt, as played by Horowitz, a record of that kind—to show a consummate virtuoso and, at the same time, the control of immense musical forces.

R.H.   You mentioned Oriental music. Do you think such music has particular relationship to young people today or to the age we are living in? Or do you think it's important for an understanding of all music in general?

M.T.T.   All three reasons. Besides, I think Oriental music develops certain kinds of things which are not very much developed in Western music, or at least weren't until recent times. For example, if you compare *The Play of Daniel*, which is a piece from the twelfth century, with the UNESCO series of records of Japanese Gagaku music, music which dates from at least 350 years *earlier,* you realize what an astounding kind of already-developed sense of rhythmic structure and variation preceded us.

R.H.   But for somebody just starting out—especially a young person who says he knows nothing about music—what are the advantages of going this far back? Is it just for historical comprehension?

M.T.T.   And the perspective. I agree with a comment that Stravinsky once made that nothing is as boring as the recent past. And I think the kind of music which might, in the full sense of being "interesting," *not* turn off a young person today is something completely different from the kind of commercially available, "non-heard" music that's everywhere around us today—as backgrounds for movies or that's piped into restaurants or elevators or wherever you go. That's why I think young people will find this kind of music very exciting. Look at the tremendous appeal that Hindu music has had in the past few years on college campuses. It's an immense shock to be suddenly confronted with the full-blown development of something so utterly unique and marvelous. Personally, I would rather do nothing but listen to many pieces by Mahler, but I wouldn't particularly recommend these pieces to a beginner. I know, too, from some of the youth concerts that I've done in Los Angeles, that people in their teens and early 20's seem to react very, very well to music of the Classical and Baroque periods, and also to present-day new music.

R.H.   Do you think any of the things that the Beatles and other pop groups have done, utilizing Baroque music or Oriental instruments, has had any influence on making young people more receptive to serious music today?

M.T.T.   Certainly. But what I think is most marvelous is that *all* the barriers are breaking down. All the differentiations are collapsing, so that we are no longer living in a time when, because one liked Wagner, one therefore couldn't like Brahms. Today you just simply decide what it is that *you* like. It may be only one piece by some particular composer, but that's fine. You listen to that because *you* want to.

• *TAMAS VASARY*

Hungarian pianist, now living in Switzerland.

T.V.   I would certainly recommend that he or she buy works that represent different styles—something Classical, something Romantic, something Impressionistic, and something modern. Let's say not *too* modern. Maybe a Bartók work that is still tonal. I wouldn't give someone atonal music to start with. Instead, I'd choose from the great classics: Bach, Mozart, and Beethoven. Then one Chopin and one Debussy.

R.H.   Any specific works by these composers?

T.V.   For Bach, maybe a two-part invention for piano, maybe the first two-part invention. Or maybe something from the first book of the *Well-Tempered Clavier*, the C major Prelude and Fugue. For Mozart: *Eine Kleine Nachtmusik*. For Beethoven: one of the symphonies, maybe the Fifth. Then one Chopin work: the F minor Ballade. And for Bartók, the Third Piano Concerto.

R.H.   And your reasons for picking these pieces?

T.V.   As you can certainly see, I have chosen pieces which are very popular. I believe in popularity. If a work holds onto its popularity over the years, it means it is something special, something really of genius. I think every composer dreams of writing striking tunes, striking rhythms, or striking moments which will be remembered for years and years by others. Almost anyone can learn how to compose a prelude and fugue, or a sonata—but *what* really makes the difference, *what* makes people react to it, you cannot always tell. If you asked me *why* do I like my favorite pieces, I could probably talk about the structure, or the harmonic progression, or things like that. But that's not why it might appeal to *you*. It's exactly like one's reaction to a woman. A man may see a certain woman as beautiful and fall in love with her—but to others she may be less beautiful. The difference is that, in music, the whole public falls in love with certain works. And the public is, as a whole, a marvelous critic—a better critic than we, as individual musicians, often are.

• *ROGER VOISIN*

Leading trumpet player with the Boston Symphony Orchestra and Boston Pops Orchestra until his retirement in 1973. He has also conducted recordings of Baroque and other music.

R.V.　The first thing I would say is get some Bach. Particularly some of Bach's keyboard music. I find this not only obviously very musical, but also something in which you hear something else every time you hear it. And, of course, the Beethoven quartets—particularly the late Beethoven quartets. Personally, I myself prefer music played by a small group instead of by a big group. But I would still recommend a Mahler or Bruckner symphony—to experience the *tremendous* sound of a great orchestra. Maybe, too, some music of Prokofiev, which is really wonderful music. I feel that a young person of today, particularly, would find the type of coloring in Prokofiev very intriguing and very entertaining. I'd also suggest Mussorgsky's *Pictures at an Exhibition* (the orchestral version) as a very good piece of descriptive music. Then some of the great French music—like Ravel's *Daphnis and Chloé*, a tremendous piece. Or Debussy's *Pelléas et Mélisande*—for color and to show that you can have a very different musical atmosphere with very little action.

Now for performers. For an instrumentalist, of course something by Heifetz—to see what can be achieved on the violin. And then pianists like Horowitz or Rubinstein, to see what can be achieved on the keyboard. And young Jacqueline du Pré on the cello. I think I would even flirt a bit into another field: Doc Severinsen, for instance, is a very wonderful trumpet player. You wouldn't call him classical, certainly—but to me it is very interesting to see what he can achieve on his instrument. There's also a wonderful Frenchman, a classical trumpet player named Maurice André.

Now, back to works—naturally, one of the Beethoven symphonies! I'd say the Ninth, because of the popular song taken from it, "The Song of Joy." The last time I played the Ninth with the Boston Symphony, I couldn't help but think how surprised some young people were going to be when they heard the *whole* Ninth

Symphony for the first time. You know, I used to have a tendency—and I'm ashamed to admit it—to say let's give young people a lot of the quick and simple pieces. I don't anymore. And I find, strangely enough, that the young audience today seems to like Beethoven especially.

R.H.   You mentioned Bach keyboard music. Would you single out any one specific work?

R.V.   Probably something from the *Art of the Fugue* or the *Well-Tempered Clavier*. It is a difficult choice for me to make. For Prokofiev, *anything* by Prokofiev! I think the *Love for Three Oranges* is a marvelous piece, or any of his piano concertos.

R.H.   You've mentioned two operas, Debussy's *Pelléas et Mélisande* and now Prokofiev's *Love for Three Oranges*. Do you think people should start by trying to listen to a whole opera or to just an album of highlights?

R.V.   I think they should start with that wonderful record Anna Russell made some years ago explaining Wagner's *Ring* [Columbia MG 31199, *mono only*]. It is a most wonderful record. And it's not making fun of music. I think Anna Russell really brings it all to reality, taking so much of the stuffiness out of it. I would break somebody into opera that way.

• *ALEXIS WEISSENBERG*

Bulgarian-born, U.S.-educated pianist, now living in Paris.

A.W.   I would try to get not so much certain composers as the right performers. I think we must consider the image of certain artists like Van Cliburn, who is virtually a national hero, or Leonard Bernstein, who has done such phenomenal work on TV, particularly for young people. I think, therefore, that whatever symphony you buy performed by Bernstein is more important than who the composer is. It brings people much closer to him because they've *seen* him. They may listen more carefully and more attentively to a recording of his than to the same symphony by any other conductor. It's unbelievable how much you can bring music *up* to people—and I don't say down to people!—if they know something about the artist producing it.

R.H.   What other artists besides Bernstein and Cliburn would you include?

A.W.   Artur Rubinstein, of course. And Vladimir Horowitz. Since they've both had TV specials, I think many people are getting to know who they are and what they mean. I would stress again that the interpreter in this case is extremely important.

R.H.   What Weissenberg recordings?

A.W.   I can't answer that. But I would stress that young people should not buy five or six or even three *long* recordings. I think young people today are nervous. They can easily become inattentive, and can rarely concentrate on something unfamiliar that lasts more than thirty minutes. So they should try short pieces first—such as Chopin *Nocturnes*, played by Rubinstein for example. Or maybe some ballet music, *before* the big symphonies. I think it is wrong to give young people the big, fat, solid pieces first, because then they start hating music rather than liking it.

Summary

Trying to summarize the foregoing fifty interviews statistically is complicated by the different ways in which the musicians phrased their responses, and by the varying degrees of emphasis they gave certain choices.

But for those interested in knowing which composers were most frequently mentioned, here is how it breaks down—at least the composers named by five or more different people. (The numbers refer to the individual interviews in which one or more works by that composer was recommended.)

Beethoven, 35. Mozart, 29. Bach, 23. Stravinsky, 20. Tchaikovsky, 18. Bartók, 15. Brahms, 11. Debussy, 8. Chopin, 7. Prokofiev, 7. Puccini, 7. Ravel, 7. Mahler, 6. Berg, 5. Berlioz, 5. Copland, 5. Handel, 5. Haydn, 5. Rachmaninoff, 5. Schoenberg, 5. Schumann, 5. Strauss, 5.

The most frequently named individual works were: Beethoven Fifth Symphony, 13. Stravinsky *Le Sacre du Printemps*, 9. Beethoven Ninth Symphony, 8. Bach Brandenburg Concertos, 7. Mozart *Don Giovanni*, 6. Stravinsky *Firebird*, 6. Bartók Concerto for Orchestra, 5. Mozart *Marriage of Figaro*, 5.

If the responses reveal any summary proposition it is, I believe, how many different approaches there are to discovering music—and how valid each approach is according to individual tastes.

That, to me, is the unique and special joy of classical music—finding out what *you* like and what *you* believe to be the best. The rest of this book is designed to help you do just that.

PART TWO

Fifty Composers and their Major Works

How to Use This Section

Any "basic" music list can never hope to please everyone. Musical tastes are quite individual, and *should* be. But for those seeking general guidance about leading composers and their works, this section seeks to provide concise, pertinent information.

The composers discussed in this section represent those generally recognized today as major figures, those most often featured on concert programs. They are arranged chronologically by date of birth, from the Baroque period to today's contemporary scene. An introductory chapter on early music is also included.

A brief biographical sketch of each composer is followed by a listing of several of his major works. In general, they are the ones most likely to be encountered on symphony programs, although certain chamber, solo, or vocal works are also included.

A list of preferred recordings is then given for each work. Only the best available performances as of 1974 are indicated. In most cases, the performances are on stereo discs. If the performance is available only in a monaural edition, it is so noted. Wherever tape cassettes, tape cartridges, or quadrasonic versions are available, they are indicated.

Critical evaluations of these performances follow. These evaluations are intended for the average listener, *not* musical experts, and thus reflect the quality or feeling of the performance in non-technical terms. These evaluations, admittedly, rely heavily on descriptive adjectives—chosen to summarize the recordings in the most concise manner and to indicate basic differences between the performances.

The listing of various (and interpretively different) performances is not intended to make a newcomer's choice more difficult, but to indicate the wealth and variety of good recorded performances available—and possible with classical music. The author hopes that the reader will use his or her own judgment in deciding which descriptive comments come closest to his own tastes.

The listing, however, is in a sequence representing the author's own preferences, and the symbol ★ precedes the author's first choice among the available versions.

The symbol **b** before a listing indicates it is a so-called budget-label recording, generally selling for less than $3.50 a disc.

If a recording involves more than a single disc or tape, the number of discs or tapes in the set is indicated.

Other works included on the same disc or tape are referred to as the "coupling" or as "overside."

The first name in the listing of strictly orchestral works is that of the conductor. In opera recordings, the conductor's name is first, followed by the principal singers. In recordings of concertos and other works involving soloists, the soloists' names are listed *before* the conductor.

Wherever actual recording dates were not confirmable through the record company involved, the year in which the recording was released is given. Classical recordings are usually released one to three years after the recording session.

A "postscript" chapter at the end of this section lists an additional group of composers of works that remain popular on records or that may be of special interest.

But First a Few Words about Early Music

Trying to narrow down the wealth of good music composed over the centuries to fifty major composers is a difficult and, inevitably, arbitrary process. But deciding on a specific composer with whom to begin is even more difficult.

Until recent years, concert programs rarely featured music composed before the 18th century. But beginning in the 1950's there has been a vast reawakening of interest in music of the Renaissance and Baroque periods—spurred on to a large degree by recordings by instrumental ensembles and vocal groups dedicated to unearthing and preserving works that have long been neglected.

Accordingly, some introductory comments about early music are in order—first, to help newcomers discover some of the extraordinary works of these early periods and, second, to provide a brief historical background for understanding the development of music by the later composers discussed in the remainder of this section.

Until the Renaissance, European music was primarily vocal music. It generally took two forms: *church music*, usually hymns or psalms sung to Biblical or other religious texts; and *folk songs* such as lullabies, spinning songs, drinking songs, harvest songs, and so on. Originally, both forms of this music were very simple—with one line of melody, called monophony (one voice), predominating. Very little of this early music was written down, for there was no consistent system of musical notation until the late 10th and early 11th centuries, when Pope John XIX endorsed the system organized by Guido of Arezzo—a system that still forms the basis of modern musical notation.

As time went on, and particularly as new churches and cathedrals rose throughout Europe, church choirs began to embellish their singing. Like the woodcarvers and goldsmiths of their day, the choirs developed more intricate and ornate patterns. And more and more of this music came to be written down.

The Renaissance witnessed a rich and profuse development of the art of music. Literally thousands of pieces of music were composed by such masters as Jacob Obrecht (c.1450–1505), Heinrich Isaac (c.1450–1517), Josquin des Prez (c.1445–1521), Pierre de la Rue (c.1460–1518), Giovanni di Palestrina (1524–1594), Roland de Lassus (1532–1594), and William Byrd (1543–1623).

Sacred music dominated—in the form of the *Mass* and the *motet* (settings of Latin sacred texts). But secular music also thrived—in the *madrigal* in England and Italy, the *chanson* in France, and the *minnesong* in Germany.

The essential feature of Renaissance vocal music was its polyphonic texture—that is, simultaneous melodic lines, with all of them having roughly the same degree of activity and importance so that no one of them dominated for any appreciable length of time. (In contrast, later musical styles tended to emphasize one melodic line with everything else subjected to a definite secondary or accompanying function.)

Renaissance vocal music was further characterized by its continuous flow, with only rare complete resting points within a piece. Its rhythm was steady and continuous, lacking in extreme contrasts. Its harmony was mild, and its melodic lines restrained and carefully balanced. In comparison to later styles, this music was cool and non-dramatic, although beautiful in its own terms. A good example of Renaissance sacred polyphony is found in a recording of selected works by Josquin des Prez by the New York Pro Musica (Decca stereo disc DL-79410). This recording also demonstrates aspects of instrumental music of the Renaissance.

Instruments performed a variety of functions during this time. More often than not, they were used in conjunction with vocal music—sometimes duplicating a part being sung and sometimes replacing the voice altogether.

The instruments of the period were many and varied, but were rarely standardized. They included the lute (a multi-stringed, plucked instrument that came in varying sizes and shapes), the viol (a multi-stringed, bowed predecessor of the violin), the recorder (a reedless woodwind instrument similar to a flute), various other woodwind and brass instruments, and keyboard instruments of the harpsichord type.

Purely instrumental music began to come into its own during the Renaissance, although it occupied a secondary position to choral music. Music for the courtly dance was important, and the Renaissance dance suite was a notable forerunner of the more elaborately worked out and sophisticated instrumental music of the Baroque and later periods. A good example of this type of early dance piece is found in a 1960 recording of Dances from *Terpsichore* (Deutsche Grammophon Archive stereo disc ARC-198166; cassette 923-002; cartridge 88-166) by the German composer Michael Praetorius (1571–1621).

During the 16th century, kings, princes, counts, dukes, and other nobles increasingly sought out musicians to compose and perform for their courts. They also began to train more and more instrumental players as well as singers. And the development of music printing made possible the increasingly wide distribution of musical works.

The early 17th century ushered in vast changes in musical style—changes so great that the course of music history was profoundly affected. The period of music history known as the Baroque was born in Italy. It grew out of the work of a group of Florentine scholars and musicians who have come to be known as the Camerata. This group, rejecting the tenets of the vocal polyphony of Renaissance sacred music, developed what they called the "new music." Its basic feature was the prominence of one voice part sung by a solo singer, with a single instrumental accompaniment (the *continuo*) which supplied an unobtrusive harmonic support for the voice.

The new music of the Camerata was secular rather than sacred, dramatic and passionate rather than ceremonial. Its rhythms were generally lively, its harmonies expressive, its melodies designed to reflect the meaning and spirit of the words.

The work of the members of the Camerata resulted in new techniques of composition which eventually culminated in the great vocal forms that characterize the Baroque: the *cantata,* the *oratorio,* and the *opera.* Among the first composers to employ these new techniques was Claudio Monteverdi—at whom we shall take a closer look on following pages.

But the Baroque also stands as the era in which instrumental music came into its own, achieving a status at least equal to vocal music. The instruments themselves underwent considerable improvement in design and construction, and composers began to write for the particular individual quality and distinctive characteristics of each instrument. The pipe organ and harpsichord became basic keyboard instruments, and violins fashioned by such craftsmen as Nicolo Amati (1569–1684), Giuseppe Guarneri (1681–1742), and Antonio Stradivari (1644–1737) became world famous.

With these advances appeared new forms of instrumental composition: the *suite,* the *sonata,* the *concerto grosso,* and the *solo concerto.*

The Baroque suite was actually not a new form but an expansion of the dance suite of the Renaissance—a set of contrasting dance movements imbued with the new Baroque style and adapted to either the keyboard or an instrumental ensemble.

The sonata was cultivated in two forms: the *ensemble sonata,* a work in several movements for several instruments; and, more importantly, the *solo sonata,* a work in several movements for a solo instrument (often the violin) with accompaniment provided by a keyboard instrument (usually the harpsichord).

The Baroque *concerto grosso* provides one of the richest bodies of music that has come down to us from the early periods of music. The concerto grosso is a work in several movements for a group of solo instruments (the concertino) and a larger, contrasting group (the ripieno).

Among the earliest known and finest concerti grossi are those of the Italian composer Arcangelo Corelli (1653–1731). In his Twelve Concerti Grossi (Op. 6), written in 1682, the solo group consists of two violins and a cello contrasted with a string orchestra with continuo (together making up the ripieno). The contrast involved can be described primarily in terms of soft vs. loud, light vs. heavy, or thin vs. thick. Among recorded versions of this work, two stand out: (1) a single disc 1967 release of four of the twelve concerti grossi, including the most popular ("Christmas," No. 8 in G minor), played with verve and full-blooded style by the Virtuosi di Roma led by Renato Fasano (Angel stereo disc S36130), and (2) a 3-disc budget-priced album of all twelve, played with refined style and spirit by the Vienna Sinfonietta under Max Goberman (Columbia Odyssey 3-disc set 32360002) and recorded in the early 1960's.

For Follow-Up Consideration

The Seraphim Guide to Renaissance Music, a 3-disc, budget-priced album released in 1970, made up of seventy-two short vocal and instrumental (but no choral) works spanning the 13th to 17th centuries. It includes works by Perotin, Tassin, Machaut, Dufay, Lorenzo da Firenze, Jacopo da Bologna, Henry VIII, Othmayr, Sweelinck, Josquin des Pres, and others (some anonymous)—performed by the Syntagma Musicum, an excellent young Dutch group (named after a famous treatise on music written in the early 1600's by Michael Praetorius). Inevitably, as with any grab-bag set covering so much territory, the standard varies from work to work. But considering the price this is a distinctly worthwhile collection, with generally good sound engineering (Seraphim stereo 3-disc set SIC-6052).

Madrigal Masterpieces, the first of several excellent discs made in the early 1960's by countertenor Alfred Deller and the Deller Consort, with madrigals by Monteverdi, Gesualdo, Byrd, Lassus, Morley, and others (Vanguard stereo disc 5031).

English Music for Recorders and Consort Viols, a delightful and varied collection of short English works ranging from mid-Renaissance to early Baroque, led by Frans Brueggen in this 1967 recording (Telefunken stereo disc SAWT-9511).

Baroque Guitar, a group of excellent works by Sor, Sanz, Weiss, Visée, and Bach, performed by the outstanding English guitarist Julian Bream, in a 1966 release that shows the unique lyric beauty and rhythmic pulse of the guitar in this type of music (RCA Red Seal stereo disc LSC-2878; cartridge R8S-1060).

Top Hits . . . c.1420–1635 A.D., for all its deliberately commercial title, this 1967 release by Enoch Light's Project-3 company (famous for its stereo showpiece albums of today's pop hits) is a good collection of Renaissance pieces, stylishly played by a group called the Renaissance Quartet, and recorded in ultra-crisp stereo (Project-3 stereo disc PR-7000).

• CLAUDIO MONTEVERDI

Pronounced: mahn-tih-*vayr*-dee. Born May 15, 1567, in Cremona, Italy. Died November 29, 1643, in Venice, Italy.

SIGNIFICANCE: Composer of early operas, madrigals, and church music, and among the first to write out accompaniments for vocal music in which he not only used a large number of instruments but also specified exactly which instruments were to play which notes.

BACKGROUND: The eldest son of a doctor, Monteverdi began his musical career at an early age, as a choirboy in his native Cremona—the same town in which the Amati family was then earning its reputation for great violin-making. Monteverdi published his first works when he was seventeen. Most of them were madrigals on religious themes, and many were daringly original in form. At the age of twenty-five, he entered the service of the Duke of Mantua as a singer, viol player, and composer. The duke, an active patron of the arts, had a small orchestra which performed not only for balls and fêtes, but also for plays and ballets. Over the next eleven years, Monteverdi composed prolifically for the duke, often experimenting with new forms and with combinations of different instruments to convey different moods of expression.

His experiments led him to compose in 1607 what is generally accepted as the first successful opera: *Orfeo*. It was by no means the first opera (a 1594 work by two

Florentines, Jacopo Peri and Giulio Caccini, is usually accorded that honor), but *Orfeo*'s difference from its predecessors was enormous. Instead of a simple accompaniment to the singers, to be played on a keyboard instrument with sketchily indicated background for a handful of other instrumentalists, Monteverdi employed thirty-six pieces in his orchestra, and set down exact notes for each of them. Moreover, his orchestra became important for its own sake—having independent themes designed to reinforce the meaning or expressiveness of a scene. As for the vocal line itself, Monteverdi combined the new Baroque techniques of *recitative* (a kind of singing speech in which the words are the most important element) and *arioso* (a more lyrical kind of music in which the melodic line holds primary interest).

Orfeo was such a success that the duke commissioned a second opera, *Arianna*—which became one of the most popular works of its time. Six thousand people are reported to have seen its first performance in 1608 in an immense theatre built especially by the duke to celebrate his son's wedding.

Shortly thereafter, the duke died and Monteverdi went to Venice to become *maestro di cappella* (choir master) at St. Mark's Cathedral, then one of the most prestigious posts in all Italy. He raised the standard of performance to the highest then known in Europe, and remained in the post until his death. He wrote mostly church music during this period, and eventually took orders as a priest in 1630 (his wife had died five years before he moved to Venice).

But the opening of Europe's first public opera house in Venice in 1637 turned his creative interests again toward opera, even though he was then 70. For the house he wrote his last two works: *The Return of Ulysses* (*Il ritorno d'Ulisse*) and *The Coronation of Poppea* (*L'Incoronazione di Poppea*), usually regarded as his crowning achievements. When he died he was the most famous musician of his time. His work had not only fused choral and instrumental forms in a new way, but had also taken it on newly expressive paths.

Vespro della Beata Vergine (Vespers of the Blessed Virgin)

Composed in 1610 and dedicated to Pope Paul V, the Vespers are considered not only Monteverdi's finest sacred work but also a marvelous combination of Renaissance and Baroque techniques and stylistic elements all rolled into a new kind of religious musical expression. The use of solo voices, the rich instrumental ensembles, the harmonic expressiveness, and the rhythmic liveliness of early Baroque opera are effectively fused with such Renaissance traditions as the use of plainchant and polyphonic texture. The Vespers are scored for a number of vocal soloists, two choruses, and a large instrumental ensemble of strings, winds, and brasses, with other instruments (such as harp, lute, harpsichord, and organ) used as continuo instruments. This is, as far as modern historians know, the first sacred work to use an "operatic" orchestra. Its fourteen large movements vary in style and design. There has long been disagreement over whether Monteverdi intended the Vespers as a unified work or as a collection from which individual parts were to be chosen on different occasions. The total length of the Vespers is nearly two hours. Each of the fourteen movements, however, stands as an individual entity—with the final two movements being alternate settings of the "Magnificat." Accordingly, it is not uncommon for the work to be performed on concert programs as "Selections from Vespro della Beata Vergine."

Recommended Recordings

★ Craft, Columbia Baroque Ensemble, Gregg Smith Singers, Texas Boys' Choir, soloists (Columbia stereo 2-disc set CSP-2S-763)

Harnoncourt, Vienna Concentus Musicus, Vienna Boys Choir, Hamburg Monteverdi Chorus, soloists (Telefunken stereo 2-disc set S-9501/2).

b Stevens, Orchestra of the Accademia Monteverdiana, Ambrosian Singers, soloists (Vanguard/Cardinal stereo 2-disc set VCS-10001/2).

Comments

Since Monteverdi's music survives only in sketches comprising the vocal parts plus some of the instrumental parts and a figured bass, what we hear today is usually a performing edition put together in this century by scholars, musicologists, and practicing musicians. Moreover, performance practice varies widely in the use of either contemporary instruments or authentic period ones.

Robert Craft uses his own edition of the Vespers, performing thirteen of the pieces in rearranged order and omitting some of the liturgical responses so as to heighten the dramatic impact. Purists may disapprove of this, as well as the fact that he uses modern instruments. But newcomers to Monteverdi are likely to find Craft's recording more accessible and quite beautiful. The choirs and soloists sing expressively, and the 1967 sound engineering is excellent, especially in the echo passages. And far down among the credits appears the name Michael Tilson Thomas as harpsichordist—one of the first recordings the young conductor made during his student days in Los Angeles.

Nikolaus Harnoncourt also uses his own edition for his mid-1960's recording, and also offers thirteen of the pieces. He includes the responses Craft omits. Harnoncourt further uses a whole array of ancient instruments including recorders, lutes, virginals, and Baroque trombones, so that the sound is much closer to that of Montverdi's own time. The performance is a bit more stiff and scholarly than Craft's, but the choral singing is outstanding, and one of the tenors, Nigel Rogers, is particularly impressive.

Denis Stevens approaches the Vespers as a collection rather than a whole for his 1967 release, using his own edition for eight of the pieces, with modern instrumentation. The performers are not always as polished as Craft's or Harnoncourt's, and the tempos are generally slower, but the overall effect is deeply expressive, and at budget prices the set has considerable merit.

For Follow-Up Consideration

L'Incoronazione di Poppea, (*The Coronation of Poppea*), considered by some critics to be not only Monteverdi's greatest theatrical work but also an astonishingly modern one in its probing of the innermost aspects of human character, particularly in relation to the conflicting values of society and the individual. The story, set in Nero's Rome, deals with Poppea's schemes to become Nero's empress. RECOMMENDED RECORDING:

Pritchard conducting, Royal Philharmonic Orchestra, Glyndebourne Festival Chorus, Laszlo (Poppea), Richard Lewis (Nero), Dominguez (Arnalta), Bible (Ottavia), Cuénod (Lucano), other soloists (Seraphim stereo 2-disc set S1B-6073), originally released on Angel in 1965 and reissued on budget-priced Seraphim in 1972; an abridged version by Raymond Leppard prepared for the Glyndebourne Festival, with the emphasis less on faithfulness to Monteverdi's instrumentation and more on modern theatrical impact. Taken on those terms, it is a beautifully sung, dramatically compelling performance, with excellent sound engineering.

Orfeo, Monteverdi's pathbreaking opera of 1607, based on the ancient Greek legend of Orpheus and Eurydice. RECOMMENDED RECORDING: Harnoncourt conducting, Concentus Musicus and Capella Antiqua (of Germany), Kozma (Orfeo), Hansmann (Eurydice), other soloists (Telefunken stereo 3-disc set SKH-21), a 1967 recording the first complete version using authentic instruments; a splendidly sung, stylistically correct performance with a chamberlike quality appropriate to the work, and with very good sound engineering.

• ANTONIO VIVALDI

Pronounced: vee-*vahl*-dee. Born March 4, 1678 in Venice. Died July 28, 1741, in Vienna.

SIGNIFICANCE: Italian priest, composer, and violinist, one of the masters of Italian Baroque music, and the principal hero of the Baroque revival of recent decades.

BACKGROUND: The term Baroque (from the Portuguese *barocco,* a pearl of irregular shape) is sometimes simplified to mean a type of music that is "elegantly and irregularly fashioned" (like the gilt scroll ornamentation that decorates Baroque architecture). One of the most prolific of the composers of such music was Vivaldi. He wrote many oratorios, operas, and several hundred instrumental pieces, most of them concertos for almost every instrument known at that time (as well as combinations of them). According to harpsichordist Igor Kipnis, "A wag once observed that Vivaldi didn't write 400 concerti, but merely wrote one concerto 400 times; though exaggerated, the comment has a slight touch of truth." Baroque composers did indeed frequently rework their own material, as well as that of other composers, not because of lack of imagination but as a common compositional procedure of the period to use and re-use easily recognizable musical idioms. Bach so admired Vivaldi that he transcribed or extended more than a dozen of Vivaldi's works for different instruments; for example, Bach's Concerto for Four Harpsichords and Strings is a transcription of Vivaldi's Concerto for Four Violins and Strings.

Little is known about Vivaldi's life. His father was a violinist at San Marco in Venice, and presumably Vivaldi's first music teacher. Sometime before 1703 he entered the Roman Catholic priesthood, but he continued his musical studies at the same time.

In 1703 he became a teacher at a famous Venice foundling school for girls, the Seminario Musicale dell' Ospitale della Pietà, where he had the nickname of the "red priest" (for the color of his hair). In 1709 he became director of the school's concerts, and remained at least nominally in that post until about 1740. He is known to have traveled extensively throughout Italy and other parts of Europe between 1725 and 1736, performing his own works. In 1740 he settled in Vienna, hoping to win favor at the court of Charles VI as a composer. But he died three years later, unsuccessful in his goal and apparently in poverty.

After his death, most of his music slipped into obscurity, lying forgotten in libraries and various archives until the Baroque revival of recent years led scholars and others to seek it out.

Le Quattro Stagioni (The Four Seasons)

Perhaps the most popular of all Baroque instrumental works, *The Four Seasons* is a series of four short violin concertos in the Baroque style, each concerto representing one of the seasons (spring, summer, fall, winter). The strict fast-slow-fast scheme of the Baroque concerto is maintained for each of the successive movements, and Vivaldi's score is sprinkled with terms designed to set the mood of specific sections. For example, the phrase "*languidezza per il caldo*" (languidness because of the heat) appears over the opening bars of the second concerto, "Summer." In 1950 there were two recordings of *The Four Seasons* listed in the Schwann catalog; by 1974 there were twenty-three (one less than the Tchaikovsky Sixth Symphony, but three more than the Beethoven Fifth Symphony)—dramatic testimony to the recent Baroque revival.

Recommended Recordings

★ Fasano, Virtuosi di Roma (Angel stereo disc S-35877; cassette 4XS-35877; cartridge 8XS-35877)

b Goberman, New York Sinfonietta (Odyssey stereo disc 32160132)

Bernstein, members of the New York Philharmonic (Columbia stereo disc MS-6744)

Zukerman, English Chamber Orchestra (Columbia stereo disc M-31798; cassette 4XS-31798; cartridge 8XS-31798)

Comments

The Virtuosi di Roma have long specialized in Vivaldi's music, and their early 1960's recording is exceptionally good—stylistically correct, vibrant, expressive, and with beautiful ensemble playing.

Goberman's recording from the mid-1950's, reissued in 1967 on budget-priced Odyssey, holds up fairly well in terms of sound, and rates highly in terms of style and spirit.

Bernstein, conducting from the harpsichord with John Corigliano (then the Philharmonic's concertmaster) as violin soloist, leads a strongly virtuosic performance recorded in 1962, with some incredibly fast finales and some highly individual melodic flourishes. Purists of Baroque style may find it too "modern" an approach, but others should find it exciting.

Zukerman's 1973 release falls somewhere between Bernstein's and the others. The English Chamber Orchestra plays with style and grace, and Zukerman (violin soloist as well as conductor) digs in with a full-blooded gusto that may be more Romantic than Baroque but is nonetheless most effective.

For Follow-Up Consideration

Gloria in D, one of the best examples of Vivaldi's musical settings of a religious text. RECOMMENDED RECORDING: Robert Shaw, Adele Addison, Saramae Endich, Florence Kopleff, Robert Shaw Chorale (RCA stereo disc LSC-2883, cartridge R8S-5040), a superbly spirited, reverent mid-1960's performance featuring three of the finest American concert and oratorio singers. The disc edition also includes Vivaldi's Kyrie; the cartridge edition includes the Kyrie and also Bach's Motet No. 3, sung by the Shaw Chorale.

Concerto in D for Guitar and Orchestra, originally written for the lute but usually played by concert guitarists today. RECOMMENDED RECORDING: John Williams, English Chamber Orchestra (Columbia stereo disc MS-7327), a beautifully played performance with considerable rhythmic verve, coupled with Vivaldi's Concerto in A for Mandolin and Strings, and an interesting Concerto for Guitar and String Orchestra by Mauro Giuliani (1781–1828).

Concertos for Two Violins and Orchestra, of which Vivaldi wrote no fewer than twenty-three, obviously intrigued with the possibilities of adding to the virtuoso aspects of different harmonies and counterpoint not possible for a single soloist. RECOMMENDED RECORDING: Stern, D. Oistrakh, Ormandy, Philadelphia Orchestra (Columbia disc MS-6204), a historic recording of four of these concertos by the U.S. and Soviet violinists, made while Oistrakh was on a cultural exchange tour of the U.S. in 1959. The playing is exceptionally beautiful and expressive.

• *GEORGE FREDERICK HANDEL*

Pronounced: *han*-d'l. Born February 23, 1685, in Halle, Saxony (Germany). Died April 14, 1759, in London, England.

SIGNIFICANCE: German-born composer and organist who moved to England in his 20's and stayed to become the most famous composer of English oratorios on Biblical themes.

BACKGROUND: Handel taught himself to play the organ and harpsichord when he was seven. But his father, a Saxon barber, was determined that his son become a lawyer. He discouraged his son's musical ambitions—even after a prominent duke persuaded him to allow the boy to study music together with law. When his father died,

Handel, then eighteen, promptly dropped his law courses and concentrated full time on music. He served several years' musical apprenticeship in Hamburg, playing violin in the opera orchestra and composing. At twenty-one, following a duel with a rival musician, Handel left Germany for Italy, where he became a close friend of Domenico Scarlatti, the composer and harpsichordist, and began composing operas in the Italian style.

In 1711 he was invited to produce his opera *Rinaldo* in London. It was successful, and he stayed in England for the rest of his life—becoming a naturalized British subject in 1726 and formally Anglicizing the spelling of his name (originally Georg Friedrich Händel). For more than ten years he directed opera productions at the Royal Academy of Music, hired the singers, and composed about fifteen Italian-style operas for them. But in the 1730's public enthusiasm for opera waned, and the Royal Academy went bankrupt. Then, at fifty-two, Handel suffered a paralytic stroke.

After long months of rest, as his health improved, Handel became determined to regain his lost prestige—and to do so by way of the oratorio, then little known in England. These large-scale, dramatic musical settings of religious or mythological stories (for solo voices, chorus, and orchestra), sung in the vernacular rather than Latin, were presented in concert style, without scenery or costumes. Although Handel's first two oratorios failed to win the public, *Messiah* (1742) was an enormous success—particularly after King George II rose to his feet at the "Hallelujah Chorus." (It has since become a custom for audiences to stand at this part of *Messiah* performances.) Thereafter Handel produced one, sometimes two new oratorios every year until 1751, greatly expanding both the form and expressive depth of his choral writing. Illness and finally blindness plagued the last years of his life, but at the time of his death he was England's most popular and respected musician, and he was buried among England's great in Westminster Abbey.

Messiah

Messiah is a work of musical majesty and spiritual nobility, best-known for its joyous "Hallelujah Chorus." The work is in three parts, consisting of more than fifty individual pieces—dealing with the prophecy, advent, nativity, mission, sacrifice, atonement, ascension, and resurrection of Jesus. Over the years its instrumentation and ornamentation have been reworked by various conductors, choral directors, and soloists, so that few performances are ever alike. Moreover, in his own lifetime Handel often modified the score to meet the needs of individual performances or soloists, so that musicologists rarely agree on what the composer himself sanctioned.

Recommended Recordings (Complete)

★ Davis, London Symphony Orchestra and Chorus, with Harper, Watts, Wakefield, Shirley-Quirk (Philips stereo 3-disc set SC 71AX300)

Mackerras, English Chamber Orchestra, Ambrosian Singers, with Harwood, Baker, Esswood, Tear, Herincx (Angel stereo 3-disc set SCL-3705)

Shaw, Robert Shaw Orchestra and Chorale, with Raskin, Kopleff, Lewis, Paul (RCA Red Seal stereo 3-disc set LSC-6175)

b Somary, English Chamber Orchestra, Amor Artis Chorale, M. Price, Minton, Young, Diaz (Vanguard/Cardinal stereo 3-disc set VCS-10090)

Beecham, Royal Philharmonic and Chorus, Vyvyan, Sinclair, Vickers, Tozzi (RCA Red Seal 4-disc set LDS-6409)

Recommended Recordings (Highlights)

★ Davis, London Symphony, etc., as above (Philips stereo disc 900214; cassette PCR4-900-214; cartridge PC8-900-214)

Mackerras, English Chamber Orchestra, etc., as above (Angel stereo disc S-36530)

Shaw, Robert Shaw Orchestra and Chorale, etc., as above (RCA Red Seal stereo disc LSC-2966)

Beecham, Royal Philharmonic, etc., as above (RCA Red Seal stereo disc LDS-2447)

Comments

Handel comes vividly alive under Davis, whose 1966 release stands out for the fire and intensity of the performance, as well as for its attempt at authenticity in following instructions in scores from Handel's own time.

Beecham goes almost to the other extreme, using an edition almost Wagnerian in its scope and color. Yet there is no denying that Beecham's is a thrilling performance. Originally released in the late 1950's, the recording was officially withdrawn from RCA's active catalog in 1972, but may still be available in many stores. (There are also reports it may be reissued on the Seraphim budget label.)

Mackerras' 1967 release uses five soloists (including a countertenor) instead of the usual four, and is very dramatic, close to Davis' performance in style if not always in feeling, and the chorus is excellent.

Shaw's mid-1960's recording rearranges the sequences of some sections (sometimes in ways Handel himself later did) to offer an uncommonly dynamic performance, thrillingly sung.

Somary's 1970 recording is the most chamberlike in feeling, using a superb chorus that numbers only about thirty-two voices. Somary, a Handel specialist, bases his interpretation on the performing styles of Handel's time, and the solo work of Margaret Price and Diaz is particularly good.

All of the above performances are sung in English.

Water Music

Originally a suite of twenty short movements, the *Water Music* is a set of rhythmically contrasting orchestral pieces written for a royal festival on London Thames River in 1717. For many years it was best known in an arrangement of six movements made in 1922 by the late English conductor Sir Hamilton Harty, but in recent years conductors have begun to favor the more complete and authentic version by H. F. Redlich. This edition divides 18 of the pieces into three suites. The first suite (nine pieces) is made up of the music intended to be played as the King's boat journeyed along the Thames from Whitehall to Chelsea. The second, more intimate suite (four pieces) consists of the pieces written to accompany the royal supper. The third suite (five pieces) is the music intended for the return journey, and introduces trumpets into the music for the first time.

Recommended Recordings

★ Leppard, English Chamber Orchestra (Philips stereo disc 6500047; cartridge 7300060)
   Collegium Aureum (BASF/Harmonia stereo disc HB-20341)
b Boulez, Hague Philharmonic Orchestra (Nonesuch stereo disc 71127)
   Kubelik, Berlin Philharmonic Orchestra (Deutsche Grammophon stereo disc 138799; cassette 923-015; cartridge 88-799)

Comments

Leppard's 1971 release is stylistically faithful to the 18th century (much of it is based on Leppard's own research), and is played with considerable verve and supple embellishments. The sound engineering is excellent.

The Collegium Aureum, a German chamber ensemble with Franz-Josef Maier as concertmaster, features old wind and string instruments (*"auf Originalinstrumenten"* the album cover proclaims) in a mellow, pleasantly easy-going performance released in the U.S. in 1973.

Boulez's 1966 release is the most lively and crisp (sometimes almost stridently so), and certainly the most festive by contemporary standards.

Kubelik's 1963 recording has the most polished orchestral playing and the most resonant sound engineering for his elegant if sometimes stolid performance.

For Follow-Up Consideration

Royal Fireworks Music, a set of pieces written to accompany a royal fireworks display (some of the pieces have descriptive titles such as "Peace" and "Rejoicing"). Handel wrote two arrangements: the original one for large wind band and percussion, and a second one for normal Baroque orchestra. RECOMMENDED RECORDING OF THE ORIGINAL VERSION: Mackerras, ensemble of sixty-four winds, nine percussion instruments (Vanguard disc S-289), a spirited, sometimes thunderous performance about which the reviewer in *High Fidelity* magazine said at the time of its release in 1963, "You won't have to invite your neighbors in—they'll be able to hear it where they are." RECOMMENDED RECORDING OF THE SECOND VERSION: Menuhin, Menuhin Festival Orchestra (Angel stereo disc S36604; cassette 4XS36604; cartridge 8XS36604), an elegant, stylish performance, released in 1969, coupled with Handel's Concerto in B-flat for Two Wind Choirs and Strings, which is really a transcription (by Handel himself) of themes from *Messiah, Belshazzar,* and other oratorios.

Julius Caesar (Giulio Cesare), one of the finest examples of Handel's opera style, based on the story of Caesar and Cleopatra. RECOMMENDED RECORDING: Rudel (conductor), Treigle (Caesar), Sills (Cleopatra), Forrester (Cornelia), Wolff (Sesto), New York City Opera Orchestra and Chorus (RCA Red Seal stereo 3-disc set LSC-6182, or highlights on stereo disc LSC-3116), an excitingly sung 1967 version of one of the New York City Opera's most highly acclaimed productions.

• *JOHANN SEBASTIAN BACH*

Pronounced: *bahkh.* Born March 21, 1685, in Eisenach, Saxe-Weimar (Germany). Died July 28, 1750, in Leipzig.

SIGNIFICANCE: German organist and composer, an unsurpassed master of counterpoint and other stylistic principles of Baroque music, who brought to his works a maturity, a depth of expression, and a grand design unequaled by his predecessors.

BACKGROUND: Although widely known in his lifetime as an organ virtuoso, Bach did not win world renown as a great composer until the early nineteenth century. One of his first important champions was Felix Mendelssohn who, at the age of twenty, discovered the manuscript of the *Passion According to St. Matthew* (unheard since Bach's own time) and created a sensation when he conducted it in Leipzig in 1829. Over the following decade, other works were uncovered, but it was not until 1850—one hundred years after Bach's death—that a society was formed to publish Bach's complete works. How incredible that now seems to those of us born in the twentieth century who have invariably heard Bach described as one of the greatest composers— if not *the* greatest—of all time.

Bach came from a long line of musicians (seven preceding generations of Bachs had included town musicians and organists). Orphaned at the age of ten, he went to live with an elder brother, an organist who gave him his first organ lessons. At fifteen he won a scholarship to become a chorister in St. Michael's Church at Lüneburg. His three years at Lüneburg were significant in his musical development, especially the influence of the eminent organist Georg Böhm at the nearby St. Catherine's Church. On more than one occasion Bach also traveled more than thirty miles on foot to Hamburg to hear the great Dutch organist Reinken. At St. Michael's, he studied, copied, arranged, and reworked the styles and techniques of as many different composers as he could. He also damaged his eyes permanently—copying manuscripts of forbidden "radical" composers by moonlight.

In his adult years, as his reputation as an organist spread, Bach held church or court posts as organist at Weimar, Arnstadt, Mühlhausen, Cöthen, and Leipzig. He composed many works as part of his official duties. They include nearly three hundred church (Lutheran) cantatas, Christmas and Easter oratorios, the St. John, St. Luke, and St. Matthew *Passions,* many preludes, fugues, and other works for organ, the *Goldberg Variations, The Well-Tempered Clavier,* and other works for harpsichord and clavichord.

Aside from his reputation for an irascible temper, Bach was known as a relatively simple, hard-working organist whose home and children meant much to him. His first wife bore him seven children. After she died, he remarried, and his second wife bore him thirteen more. Two of his children became well-known composers in their own right: Carl Philipp Emanuel Bach (1714–1788) and Johann Christian Bach (1735–1782). In 1749 Bach underwent an operation to help restore his increasingly troublesome sight. It left him totally blind. The following year he died of a paralytic stroke.

Speaking of Bach's musical legacy, composer Paul Hindemith said: "Recognition of human excellence in its highest form, knowledge of the path that leads to it, the necessary done with dutifulness and driven to that point of perfection where it outgrows all necessity—this knowledge is the most precious inheritance given us with Bach's music."

Brandenburg Concerto No. 5

Bach's six *Brandenburg* Concertos (so named because of their dedication to the Margrave of Brandenburg) are characteristic of the Baroque concerto grosso, in which musical ideas are developed by pitting a small group of instruments (concertino) against a larger group (ripieno). Each of these concertos is scored for a different combination of instruments, and performances today vary from those using "authentic" instruments of the period (recorders, violas da gamba, baroque oboes, etc.) to those choosing more contemporary ones (including a saxophone used in a Casals performance at Marlboro in the 1960's!). The Concerto No. 5 is perhaps the most ambitious of the six *Brandenburgs* in its keyboard writing. It is scored for a concertino of harpsichord, flute, and violin—with the harpsichord having probably its most significant solo use to that time in a concerto. Author-critic Martin Bookspan has referred to "the long, tension-laden cadenza for the harpsichord in the first movement" as being "one of the most breathtaking moments in all music."

Recommended Recordings

★ **b** Ristenpart, Saar Chamber Orchestra (Nonesuch 2-disc stereo set 73006; cassette N5-73006)

  b Collegium Aureum (RCA Victrola 2-disc stereo set VICS-6023)

    Britten, English Chamber Orchestra (London 2-disc stereo set CSA-2225; cassette D10223)

    Richter, Munich Bach Orchestra (Deutsche Grammophon-Archive stereo 2-disc set ARC-2708013)

    Saidenberg, Baroque Chamber Orchestra (Decca stereo disc 710130)

    Loussier, Royal Philharmonic (London stereo disc 21044; cassette M-94044; cartridge M-95044)

Comments

Complete sets of the *Brandenburg* Concertos appear to be among the most recorded of all Baroque works (by 1974 there were twenty-one different versions listed in the Schwann catalog). Two of the best are on budget-priced labels. Ristenpart's (from the mid-1960's) is especially stylish and lucid, with excellent solo and instrumental balances, and an exceptionally good group of soloists. The Collegium Aureum's (from the late 1960's) is notably animated and tasteful, with fine ornamental embellishments by the soloists. Both performances are available only in sets of the complete *Brandenburgs*.

Among the standard-priced sets, two stand out: (1) the 1968 recording by Britten, using a larger ensemble, modern instruments, and a more subtly Romantic approach;

and (2) the lively, well-balanced performance by Richter from the late-1960's, using more authentic instruments. Both are available only in sets of the complete *Brandenburgs*.

Among single-disc editions of the Fifth *Brandenburg* alone, the 1966 Saidenberg release is notable. It has both style and spirit, and the harpsichord playing of Sylvia Marlowe is particularly good. The coupling is a Haydn harpsichord concerto, also well played by Miss Marlowe.

The Jacques Loussier release of 1970 is included here as an offbeat but interesting jazz edition of the *Brandenburg* No. 5. Loussier is famous for his "Play Bach" jazz albums, and in this album his trio (piano, bass, drums) replaces the traditional concertino—playing jazz variations on Bach's themes while members of the Royal Philharmonic play them straight. His late 1960's album is filled out with similar treatments of Bach's "Air for the G-String" and the Prelude No. 2 from *The Well-Tempered Clavier*.

Concerto in D minor for Two Violins and Orchestra

This so-called "Double Concerto" is particularly outstanding among Bach's works for its rhythmic vitality and its melodic lines. The two soloists constantly cross parts, questioning and answering each other, copying and contradicting each other. The concerto is well known among ballet fans as the score for George Balanchine's *Concerto Barocco* in the repertory of the New York City Ballet.

Recommended Recordings

★ Zukerman, Perlman, Barenboim, English Chamber Orchestra (Angel stereo disc S-36841; cassette 4XS-36841; cartridge 8XS-36841)

Heifetz, Friedman, Sargent, New Symphony Orchestra of London (RCA Red Seal stereo disc LSC-2577)

David and Igor Oistrakh, Goossens, Royal Philharmonic Orchestra (Deutsche Grammophon stereo disc 138820; cassette 923-087; cartridge 88-820, or Deutsche Grammophon stereo disc 138714; cassette 923-073)

Comments

Zukerman, Perlman, and Barenboim bring youthful vitality and an almost Romantic tonal feeling to their collaboration, made when they were all still in their 20's in 1972. They round off the disc with similarly extroverted performances of Bach's Violin Concerto No. 2 in E major (Perlman) and Gustav Schreck's reconstruction for violin (in G minor) of Bach's Clavier Concerto in F minor (Zukerman). Some traditionalists may debate the stylistic approach, but the young performers do succeed in bringing each of the three concertos vividly alive. Excellent sound.

Heifetz and his young protégé, Erick Friedman, offer a stylistically cooler, impressively elegant, dynamic performance dating from the early 1960's. The coupling is a fine-grained Heifetz performance of Beethoven's Violin Sonata No. 9.

The father-son Oistrakh team is sensitive, lyrical, warmer than Heifetz–Friedman but less vivid than Zukerman–Perlman. The Deutsche Grammophon sound engineering, also dating from the early 1960's, is more mellow than RCA's or Columbia's. The performance is available with two different couplings; one (138820) offers excellent Oistrakh performances of two solo Bach violin concertos, the other (138714) a Vivaldi concerto for two violins. (Note: This Oistrakh recording should not be confused with several mono-only releases formerly available on imported Russian labels, featuring the Oistrakhs with Moscow orchestras, and with inferior sound engineering.)

Suite No. 3 for Orchestra

The simple, tenderly beautiful "Air," now popularly called "Air for the G-String," from this suite remains one of Bach's most widely loved compositions. The rest of the suite is made up of four lively dances (two gavottes, a bourrée, and a gigue) preceded by an extended overture. Of Bach's suites, Albert Schweitzer once said: "Their charm resides in the perfection of their blending of strength and grace."

Recommended Recordings

★ Richter, Munich Bach Orchestra (Deutsche Grammophon-Archive stereo 2-disc set ARC-198272/3; cassette 924-005)

Leppard, English Chamber Orchestra (Philips stereo 2-disc set 839792/3; cassette 7505004)

Harnoncourt, Vienna Concentus Musicus (Telefunken stereo 2-disc set S-9509/10)

Ansermet, Suisse Romande Orchestra (London stereo disc CS-6243)

Comments

Richter's performance is distinguished by stylish playing, good tempos, and fine recorded sound (from the early 1960's). It is available on disc only as part of a 2-LP album of all four Bach Suites, although the cassette edition couples the Second and Third Suites alone.

Leppard's 1970 release has the best sound, and his performance is animated and precise, with interesting dynamic variations. It is included in a 2-disc set with all four Bach suites.

Harnoncourt's ensemble uses authentic 17th- and 18th-century instruments, which give a warm, beautiful sound, but the performance is not as buoyant as Richter's or Leppard's. This is also part of a set of all four suites, recorded in 1966.

Ansermet avoids the overblown symphonic approach of which a number of other "major" conductors (such as Karajan) are guilty. In this early 1960's recording, he couples the Third Suite with a lovely performance of the Second Suite.

For Follow-Up Consideration

The Passion of Our Lord According to St. Matthew, a large-scale setting of the Biblical text for solo voices, chorus, and orchestra; considered by many critics Bach's most eloquent and deeply moving choral masterpiece. RECOMMENDED RECORDINGS: Richter, Seefried, Töpper, Haefliger, Fischer-Dieskau, Munich Bach Orchestra (Deutsche

Grammophon 4-disc set ARC2712-001), a beautifully sung, noble, and vibrant performance dating from the late 1950's; or Harnoncourt, Esswood, Bowman, Rogers, Ridderbusch, Vienna Choir Boys, Kings College Choir Concentus Musicus of Vienna (Telefunken 4-disc set S-9572/5), an outstanding 1971 release of the "original instrument" version, using two countertenors and other soloists who display exceptional understanding of the stylistic requirements of their parts. Both recordings are sung in the original German.

Modern Transcriptions of Bach Works

Earlier in this century there was a rash of orchestrated versions of some of Bach's organ works by Leopold Stokowski, Ottorino Respighi, and others. These transcriptions have always been controversial. Their critics say they distort or vulgarize Bach's music. Defenders argue that they have added new dimensions of modern orchestral colors to the works and helped introduce Bach to listeners who are accustomed to the sound of the large, modern orchestra.

The best example of orchestrated Bach is a Capitol release (Capitol disc SP8489) by Leopold Stokowski's Orchestra; although the disc was deleted from the active catalog in the early 1970's, it may still be available in some stores. Several of Stokowski's Bach transcriptions are also included in a diverse 1971 budget collection called *Stokowski's Greatest Hits* (RCA Victrola 2-disc set VCS-7077; cassette RK-5072; cartridge R8S-5072).

Guitar transcriptions of Bach works have been popularized by the great Spanish guitarist Andrés Segovia, and are included in Decca disc 79751; cassette 673-9751; cartridge 6-9751. The young American guitarist Christopher Parkening also features excellent performances of several of Segovia's and his own Bach transcriptions in a 1972 release (Angel stereo disc S-36041; cassette 4XS-36041; cartridge 8XS-36041).

One of the most talked-about releases of the early 1970's was an LP called *Switched-On Bach* (Columbia stereo disc MS-7194; cassette 16-11-0092; cartridge 18-11-0092), in which electronic composer Walter Carlos "realized" harmonically subtle and pitch-correct performances of ten short Bach works completely without human instrumentalists, using the electronic synthesizer developed by Robert Moog. Many have hailed the album as an exciting and enjoyable example of electronic music-making. Others have denounced it as "the last straw" in the mechanization or computerization of man and his culture. It has been not only one of the best-selling albums of the 1970's but also in all recording history.

• *FRANZ JOSEF HAYDN*

Pronounced: *high*-d'n. Born March 31, 1732, in Rohrau, Austria. Died May 31, 1809, in Vienna.

SIGNIFICANCE: Austrian composer, generally known as the "father of the symphony" because of the way he developed and expanded the form even though he did not invent it, and a major force in the development of the symphony orchestra.

BACKGROUND: Haydn, at age eight, was sent to Vienna to sing in the boys' choir of St. Stephan's Cathedral. There he also learned to play the violin and other instruments. About the time his voice broke, he reportedly pulled a prank that got him thrown out of the choir school (he cut off the pigtail of a chorister in front of him). He wandered penniless through the Vienna streets, finally joining a group of serenading musicians in order to earn money for food. (It was then a custom in Vienna for people to hire musicians to play under the window of a lady on her birthday or other festive occasion.) Several years later he joined the orchestra of Count Morzin, who had a large estate near Pilsen, in Bohemia (now Czechoslovakia), and for it he composed his first symphony in 1759.

Word of his talent spread among the aristocracy, and in 1761 Haydn was invited to join the service of Prince Esterhazy, the richest and most powerful of all the Hungarian nobility, and whose estate was the most elaborate east of Versailles. Haydn was never again to know hunger. He remained with the Esterhazy family for almost thirty years, conducting and composing more than sixty symphonies, eleven operas, five masses, and hundreds of chamber works. As the fame of his symphonies spread throughout Europe, instrumental music became the chief symbol of 18th-century German culture, just as vocal music was of Italian.

Between 1785 and 1786, Haydn composed a group of symphonies on commission from Paris, but it was not until 1790 that he left Austria-Hungary. In England he received an honorary degree from Oxford, and heard some of Handel's oratorios for the first time. Under their influence, he wrote his own oratorio, *The Creation.* For a London concert manager, J. P. Salomon, Haydn also wrote his last twelve symphonies (since known as the "London" or the "Salomon" symphonies and considered among his finest, most fully developed ones)—bringing the total to 104! As his health failed, he went into retirement. His death in 1809 is said to have been partly caused by the shock of Vienna's bombardment by the French during Napoleon's conquests.

Symphony No. 94 in G major ("Surprise")

As a whole, the 94th splendidly represents the uncomplicated melodies and clear-cut rhythms that distinguish Haydn's music. It was nicknamed the "Surprise" Symphony because there is a loud chord in the midst of the quiet and peaceful second movement that Haydn is reported to have puckishly said "will make the ladies jump," referring to the fact that the noble ladies often fell asleep during the long concert programs fashionable in the late 18th century.

Recommended Recordings

★ Szell, Cleveland Orchestra (Columbia stereo disc MS-7006)

   Giulini, Philharmonia Orchestra (Angel stereo disc S-35712)

   Bernstein, New York Philharmonic (Columbia stereo disc M-32101; cassette MT-32101)

b Krips, Vienna Philharmonic (London Stereo Treasury disc STS-15085)

Comments

Szell performs the 94th with tremendous thrust and cleanness, and the fairly large body of Cleveland strings plays with an almost chamber music clarity. The 1967 recording is coupled with a similarly crisp Szell account of the Haydn Symphony No. 93.

Giulini's 94th has sparkle, force, and a distinctively warm glow. His late 1950's release is coupled with two interesting and rarely played works by Boccherini (1743–1805): Overture in D and Symphony in C minor.

Bernstein has shown a special knack in a number of Haydn recordings for making the most of the contrasting "courtly" and "peasant" elements in Haydn's music—and he has rarely done so better than in this 1972 release, even if the orchestral playing is not as good as that on Szell's and Giulini's discs. Bernstein's coupling is the same as Szell's.

Krips' recording, dating from the late 1950's and reissued on London's budget label in 1971, is beautifully suave and spirited. The coupling is Haydn's Symphony No. 99, also well played.

Symphony No. 88 in G major

This is one of Haydn's most immediately appealing symphonies, and one of his most perfectly constructed. It is filled not only with sunny melodies and rhythmic vitality, but also with much evidence of Haydn's delightful sense of humor.

Recommended Recordings

★ **b** Reiner, Chicago Symphony (RCA Victrola stereo disc VICS-1366)
   Bernstein, New York Philharmonic (Columbia stereo disc MS-7259)
 b Furtwängler, Berlin Philharmonic (Heliodor disc 25073, *mono only*)

Comments

Reiner's performance from the mid-1950's combines vitality and sensitivity, and the sound engineering of this budget release holds up better than some more recent editions. Overside, Reiner offers a first-rate performance of Mozart's "Jupiter" Symphony.

Bernstein's 1963 recording bears the conductor's individual stamp—the melodies lingered over warmly and the faster sections taken at quite a clip. It all adds up to a delightful if less than classically pure performance, with somewhat strident string tone. The same holds true of the Haydn No. 102 overside.

Furtwängler's 1951 performance, in mono only, remains one of the best examples of Furtwängler's approach to the Classical style on records, and is coupled with a distinctive performance of Schumann's Symphony No. 4 overside.

For Follow-Up Consideration

Symphony No. 22 ("The Philosopher"), one of the most delightful of Haydn's earlier symphonies (1764). It has an unusual opening for an 18th-century symphony—a quiet, chorale-prelude-like theme (hence its nickname)—but then goes on to more spirited themes in Haydn's typical combination of elegance and sportiveness. RECOMMENDED RECORDING: Leppard, English Chamber Orchestra (Philips stereo disc 839796), a brisk yet genial performance, released in 1971, coupled with similarly stylish performances of Haydn's rarely played Symphonies No. 39 and 47.

Symphony No. 60 ("Il Distratto"), one of the most vivacious of Haydn's "middle period" symphonies; a six-movement work of 1776 which originally served as incidental music for Regnard's comedy *Il Distratto* (*The Absent-Minded One*), and filled with unexpected, sometimes tongue-in-cheek departures from the purely Classical style. RECOMMENDED RECORDING: Blum, Esterhazy Orchestra of New York (Vanguard stereo disc HM-27), a spirited, well-recorded 1963 performance, coupled with a good performance of Haydn's more muted and serious Symphony No. 52.

Symphony No. 101 ("The Clock"), one of the most popular of Haydn's late symphonies (1794) because of the tick-tocking lyricism of its second movement; overall one of Haydn's most relaxed and mellow symphonies. RECOMMENDED RECORDING: Reiner, Chicago Symphony (RCA Red Seal stereo disc LSC-2742), Reiner's last recording (1963) and a glowingly animated one, coupled with a first-rate performance of the Symphony No. 95.

The Creation (*Die Schöpfung*), the most famous work of Haydn's late years, composed between 1796 and 1798, and based on the Genesis section of the Bible and on Milton's *Paradise Lost*. Most critics regard the work more highly for its solo passages (especially those for Adam and Eve) than for its choral writing, although one very popular chorus, "The Heavens Are Telling," has become part of the standard choral repertory. RECOMMENDED RECORDING: Karajan, Berlin Philharmonic, Vienna Singverein, with Janowitz, Wunderlich, Fischer-Dieskau, Berry, Ludwig, Krenn as soloists (Deutsche Grammophon stereo 2-disc set 2707044; cassette 3370-001), a spacious, well-paced, reverent 1966 performance, with particularly outstanding soloists. Wunderlich was killed before completing the recording; he had recorded all the arias but not the recitatives, which were so expertly interpolated by Werner Krenn.

Special Note on the Complete Recordings of Haydn's Symphonies: In 1974 London Records issued the final album in its special project to record all 104 of Haydn's symphonies with the same orchestra and conductor—the Philharmonia Hungarica led by Antal Dorati. While complete sets of a composer's works (especially one this extensive) generally appeal more to experienced collectors than to beginners, this particular set has much to recommend to those who find they really like Haydn's music. First of all, it is on the budget-priced London Stereo Treasury Series (STS) label. The eight volumes vary from four to six discs each, are all very well engineered, and include excellent annotations by the distinguished Haydn scholar H.C. Robbins Landon. Dorati leads consistently good, spirited, stylish performances. The orchestra is made up of members of leading Hungarian symphony orchestras who fled their homeland during the 1956 revolution and established the Philharmonia Hungarica as an orchestra-in-exile, with a home base in West Germany (it has toured the United States several times).

• *WOLFGANG AMADEUS MOZART*

Pronounced: *moh*-tsart. Born January 27, 1756, in Salzburg, Austria. Died December 5, 1791, in Vienna, Austria.

SIGNIFICANCE: Austrian composer of forty-one symphonies, twenty-seven piano concertos, twenty-three string quartets, eighteen Masses, more than ten operas, and numerous other chamber and solo works, most of them unequaled in their Classical style, elegance, subtlety, and melodic imaginativeness.

BACKGROUND: Mozart began to show his musical genius at age three in his native Salzburg, where his father was a well-known violinist and composer (Leopold Mozart, composer of the popular "Toy Symphony," a work long wrongly attributed to Haydn). When he was seven, Mozart was taken by his father on a tour to Paris, London, Amsterdam, and other cities, chiefly as a harpsichord prodigy, and he delighted royalty and impressed musicians with his feats of sight-reading and improvisation. By the age of twelve he had composed an opera (*Bastien and Bastienne*), a Mass, an oratorio, and several sonatas, and had made his debut as a conductor.

In his teens he traveled to Italy to study and concertize, and then returned to Salzburg to settle in the service of the archbishop. After a quarrel, he left this service in 1781 (at age twenty-five), moved to Vienna, married, and had a difficult time over the following years making ends meet for his wife and six children—even though he continued to compose prolifically and to have his works performed. His greatest successes included the operas *The Marriage of Figaro* (Vienna, 1786), *Don Giovanni* (Prague, 1787), and *The Magic Flute* (Vienna, 1791). Despite favor at court, his income was meager and he died penniless at age thirty-five, and was buried in an unmarked pauper's grave.

A note about those **K.** *numbers:* In the 19th century the Austrian scholar Ludwig von Köchel compiled a complete catalog of Mozart's works in the correct compositional sequence (revised in this century by Alfred Einstein), and it is now standard to refer to Mozart's works as "K. (followed by a number)"—for example, Piano Concerto No. 23, K. 488 (the German usage is sometimes "K.V." for Köchel-Verzeichnis—that is, Köchel Index).

Piano Concerto No. 21 in C major (K. 467)

This concerto has been nicknamed the "Elvira Madigan Concerto," after Geza Anda's recording of the slow movement (*andante*) was used as background music in the hit Swedish film *Elvira Madigan* in the late 1960's. Like most of Mozart's late piano concertos, No. 21 mixes elegance and an intimate expressiveness with great subtlety, delicacy, and rhythmic spirit. It represents, together with all the Mozart concertos between No. 15 and 27, the "coming of age" of the piano concerto.

Recommended Recordings

★ Anda, Salzburg Camarata Academica (Deutsche Grammophon stereo disc 138783; cassette 923-052; cartridge 88-783)

Barenboim, English Chamber Orchestra (Angel stereo disc S-36814; cassette 4XS-36814; cartridge 8XS-36814)

Rubinstein, Wallenstein, RCA Symphony (RCA Red Seal stereo disc LSC-2634; cassette RK-1263; cartridge R85-1263)

Lipatti, Karajan, Lucerne Festival Orchestra (Angel disc 35931, *mono only*)

Comments

Anda, both piano soloist and conductor, offers a supple, poetic, beautifully contemplative performance; the 1961 sound engineering is appropriately mellow. This is the recording used for the sound track of the film *Elvira Madigan*. Anda, incidentally, has recorded *all* 25 of Mozart's piano concertos, available in a 12-disc album (Deutsche Grammophon 2720630); of the several pianists who have attempted an integral set of all the concertos, Anda's is the superior.

Barenboim, too, doubles as pianist and conductor for a 1972 performance notable for its fluency, elegance, and (something not always associated with Barenboim) airiness.

Rubinstein is not as dreamy as Anda or as melancholic as Barenboim in the *andante,* bringing to it a more crystal-clear grace. He also brings more sparkle and sweep to the other movements in his 1961 recording.

Both Anda's and Rubinstein's recordings are coupled with other Mozart concertos—Anda's with a lovely No. 17, Rubinstein's with a spirited No. 23. Barenboim's coupling is Mozart's Symphony No. 40 in G minor, in a rhythmically forthright, lyrically expressive performance.

The Lipatti performance dates from a 1950 broadcast just a few months before the young Rumanian pianist's death. Despite its sonic limitations (it is based on amateur tapes found by Lipatti's widow in 1959), it remains a remarkable performance, matching tenderness and strength in a very special way.

Symphony No. 35 in D major, "Haffner" (K. 385)

The ease with which Mozart apparently tossed off masterpieces is illustrated by the story of the origin of this symphony: In 1782, Mozart's father Leopold was asked by one of Salzburg's prominent citizens, Sigmund Haffner, to write an orchestral serenade for a special festivity. Leopold Mozart turned the commission over to his son, who had recently married and needed the money. Young Mozart wrote a six-movement serenade in two weeks and sent it to Haffner. Some months later, Mozart needed a new symphony for a concert program he was to conduct in Vienna, and wrote to his father urgently requesting the score of the serenade, to see if any of the material could be adapted to the symphony. When Mozart conducted his new symphony a few weeks later, it consisted basically of four of the six movements of the serenade, rescored for a larger orchestra. It was so well received at its first performance that it had to be repeated—and has remained one of Mozart's most popular works ever since. The "Haffner" is generally a bright, energetic, and lighthearted work, and is perhaps the most immediately appealing of Mozart's great symphonies.

Recommended Recordings

★ Barenboim, English Chamber Orchestra (Angel stereo disc S-36512)

Böhm, Berlin Philharmonic (Deutsche Grammophon stereo disc 138112)

Szell, Cleveland Orchestra (Columbia stereo disc MS-6969)

Comments

Barenboim's performance is brimming with vitality and buoyancy. His 1968 release is coupled with similarly vibrant performances of the Symphony No. 38 ("Prague") and the short Symphony No. 32.

Böhm starts off more restrainedly, but zips through the finale with enormous dash. The coupling on his 1959 version is the same as Barenboim's: Nos. 32 and 38, both very animatedly and warmly played.

Szell projects a cooler view of the symphony in his late 1960's release, notable for its forward-moving energy and orchestral polish. The coupling is a similarly vivid "Jupiter" Symphony (No. 41).

Symphony No. 41 in C major, "Jupiter" (K. 551)

A London publisher nicknamed Mozart's last symphony the "Jupiter" because of its "loftiness of ideas and nobility of treatment." Its nobility is evident throughout, along with Mozart's special ability to contrast forceful and gentle themes. The fugue in the last movement is considered one of the great achievements in counterpoint.

Recommended Recordings

★ b Reiner, Chicago Symphony (RCA Victrola stereo disc VICS-1366)

Böhm, Berlin Philharmonic (Deutsche Grammophon stereo disc 138815; cassette 923056; cartridge 88-815)

Szell, Cleveland Orchestra (Columbia stereo disc MS-6969)

Comments

Reiner's performance, dating from 1955, remains an outstanding one both in the quality of the interpretation and in the playing of the Chicago Symphony. It has strength, grandeur, and lucidity. Coupled with Reiner's first-rate Haydn Symphony No. 88, this is an especially worthwhile budget-label bargain.

Among the newer, standard-priced recordings, Böhm's (recorded in the mid-1960's) stands out for its combination of animation and forcefulness, classical elegance and warmth. It is coupled with Böhm's similarly vivid Mozart Symphony No. 40.

Szell has a particularly fine feeling for the work's architecture in his cooler, beautifully polished performance dating from 1963. His coupling is a spirited performance of the "Haffner" Symphony (No. 35).

Le Nozze di Figaro (The Marriage of Figaro) (K. 492)

One of the greatest, if not *the* greatest, of all comic operas, Mozart's *Figaro* is distinguished by its wealth of melody, its wit, and its spirited, stylish sense of fun. In its time, Beaumarchais' original French comedy (on which the libretto was based) did not sit well with much of the aristocracy because of its sardonic view of their manners and morals. But bans against its public performance merely helped spread its popularity throughout Europe (Marie Antoinette is even reported to have delighted in attending a private performance). Mozart's librettist, Lorenzo da Ponte, persuaded the Austrian emperor to rescind the ban in Vienna, where the opera achieved only a mild success in 1786. Shortly afterward it scored a bigger hit in Prague, and led to the Prague opera's commission of Mozart's *Don Giovanni.* The original libretto is in Italian, although a German libretto is widely used in parts of Europe (*Figaros Hochzeit*) and on some recordings.

Recommended Recordings (Complete)

★ Giulini (conductor), Schwarzkopf (Countess), Wächter (Count), Moffo (Susanna), Taddei (Figaro), Cossotto (Cherubino), Philharmonia Orchestra & Chorus of London (Angel stereo 4-disc set S-3608; in Italian)

   Davis (conductor), Norman (Countess), Wixell (Count), Freni (Susanna), Ganzarolli (Figaro), Minton (Cherubino), BBC Symphony Orchestra and chorus (Philips stereo 4-disc set 6707014; cassette 7675001; in Italian)

b Suitner (conductor), Gueden (Countess), Prey (Count), Rothenberger (Susanna), Berry (Figaro), Mathis (Cherubino), Dresden State Opera Orchestra and Chorus (Seraphim stereo 3-disc set S-6002; in German)

   Kleiber (conductor), Della Casa (Countess), Poell (Count), Gueden (Susanna), Siepi (Figaro), Danco (Cherubino), Vienna Philharmonic and Vienna State Opera Chorus (London *mono only* 4-disc set OSA-1402; in Italian)

Recommended Recordings (Highlights)

★ Giulini, Schwarzkopf, Wachter, Moffo, etc., as above (Angel stereo disc S-35640)

   Davis, Norman, Wixell, Freni, etc., as above (Philips stereo disc 6500434; cassette 7300186)

   Kleiber, Della Casa, Siepi, Gueden, etc., as above (London disc OS-25045, *mono only*)

Comments

Giulini brings the most overall warmth and supple style to his 1960 edition. Schwarzkopf and Moffo are especially moving in their characterizations, as well as singing with lovely tone colors; the male singers are good if less inspired.

Davis leads a spirited, elegantly playful performance released in 1972, with beautiful if sometimes a bit impersonal singing by most of his principals. The sound engineering is particularly good.

The Suitner version (dating from 1961, although not released in the U.S. until 1966) has lots of verve and sparkle, plus the advantage of being on only 3 LPs—and on a budget-priced label too. But it is sung in German rather than the original Italian. For those to whom this point is not significant, there is much to recommend in the first-rate singing of an excellent cast, particularly Prey, Berry, and Mathis.

The Kleiber mono recording, dating from the 1950's, set a high standard for a performance of this opera for many years. Despite aging sound, it still has many outstanding qualities, especially Kleiber's stylishly spirited pacing, and the elegant singing of Della Casa, Gueden, and Siepi.

Don Giovanni (K. 527)

Some critics call this opera the Western world's finest single piece of musical art. Few others doubt that it is surely one of the landmark achievements in all opera. Based on a Spanish version of the Don Juan legend, Mozart's opera (again with an Italian libretto by Lorenzo da Ponte) was begun as a comic opera, but was broadened into a drama of much more profound human irony. It might well be subtitled "The Last Days of a Rake," for it deals with Don Juan after his luck as a great lover has run out. In some ways it remains essentially a comic opera, surrounded by a serious beginning and a tragic ending—and, accordingly, it creates many difficult challenges for singers and conductors in the way of interpretation. Musically, some of Mozart's arias are extremely difficult to sing, but they also include some of his finest melodies, supported by some of his subtlest orchestral writing.

Recommended Recordings (Complete)

★ Giulini (conductor), Wächter (Giovanni), Sutherland (Donna Anna), Schwarzkopf (Donna Elvira), Sciutti (Zerlina), Taddei (Leporello), Philharmonia Orchestra of London (Angel stereo 4-disc set S-3605)

Klemperer (conductor), Ghiaurov (Giovanni), Watson (Donna Anna), Ludwig (Donna Elvira), Freni (Zerlina), Berry (Leporello), New Philharmonia Orchestra of London (Angel stereo 4-disc set S-3700)

Böhm (conductor), Fischer-Dieskau (Giovanni), Nilsson (Donna Anna), Arroyo (Donna Elvira), Grist (Zerlina), Flagello (Leporello), Prague National Theater Orchestra (Deutsche Grammophon stereo 4-disc set 2711006)

Recommended Recordings (Highlights)

★ Giulini, Wächter, Sutherland, Schwarzkopf, etc., as above (Deutsche Grammophon stereo disc S-35642)

Böhm, Fischer-Dieskau, Nilsson, Arroyo, etc., as above (Angel stereo disc 136282)

Comments

None of the present recordings is completely satisfactory, but each of the ones listed has its strong points as well as some weak ones.

Giulini (recorded around 1960) and Böhm (1967) are generally spirited and dramatic conceptions, whereas the Klemperer (1966) performance is paced more deliberately.

Ghiaurov and Wächter are effective if not always deeply penetrating in their singing of the title role. The usually impressive Fischer-Dieskau is disappointing—he sings the role more like a villain than a tragic hero.

Among the sopranos, Schwarzkopf and Ludwig bring the finest style and most beautiful sounds to the difficult role of Donna Elvira. Sutherland and Nilsson may be "star" names, but neither is at her best as Donna Anna.

On balance I recommend the Giulini—especially for someone who doesn't know *Don Giovanni* at all and wants somewhere to start.

All of the above are sung in the original Italian.

For Follow-Up Consideration

Eine Kleine Nachtmusik (Serenade No. 13 in G for strings, K. 525), one of Mozart's most popular works and considered by some to be the epitome of graceful 18th-century Classicism. The title translates roughly as "A Little Night Music." RECOMMENDED RECORDING: Davis, Philharmonia Orchestra (Seraphim stereo disc S-60057), a suave and sensitive performance, first released in the U.S. on the budget Seraphim label in 1967 but apparently originating earlier than that, and coupled with a fine performance of Mozart's lovely Serenade No. 6 (*Serenata Notturna*).

The Magic Flute (*Die Zauberflöte*) (K. 620), Mozart's last opera, a sometimes bewildering and complicated mixture of fantasy and symbolism—with many references to Freemasonry—containing some of Mozart's most poetic and eloquent music. (Beethoven declared it to be Mozart's greatest work.) RECOMMENDED RECORDING OF THE COMPLETE OPERA: Solti (conductor), Lorengar (Pamina), Burrows (Tamino), Prey (Papageno), Deutekom (Queen of the Night), Talvela (Sarastro), Fischer-Dieskau (Speaker), Vienna Philharmonic and Chorus (London stereo 3-disc set OSA-1397), sung in the original German; a 1971 release, superbly led by Solti with a generally good cast, and including the spoken dialogue (in German) missing in some other recordings. RECOMMENDED RECORDING OF HIGHLIGHTS ONLY: Böhm (conductor), Lear (Pamina), Wunderlich (Tamino), Fischer-Dieskau (Papageno), Peters (Queen of the Night), Berlin Philharmonic and Chorus (Deutsche Grammophon stereo disc 136440, cassette 922014), a more unevenly sung but warmly led set of excerpts taken from a complete 1964 recording (sung in German), and with the late Fritz Wunderlich in particularly good form.

Cosi Fan Tutte (K. 588), a comic opera sometimes given the English title *Women Are Like That* (the Italian title translates roughly as "Thus Do They All"), about two love-stricken young men who agree to test their fiancées' faithfulness, and end up disillusioned but wiser. RECOMMENDED RECORDING: Böhm (conductor), Schwarzkopf (Fiordiligi), Ludwig (Dorabella), Kraus (Ferrando), Berry (Alfonso), Taddei (Guglielmo), Philharmonia Orchestra and Chorus (complete on Angel stereo 4-disc set S-3631, or highlights only on Angel stereo disc S-36167), a wonderfully spirited, stylish, and beautifully sung (in Italian) performance from the early 1960's.

Requiem (K. 626), one of the most profoundly moving of religious works by any composer, and the last music Mozart wrote (there has long been uncertainty over how much of it Mozart himself completed and how much is the work of his pupil, Süssmayr, who was privately engaged by Mozart's widow to complete it so she could collect the promised fee). RECOMMENDED RECORDING: Davis conducting, with Donath, Minton, Davies, Nienstedt, BBC Symphony and John Alldis Choir (Philips stereo 2-disc album 802862, cassette PCR4-900-160; cartridge PC8-900-160), a subtly phrased, beautifully flowing and animated 1968 performance.

Quintet for Clarinet and Strings in A major (K. 581), one of the loveliest works in the entire chamber music repertory. Mozart had loved the sound of the clarinet ever since he first heard one in the orchestra at Mannheim when he visited that Rhineland city. He wrote to his father: "If only we had clarinets in our orchestra! What wonderful things one can do with them." Mozart indeed proved the last point in this quintet. Although the solo part requires exceptional agility on the part of the clarinetist, the quintet is essentially a serene and mellow work. RECOMMENDED RECORDING: De Peyer (clarinet), with members of the Melos Ensemble (Angel stereo disc S36241), a warmly elegant, beautifully phrased mid-1960's performance by the fine English clarinetist. Overside, De Peyer is also featured in an appealing performance of Mozart's Trio in E flat major for clarinet, piano, and viola (K. 498).

• LUDWIG VAN BEETHOVEN

Pronounced: *bay*-toh-ven. Born December 16, 1770, in Bonn, Germany. Died March 26, 1827, in Vienna.

SIGNIFICANCE: German composer and pianist who has ranked for more than 150 years as the titan of Western music, and is generally regarded today as the most widely popular of all composers; in creating a new "heroic" style he raised instrumental music to previously unimagined heights of grandeur, marked by a new expressiveness, yet still maintaining basically Classical structures.

BACKGROUND: The son and grandson of musicians, Beethoven had started to play both the piano and violin by the age of four. His father, a minor singer in the court of the Archbishop of Cologne, pushed his son in hopes he would become a child prodigy like Mozart. But Beethoven's talent was slow to ripen, and he showed none of the personal charm of the young Mozart. So the family continued to live in poverty and unhappiness, aggravated by the father's alcoholism. To supplement the family income, Beethoven, at eleven, began to play in a theatre orchestra. At thirteen he became assistant to the organist at the court chapel.

As his musical talents developed during his late teens, he won the favor of the archbishop, who finally aided him in going to Vienna to continue his studies. At first Beethoven studied with Haydn, but according to some reports of the time, they did not get along too well. Over the years, the growing fame of Beethoven's piano improvisations made him a performer much sought after by Viennese aristocrats—despite (and sometimes perhaps because of) his reputation as a "country bumpkin." Although most of his first successful works were for the piano, Beethoven earnestly sought to expand his creative activities to symphonies, trios, and quartets during his first ten years in Vienna.

He composed slowly and with great effort. And in 1799 he became aware of one of the worst calamities that can strike a performing musician: he was going deaf. At one point he seriously considered suicide. But then he vowed in a letter: "I will take Fate by the throat." He continued to compose—and there are some who believe that it was because of his growing deafness that Beethoven poured so much emotion and intensity into his music, thus expanding the Classical forms of his predecessors and paving the way for the Romantics who followed him. By 1822—after the completion of the Ninth Symphony but before the last three string quartets—Beethoven was completely deaf. Though he never married, Beethoven was known throughout Vienna for many love affairs (his popular "Moonlight Sonata," for example, is dedicated to Giulietta Guicciardi).

Symphony No. 5 in C minor

The Olympian grandeur and driving power of this work have kept it one of the most popular of all symphonies. During World War II its opening theme was used as a symbol of the Allied forces fighting the Nazis (a use still reflected in many of the films of that period that appear regularly on TV). Beethoven himself suggested, many years after the first performance, that the opening theme signified the summons of Fate.

Recommended Recordings

★ Bernstein, New York Philharmonic (Columbia stereo disc MS-6468; cassette 16-11-0036; cartridge 18-11-0036)

Karajan, Berlin Philharmonic (Deutsche Grammophon stereo disc 138804; cassette 923-011)

Szell, Amsterdam Concertgebouw (Philips stereo disc 802769)

Ozawa, Chicago Symphony (RCA Red Seal stereo disc LSC-3132)

b Toscanini, NBC Symphony (RCA Victrola disc VIC-1607, *mono only;* also included in complete 8-disc set of Beethoven's nine symphonies, VIC-8000)

Gould, piano version arranged by Franz Liszt (Columbia stereo disc MS-7095)

Comments

Bernstein gives a robust, stirring performance, full of drama and kinetic energy. Overside is an adapted version of one of Bernstein's most highly praised TV lectures, about the Beethoven Fifth ("How a Great Symphony Was Written")—making this 1961 edition especially recommended for a first purchase.

Karajan gives a blazingly alive, thrillingly surging performance, one of his all-time best, released in 1963 and superbly engineered. However, unlike the other versions on this list, it is spread over two full sides of the disc.

Szell's famous razor-edged precision and rhythmic urgency fit the Fifth splendidly, especially in combination with the dark, spacious tonal colors of the Amsterdam orchestra. This 1967 version is preferable to Szell's Cleveland Orchestra recording of the Fifth formerly on Epic and now on Columbia. It is coupled with a refined, energetic Szell–Amsterdam performance of Mozart's Symphony No. 34.

Ozawa's 1970 performance has spirit and intensity despite a few instances of curious phrasing. The playing of the Chicago Symphony is particularly impressive. The coupling is a genial, lyrical performance of Schubert's "Unfinished" Symphony.

Among the budget-priced editions, Toscanini's (taken from a 1952 Carnegie Hall broadcast) still packs a tremendous wallop through its sheer power and incisiveness, even if its sound is not up to today's standards.

A century ago, piano transcriptions of operatic and orchestral works were as common as Kostelanetz or Fiedler orchestrations of today's pop tunes. But the 1967 Glenn Gould performance of Liszt's piano transcription of this symphony is much more than a curio—for Gould plays it with such expressiveness and artistry that it becomes more than a mere "stunt"—and emerges close in feeling to the great Beethoven sonatas. The liner notes on the album are a different matter—sheer (and sometimes wild) spoofing, presumably ghost-written by Gould himself.

Symphony No. 7 in A major

Various critics have linked this symphony (written in 1811 and 1812) to descriptions of a rustic wedding, a royal hunt, a knightly battle, a masquerade party, a sweeping political revolution, and even "the love-dream of a sumptuous odalisque." Beethoven himself disowned all such attempts to attach a program to his Seventh. Yet Wagner's reference to it as an "apotheosis of the dance" has stuck through the years. Rhythmic energy does indeed dominate the symphony, with each of the four movements built around a different rhythmic pattern. The entire symphony bristles with vim and vigor, and occasionally with a gruff kind of humor.

Recommended Recordings

★ Bernstein, New York Philharmonic (Columbia stereo disc MS-7414 or MS-6112; cassette 16-11-0158)

Karajan, Berlin Philharmonic (Deutsche Grammophon stereo disc 138806; cassette 923-119)

Szell, Cleveland Orchestra (in Columbia 7-disc set M7X-30281)

b Toscanini, NBC Symphony (RCA Victrola disc VIC-1658E; also included in a complete 8-disc mono set of Beethoven's nine symphonies VIC-8000)

Comments

Musically the most exciting performance remains Toscanini's (from 1951), but it is a mono recording available only as part of an 8-LP, budget-priced set of the complete

Beethoven symphonies or in an electronically "reprocessed" single disc version. Its rhythmic cleanness and white-heat propulsion have yet to be equaled in any of the later, better-recorded stereo editions by other conductors.

Among the latter, Bernstein offers the most dramatically urgent, energetic, virile performance. He has recorded the symphony several times. An earlier performance from the late 1950's is still available singly (MS-6112), whereas a 1964 one is part of his 8-disc set of the complete Beethoven symphonies (D8S-815) as well as being available singly (MS-7414). The interpretations are basically the same.

Karajan's 1963 release is also dramatically forceful, but with more subtle shadings and accents, and a deeper sense of tone color overall. The sound engineering is unusually spacious.

Szell's performance, from about 1959, is crisp and vigorous, and less intense than the others listed (it's for those who like a "cooler" Beethoven). The original Epic single release has recently been withdrawn (it may still be available in some stores) and transferred to Columbia as part of a 7-disc set of the complete Beethoven symphonies as played by Szell and the Cleveland Orchestra.

Symphony No. 3 in E flat ("Eroica")

As a child, Beethoven had been fascinated by stories about the American and French Revolution. Later, even though he had many friends in the aristocracy, he became a vigorous champion of some of the revolutionary movements of his day. This is musically reflected in two of his major works—the "Eroica" Symphony and his only opera, *Fidelio*. Beethoven so admired Napoleon as a revolutionary leader and liberator that he originally inscribed his Third Symphony to Napoleon in 1804. But when it was published it bore a more general inscription: "Heroic Symphony, composed to celebrate the memory of a great man." The reasons for the change have long been disputed by scholars. Some say Beethoven became angry and disillusioned when Napoleon took the title of Emperor. But others point to letters written by Beethoven *after* the first performances of the "Eroica" in 1810 suggesting that he might still dedicate a work to Napoleon. In any event, the "Eroica" is a symphony on a grand scale, and twice the length of the average Haydn or Mozart symphony. Berlioz said it "is so mighty in conception and execution, its style so terse and constantly exalted, its form so poetic, that it is equal to the greatest works of its great creator."

Recommended Stereo Recordings

★ Karajan, Berlin Philharmonic (Deutsche Grammophon stereo disc 138802; cassette 923-063; cartridge 88-802)

Bernstein, New York Philharmonic (Columbia stereo disc MS-6774)

Leinsdorf, Boston Symphony (RCA Red Seal stereo disc LSC-2644; cassette RK1058; cartridge R8S-1058)

b Toscanini, NBC Symphony (RCA Victrola, *mono only,* included in complete 8-disc set of the nine Beethoven symphonies VIC-8000)

Comments

Karajan's 1963 release is a taut, stirring, majestic declaration, conceived and played on a large scale. The sound engineering is especially good.

Bernstein's 1964 recording has more dramatic tension and intensity. He tends to rush the Funeral March (second movement), but his opening and final movements are unusually vivid.

Leinsdorf's recording was one of the first he made with the Boston orchestra (in 1963) when he had not yet become as mannered and antiseptic as he later did. His performance is vigorous and beautifully proportioned throughout.

Despite aging sound, Toscanini's 1953 performance is still a brilliant, heavens-storming, exciting musical experience, one of the finest of all of Toscanini's recordings.

Symphony No. 9 in D minor ("Choral")

This gigantic symphony was the first symphony to combine a huge choral part with purely orchestral movements. The text of the choral section is based on the "Ode to Joy" by the German poet Schiller. Beethoven had read Schiller's poem as a youth and apparently wanted to set it to music from the start. Its appeal to youth apparently continues strongly into our own days, for in the early 1970's a pop version of the Ninth's finale made its way to the top of the "pop charts" as "The Song of Joy." (Since then some record shops have even advertised the "original version" as a way to sell various complete versions of the Beethoven Ninth!) The late Lawrence Gilman, for many years program annotator of the New York Philharmonic, described the special qualities of the Ninth as "its strange blend of fatefulness and transport, wild humor and superterrestrial beauty, its mystery and exaltation, its tragical despair and its shouting among the stars."

Recommended Recordings

★ Leinsdorf, Boston Symphony, Marsh, Veasey, Domingo, Milnes, New England Conservatory Chorus & Chorus Pro Musica (RCA Red Seal stereo 2-disc set LSC-7055)

Solti, Chicago Symphony, Lorengar, Minton, Burrows, Talvela, Chicago Symphony Chorus (London stereo 2-disc set CSP-8).

Karajan, Berlin Philharmonic, Janowitz, Rössel-Majdan, Kmentt, Berry, Vienna Singverein (Deutsche Grammophon stereo 2-disc set 2707013)

b Toscanini, NBC Symphony, Farrell, Merriman, Peerce, Scott, Robert Shaw Chorale (RCA Victrola disc VIC-1607; also included in the complete 8-disc set of Beethoven's nine symphonies, VIC-8000, *mono only*)

b Fürtwangler, Bayreuth Festival Orchestra and Chorus, Schwarzkopf, Höngen, Hopf, Edelmann (Seraphim 2-disc set IB-6068, *mono only*)

Comments

Leinsdorf's 1969 recording is full of kinetic energy and spirit, and the chorale finale is exceptionally rousing. His set also includes Schoenberg's *A Survivor of Warsaw*, a brief but profoundly moving "music-drama" about the Nazi slaughter of Warsaw's Jews in 1943. The coupling thus provides in one album a provocative contrast of man's nobility and ignobility expressed in music.

Solti's 1973 release is lyrically surging and dramatic throughout, and builds militantly to a soaring finale. Sound engineering is also outstanding.

Karajan's 1963 release has the most plastic tonal qualities in the purely orchestral movements, and his finale is both noble and stirring.

Toscanini's 1952 recording created a sensation when first released because of its overwhelming power and intensity. Despite aging sound, it remains as exciting as any Ninth on records—and its reissue on a single disc in 1971 makes it an especially worthwhile budget-label bargain.

Fürtwangler's 1951 Bayreuth performance, reissued in 1971, also holds historic interest. It has been acclaimed by many critics for its lofty grandeur, and downgraded by others for its heaviness and slowness. Despite aging sound, it remains a fascinating example of Fürtwangler's individual approach.

All of the above performances are sung in German (English translations are included in the albums).

Piano Concerto No. 5 in E flat ("Emperor")

From its majestic opening theme to its spirited, dramatic finale, this is the classical concerto at its noblest. It tests not only the technical ability but also the emotional depth of any pianist. The nickname "Emperor" was not Beethoven's, but is reported to have come from a prominent piano-maker who called it "an Emperor among concertos." Before he composed the "Emperor," Beethoven had always performed his own piano concertos, but because of his growing deafness he chose not to perform this one. He insisted instead that the pianist follow his intricate score exactly, and instead of allowing him to improvise the cadenza—then a traditional procedure—he wrote his down. What was probably meant only to protect the integrity of one composition soon set a trend, and subsequent composers continued to write out cadenzas for their concertos, too.

Recommended Recordings

★ Serkin, Bernstein, New York Philharmonic (Columbia stereo disc MS-6366 or M-31807; cassette MT-31807; cartridge MA-31807)

Gilels, Szell, Cleveland Orchestra (Angel stereo disc S-36031; cassette 4XS-36031; cartridge 8XS-36031)

Barenboim, Klemperer, New Philharmonia of London (included in Angel stereo 4-disc set S-3752)

Cliburn, Reiner, Chicago Symphony (RCA Red Seal stereo disc LSC-2562; cassette RK-1008; cartridge R8S-1008)

Gould, Stokowski, American Symphony (Columbia stereo disc MS-6888)

b Horowitz, Reiner, RCA Symphony (RCA Victrola disc VICS-1636)

b Fleischer, Szell, Cleveland Orchestra (included in Columbia stereo 4-disc album M4X-30052)

Comments

Serkin offers a robust, virile, thoroughly brilliant performance recorded in 1962. He is well matched by Bernstein's dramatic accompaniment.

Gilels finds more poetry in the "Emperor" than most others, and Szell matches him in insight and grandeur in their 1968 collaboration.

Barenboim plays like the strong young titan he is, and the venerable Klemperer accompanies majestically. This 1969 edition is available only in a 4-LP set of the complete Beethoven piano concertos by Barenboim and Klemperer, but may possibly be released separately at a later date.

Cliburn's 1961 recording is in his most grand manner, polished and elegant, with a compelling accompaniment from Reiner.

Both Glenn Gould and Stokowski are famous (or is it infamous?) for the individuality of their performances, but they collaborate marvelously on a 1966 recording emphasizing the heroic substance and self-confident nobility of this work.

Among older recordings still available on budget labels, Horowitz's (from the early 1950's) remains exceptional—a dynamic, brilliant performance, well matched by Reiner's accompaniment. The 1972 reissue has been electronically reprocessed from its mono original to simulate an acceptable stereo effect.

Fleischer's performance (from 1961) is especially clean-cut and propulsive, and Szell contributes a vividly lucid accompaniment. The recording, much admired a decade ago but long unavailable, was reissued as part of the Beethoven Bicentennial in 1970, in a reduced-priced album of all five Beethoven Piano Concertos superbly played by Fleischer and Szell, but there is no knowing how long it will remain available in that edition.

Violin Concerto in D major

Although almost perfectly Classical in structure, the mood of this concerto is more Romantic than most of Beethoven's works. Some of its special character may be due to the violinist Beethoven wrote it for. Franz Clement was a violinist who used to play as an encore a work of his own while holding his violin upside down—a feat about which author-critic Martin Bookspan has quipped: "Were he alive today [he] would be a natural for the Ed Sullivan Show!" Tricks or no tricks, violin concertos were not as popular in Beethoven's day as piano concertos, and Beethoven even recast this violin concerto as a piano concerto. The piano version occasionally turns up on concert programs even today. However, over the past century the original version has become one of the most popular of all violin concertos.

Recommended Recordings

★ Stern, Bernstein, New York Philharmonic (Columbia stereo disc MS-6093; cassette MGT-31418)

Ferras, Karajan, Berlin Philharmonic (Deutsche Grammophon stereo disc 139021; cassette 923-026; cartridge 89-021)

Heifetz, Munch, Boston Symphony (RCA Red Seal stereo disc LSC-1992; cassette RK-1045; cartridge R8S-1045)

Oistrakh, Cluytens, French National Orchestra (Angel stereo disc S-35780)

Menuhin, Klemperer, New Philharmonia of London (Angel stereo disc S-36369; cassette 4XS-36369; cartridge 8XS-36369)

b Szerying, Thibaud, Paris Conservatory Orchestra (Monitor stereo disc S-2093)

Comments

Preferences among recordings of this concerto depend to a large extent on whether a listener prefers a cooler approach, emphasizing the concerto's Classical line, or a warmer, more Romantic approach. In the latter category, Stern, Ferras, or Oistrakh are recommended; in the former, Heifetz, Menuhin, or Szerying.

Stern gives the concerto a full-blooded, richly toned performance dating from about 1960, well matched by Bernstein's orchestral accompaniment.

Ferras and Karajan linger expressively over the concerto's lyric beauty, and the sound engineering of this 1967 release is caressingly mellow.

Oistrakh is also uncommonly expressive, if more rhapsodic, in his 1959 release, and has a beautifully singing tone.

Heifetz and Menuhin have a more detached Classical approach. Heifetz plays with spirit and incisiveness and with his always-dazzling technical *élan,* in a recording dating from the mid-1950's. Menuhin is more leisurely than usual (Klemperer's influence?) in this 1966 release, with an emphasis on a lyrical, noble interpretation.

There are as yet no budget-priced recordings that equal in sound any of the above, but Szerying's strong, beautifully lyrical version (from around 1959) has many merits, and is conducted by one of the great violinists of an earlier generation, Jacques Thibaud.

For Follow-Up Consideration

Symphony No. 6 in F major "Pastoral," Beethoven's only programmatic symphony, describes a day in the country (its movements are subtitled "Awakening of Pleasant Feelings Upon Arriving in the Country," "Scene at the Brook," "Peasant's Merrymaking," "The Storm," and "Shepherd's Hymn of Thanksgiving After the Storm"), but it is meant to be "more an expression of feeling than a painting in sound" (to quote Beethoven himself). RECOMMENDED RECORDING: Reiner, Chicago Symphony (RCA Red Seal stereo disc LSC-2614; cassette RK-1094; cartridge R8S-1094), one of Reiner's last recordings (recorded in 1961), with a marvelously mellow and flowing feeling in the first movements and a climactic thunderstorm that really hurls musical thunderbolts from the grooves.

Symphony No. 4 in B flat, sometimes called Beethoven's "Romantic" symphony, more graceful, tender, and sunny than some of Beethoven's other symphonies. Schumann likened the Fourth to "a slender Greek maiden between two Norse giants," the giants being the Third and Fifth symphonies. RECOMMENDED RECORDING: Karajan, Berlin Philharmonic (Deutsche Grammophon stereo disc 138803; cassette 3300257; cartridge 88-803), a sunny and spirited performance dating from 1962.

Piano Concerto No. 4 in G, like the Fourth Symphony more poetically "Romantic" in its basic feeling than Beethoven's other piano concertos, and next to the "Emperor" his most popular concerto. RECOMMENDED RECORDING: Rubinstein, Leinsdorf, Boston Symphony (RCA Red Seal stereo disc LSC-2848), a warm yet elegant and always colorful performance, recorded in 1964.

Triple Concerto in C for piano, violin, cello, and orchestra, belonging to the same period as the "Eroica" Symphony and the violin concerto but long underrated, perhaps because it is less flashy and more traditional in style. Yet it has some of Beethoven's most appealing and melodious concerto writing. RECOMMENDED RECORDING: Richter, Oistrakh, Rostropovich, Karajan, Berlin Philharmonic (Angel stereo disc S-36727; cassette 4XS-36727), a 1970 collaboration between the three Soviet musical giants and Karajan's Berliners that is deeply lyrical and elegantly polished throughout.

Quartets No. 12, 13, 14, 15, 16, Beethoven's last quartets are considered by many critics as ranking at or near the top of all his compositions. Conductor Carlo Maria Giulini has said, "I think he only fully expressed himself in the late quartets." Some have also compared them to abstract paintings in their remoteness, fragmentation, sense of color, intellectual depth, and mystery. RECOMMENDED RECORDING: Budapest String Quartet (Columbia 5-disc set M5S-677), a superbly eloquent set recorded in 1961 by the quartet closely identified with these works for more than thirty years; the *High Fidelity* magazine reviewer called the set "the finest thing the Budapest has ever given us (and that covers a great many memorable recordings)."

Special Note on Complete Recordings of All Nine Beethoven Symphonies

In 1952 Columbia issued an album combining all of its previously released recordings of the nine Beethoven symphonies as conducted by the late Felix Weingartner. Several years later RCA issued a similar "special package" featuring Toscanini's interpretations. Since then it has become something of a status symbol among conductors to record *all* of the Beethoven symphonies and to have them released in "deluxe albums." As a result, there are now many complete Beethoven symphony sets—by Ansermet, Bernstein, Böhm, Jochum, Karajan, Klemperer, Krips, Leinsdorf, Ormandy, Steinberg, Szell, Walter, and a few others.

Except for the most loyal fans of the individual conductors involved, most of these sets are *not* recommended for a beginning collector. A conductor who may be at his best in the Fifth or Seventh Symphonies may just not be as good in the very different Second or Sixth—or vice-versa, of course.

At present there are only three complete sets that challenge that position: those of Toscanini (RCA Victrola, *mono only*, VIC-8000, eight discs), Szell (Columbia M7X-30281, seven discs), and Karajan (Deutsche Grammophon 2720007, eight discs).

All three conductors have something worthwhile to say about *each* of the symphonies —and although they too are better in certain of the symphonies than in others, the discrepancies are less troublesome with them than with other conductors.

• *FRANZ SCHUBERT*

Pronounced: *shoo*-bert. Born January 31, 1797, in Lichtenthal, near Vienna. Died November 19, 1828, in Vienna.

SIGNIFICANCE: Austrian composer, an important bridge between Classical and Romantic music, and the first great master of the Romantic 19th-century German art song.

BACKGROUND: One of fourteen children of a village schoolmaster in Lichtenthal, Schubert became a choirboy in the Vienna court choir and a member of its student orchestra when he was eleven. By fifteen he had written many songs and piano pieces, by sixteen his first symphony, and by seventeen his first Mass. To avoid military conscription he became a teacher for several years, but he hated the routine, and was frequently reprimanded for scribbling music in his notebooks during classes.

He composed quickly, and had written six symphonies by age twenty-one. But he was badly paid by his publishers, and was involved in a number of financially disastrous stage productions, and so lived most of his life on the verge of starvation. His health finally could not stand the pace of his daytime writing frenzy combined with too little food and too much nighttime revelry, and he died of typhus at age thirty-one. So little was he appreciated at his death that the five hundred manuscripts found in his room were valued at about $2 by the investigating authorities. It was not until many years later that the significance of his works was recognized, partly through the efforts of Mendelssohn and Schumann.

Symphony No. 8 in B minor ("Unfinished")

Musicians and scholars have long debated why this symphony was never completed— if indeed it was ever meant to be. Some hold that Schubert, unconcerned about traditional form, *intended* the symphony to be in only two movements rather than the customary four. Others argue that Schubert's disordered working habits kept him from completing it. A piano sketch of most of a projected third movement was found among Schubert's papers many years after his death (and was orchestrated and recorded in the 1960's by Australian conductor Denis Vaughan). But scholars feel that it is so far inferior to the first two movements that Schubert himself probably abandoned it as unworthy. There have, of course, been a number of fictionalized, highly romantic stage and film stories involving the writing of the Eighth. It was not performed until nearly forty years after Schubert's death, and then, ironically, became an immediate success. The symphony, from its soft, reflective, dark-hued opening, is full of melting melody. It remains one of the most appealing of all early Romantic works.

Recommended Recordings

★ Bernstein, New York Philharmonic (Columbia stereo disc MS-7057)

b Munch, Boston Symphony (RCA Victrola disc VICS-1035; cartridge V8S-1005)

Karajan, Berlin Philharmonic (Deutsche Grammophon disc 139001; cassette 923-057; cartridge 89-001)

Fischer-Dieskau, New Philharmonia of London (Angel stereo disc S-36965)

b Cantelli, Philharmonia Orchestra of London (Seraphim disc 60002, *mono only*)

Comments

Bernstein gives a beautifully expressive, intensely lyrical performance. His 1963 version is coupled with a buoyant account of Mendelssohn's "Italian" Symphony (No. 4).

Munch leads a radiantly warm, poetic performance dating from the mid-1950's, with splendid Boston Symphony tonal colors. Overside he leads a vivid, intense Beethoven Fifth, marked by some rhythmic irregularities.

Karajan molds a long-lined, subtly shaded, beautiful performance. His 1965 release is coupled with three well-played Beethoven overtures, including the popular "Leonore No. 3."

Fischer-Dieskau's warm, genial, more intimately phrased performance marks the impressive conducting debut of the baritone long noted for his interpretation of Schubert *lieder*. The 1974 release is coupled with a spirited, elegant performance of the Schubert Fifth Symphony.

Cantelli's mono performance, dating from the early 1950's, remains a glowing, poetic account—one of the few recorded testaments of a promising career left tragically "unfinished" by the premature death of the conductor at almost as early an age as Schubert. It is coupled with a vivacious Cantelli performance of Mendelssohn's "Italian" Symphony.

Symphony No. 9 in C ("Great")

The nickname "Great" is used primarily to distinguish the Ninth from a smaller-scaled, earlier Schubert symphony in the same key (No. 6, usually called the "Little" C major). However, the Ninth's nickname applies as much to the grand sweep and monumental strength of the music. Next to Beethoven's symphonies, it represents the large-scaled early 19th-century symphony at its most eloquent.

For many decades the Schubert Ninth was called the Seventh, since it was the seventh of his symphonies to be published. This caused no end of confusion, leading many to assume it was written *before* the "Unfinished" Eighth, whereas it actually had been composed six years *after* the "Unfinished," in the final year of Schubert's life. Recently it has become standard to number the Schubert symphonies in chronological sequence, which makes the incompleted Symphony in E major No. 7, the popular "Unfinished" (in B minor) No. 8, and the final C major Symphony No. 9.

Recommended Recordings

★ b Szell, Cleveland Orchestra (Odyssey stereo disc Y-30669)

Szell, Cleveland Orchestra (Angel stereo disc S-36044; cassette 4XS-36044; cartridge 8XS-36044)

b Skrowaczewski, Minneapolis Symphony (Philips World Series stereo disc WS-9044)

Steinberg, Boston Symphony Orchestra (RCA Red Seal disc LSC-3115; cartridge R8S-1159)

Toscanini, Philadelphia Orchestra (RCA Red Seal disc LD-2663, *mono only*)

b Furtwängler, Berlin Philharmonic (Heliodor electronic-stereo disc 25074)

Comments

This symphony was for a long time one of Szell's specialties, and he projected it with exceptional excitement—particularly in the 1957 recording originally released on Epic and reissued on the budget-priced Odyssey in 1972. The Angel version, recorded in 1969, is a little less crisp but still outstanding for its surging, robust power.

Skrowaczewski's 1966 recording has dynamic rhythmic thrust and impressive clarity of orchestral detail. It was recently deleted from the active catalog, but still may be available in some stores.

Steinberg's 1969 recording, his first as the Boston Symphony's music director, is more relaxed than Szell's or Skrowaczewski's, but is uncommonly noble and stirring.

Both the Toscanini and Furtwängler are historic releases, very different in interpretation, and each in its own way a testament to two of this century's greatest conductors. Toscanini, in a rare appearance with the Philadelphians, has a hard-driving, rhythmically crisp approach, similar to his approach to Beethoven—in contrast to the slower tempos, sentimental phrasing, yet vibrant interpretation of Furtwängler. The Toscanini LP is specially packaged with an elaborate booklet which includes a fascinating explanation of the technical problems as to why the original 1941 recording was never released until 1963. What finally did emerge is one of the great recordings of the century, with remarkably serviceable sound, considering how far hi-fi has come since 1941. Heliodor has judiciously "doctored" the sound of Furtwängler's original Deutsche Grammophon recording (dating from the early 1950's) and it, too, is remarkably serviceable—especially at a budget-label price.

For Follow-Up Consideration

Die Schöne Müllerin (The Fair Maid of the Mill), a song cycle of twenty vividly beautiful *lieder,* written in 1823, and built on the story of a young miller who loses a beautiful but fickle girl to a handsome hunter. RECOMMENDED RECORDING: Wunderlich, Giesen (Deutsche Grammophon stereo disc 2707031), one of the German tenor's last recordings before his accidental death in 1968 and a fine vehicle for his rich, beautifully lyrical voice.

Winterreise (Winter's Journey), a cycle of twenty-four deeply melancholy songs, written in 1827, describing the winter journey of a broken-hearted man toward death;

the cycle is considered by some critics to consist of the finest *lieder* ever written. RECOMMENDED RECORDING: Fischer-Dieskau, Demus (Deutsche Grammophon stereo disc 2707028), Fischer-Dieskau's third recording of the cycle (made in 1965) and the finest in both the depth of his interpretation and the sound engineering.

Symphony No. 2 in B flat, written when Schubert was eighteen and with the shadow of Haydn and Mozart looming clearly over it, yet with equally clear evidences of Schubert's fresh melodic and rhythmic sense. RECOMMENDED RECORDING: Munch, Boston Symphony (RCA Victrola stereo disc VICS-1436), a bright, animated performance from the mid-1950's of one of Munch's personal specialties, coupled on this budget-priced reissue with a similarly bright performance of Schumann's First ("Spring") Symphony.

Symphony No. 5 in B flat, from its opening measures a generally joyous symphony, with one of Schubert's loveliest slow movements. RECOMMENDED RECORDING: Böhm, Berlin Philharmonic (Deutsche Grammophon stereo disc 139385; cartridge 89-385), a warmly lyrical, beautifully proportioned 1966 performance, coupled with a genially spirited performance of Mozart's Symphony No. 33.

• *HECTOR BERLIOZ*

Pronounced: *bare*-lee-ohz. Born December 11, 1803, in La Côte-St. André, near Grenoble, France. Died March 8, 1869, in Paris.

SIGNIFICANCE: French composer, conductor, and critic, sometimes called the "father of modern orchestration"; one of the first composers to give an orchestral work a "program" (a plot or sequence of events), and an early Romantic who favored super-scaled works scored for bigger and bigger orchestras.

BACKGROUND: Although he was sent to Paris to study medicine (his father's profession), Berlioz decided to accept disinheritance in order to take up music instead. Twice Berlioz was denied admission to the Paris Conservatory because he did not meet their standards for previous formal musical training (he could only play guitar and flute). Finally, after he borrowed the money to pay for a successful performance of a Mass he had written (the *Messe Solonelle*), he was accepted by the Conservatory. There he immediately established a reputation as a rebel, expounding what his teachers considered subversive ideas about harmony and structure.

Stories about his fiery behavior abound. The most famous concerns his stormy wooing of the English Shakespearean actress Harriet Smithson, commemorated in his *Symphonie Fantastique*. Later he married her, but the romance soon cooled and they ended up living apart. His personal and professional life was a series of such ups and downs. He constantly charged ahead romantically with some grandiose idea or other, never quite sure where he was heading yet trusting it would all turn out right. Sometimes it did. Mussorgsky, the Russian composer, said soon after Berlioz's death: "There are two giants in music, the thinker Beethoven and the super-thinker Berlioz."

Symphonie Fantastique (Fantastic Symphony)

In one of his popular TV broadcasts, Leonard Bernstein called this work "the first psychedelic symphony in history, the first musical description ever made of a trip"—a narcotics trip that ends up taking its hero through hell. As Bernstein puts it, even for 1830 Berlioz "tells it like it is—you take a trip and you end up screaming at your own funeral." Berlioz's symphony, one of the first to have a specific "program," depicts a young man's opium dream after an unhappy love affair with a famous actress, with the real and the imagined intertwined—particularly in the frenzy of the final "Witches' Sabbath" movement. The symphony's five movements are unified by a recurring theme—the *idée fixe*—representing the hero's beloved. The movements have the following titles: "Reveries, Passions"; "A Ball"; "Country Scenes"; "March to the Scaffold"; "Dream of a Witches' Sabbath."

Recommended Recordings

★ Munch, Boston Symphony (RCA Red Seal stereo disc LSC-2608; cartridge R8S-5050)

Ozawa, Boston Symphony (Deutsche Grammophon stereo disc 2530358; cassette 3300316; cartridge 89467)

b Ozawa, Toronto Symphony (Odyssey stereo disc Y-31923)

Ansermet, Suisse Romande Orchestra (London stereo disc CSA2101)

Boulez, London Symphony (Columbia stereo disc M-30587)

Davis, London Symphony (Philips stereo disc 835188; cassette PCR4-900101)

Comments

Munch made the *Symphonie Fantastique* one of the most passionate and exciting *tours de force* of his conducting career, recording it four times. His second recording with the Boston Symphony (dating from 1962) is his best, and is much superior to a later recording made with the Orchestre de Paris in 1968 (Angel stereo disc 36517). His approach to the *Fantastique* is a striking mixture of fieriness and sensitivity, and only the most virtuoso orchestral playing could pull off some of Munch's breathtaking tempos and coloristic effects—which the Bostonians do superbly.

Ozawa, probably influenced by Munch during his Tanglewood student days, gives a similarly supercharged performance, with an inner rhythmic drive that is especially outstanding. In a few places he is perhaps too intense (the ball scene, for example, could be lighter), but his final "Witches' Sabbath" rivals Munch in sheer excitement. Ozawa's 1973 recording with the Boston Symphony is superior in both orchestral playing and sound engineering to his 1966 Toronto recording, but the latter is still quite good.

Ansermet's 1967 recording includes two bonuses—a fine performance of Berlioz's "Corsair" Overture plus an additional (free) LP made up of snatches from Ansermet's rehearsals of the symphony (which will have meaning mostly to music students and those who understand French). Ansermet's performance is less frenetic than Munch's or Ozawa's, and has subtler insights into its musical form. Ansermet also has some unorthodox ideas about the way the famous church bells in the finale should sound (low and distant and eerily out of tune). In terms of sound engineering, London's recording is clearly the best.

In his 1967 version Boulez, like Ansermet, puts the emphasis on the clarity of inner musical voicings, which is fascinating until the finale when the expected fireworks never materialize. However, Boulez is the only conductor to offer Berlioz's sequel to the *Fantastique* in a companion album: *Lélio* (*The Return to Life*), a "lyrical melologue" for narrator, orchestra, chorus, and soloists (Columbia stereo disc M-30588). Built around the theme of the composer's love for the same actress who inspired the *Fantastique*, it is a more diffuse, "variety show" sort of work, but Boulez's performance, and especially that of Jean-Louis Barrault as narrator, manages to make most of it absorbing.

Colin Davis' 1966 recording has also been widely praised by many critics for its lucidity of orchestral textures and Classical sobriety. Although some may find its overall feeling a bit earth-bound, it will appeal to those who prefer Classical constraint to Romantic excesses.

Romeo and Juliet

Composed in 1839, Berlioz's "dramatic symphony" preceded Gounod's opera based on Shakespeare's play by twenty-eight years, Tchaikovsky's famous "overture-fantasia" by thirty, and Prokofiev's ballet by nearly a century. Berlioz's work remains, however, the most penetrating musical approach to Shakespeare's romantic tragedy. The complete score calls for three vocal soloists (a mezzo-soprano, a tenor, and a bass-baritone) plus a chorus in addition to full orchestra. Frequently the orchestral sections are performed alone in concert programs, and most critics agree that they are the greatest parts, especially the technically difficult "Queen Mab Scherzo."

Recommended Recordings (Complete)

★ b Munch, Boston Symphony, New England Conservatory Chorus, Elias, Valletti, Tozzi (RCA Victrola stereo 2-disc album VICS-6042)

Davis, London Symphony Orchestra and Chorus, Kern, Tear, Shirley-Quirk (Philips stereo 2-disc album 839716-7)

Toscanini, NBC Symphony, Chorus, Swarthout, Garris, Moscona (RCA Victor 2-disc album LM-7034, *mono only*)

Recommended Recordings (Orchestral Sections only)

★ Giulini, Chicago Symphony (Angel stereo disc S-36038; cassette 4XS-36038)

Bernstein, New York Philharmonic (Columbia stereo disc MS-6170)

b Toscanini, NBC Symphony (RCA Victrola disc VIC-1398, *mono only*)

Comments

Munch is passionate and colorful in his 1961 performance of a score he obviously loved. His soloists are all excellent, and the sound engineering is very good. (The recording was transferred to the Victrola budget label in 1971.)

Davis' 1968 performance is more relaxed, yet deeply expressive and compelling. His soloists range from fair to good, and the chorus is very good. The sound engineering is excellent.

Toscanini's performance is musically the finest, but the sound is dated. His complete version is taken from two historic broadcasts of 1941—they were the first complete performances of the work in the U.S. in this century—whereas the orchestral fragments were recorded in 1946. Dated though the sound may be, both of these Toscanini performances are still highly recommended, especially since the orchestral excerpts were shifted in 1969 to the budget-priced Victrola label (coupled with a hair-raising Toscanini performance of the Prologue to Boito's opera *Mefistofele*).

Giulini's set of orchestral excerpts, released in 1970, are warmly and dynamically projected, and the playing of the Chicago orchestra is outstanding.

Bernstein's late 1950's account of the orchestral sections is more colorful and fervent, but the orchestral playing is not as polished as the Chicagoans.

All of the vocal versions listed above are sung in French. (English translations are included in each album.)

Harold in Italy

Though called a symphony, this is in some ways a "program concerto" for viola and orchestra, written on a commission from the great 19th-century violin and viola virtuoso Paganini. Based loosely on Byron's *Childe Harolde*, the work depicts a series of scenes that pass before the wandering Harold's eyes ("Harold in the Mountains," "March of the Pilgrims," "Serenade of a Mountaineer to His Sweetheart," and "Orgy of the Brigands"). The symphony is richly lyrical and expressive, with its chief theme recurring throughout the work. Unlike the recurring *idée fixe* of the *Symphonie Fantastique*, however, this theme interposes itself on other themes, modifying them or being modified in the process.

Recommended Recordings

★ Primrose, Munch, Boston Symphony (RCA Red Seal stereo disc LSC-2228)

Menuhin, Davis, Philharmonia Orchestra (Angel stereo disc 36123)

Lincer, Bernstein, New York Philharmonic (Columbia stereo disc MS-6358)

Comments

Munch and Primrose are ardent and colorful in their 1958 release, although there are moments when Munch drives the orchestra to overwhelm his soloist. Those who interpret the work literally as a symphony with viola *obbligato* may not object.

Davis and Menuhin have better sound and are stylish and sensitive in their 1968 release, with Menuhin in a rare performance as a violist rather than violinist.

Bernstein and Lincer (from about 1962) are dramatic and sensitive, with the viola recorded less "close-up" than in the RCA or Philips editions, thus contributing to a more distinctly symphonic blend than the others.

For Follow-Up Consideration

Overtures to *The Corsair, Benvenuto Cellini, Beatrice and Benedict,* and *The Roman Carnival,* all fiery, colorful orchestral showpieces. RECOMMENDED RECORDING: Munch, Boston Symphony (RCA Red Seal stereo disc LSC-2438; cartridge R8S-5050), which includes all four overtures in an exciting set of 1960 performances played at breakneck tempos which few other orchestras could pull off with such incisiveness and tonal splendor. The disc is coupled with Berlioz's "Royal Hunt and Storm Music" (without the choral parts) from *The Trojans,* while the cartridge is coupled with Munch's performance of the *Symphonie Fantastique.*

Nuits d'Été (*Summer Nights*), one of Berlioz's most intimate and least grandiose works; a graceful, sensitive, lyrical setting, for soprano and orchestra, of six poems by the arch-Romantic Theophile Gautier. RECOMMENDED RECORDING: Crespin, Ansermet, Suisse Romande Orchestra (London stereo disc CS-25821), a shimmeringly beautiful and expressive performance by both soprano and conductor, released in 1963; the coupling is a similarly superb Crespin-Ansermet performance of Ravel's haunting song cycle, *Shéhérazade.*

Requiem, or the *Grande Messe des Morts,* one of the most spectacularly scored Masses of all time (requiring, for example, sixteen brasses instead of the usual four), yet at its heart a reverent and lyrical work, in some sections disarmingly simple and quiet. RECOMMENDED RECORDING: Munch, Simoneau, Boston Symphony and New England Conservatory Chorus (RCA Victrola stereo 2-disc set VICS-6043), an alternately stirring and eloquently restrained performance from 1959, superior to a later (1968) Munch–Schreier performance recorded in Munich (Deutsche Grammophon stereo 2-disc set 2707032).

• *FELIX MENDELSSOHN*

Pronounced: *men*-dell-sone. Born February 3, 1809, in Hamburg, Germany. Died November 4, 1847, in Leipzig.

SIGNIFICANCE: German composer, conductor, pianist, and organist. In his elegant and finely sculptured music he sought to reconcile Romantic content with Classical form.

BACKGROUND: Compared to some early 19th-century composers, Mendelssohn led a uniquely happy, comfortable, successful life. He was the grandson of Jewish philosopher Moses Mendelssohn, who waged a lifelong battle to reconcile Christians and Jews, and the son of a Hamburg banker who used the name Mendelssohn-Bartholdy to distinguish himself as a Christian. Young Mendelssohn began formal study of music at the age of ten, and became widely known as a child prodigy. On Sundays a small orchestra performed at his father's rambling house in Berlin, and it eventually became a vehicle for the boy's composing and conducting. At twenty, he conducted the first public performance since Bach's death of the *St. Matthew Passion*, and began a great crusade to take Bach out of obscurity and gain him the reputation he now holds.

By twenty-six he held the most important musical post in Germany: director of the Leipzig Gewandhaus Orchestra. In 1841 he married the daughter of a French Protestant clergyman, and they subsequently had five children. He traveled frequently to conduct in Berlin and Dresden, and to perform as both pianist and organist. Some of his works were inspired by his travels (the "Scotch" Symphony, the "Italian" Symphony, the "Hebrides" Overture). He also wrote works that reflected his dual religious loyalties (the "Reformation" Symphony dedicated to Martin Luther, and the oratorio *Elijah*). Returning from a successful English tour in 1847, he was mistaken for a Dr. Mendelssohn wanted for revolutionary political activity, and was detained and interrogated at the Prussian border. A few hours after his release he learned suddenly that his most beloved sister Fanny had died, and he collapsed with a ruptured cerebral blood vessel. He never recovered, and died a few months later at age thirty-eight.

Violin Concerto in E minor

One of the most popular and immediately appealing of all violin concertos with—as one Mendelssohn biographer once said—"the charm of eternal youth." It is Romantic in mood but Classical in form—except that there are no breaks between its three movements. The concerto moves instead in a continuous line, but with changing melodies and rhythms.

Recommended Recordings

★ Zukerman, Bernstein, New York Philharmonic (Columbia stereo disc MS-7313; cassette 16-11-0162)

Stern, Ormandy, Philadelphia (Columbia stereo disc MS-6062; cassette 16-11-0126; cartridge 18-11-0126)

Heifetz, Munch, Boston Symphony (RCA Red Seal stereo disc LSC-2314; cartridge R8S-1083)

b Laredo, Munch, Boston Symphony (RCA Victrola stereo disc VICS-1033)

Comments

Zukerman's debut recording, recorded in 1969 when he was twenty-one, explains why there's been so much excitement about this young violinist. His tone is beautiful, his technique impeccable, and he plays with an interpretive flair and warmth of feeling that few others equal. Overside, he is just as impressive in Tchaikovsky's Violin Concerto.

Stern plays with a broadly lush, unabashedly Romantic flair in a recording dating from the late 1950's. Overside on the disc version he offers a similarly styled Tchaikovsky Violin Concerto; the cassette version is coupled with a group of short Mendelssohn works played by Rudolf Serkin, Kostelanetz, and others.

Heifetz is, as always, impressive technically, and although he seems less involved with the Romanticism of the score, his finale is dashingly brilliant. His late 1950's release is coupled with a superbly played Prokofiev Violin Concerto No. 2.

Young Laredo, in one of the first recordings he made in the early 1960's, gives a freshly lyrical, beautifully expressive performance. It is coupled with a warm, flowing account of the Romantic Bruch Violin Concerto No. 1.

Symphony No. 4 in A major ("Italian")

Mendelssohn himself once called this "the most sportive piece I have composed." It was begun while the composer was on a lengthy holiday in Italy in 1831 (during his twenty-first year), visiting Rome, Naples, Capri, Sorrento, and Amalfi. In general it is a sunny symphony, filled with appealing melodies and spirited rhythms. Its slow movement has a "walking bass" figure usually taken to depict a religious procession or pilgrims' march. Although commonly called Mendelssohn's Fourth symphony (because it was the fourth to be published), it was actually his third—*if* you count only the five symphonies Mendelssohn composed as an adult (and not the twelve or more he wrote as a teenager, mostly works for strings alone).

(For the record, the correct compositional sequence of the Mendelssohn symphonies is as follows, with the numbers referring only to the order in which they were published: No. 1 in C minor, 1824; No. 5 in D minor, the "Reformation," 1832; No. 4 in A major, "Italian," 1833; No. 2, "Lobgesang," with voices, 1840; and No. 3 in A minor, "Scotch," 1842.)

Recommended Recordings

★ Abbado, London Symphony (London stereo disc CS-6587)

Bernstein, New York Philharmonic (Columbia stereo disc M-31819; cassette MT-31819)

Munch, Boston Symphony (RCA Red Seal stereo disc LSC-2221)

Ansermet, Suisse Romande Orchestra (London stereo disc 6436)

b Cantelli, Philharmonia Orchestra (Seraphim disc 60002, *mono only*)

Comments

Abbado serves up a bright, animated performance, marked by a splendid balance between rhythmic incisiveness and melodic flow. His 1968 release is coupled with a similarly lively performance of Mendelssohn's "Scotch" Symphony.

Bernstein gives a wonderfully vivid and sunny performance, dating from the late 1950's. It is coupled with a beautifully expressive performance of Schubert's "Unfinished" Symphony.

Munch leads an unusually exhilarating, virtuoso performance also dating from the late 1950's, with an eloquent performance of Mendelssohn's "Reformation" Symphony overside.

Ansermet gives a more relaxed yet tonally sparkling performance recorded in 1964. It is coupled with his first-rate performances of Mendelssohn's "Hebrides," "Fair Melusina," and "Ruy Blas" overtures.

Cantelli's mono-only recording dates from the mid-1950's, but it remains a vivacious, warmly singing performance, and the sound is still serviceable. It is coupled with a most poetic performance of Schubert's "Unfinished" Symphony.

For Follow-Up Consideration

A Midsummer Night's Dream (Incidental Music), begun when Mendelssohn was seventeen and added to in his later years; an airily merry and charming set of pieces to accompany Shakespeare's play. A really satisfactory performance of the complete score (with choruses, soloists, etc.) has yet to be released. A nearly complete 1963 effort by Leinsdorf and the Boston Symphony (RCA Red Seal stereo disc LSC-2673), with some of Shakespeare's lines spoken by actress Inga Swenson to provide desirable continuity, is spoiled by the rather arch approach of both conductor and narrator. A somewhat leaden Klemperer 1962 release (Angel stereo disc S-35881) has beautiful singing by Heather Harper and Janet Baker. Kubelik's 1964 recording with the Bavarian Radio Orchestra and Chorus (Deutsche Grammophon stereo disc 138959; cassette 923-010) has both warmth and sparkle, plus fine singing by Edith Mathis and Ursula Boese, but Shakespeare's text is unfortunately used in a German translation.

Symphony No. 3 ("Scotch"), an alternately dark and spirited symphony which mixes pastoral images with those of warlike Scottish clans, supposedly inspired by a visit to the ruins of Mary Stuart's Holyrood Castle in 1829 but not completed until thirteen years later. RECOMMENDED RECORDING: Maag, London Symphony Orchestra (London Stereo Treasury disc STS-15091), a colorful, spacious, lithely spirited performance from the early 1960's (reissued in its budget-label edition in 1972); the coupling is a fine Maag performance of the "Hebrides" Overture, fittingly placed *before* the symphony.

• *FREDERIC CHOPIN*

Pronounced: *show*-pan. Born February 22, 1810, in Zelazowa Wola, near Warsaw. Died October 17, 1849, in Paris, France.

SIGNIFICANCE: Polish composer and pianist, the great Romantic poet of the piano.

BACKGROUND: The son of a French father and a Polish mother, Chopin grew up in Poland but spent most of his adult life in Paris. His musical studies began at his father's private school for young noblemen in Warsaw, and he gave his first piano recital at the age of nine. From then on, the piano was to be his life. By nineteen he had written two piano concertos, some of his most famous polonaises, waltzes, and mazurkas.

At twenty-one he visited Paris and met with such success with his first concerts that he stayed there permanently. He never married, but he had a long, stormy affair with the French authoress Aurore Dudevant, who wrote under the name George Sand. He never revisited Poland after 1831 (it was then under Russian occupation), but he was widely known in Paris as a Polish patriot and an expert on Polish literature. Tuberculosis, allegedly aggravated by his social high life, led to his death at the age of thirty-nine.

Chopin composed almost exclusively for the piano and was one of the first to introduce Slavic elements into Classical forms.

Waltzes

Chopin wrote his first three waltzes when he was nineteen, after his first visit to Vienna—at a time when the waltzes of Johann Strauss, Sr. were the rage of that city. Yet Chopin's waltzes are of a completely different sort. Instead of invoking the atmosphere of the ballroom, they are poems in music more closely akin to his etudes and other solo piano works. They are often deeply romantic, sometimes melancholy, sometimes gay, and filled with elegance and wit. Says pianist Artur Rubinstein about Chopin's waltzes: "The point is not to try to define them all in a word or phrase, or to make them all sound 'like Chopin waltzes,' but to consider each of them as a unique event and listen very attentively to what each has to say." Chopin wrote several sets of waltzes between 1829 and 1847, the most famous bearing the publisher's opus numbers 18, 34, 42, 64, and 70. Pianists rarely play them in compositional sequence, preferring to group the various waltzes according to their own tastes for mood, color, or dramatic effect. Some have acquired descriptive subtitles—such as the "Minute Waltz" (Op. 64, No. 1, in D flat), "Farewell Waltz" (Op. 69, No. 1, in A flat—written as a farewell gift to Marya Vodzhinska, a Polish girl Chopin almost married), and several "Valses brillantes" (Op. 34, Nos. 1, 2, 3, in A flat, A minor, and F major respectively).

Recommended Recordings

★ b Lipatti (Odyssey disc 32160058, *mono only*)

    Lipatti (Angel 2-disc set S-3556, *mono only*)

    Rubinstein (RCA Red Seal stereo disc LSC-2726; cassette RK-1071; cartridge R8S-1071)

    Anievas (Angel stereo disc S-36598; cassette 4XS-36598; cartridge 8XS-36598)

    Vasary (Deutsche Grammophon stereo disc 136485)

Comments

Lipatti's two recordings are among the most memorable of the century, by a pianist capable of exceptional light and lightness, caressing lyricism, and rhythmic subtlety. The Odyssey release (fourteen waltzes) dates from the late 1940's and, accordingly, is "low fidelity," but not enough to detract from the beauty of the playing. The 2-disc Angel release is taken from a live 1950 recital—Lipatti's last—and includes works by Bach, Mozart, and Schubert in addition to thirteen Chopin waltzes—all beautifully played despite the physical pain Lipatti suffered during the recital (from the leukemia which claimed his life a few months later) and which made it impossible for him to perform the scheduled fourteenth waltz.

The Polish-born Rubinstein has long specialized in Chopin's music. He brings a special elegance and grace to the waltzes, as well as tonal color and rhythmic vibrancy. This 1963 recording of fourteen waltzes is in compositional sequence.

The performances of two young pianists—Anievas and Vasary—are both excellent. Each plays with sensitivity, elegance, taste, and poetry, with Vasary perhaps also the most subtle. Vasary's recording dates from the mid-1960's, Anievas' from 1969. Both pianists include several less frequently performed waltzes discovered after Chopin's death, and not included in Lipatti's or Rubinstein's sets. Vasary plays a total of seventeen waltzes, Anievas nineteen.

Piano Concerto No. 1 in E minor

Chopin wrote only two piano concertos, both during his late teens. Actually the concerto published as No. 2 (in F minor) was written first, the one published as No. 1 (in E minor) coming within the following year. Some critics maintain that the concertos are not as cohesive as Chopin's solo works, that Chopin was essentially a miniaturist who did not handle the larger forms as well. There are others, however, who find the concertos a remarkably original pair—particularly considering Chopin's remoteness (in his teen years in Poland) from the musical centers of his day. Both concertos stand out for their grace and elegance, and for their early Romantic expressiveness. The E minor concerto, in spite of its episodic structure, is colorful, charming, richly melodic, and technically demanding.

Recommended Recordings

★ Rubinstein, Skrowaczewski, New Symphony of London (RCA Red Seal stereo disc LSC-2575; cassette RK-1004; cartridge R8S-1004)

b Lipatti, unnamed conductor and orchestra (Seraphim disc 60007, *mono only*)

Argerich, Abbado, London Symphony (Deutsche Grammophon stereo disc 139383; cassette 923-083; cartridge M-89383)

b Pollini, Kletski, Philharmonia (Seraphim stereo disc S-60066)

b Graffman, Munch, Boston Symphony (RCA Victrola stereo disc VICS-1030; cartridge V8S-1041)

Comments

Rubinstein has recorded this concerto at least three times. His latest, dating from 1961, is superb in every respect—deeply expressive yet always elegant and sensitive, and with an accompaniment by Skrowaczewski that is rich in detail and nuance.

Lipatti's performance (mono only) is from the late 1940's, and reportedly used a well-known conductor who could not be credited because of a contractual conflict (rumors say either Ansermet or Karajan). The sound is dated but not unbearably so, and the quality of Lipatti's performance is so compelling that one quickly forgets about the limited sonics. Here is a beautifully flowing, subtly expressive, yet continually animated performance.

Argerich's 1968 recording is an exciting one. The young Argentinian collaborates with Abbado on a beautifully meshed, youthfully exuberant and vibrant performance.

DG not only provides outstanding sound engineering, but also includes a first-rate coupling of the Liszt Piano Concerto No. 1, again teaming Argerich and Abbado.

Pollini recorded this concerto just after he won the 1960 International Chopin Competition in Warsaw at the age of eighteen. It was an impressive recording then, full of virility, warmth, and poetry—and it still is impressive. Apparently it did not sell well enough to lead to any further Pollini recordings until 1973, but perhaps its reissue on the budget-priced Seraphim label will encourage more listeners to investigate an excellent talent.

Graffman's late 1950's performance is also a splendid combination of virility and poetry, with a warm Munch accompaniment. The coupling is a vivid Graffman performance of Mendelssohn's *Capriccio Brillant*.

For Follow-Up Consideration

Polonaises, over fifteen in all (the first one written when Chopin was eight, and his first published composition; the last one, the "Fantaisie Polonaise," his last large composition). They blend the rhythms of a Polish folk dance with a more martial, patriotic feeling. RECOMMENDED RECORDING: Rubinstein (RCA Red Seal stereo 2-disc set LSC-7037), a 1965 release that includes eight of the polonaises—the first and last, and the popular "Military" Polonaise—together with a group of four Impromptus, all played with an insight, skill, and Romantic fervor that few pianists can match in these pieces.

Nocturnes, the most popular of Chopin's works during his lifetime. A series of atmospheric piano pieces with something of the poetic feeling traditionally linked to the idea of nightfall, and ranging in mood from calm, moonlit reveries to moments full of clouds and turbulence. RECOMMENDED RECORDING: Weissenberg (Angel stereo 2-disc set S-3747), whose restrained yet elegant and expressive 1969 recording is the most complete—the nineteen Nocturnes found in most standard editions, plus two additional ones found among the composer's unpublished manuscripts after his death.

Preludes, a set of twenty-four short, atmospheric pieces, mostly composed during the winter of 1838–39 while Chopin was trying to recover from a lung ailment on the island of Majorca. RECOMMENDED RECORDING: Moravec (Connoisseur Society stereo disc CS-1366), one of the Czech pianist's finest recordings (released in 1967), played with warmth, elegance, and grandeur.

• *ROBERT SCHUMANN*

> Pronounced: *shoo*-muhn. Born June 8, 1810, in Zwickau, Saxony. Died July 29, 1856, in Endenich, near Bonn, Germany.

SIGNIFICANCE: German composer and critic, one of the leading figures in the 19th-century Romantic movement; his compositions, mostly short, poetic works with literary allusions, helped to expand the expressive power of the movement.

BACKGROUND: Although Schumann began to study piano at the age of six, the major interest of his early youth seemed to be literature—not too surprising, since his father was a publisher. But during his late teen years, his interest in music grew. On the death of his father, however, his practical-minded mother pushed him to study law. The repression of his musical ambitions strained his nerves almost to the breaking point. Finally he decided to study music despite all opposition. Impatient to improve his piano playing, he invented a device which he believed would strengthen a weak finger on his hand. Instead, it severely crippled the hand and forced him to abandon any hopes for a career as a pianist. He turned to composition.

While boarding at the Leipzig home of one of his composition teachers, Friedrich Wieck, he fell in love with Wieck's teenage daughter, Clara, a piano student. Wieck was determined to block their marriage, partly because he considered his daughter's talent greater than Schumann's. After a long series of legal battles, Schumann and Clara Wieck received court permission to marry shortly after her twenty-first birthday. Meanwhile, she had gone on to become one of Europe's most successful pianists, and frequently played Schumann's works on her programs. Their romance became one of the most famous of the period.

In addition to composing, Schumann also founded a music journal (thus combining both his musical and literary interests), and became one of Europe's foremost critics. His writings helped win public recognition for Chopin and Brahms, and to give increased importance to the Romantic movement.

In 1853, signs of insanity, which had also appeared in 1833 and 1845, forced Schumann to retire from public life. In 1854, after trying to commit suicide, he was committed to an asylum near Bonn, where he died two years later at the age of forty-six. Clara went back to concertizing, and became a legend over the next forty years for her devotion to her husband's works.

Piano Concerto in A minor

Although Schumann wrote many works for solo piano, he composed only one piano concerto—and that one didn't start out to be a concerto. A few months after his marriage in 1841, Schumann composed especially for his wife a "Fantasie" in A minor for piano and orchestra. Four years later he added an "Intermezzo" and a "Finale", thereby turning it into a three-movement concerto. The work reflects Schumann's comment, "I cannot write a concerto for the virtuoso; I must plan something else." His "something else" is more poetic and intimate than virtuosoistic, and interweaves piano and orchestral sound in a manner more often found in chamber music.

Recommended Recordings

★ b Lipatti, Karajan, Philharmonia Orchestra of London (Odyssey disc 32160141, *mono only*)

Rubinstein, Giulini, Chicago Symphony (RCA Red Seal stereo disc LSC-2997)

Serkin, Ormandy, Philadelphia Orchestra (Columbia stereo disc M-31837; cassette MT-31837; cartridge MA-31837)

Comments

The Lipatti recording of 1948 ranks as one of the great recordings of the century. Made three years before his death, it combines strength and sensitivity in a unique way. It is profoundly lyrical and beautifully phrased, and finds pianist and conductor in marvelous rapport. The sound, of course, is dated but still acceptable (the quality of English Columbia's sound was ahead of the field in 1948). Overside, Lipatti offers an excellent performance of the Grieg Piano Concerto.

Rubinstein also plays the concerto without the heaviness of so many other pianists. In his 1967 recording he gives it not only a leisurely Romantic breadth, but also a suppleness that is most beguiling. Giulini's accompaniment is excellent, though the orchestral sound is not up to the RCA-Chicago Symphony standard.

Serkin's 1965 performance (his third recorded version with Ormandy) is high-strung and dramatic, often passionately so, and Ormandy's accompaniment is appropriately strong. It is coupled with a lively account of the Mendelssohn Piano Concerto No. 1.

Symphony No. 4 in D minor

This most popular of Schumann's four symphonies was not the fourth to be composed, but rather the second—dating from 1841, the same year Schumann published his First Symphony ("Spring"). Schumann held up its publication for ten years, and it was finally published in a rescored version in 1851 as his Fourth Symphony. Although its sections follow a generally traditional four-movement pattern, there is a unity and flow to the work as a whole that in some ways anticipates the cyclic form used by later 19th-century composers. The music is melodic and dramatic, with a particularly assertive finale.

Recommended Recordings

★ Bernstein, New York Philharmonic (Columbia stereo disc MS-6256 or 3-disc set D3S-725)

Kubelik, Berlin Philharmonic (Deutsche Grammophon stereo disc 138860; cassette 923-022)

Solti, Vienna Philharmonic (London stereo disc CS-6582)

b Furtwängler, Berlin Philharmonic (Heliodor stereo disc S-25073)

Comments

Bernstein's performance, dating from the late 1950's, is vibrant and expressive. It is coupled with a dramatic account of Schumann's "Manfred" Overture on a single LP (MS-6256), and is also available in a 3-LP set (D3S-725) of all four of Schumann's symphonies—all of them ardently led by Bernstein.

Kubelik's 1963 performance is less highly wrought than Bernstein's, but is most appealing in a more lyrical way. It is coupled with a spirited performance of Schumann's First Symphony ("Spring").

Solti leads an energetic, dynamic performance, though emotionally cooler than either Bernstein's or Kubelik's. His 1968 release is coupled with a strong performance of Schumann's Third Symphony ("Rhenish"). London's sound engineering is particularly good.

Furtwängler's highly individualistic interpretation has unusual breadth and intensity. The early 1950's sound has been electronically "enhanced" for Heliodor's stereo reissue, and the result is less objectionable than in some other instances, increasing the resonance of the excellent original sound without distorting it. The same disc includes Furtwängler's vividly individualistic interpretation of Haydn's Symphony No. 88.

For Follow-Up Consideration

Symphony No. 1 ("Spring"), one of Schumann's most spontaneous and optimistic works, full of joyous melody and exuberance. RECOMMENDED RECORDING: Kubelik, Berlin Philharmonic (Deutsche Grammophon stereo disc 138860; cassette 923-022), a warm and spirited performance (from around 1963), coupled with an excellent performance of Schumann's Symphony No. 4.

Carnaval, Schumann's most popular solo piano work, written when he was twenty-five, and filled with a number of complex personal connotations (for example, No. 11 "Chiarina" represents Clara Weick; No. 13, "Estrella," Ernestine von Fricken with whom Schumann had a student romance). RECOMMENDED RECORDING: Rubinstein (RCA Red Seal stereo disc LSC-2669), a technically brilliant, interpretively compelling 1963 recording (Rubinstein's second), coupled with a beautiful Rubinstein performance of Schumann's subtle "Fantasiestücke" (Opus 12).

Cello Concerto in A minor, a darkly brooding concerto from Schumann's last years, more of a character study of the cello than a showpiece, and thus a work that grows on the listener rather than one that has immediate appeal. RECOMMENDED RECORDING: Starker, Skrowaczewski, London Symphony (Mercury stereo disc 900347), a rich-toned, soaringly melodic, deeply probing 1962 performance, superior interpretively and sonically to an earlier Starker recording with Giulini (Angel stereo disc S-35598), and coupled with a splendid Starker performance of Lalo's more buoyant and lyrical Cello Concerto in D minor.

Dichterliebe (The Poet's Love), a song cycle set to sixteen poems by Heinrich Heine, the German poet and critic; among the most dramatic and passionate of all 19th-century *lieder,* and with uncommonly rich and varied piano accompaniments. RECOMMENDED RECORDING: Fischer-Dieskau, baritone, with Demus, piano (Deutsche Grammophon stereo disc 139109), an outstanding performance on the part of both singer and pianist, with unusually subtle colorations that illuminate the deepest meanings of the poems. Overside on this 1966 release is another group of Schumann songs to Heine texts, *Liederkreis,* just as beautifully performed, if not always as interesting in content.

• *FRANZ LISZT*

Pronounced: *list*. Born October 22, 1811, in Raiding, near Odenburg, Hungary. Died July 31, 1886, in Bayreuth, Germany.

SIGNIFICANCE: Hungarian pianist, conductor, and composer, who used the term "symphonic poem" to describe extended orchestral pieces that translated into musical terms the content of a specific poem, story, or painting; he also helped develop the piano concerto into a more virtuoistic form.

BACKGROUND: Liszt was the son of a disappointed musician who served as land steward to the noble Esterhazy family of Hungary. After he showed prodigious talent as a pianist at the age of nine, a group of Hungarian counts subscribed a six-years' annuity on the boy's family to move to Vienna for him to study. Liszt started giving successful piano recitals at twelve, became a salon idol as a young man, and later won recognition throughout Europe as the first of the great piano virtuosos.

After the age of forty, however, he stopped playing publicly except on rare special occasions, and concentrated on conducting and composing. From 1848 to 1859 he was court music director at Weimar, making it one of Europe's most important music centers and using the post to become a patron of new composers such as Berlioz, Schumann, Grieg, and Wagner. Although he never married, he caused a great public scandal by living for long periods of time with, first, the Countess d'Agoult (from 1833 to 1844), with whom he had four children (one daughter, Cosima, later married Richard Wagner), then with the Princess Sayn-Wittgenstein (from 1848 to 1861).

In 1865 he took minor orders as an abbé of the Roman Catholic Church from Pope Pius IX, and sought unsuccessfully for many years to become Vatican music director. In 1870 he gave up the religious life to teach in Weimar and Budapest, and to become one of Wagner's staunchest supporters in establishing Bayreuth as the capital of Wagnerian opera. He died in Bayreuth in 1886 at seventy-five.

As a composer, he is best known for his two piano concertos, some nineteen Hungarian Rhapsodies for piano, of which six exist in orchestral versions as well, and thirteen "symphonic poems."

Piano Concerto No. 1 in E flat major

From its strong, assertive opening chords, this concerto surges with Romantic fervor and rhapsodic melody. The piano dominates throughout, but the orchestral writing is more colorful and more varied than in most concertos up to that time. It is interesting that Liszt, the most acclaimed piano virtuoso of his day, was so preoccupied with orchestral harmonies and tonal effects that he refused to publish a piano concerto until he was forty-four, when he felt he had finally begun to master orchestral techniques. He *had* written earlier concertos and performed them in his 20's and 30's, but they were not published and most are apparently lost. This first published concerto is sometimes nicknamed the "Triangle" Concerto, because of the use Liszt makes of a struck triangle in the final movement, a use that was highly controversial in Liszt's time. There is no break between the movements, which are linked thematically by what Liszt called the "transformation of themes" (a method of repeating and developing themes in various guises throughout a work), which some critics believe influenced Wagner in developing the *leitmotif* concept in his operas.

Recommended Recordings

★ Watts, Bernstein, New York Philharmonic (Columbia stereo disc MS-6955)

Richter, Kondrashin, London Symphony (Philips stereo disc 835474; cassette PCR-900-000; cartridge PC8-900-000)

Cliburn, Ormandy, Philadelphia Orchestra (RCA Red Seal stereo disc LSC-3065; cassette RK-1113; cartridge R8S-1113)

Rubinstein, Wallenstein, RCA Victor Symphony (RCA Red Seal stereo disc LSC-2068; cartridge R8S-5035)

Katchen, Argenta, London Symphony (London stereo disc CS-6033)

Comments

Watts' recording marked his disc debut in 1963 at the age of sixteen, following a highly-acclaimed performance as a substitute for an ill soloist (Glenn Gould) with the New York Philharmonic. Watts performs the concerto with a marvelously light and dashing touch, avoiding the heavy-handed thumping so many other pianists bring to Liszt. Overside he uses much the same approach for Chopin's Piano Concerto No. 2.

Richter gives the concerto an impressive blend of dazzling virtuosity and lyrical poetry, and Kondrashin matches him in the sweep and detail of the orchestral role. Overside on this 1962 release they offer an equally brilliant performance of Liszt's Piano Concerto No. 2.

Cliburn, in a 1968 recording, underplays the flamboyance of the concerto, but still projects a lucid, compelling performance. Ormandy leads a tonally lush accompaniment. Overside Cliburn and Ormandy collaborate similarly on Grieg's Piano Concerto.

Rubinstein's recording dates from the late 1950's, and thus the sound is not up to Cliburn's, but his interpretation has more flair and verve. Overside Rubinstein offers a surging, dynamic performance of Rachmaninoff's Piano Concerto No. 2. The cartridge edition also includes a beautiful, elegant Rubinstein performance of Falla's *Nights in the Gardens of Spain*.

The Katchen–Argenta performance also dates from the late 1950's and its sound holds up unusually well. Katchen's performance is vibrant and exciting, as is his version of Liszt's Piano Concerto No. 2 overside. There is a possibility that this performance may be transferred to London's budget-priced Stereo Treasury series—if it is, it will be an excellent budget choice.

Les Préludes (Symphonic Poem No. 3)

This best known and most popular of Liszt's symphonic poems is a colorful, dramatic work expressing Romantic musical ideas but having an unexplicit "program" that permits the listener great freedom in interpreting the meaning. Originally written in 1848 as a prelude to a choral work, *The Four Elements*, it was revised several times in succeeding years, until it reached its final form in 1854 as an independent orchestral work. Although Liszt used some of the thematic material of *The Four Elements*, he related the final version to the poem "Les Préludes" from Lamartine's *Méditations Poétique* (Poetic Meditations): "What is our life but a series of preludes to that unknown song whose first solemn note is sounded only by death?" Liszt depicts man's struggle for existence through various interconnected episodes: first, love ("The Enchanted Daybreak"), then the harshness of the real world ("Storms Whose Killing Breath Dispel Lovely Illusion"), a pastoral interlude ("A Pleasant Rest Amidst Nature's Moods"), a call to battle ("The Trumpets' Loud Clangor . . . The Post of Danger . . ."), and finally, self-recognition.

Recommended Recordings

★ Haitink, London Philharmonic (Philips stereo disc 839788; cassette 18464-CAA)

Karajan, Berlin Philharmonic (Deutsche Grammophon stereo disc 139037; cassette 923-049; cartridge 89-037)

Karajan, Philharmonia Orchestra of London (Angel stereo disc S-35613)

Fiedler, Boston Pops Orchestra (RCA Red Seal stereo disc LSC-2442)

Comments

Haitink's 1968 performance is vivid and warm, and beautifully spacious both in interpretation and sound. It is coupled with two other Liszt symphonic poems of 1854: the haunting and lyrically lovely *Orpheus*, and the more rambling *Tasso*, written as a prelude for a production of Goethe's play.

Karajan's two recordings are both broadly lush and strikingly dramatic. Both have good sound, though the DG edition of 1968 is about seven years newer than Angel's. The couplings are quite different. Angel offers highly polished Karajan performances of Respighi's *Pines of Rome* and Berlioz's *Roman Carnival* Overture, whereas DG includes the Liszt Hungarian Rhapsody No. 2 plus two of Smetana's finest symphonic poems, "The Moldau" and "Vyšehrad" (both from *Ma Vlast*), all beautifully played.

Fiedler leads a spirited, full-blooded performance from about 1960, coupled with a rousingly played Hungarian Rhapsody No. 2 and Liszt's Symphonic Poem No. 6, *Mazeppa*.

For Follow-Up Consideration

Totentanz (*Dance of Death*), a rousingly dramatic and colorful set of variations for piano and orchestra, based on the traditional Dies Irae theme from the Mass for the Dead, and inspired by Vorcagna's 14th-century frescoes, "The Triumph of Death," that Liszt saw at Pisa. RECOMMENDED RECORDING: Lewenthal, Mackerras, London Symphony Orchestra (Columbia stereo disc MS-7252), a brilliantly flamboyant 1969 performance in which pianist Lewenthal reinstates Liszt's original church-bell opening and a slow, rhapsodic "De Profundis" section that Liszt cut out of his final version;

Lewenthal makes a good argument for his alterations in a brief talk on a 7-inch bonus record that comes free with the album. The coupling is a virtuoso Lewenthal performance of Adolf von Henselt's long-neglected and charmingly Chopinesque Piano Concerto in F minor, which Clara Schumann premiered in 1844 and which Liszt played on his concert tours.

Homage to Liszt, a recording by pianist Vladimir Horowitz (RCA Red Seal LM-2584, *mono only*), released in 1962 and made up of reissues of some of the most unforgettable earlier Horowitz performances of Liszt's Hungarian Rhapsodies Nos. 2 and 6, "Sonetto del Petrarca," "Funerailles," "Valse oubliée" No. 1, and several other pieces. There are few pianists who can play these diabolically difficult works so breathtakingly well.

The Daemonic Liszt, a 1968 recorded anthology of some of Liszt's more flamboyant but lesser-known piano works, some of them based on popular works by other composers, such as "Reminiscences of Don Juan" (after Mozart), "Waltz" (after Gounod's Faust), "Valse Infernale" (after Meyerbeer), "Reminiscences of Robert le Diable," etc., spectacularly played by Earl Wild (Vanguard/Cardinal stereo disc C-10041).

• RICHARD WAGNER

Pronounced: *vahg*-ner. Born May 22, 1813, in Leipzig, Germany. Died February 13, 1883, in Venice, Italy.

SIGNIFICANCE: German composer and conductor, who wrote "music-dramas" in which he combined complex orchestral and vocal elements built out of combinations of hundreds of individual themes (called *leitmotivs,* or leading motives) representing characters, objects, moods, situations, or ideas, which he changed in rhythm, form, etc., according to the dramatic requirements.

BACKGROUND: Wagner's father, a Leipzig police actuary, died when Wagner was quite small, and his mother took in boarders to support her family. One of the boarders was an actor whom she eventually married. Through his stepfather, Wagner became fascinated with the theatre, and as a teenager he began to write a play. At about the same time he became interested in ancient Greek literature. He was determined to become a poet for the stage. Then one day he saw a production of Beethoven's opera *Fidelio.* "From that moment," he wrote, "my life acquired its true significance"—he would write poetic dramas for the *musical* stage.

He borrowed books on music and began to teach himself composition, finally beginning formal music training at age seventeen at the Leipzig university. By twenty-one he had written two operas (*Die Feen, Das Liebesverbot*) and managed to get them produced. They were both failures. Wagner married an actress, became a theatre conductor—and continued to write operas. Finally, in the early 1840's, the first performances of his *Rienzi* and *The Flying Dutchman* (*Der Fliegende Holländer*) were so successful that Wagner was made conductor of the opera house in Dresden. He remained there, producing *Tannhäuser* and *Lohengrin*, until he got into political difficulties when he threw in his lot with the revolutionaries of 1848. A warrant was issued for his arrest, but he escaped to Weimar. There Franz Liszt sheltered him in his house and gave him money to go to Switzerland.

Wagner spent twelve years in exile in Switzerland, writing a book on *Art and Revolution*, composing *Tristan und Isolde*, and beginning a mammoth four-opera cycle, *The Ring of the Nibelungs* (*Der Ring des Nibelungen*).

The *Ring*, based on his own adaptations of Teutonic legends, occupied Wagner off and on for more than twenty years (1853–74). During these years, Wagner experienced many ups and downs. His exile was finally ended and he was allowed back to Germany as a conductor. But he accumulated large debts that almost landed him in debtor's prison. And his personal habits won him as many enemies as friends. Some considered him the most amoral, self-absorbed egotist of all time. Particularly scandalous at this time was his love affair with Liszt's daughter, Cosima. She bore him three children before they could be married, which came only after Wagner's first wife died and Cosima divorced her husband, the famous conductor Hans von Bülow.

Finally, when his personal fortunes seemed at their lowest ebb, the nineteen-year-old King Ludwig II of Bavaria came to his rescue, becoming his patron and encouraging his plans to build his own theatre big enough for his grandiose scheme of opera production. Cosima is credited with picking the site in the foothills of the Bavarian Alps, the town of Bayreuth. Despite widespread controversy over Wagner's works, philosophy, and personal life, there were enough pro-Wagner societies to raise the funds to complete the theatre by his sixty-third birthday. He devoted his last years to Bayreuth, producing for it not only the *Ring* but his last opera, *Parsifal.* In 1883, in poor health, he died suddenly while on a visit to Venice with Cosima, who brought his body back to Bayreuth to be buried in the gardens there.

Orchestral Music

Since Wagner's operas tend to be long and complex, a good introduction to them is through their orchestral music—some of the most resplendent, dramatic, and exciting music in all opera. Conductors renowned for their performances of Wagnerian opera have frequently played orchestral excerpts on their concert programs (Toscanini, Furtwängler, Szell, Leinsdorf, Solti, Böhm, etc.). Several have prepared extensive "orchestral syntheses" of individual operas for concert performances (Stokowski, Leinsdorf)—though unfortunately, few of the latter have been recorded.

Recommended Recordings

- ★ *Great Orchestral Highlights from The Ring of the Nibelungs*: Szell, Cleveland Orchestra (Columbia stereo disc MS-7291; cassette 1611-0190)
- ★ *The Sound of Wagner*: Stokowski, Symphony of the Air & Chorus (RCA Red Seal stereo disc LSC-2555; cartridge R8S-5002)

Solti Plays Wagner: Solti, Vienna Philharmonic (London stereo disc CS-6245)

b *Toscanini Conducts Wagner*: Toscanini, NBC Symphony (RCA Victrola VIC-1247 and VIC-1278, *mono only*)

b *A Wagner Concert*: Furtwängler, Vienna & Berlin Philharmonic (Seraphim 2-LP set IB-6024, *mono only*)

Overture & Venusberg Music from Tannhäuser: Leinsdorf, London Symphony & Chorus (London Phase-4 disc S-21037; cassette M-94037; cartridge M-95037

Comments

Szell has put together an outstanding orchestral "synopsis" of Wagner's great four-opera *Ring* cycle. It includes the "Entrance of the Gods into Valhalla" (from *Das Rheingold*), the "Ride of the Valkyries" and "Magic Fire Music" (*Die Walküre*), "Forest Murmurs" (*Siegfried*), "Siegfried's Rhine Journey," "Funeral Music," and "Brünnhilde's Immolation" (*Götterdämmerung*). Not since the days of Toscanini has Wagner blazed so magnificently under anyone's baton, and Toscanini certainly didn't have the kind of stereo engineering Szell had for this 1969 release.

Stokowski's 1961 recording is one of his all-time bests, and it *sounds* gloriously. This is not one of Stokowski's reworked orchestral "syntheses," but a set of excerpts for which he uses the original choral parts and a first-rate group of soloists (including Verrett, Allen, and Arroyo—all virtually unknown at the time of the recording). The excerpts are the "Entrance of the Gods into Valhalla" (*Das Rheingold*), the "Ride of the Valkyries" (*Die Walküre*), the Prelude to Act 3 of *Tristan und Isolde*, and the Overture and Venusberg Music (Paris version) from *Tannhäuser*. The cartridge edition has an outstanding dividend—it adds to these performances those of another Stokowski album, including a superb performance of Smetana's "The Moldau" (from *Ma Vlast*) plus several rhapsodies by Liszt and Enesco.

Solti's 1963 release is unique in that it offers the two versions of the *Tannhäuser* Overture: the original 1845 Dresden version, and the later 1861 Paris version (which expands the "Venusberg Bacchanale" and includes a chorus). Both are played with stunning intensity, and the sound engineering is excellent. Overside, Solti offers vigorous performances of the overtures to *Rienzi* and *The Flying Dutchman*.

Toscanini's Wagner was long unexcelled in this century for its intensity, fire, and power (his last public concert in 1954 was an all-Wagner program with the NBC Symphony), but its recorded accounts have been overshadowed by advances in sound engineering since then. Still, the musical glow of his interpretations shines through the early 1950's mono performances RCA has transferred to its budget Victrola label. The Preludes to *Die Meistersinger* and *Lohengrin*, *A Faust Overture*, and the *Siegfried Idyll* are on VIC-1247; the Prelude and "Good Friday Spell" from *Parsifal*, and the Prelude and "*Liebestod*" from *Tristan und Isolde* are on VIC-1278.

Because Furtwängler was the leading German conductor during most of the Nazi period (1933–45), and because Hitler's propaganda sometimes linked the Nazi cause with Wagnerian concepts of German superheroes, many Americans have tended to shun Furtwängler's Wagner recordings. This is unjust, not only because of Furtwängler's postwar clearance by the Allies of all charges of Nazi collaboration, but also

126 • *Discovering Music*

because Furtwängler brought a unique depth and radiance to Wagner's music. The 2-LP, budget-priced Seraphim set preserves for contemporary audiences some of the best: the *Parsifal* Prelude and "Good Friday Spell" and the *Tristan und Isolde* Prelude and *"Liebestod,"* as recorded in Berlin in 1938, and *The Flying Dutchman* Overture, the *Lohengrin* and *Meistersinger* Preludes, the *Walküre* "Ride of the Valkyries," and the "Siegfried Idyll," as recorded in Vienna between 1949 and 1954. The sound is dated, but not uncomfortably so.

Considering how many superb Wagner performances Leinsdorf has led over the years, particularly during the 1960's as conductor of the Boston Symphony, it is regrettable that his Wagner recordings have been so few and so disappointing. Most worthwhile is a 1968 recording of the *Tannhäuser* music (Paris version, with an uncredited chorus). It is a spacious, crystalline performance, beautifully recorded. Overside, Leinsdorf offers a sonically splendid but interpretively restrained *Rosenkavalier* Suite by Richard Strauss.

Tristan und Isolde

Here is *the* Romantic masterpiece in German opera—an intense, soaringly beautiful, elaborately scored music-drama based on a tragic Celtic legend dating from the thirteenth century. Its libretto is Wagner's most complicated and subtle—filled with secret love potions, royal intrigue, etc.—causing critic Ernest Newman to write: "While there are few operas more popular, there probably is not one that is the subject of so much misconception on the part of its admirers." The opera's popularity rests clearly on its music, particularly the fervid, impassioned Love Duet of Act 2 and the poignant *"Liebestod"* ("Love-Death") of Act 3.

Recommended Recordings (Complete)

★ Böhm (conductor), Nilsson (Isolde), Windgassen (Tristan), Ludwig (Brangäne), Wächter (Kurvenal), Bayreuth Festival (Deutsche Grammophon stereo 5-disc set 2713001)

Solti (conductor), Nilsson (Isolde), Uhl (Tristan), Resnik (Brangäne), Krause (Kurvenal), Vienna Philharmonic (London stereo 5-disc set OSA-1502)

Furtwängler (conductor), Flagstad (Isolde), Suthaus (Tristan), Thebom (Brangäne), Fischer-Dieskau (Kurvenal), Philharmonia of London (Angel 5-disc set 3588, *mono only*)

Recommended Recordings (Highlights)

★ Böhm, Nilsson, Windgassen, Ludwig, etc., as above (Deutsche Grammophon stereo disc 136433; cassette 922-029)

Solti, Nilsson, Uhl, Resnik, etc., as above (London stereo disc 25938)

b Furtwängler, Flagstad, Suthaus, Thebom, etc., as above (Seraphim disc 60145, *mono only*)

b Rodzinski, Leinsdorf, Traubel, Melchior, Janssen, New York Philharmonic, Colon Opera Orchestra (Odyssey disc 3216-0145, *mono only*)

Recommended Recording (Orchestral Synthesis)

★ Stokowski, Philadelphia Orchestra (Columbia stereo disc MS-6147)

Comments

Today's Wagnerian "superstar," Swedish soprano Birgit Nilsson, has made two complete recordings of this opera: the first for London in 1960, the second for Deutsche Grammophon in 1966. The latter is the better one—in fact, possibly the best recording ever made of any Wagnerian opera. Taken from a series of performances and rehearsals at the 1966 Bayreuth Festival, it has a first-rate cast in addition to Nilsson. The "star" and driving force is clearly conductor Karl Böhm. His overall pacing, dramatic emphasis, and ardent expressiveness are the core of the album's triumph. He draws from Nilsson, in particular, one of the most impressive performances she has ever given anywhere. The single highlights album taken from the complete set includes the Love Duet and *"Liebestod"*—and is easily the best highlights album available from this opera.

Solti's 1960 recording has many splendors, especially Solti's intensity and sense of pacing. Nilsson is vocally splendid, but cooler than she is in the 1966 Böhm performance. The sound engineering favors the orchestra over the singers.

The Flagstad–Furtwängler recording from 1952 is still a classic in its own right, capturing two of the century's greatest Wagnerian interpreters in good sound, though certainly not as good as later stereo brought. Furtwängler is less impassioned than Böhm, although he projects the score with an enormous depth of feeling. Flagstad brought a clear, cool vocal beauty to the role of Isolde. The rest of the cast is good, although the Tristan of Ludwig Suthaus is not as exciting as was Lauritz Melchior in some earlier (1939) excerpts he recorded with Flagstad (still available on an RCA Victrola budget-priced mono reissue, VIC-1681).

Melchior, who retired in 1950 and who still remains unrivaled as the century's greatest Tristan, recorded a fair amount of the role in 1942 and 1943. These excerpts have been coupled with several scenes that Helen Traubel recorded in 1945—on one of the budget-priced Odyssey's "Legendary Performances" reissues. The excitement of Melchior's singing, and the warmth and richness of Traubel's, shine through the dated sound.

Among orchestral "syntheses" of the *Tristan* score, Stokowski's remains unique for its lush Romantic fervor and tonal beauty. His 1960 stereo recording with the Philadelphians is not as extensive as an earlier (and discontinued) mono recording he made in the late 1940's for RCA (LM-1174), but it does provide a luminous account of the "Love Music" from Act 2, leading directly into the Act 3 *"Liebestod."* Overside Stokowski offers a stunning version of Falla's *El Amor Brujo* with Verrett as soloist.

For Follow-Up Consideration

Die Walküre (*The Valkyrie*), the second and most popular of the four music-dramas in the *Ring of the Nibelung* cycle; this one contains the well-known "Ride of the Valkyries" (Act 3), the impassioned love duet of Siegmund and Sieglinde (Act 1), and the poignant farewell of the god Wotan to his daughter Brünnhilde, followed by the dramatic "Magic Fire Music" (Act 3). RECOMMENDED RECORDING: Böhm (conductor), Nilsson (Brünnhilde), Rysanek (Sieglinde), King (Siegmund), Adam (Wotan), Dernesch (Ortlinde), Bayreuth Festival Orchestra and Chorus (Philips stereo 4-disc set 6747047), a 1973 release taken from live Bayreuth performances of 1966; a stirring, at times incandescent performance, with Nilsson and most of the principals in peerless form, and with Böhm's ardent feeling for its surging drama always dominant. (This is, incidentally, the only complete stereo *Walküre* on four discs; the others take five).

Götterdämmerung (*The Twilight of the Gods*), the fourth and last of the four *Ring* music-dramas, and on stage the most spectacular (Valhalla, the home of the gods, is destroyed by fire as the waters of the Rhine rise so that the Rhinemaidens can recapture the magic ring). The opera contains some of Wagner's most sublime and exciting music, including two of the *Ring's* best-known orchestral passages, "Siegfried's Rhine Journey" and "Siegfried's Funeral Music," as well as perhaps the most dramatic of all Wagnerian soprano arias, "Brünnhilde's Immolation." RECOMMENDED RECORDING: Solti (conductor), Nilsson (Brünnhilde), Windgassen (Siegfried), Fischer-Dieskau (Gunther), Ludwig (Waltraute), Vienna Philharmonic (London stereo 6-disc set OSA-1604; cassette P31098), a monumentally splendid 1964 recording, powerfully led by Solti, excitingly sung by Nilsson, and sonically a real blockbuster. The closing scene from this recording is available on a single disc (London stereo disc OS-25991), together with the "Dance of the Seven Veils" and the closing scene from Strauss' *Salome* as sung by Nilsson with Solti conducting the Vienna Philharmonic—thereby combining two of the most spectacular closing scenes in all opera in spectacular Nilsson-Solti performances with spectacular sound engineering.

An Introduction to the "Ring of the Nibelungs" (London 4-disc stereo set RDNS-1). Students or others seriously interested in Wagnerian opera should not miss this analysis (in English) of how Wagner weaves recurrent themes, motives, and symbols throughout his monumental twenty-hour *Ring* cycle. The musical examples are from the Solti–Vienna Philharmonic recordings of the complete cycle. Included is a forty-two-page booklet with excerpts from the score. If you don't understand the whole *Ring* after this, then you'd better cancel that reservation to Bayreuth.

All the recordings cited above are sung in German.

• GIUSEPPE VERDI

Pronounced: *vair*-dee. Born October 10, 1813, in Le Roncole, near Busseto, Italy. Died January 27, 1901, in Milan.

SIGNIFICANCE: Italian composer of the grandest of grand operas, noted for their melodic vigor, idealized arias, and resourceful orchestration.

BACKGROUND: Verdi was the son of a poor innkeeper. At first, he was rejected as a student by the Milan Conservatory. But unwilling to give up, he studied with private teachers, meanwhile attending as many operas at Milan's La Scala Opera as he could. He began composing at twenty-three, but most of his earliest works met with failure.

Following the death of his wife and two of his children, all within three months when he was twenty-seven, Verdi's grief was so great that he renounced composing. Two years later, the director of La Scala persuaded him to come to the rescue of a work another composer (Nicolai) had turned down. Verdi agreed, and the result was *Nabucco*—his first success.

Over the following years Verdi wrote opera after opera, becoming Italy's most popular composer with *Rigoletto, La Traviata, Il Trovatore, Aïda, Don Carlo, Otello,* and *Falstaff.* The last two were written when he was more than seventy and reflect a "radical" stylistic tendency away from the set arias of his earlier works.

Because he was known throughout his life as a fierce nationalist, patriot, and democrat, Verdi's early operas frequently ran into censorship problems because of their suspected political implications. From 1860 to 1865 he sat as a deputy in that part of Italy already unified. When he died he left the bulk of his fortune to found a home for aged musicians in Milan.

Aïda

Aïda (pronounced ah-*ee*-dah) is the most impressive combination of theatrical spectacle and personal drama in all opera. The music is noble, powerful, melodic, and passionate—as Verdian and Italian as *Tristan und Isolde* is Wagnerian and German. *Aïda* was commissioned by the Khedive of Egypt to open his new Grand Opera House in Cairo at the time of the dedication of the Suez Canal in 1871. Set in ancient Egypt at the time of the pharaohs, it tells the story of an Egyptian war hero who spurns the love of the king's daughter for that of a captive Ethiopian princess (Aïda). But he is tricked by her father into a treasonous revelation of secret battle plans, and is condemned to be buried alive. At the end he finds Aïda has secreted herself in the burial tomb to die with him.

Verdi's plan for the opera permits all the pomp and ceremony of its historical period to blend with his human drama—including a spectacular Triumphal March in Act 2 and several exotic dance sequences. This, of course, has led to lavish stage productions recreating ancient Egyptian palaces and temples. But in the final analysis it is the beauty and eloquence of the music that makes *Aïda* great.

Recommended Recordings (Complete)

★ Solti (conductor), Price (Aïda), Vickers (Rhadames), Gorr (Amneris), Tozzi (Ramfis), Merrill (Amonasro), Rome Opera Chorus & Orchestra (London stereo 3-disc set OSA-1393; cassette D-31164)

Leinsdorf (conductor), Price (Aïda), Domingo (Rhadames), Bumbry (Amneris), Milnes (Amonasro), Raimondi (Ramfis), London Symphony, John Alldis Choir (RCA Red Seal stereo 3-disc set LSC-6198)

b Perlea (conductor), Milanov (Aïda), Bjoerling (Rhadames), Barbieri (Amneris), Warren (Amonasro), Christoff (Ramfis), Rome Opera Chorus & Orchestra (RCA Victrola 3-disc set 6119, *mono only*)

Karajan (conductor), Tebaldi (Aïda), Bergonzi (Rhadames), Simionato (Amneris), Mac-Neil (Amonasro), Vienna Philharmonic & Chorus, London 3-disc set OSA-1313)

Recommended Recordings (Highlights)

★ Leinsdorf, Price, Domingo, Bumbry, Milnes, etc., as above (RCA Red Seal stereo disc LSC-3275; cassette RK-1237; cartridge R8S-1237)

Karajan, Tebaldi, Bergonzi, Simionato, etc., as above (London disc 25206; cassette M-31025; cartridge M-69025)

Comments

Price's 1961 recording with Solti is one of her all-time finest. Her voice is ravishingly beautiful throughout, proud and ringing where required, and heartbreakingly melting in the more tender moments. Gorr, Vickers, and Tozzi are all impressive, and Solti is ablaze with feeling and dramatic understanding. The sound engineering, as befits an operatic spectacle, is spectacular. Originally released on RCA Victor, the recording was transferred to London Records in 1970 (under a contractual arrangement), whereupon RCA shipped Price off to England to rerecord the opera in 1971 for its own label. Her second version is very, very good, but not quite as ravishing as the 1961 one. Domingo, Bumbry, and Milnes are all exceptionally good, but Leinsdorf never "lets go" as movingly as Solti does.

Milanov's recording dates from the early 1950's, and is one of her finest. It remains, in fact, one of the most beautiful performances any singer has ever given in *any* role. Bjoerling and Barbieri are also in top form. Perlea pushes the tempos a bit, but is generally effective. The mono sound is serviceable.

Tebaldi's 1960 recording is emotionally cool but strikingly beautiful. Karajan's pacing is broad and stately, and Simionato, Bergonzi, and MacNeil are all in good form. The sound engineering is excellent.

Il Trovatore (The Troubadour)

Since its first production in Rome in 1853, *Il Trovatore* (pronounced eel troh-vah-*tor*-eh) has remained one of the most popular of all operas. It is an exciting and richly melodious opera in four acts, in which the verve and beauty of Verdi's music manage to overcome an unbelievable, over-melodramatic plot (which Gilbert and Sullivan burlesqued in part in *Ruddigore*). Briefly, the story concerns twin brothers—one the powerful Count di Luna, the other Manrico, a wandering troubadour who had been kidnapped as a baby and raised by the gypsy Azucena—who end up as opposing leaders in a civil war in 15th-century Aragon, and who love the same lady-in-waiting at the Court of Aragon (Leonora) and who are both eventually destroyed by events linked (what else?) to a witch's curse! What counts most is the wealth of thrilling music—providing more great arias and ensembles for its principal singers than two or three average operas, as well as one of the most famous choruses in all opera: the "Anvil Chorus," sung by the gypsies working at their forges.

Recommended Recordings (Complete)

★ Mehta (conductor), Price (Leonora), Cossotto (Azucena), Domingo (Manrico), Milnes (di

Luna), New Philharmonia Orchestra, Ambrosian Singers (RCA Red Seal stereo 3-disc set LSC-6194)

Basile (conductor), Price (Leonora), Elias (Azucena), Tucker (Manrico), Warren (di Luna), Rome Opera Orchestra and Chorus (RCA Red Seal stereo 3-disc set LSC-6150)

Cellini (conductor), Milanov (Leonora), Barbieri (Azucena), Bjoerling (Manrico), Warren (di Luna), RCA Victor Orchestra, Robert Shaw Chorale (RCA Victor 2-disc set LM-6008, *mono only*)

Schippers (conductor), Tucci (Leonora), Simionato (Azucena), Corelli (Manrico), Merrill (di Luna), Rome Opera Orchestra and Chorus (Angel stereo 3-disc set S-3653)

Karajan (conductor), Callas (Leonora), Barbieri (Azucena), Di Stefano (Manrico), Paneri (di Luna), La Scala Orchestra and Chorus (Angel 3-disc set 3554, *mono only*)

Recommended Recordings (Highlights)

★ Mehta, Price, Cossotto, Domingo, Milnes, etc. as above (RCA Red Seal stereo disc LSC-3203; cassette RK-1197; cartridge R8S-1197)

Basile, Price, Elias, Tucker, Warren, etc. as above (RCA Red Seal stereo disc LSC-2617)

Cellini, Milanov, Barbieri, Bjoerling, Warren, etc. as above (RCA Victor disc LM-1827, *mono only*)

Schippers, Tucci, Simionato, Corelli, Merrill, etc. as above (Angel stereo disc S-36404; cassette 4XS-36404; cartridge 8XS-36404)

Comments

Leonora has long been one of Price's best roles, and both of her recorded versions are excellent. The newest one, released in 1970 and conducted by Mehta, finds her singing more expressively, with somewhat darker tones and with more comfortable Italian pronunciation than her earlier version. The rest of the 1970 cast is a strong one, particularly Milnes. Mehta's conducting is spirited, and the sound engineering is first-rate.

Price's earlier recording was made in 1961 when she was fresh from her triumphant Metropolitan Opera debut in this role. She sings with warmth, and sails into some arias with more abandon than in the 1970 version. Tucker and Warren are both excellent, Basile's pacing is fine, and the sound holds up very well.

Milanov's version dates from the early 1950's and is thus mono only, but it has some of her most luscious singing on records. The rest of the cast is also splendid. Many sections are cut out in this performance, a relic of the days before "completeness" became an LP byword. The sound is quite dated, but the quality of the singing still equals any of the subsequent versions.

Angel's mid-1960's recording is a most commendable one, though Tucci is not as exciting vocally as Price, Milanov, or Callas. The men are the stars of this version, particularly Corelli, whose vitality and ringing tones are made for Manrico. Schippers leads a hard-driving performance, and the sound is good.

Callas' recording is also from mono days (about 1957), but it is still one of her most impressive performances. Sometimes the sounds she makes at the top of her range are shrill and unpleasant, but there is an excitement to her singing and an understanding of

Verdi's style that few singers have yet matched. The rest of the cast is uneven, but Karajan's conducting is most compelling.

For Follow-Up Consideration

La Traviata (pronounced lah *trah-vee-ah-*tah, and translatable roughly as "The Woman Gone Astray"), an 1853 opera in three acts based on Alexandre Dumas' romantic tragedy *Camille* (originally, in French, *La Dame aux Camélias*, *The Lady of the Camellias*); one of Verdi's most lyrically expressive works, and for many years one of his most popular. The story concerns a Parisian courtesan whose love for a young nobleman is thwarted by the social taboos of her time (the early 1700's, although the opera is often presented in 19th-century settings). RECOMMENDED RECORDING: Maazel (conductor), Lorengar (Violetta), Aragall (Alfredo), Fischer-Dieskau (Germont), Berlin Deutsche Opera Orchestra and Chorus (*complete opera*—London stereo 2-disc set OS-1279; cassette DS-31161; *highlights only*—London stereo disc 26193; cassette M-31192), a beautifully lyric performance, dynamically led by Maazel, with an excellent cast that had worked together in many Berlin Opera performances of the work before recording it in 1969. Moreover, London has been able to get the complete opera onto two discs (most other versions take three) while maintaining outstanding sound.

Otello, written when Verdi was in his 70's, and considered by many critics to be his most mature and most perfectly realized work; in contrast to Verdi's earlier operas, there are few arias or ensembles, and there is more emphasis on achieving characterization through the music. The libretto is based on Shakespeare's tragedy about a 15th-century Moor in the service of Venice who is destroyed by jealousy and deception. RECOMMENDED RECORDING: Karajan (conductor), Del Monaco (Otello), Tebaldi (Desdemona), Protti (Iago), Vienna Philharmonic and Vienna State Opera Chorus (*complete*—London stereo 3-disc set 1324; *highlights*—London disc 25701; cassette M31048), an intense, dramatic 1960 performance, superbly led by Karajan, with Tebaldi at her most ravishing, with Del Monaco achieving one of his finest characterizations, but with Protti weak as Iago. Excellent sound.

Requiem, a highly dramatic, profoundly moving score; written in 1874 in memory of the Italian poet and patriot Alessandro Manzoni (1785–1873) and possibly the most theatrical (some would say operatic) of Requiem Masses. RECOMMENDED RECORDING: Giulini, Schwarzkopf, Ludwig, Gedda, Ghiarov, Philharmonia Orchestra and Chorus (Angel stereo 2-disc set S-3649), a 1964 recording that superbly blends the score's devotional and theatrical elements, with exceptionally fine singing from all the soloists. (*Note:* the "Dies Irae"—"Day of Wrath"—section has become famous as a stereo showpiece, and in purely sonic respects the most electrifyingly vivid recording of this section is Solti's on London OS-1275, followed closely by Bernstein's on Columbia M2-30060, both of them in 2-disc sets of the complete Requiem released in 1971.)

• *CÉSAR FRANCK*

Pronounced: *frahnk*. Born December 10, 1822, in Liège, Belgium. Died November 8, 1890, in Paris, France.

SIGNIFICANCE: Belgian composer, organist, teacher, who developed the *cyclic form* (in which the same theme is carried over into more than one movement or section of a work) and whose mystical, symmetrical, often delicate works helped restore French instrumental music to a position of eminence.

BACKGROUND: Franck's boyhood, first in Belgium then in Paris, was spent under the influence of his strong-willed father, a bank clerk, who wanted his son to become a great pianist. And indeed Franck showed promising talent in that direction. He toured the Belgian provinces giving recitals at the age of twelve, and was accepted as a student at the Paris Conservatory at the age of fifteen. Ten years later, Franck rebelled against his father's will—at the very time Paris was going through the upheavals of the ill-fated 1848 revolution. In order to marry the daughter of a Parisian actress, he and his bride had to climb over the revolutionaries' street barricades to get to the church.

Franck then settled down to teaching and serving as a church organist, primarily at Paris' Church of St. Clotilde—although he religiously set aside 5:30 A.M. to 7:30 A.M. every morning for composing. For nearly forty years he and his wife lived frugally, never leaving Paris, and never hearing any of his music performed except for what he himself played on the organ during church services.

Finally, in 1887, a group of his students and friends arranged a concert of his works. Although only a mild success, it was enough to spur other performances of his music, and to win him increasing recognition as an important composer. But soon after, while crossing the street, Franck was struck by a bus, and never fully recovered from his injuries.

Through such students as Chausson, Chabrier, d'Indy, Lalo, and Fauré, Franck became the figurehead for a whole school of "Franckists" who dominated late 19th century French musical life until Debussy.

Symphony in D minor

When Franck's only symphony was given its first performance in 1889, composer Charles Gounod walked out, declaring the work to be "incompetence pushed to dogmatic lengths." Although radical for its time, Franck's symphony went on to become one of the most popular of all symphonies. In it, Franck introduced the cyclic form. Analysts have also suggested various mystical interpretations of the music, and have pointed out the relationship of Franck's orchestral sonorities to those of the organ. But what has appealed to the general public most of all are the symphony's noble and flowing melodies.

Recommended Recordings

★ Monteux, Chicago Symphony (RCA Red Seal stereo disc LSC-2514)

b Munch, Boston Symphony (RCA Victrola stereo disc VICS-1034; cartridge V8S-1011)
Bernstein, New York Philharmonic (Columbia stereo disc MS-6072)
b Beecham, French National Orchestra (Seraphim stereo disc S-60012)

Comments

Monteux's 1961 recording is one of the finest the late French maestro ever made. It is a profoundly moving, forthright, warm interpretation that strikes a marvelous balance between earthly tenderness and spiritual loftiness.

Munch's late 1950's recording is not as intense or driving as some of the "live" performances he gave of this work with the Boston Symphony while he was its music director (Munch often tended to "freeze up" somewhat in the recording studio). But it still has considerable fervor and glow and overall excitement.

Bernstein's performance, from about 1960, tends towards slower tempos and to stressing the emotional qualities he finds in the score.

Beecham plays down the work's intensity, approaching it with more classical coolness. Incidentally, the Seraphim release of 1967 is *not* the same performance that was available earlier with Beecham and the same orchestra on Capitol; apparently Beecham was dissatisfied with the original 1959 release and re-recorded the symphony in 1961, and that is the version now on Seraphim.

For Follow-Up Consideration

Symphonic Variations for Piano and Orchestra, a jaunty, melodic, imaginatively conceived and intricately worked-out piece which is really the equivalent of an uninterrupted three-movement piano concerto. RECOMMENDED RECORDING: Rubinstein, Wallenstein, Symphony of the Air (the former NBC Symphony) (RCA Red Seal stereo disc LSC-2234), a spirited, sweepingly joyous performance from the late 1950's, coupled with a similarly large-scaled Rubinstein performance of Saint-Saens' Piano Concerto No. 2.

Psyché, a seven-movement symphonic poem for large orchestra and chorus which some critics believe to be Franck's finest work. It was one of his last, composed in 1888. It is a cyclically structured, sensuously beautiful setting of the Greek legend of Psyché and Eros. RECOMMENDED RECORDING: Fournet, Czech Philharmonic Chorus, Prague Symphony Orchestra (Supraphon/Crossroads 22160118), a broadly lush yet sensitive performance of the complete score. Originally released in the U.S. in 1968, it was withdrawn from the active catalog in 1972, but copies may still be available in some shops. (*Note:* The fourth movement, subtitled "Psyché and Eros," is sometimes played independently on orchestral programs, and has been recorded by Toscanini, Paray, and a few others, but is much more effective when heard as part of the whole work.)

• *BEDRICH SMETANA*

Pronounced: *smeh*-ta-nuh. Born March 2, 1824, in Leitomischl, Bohemia. Died May 12, 1884, in Prague.

SIGNIFICANCE: Bohemian (Czech) composer, conductor, pianist; regarded as the founder and greatest exponent of the Czech nationalist style, which was strongly influenced by folk music.

BACKGROUND: Smetana was the son of a brewery manager. He first sought a career as a pianist, but that ended in financial disaster. With help from Franz Liszt, he opened a successful music school in Prague. But Smetana, an intense Bohemian nationalist, found it difficult to live in the repressive political environment that followed the unsuccessful 1848 revolt against Austrian rule. He went to Sweden, where he continued to compose actively. In 1859 the Austrians, following their defeat by Italian armies, granted Bohemia political autonomy. Smetana returned to Prague to become one of the leading figures in the movement to build a national opera house. He composed eight operas for it, including *The Bartered Bride* (which became an international success). But disputes over his policies, aggravated by his growing deafness, led him to resign.

He continued to compose, and after going completely deaf completed his most famous work: the six symphonic poems that make up the cycle *Ma Vlast* (My Country). The last six years of life were marked by mental illness, and he was sent to an asylum a few weeks after his sixtieth birthday. He died there two months later.

Today he is revered in Czechoslovakia as that country's greatest composer. If his international reputation is less than Dvořák's it is because he was primarily an opera composer whose librettos, in Czech, were not widely known outside his homeland. Dvořák, in contrast, composed mainly for orchestra. Each spring the famous Prague Festival traditionally begins with a complete performance of *Ma Vlast*, which today has the stature of a national epic in Czechoslovakia.

The Moldau

Next to Johann Strauss' "Blue Danube Waltz," the most famous piece ever written about a river is surely Smetana's ten-minute symphonic poem "Vltava"—better known by its German name, "The Moldau." It forms the second movement of Smetana's epic cycle *Ma Vlast* (My Country), but is often performed as a separate work. Smetana follows the flow of the river from its twin sources in the Sunava forest, past villages along the way to Prague, ending as it passes the great Vyšehrad rock outside Prague (from which the river continues on to join the Elbe). The music begins as a trickle, gradually swelling into a mighty and majestic force. Along the way, Smetana incorporates the sounds of a village wedding with its lively polka, a moonlight scene in which Rusalkas (legendary water nymphs) play on the waters, and the turbulence of the rapids of St. John. As the river reaches Prague, the majestic Vyšehrad theme of *Ma Vlast's* first movement recurs, as it does in the last movement of the complete cycle.

Recommended Recordings

★ Stokowski, RCA Symphony (RCA Red Seal stereo disc LSC-2471; cartridge R8S-5072)

Kubelik, Boston Symphony (Deutsche Grammophon stereo 2-disc set 2707054; cassette 3581008)

b Kubelik, Vienna Philharmonic (London stereo disc STS-15096/7)

Neumann, Leipzig Gewandhaus (London stereo 2-disc set 2222)

Karajan, Berlin Philharmonic (Deutsche Grammophon stereo disc 139037; cartridge M-89037; cassette 923-049)

Comments

Stokowski's 1960 performance is one of the finest of his career. The opening passage virtually oozes out of the orchestra, and the whole work is played with marvelous lilt, color, and tonal beauty. The recording is coupled with exciting performances of Smetana's Overture to *The Bartered Bride*, Liszt's Second Hungarian Rhapsody, and Enesco's *Roumanian Rhapsody*. The "Twin-Pack" 8-track cartridge offers even more, adding Stokowski's outstanding *Sounds of Wagner* album (including music from *Tannhäuser* and *Das Rheingold*)—making this one of the prize packages on Stereo-8 cartridges.

The Czech-born Kubelik gives the work a poetic, lyrical interpretation, available in two recorded versions of the complete *Ma Vlast*. The Vienna one dates from the early 1960's, the Boston one from 1971. The latter is more surging, the former more warmly mellow. Both are excellently engineered.

Another fine Czech conductor, Vaclav Neumann, recorded his vividly expressive version with the Leipzig orchestra in 1968. A few months later he quit as its conductor to protest East Germany's role in the Soviet invasion of Czechoslovakia. (The album cover is a dramatic montage of news photos of those historic days.) It is also part of a first-rate 2-LP set of the complete *Ma Vlast*.

Karajan's mid-1960's recording is sonically beautiful and poetic, and has one advantage over other performances separate from a complete *Ma Vlast*: he prefaces "The Moldau" with "Vyšehrad" (the first movement of *Ma Vlast*) so that the recurrence of the "Vyšehrad" theme at the end of "The Moldau" has more impact. Overside is an excellent performance of Liszt's *Les Préludes* and a somewhat overwrought account of Liszt's Hungarian Rhapsody No. 2.

For Follow-Up Consideration

The Bartered Bride Overture and Dances, light, appealing, and lively instrumental excerpts from the comic opera of 1863–70, still one of the most popular of all operas in central Europe. RECOMMENDED RECORDING: Neumann, Leipzig Gewandhaus Orchestra (Telefunken stereo disc SAWT-22506, a crisp, brisk performance from the late 1960's, coupled with two colorful and rarely played Czech works, Janáček's "Lachian Dances" and Dvořák's "Hell's Dance" from the opera *The Devil and Kate*.

From My Life, the subtitle of the Quartet No. 1 in E minor, which has become increasingly well known in recent years both in its original quartet form and in an orchestral transcription by George Szell. RECOMMENDED RECORDING: Guarneri Quartet (RCA Red Seal disc LSC-2887; cartridge R8S-5041), a warm and animated perform-ance from the mid-1960's; the disc coupling is Dvořák's Quartet No. 7; the cartridge also includes Mozart's Quartets No. 22 and 23. Regrettably, there is at present no recording of the Szell version, once available in a 1950's recording by Szell and the Cleveland Orchestra (Epic stereo disc SC-6015) and hopefully available for eventual reissue on the Odyssey budget label, which has reissued other Szell-Cleveland recordings from the same period.

• ANTON BRUCKNER

> Pronounced: *brook*-ner. Born September 4, 1824, in Ausfelden, Austria. Died October 11, 1896, in Vienna.

SIGNIFICANCE: Austrian composer and organist, until recently the most neglected of the major 19th-century Romantic symphonists.

BACKGROUND: After the death of his father (a poor village schoolteacher), Bruckner was sent as a very young boy to an Augustine monastery to become a chorister. His deep religious feelings remained with him for the rest of his life. He was first a schoolteacher and then court organist in Linz and Vienna. A performance of Wagner's *Tannhäuser* in 1863 turned him into an enthusiastic Wagnerite, and he sought to adopt Wagner's theories and harmonic language to the symphonic form.

But his lengthy, discursive, elaborately scored symphonies met considerable opposition from the leading Vienna critics, who idolized Brahms. This, coupled with Bruckner's lack of self-confidence and unsophisticated country ways, led to numerous revisions and modifications of his original scores—sometimes executed by well-mean-ing former pupils, colleagues, conductors, and publishers hoping to make his music more palatable to the general public. As a result, there has long been confusion and debate over various editions of Bruckner's symphonies. In recent years, the Bruckner Society has sought to eliminate the discrepancies in different published editions, and to encourage the use of Bruckner's original scores as the most faithful to his intentions and his true individuality.

Symphony No. 4 in E flat ("Romantic")

Bruckner himself named this his *Romantic* symphony, in contrast to the more Classical form of the symphonies of Brahms and others. But he was reluctant to give it a program in the manner of the Wagnerians, who considered the programmatic symphonic poems of Liszt and Berlioz's *Symphonie Fantastique* models for Romantic orchestral music. Bruckner did, however, consent to calling the scherzo (the third movement), with its many horn calls, "The Hunting of the Hare." The basic mood of the symphony is assertive. Bruckner builds his themes dramatically and often grandly, with frequent outbursts and ebbs. The complex last movement adds new themes as well as reworking themes from other movements.

Recommended Recordings

★ Haitink, Amsterdam Concertgebouw (Philips stereo disc 835385)

Karajan, Berlin Philharmonic (Angel stereo 3-disc set S-3779)

Mehta, Los Angeles Philharmonic (London stereo disc CS-6695)

Klemperer, Philharmonia Orchestra of London (Angel stereo disc S-36245)

Barenboim, Chicago Symphony (Deutsche Grammophon stereo disc 2530336; cassette 3300328; cartridge 89469)

Comments

Haitink's flair for Bruckner is outstanding among today's conductors. Using the revised 1878 edition of the score endorsed by the Bruckner Society, he leads the Fourth vividly, with just the right combination of warmth and majesty. His Amsterdam orchestra remains unmatched in conveying the spaciousness and strength that Bruckner's music requires, and the 1965 sound engineering is excellent.

Karajan, using the 1878 edition, is more broadly spacious and polished, yet he never loses the work's vital rhythmic drive. His final movement is especially imposing. However, Karajan's 1972 release takes three sides (the others listed take two), and is available only in a 3-disc set together with Karajan's performance of Bruckner's Seventh Symphony (also three sides).

Mehta, using the 1878 edition, is a shade more dramatic in his emphases, and leads a surging, colorful performance, recorded in 1970 with more close-up sound than either Haitink's and Karajan's.

Klemperer's 1965 performance, also using the 1878 edition, has conviction and dramatic insight, if less warmth than Haitink's, Karajan's, or Mehta's. But there is an overpowering feeling of rugged grandeur and solidity.

Barenboim gives a full-bodied, broadly dramatic performance, recorded in 1972, and especially impressive for the brilliance of the Chicago Symphony's massive brass onslaughts. He uses the original edition.

Symphony No. 9 in D minor

Although this symphony was left unfinished at Bruckner's death, its three completed movements are considered by some critics to be a whole "as is" (like Schubert's Eighth). Perhaps it is even appropriate for a symphony dedicated to "my dear God" to end quietly, at the conclusion of an adagio (the third movement), in a mood of peace and tranquility. It is more advanced than most works of its time in its explorations of harmony. Writes English musicologist Deryck Cooke: "Into the vast cathedral-like architecture of Bruckner's symphonic form there intruded [in the Ninth Symphony] at last something of the disturbing emotionalism of the late Romantics. There is turmoil, perplexity, and pain in this music, but at its heart stands the unshaken faith of a deeply religious man which eventually finds the peace it is seeking in the final bars of the adagio. . . ."

Recommended Recordings

★ Haitink, Amsterdam Concertgebouw (Philips stereo disc 835381)

Mehta, Vienna Philharmonic (London stereo disc 6462)

Karajan, Berlin Philharmonic (Deutsche Grammophon stereo disc 139011; cassette 923-078)

Comments

Haitink's 1965 recording is deeply moving in its total impact—noble and exciting by turns, and beautifully played by the Amsterdam orchestra.

Mehta's performance, from 1965, has marvelous color, drama, and intensity, and the Vienna Philharmonic has rarely sounded so magnificent.

Karajan's 1968 release is lyrical, beautifully sculptured, and flowingly majestic, with warmly mellow sound engineering.

For Follow-Up Consideration

Symphony No. 7, one of the first Bruckner symphonies to win widespread acceptance in Europe and the U.S., partly because of the dedication of its dirgelike second movement (an adagio) as an "In Memoriam" to Wagner. RECOMMENDED RECORDING: Walter, Columbia Symphony Orchestra (Columbia stereo 2-disc set M2S-690), one of the last recordings Walter made before his death in 1962, a performance of outstanding breadth, suppleness, and eloquence; it was withdrawn from the catalog in 1972, but may be re-released on the budget Odyssey label. If unavailable, the next recommended choice would be Haitink, Amsterdam Concertgebouw Orchestra (Philips stereo 2-disc set 802759/60), a virile, lyrical 1966 performance, coupled with Bruckner's *Te Deum*, sung by a fine group of Dutch soloists and chorus, impressively led by Haitink.

Symphony No. 8, one of Bruckner's longest and most grandiloquent scores, with one of the most heartrendingly melancholy and beautifully lyrical movements (an adagio) in any symphony. RECOMMENDED RECORDING: Solti, Vienna Philharmonic (London stereo 2-disc set CSA-2219), a 1967 release that combines sensitivity, grandeur, and dramatic thrust in just the right proportions, and with good sound engineering.

• JOHANNES BRAHMS

Pronounced: *brahmz*. Born May 7, 1833, in Hamburg, Germany. Died April 3, 1897, in Vienna.

SIGNIFICANCE: German composer and pianist, considered by many in his time as the heir to Beethoven in writing "absolute music" that needed no program or story;

working in Classical forms, but with a freer, more Romantic spirit, he composed works generally marked by deep lyric beauty and emotional gravity.

BACKGROUND: Brahms grew up in a disreputable waterfront district of Hamburg, where his father was a part-time double bass player in the Hamburg City Theatre and his mother a seamstress. From his earliest years, Brahms learned everything he could about music, and by the age of thirteen he was playing the piano in waterfront cafés to entertain the patrons. By fifteen he was giving serious piano recitals. At one of them he was heard by the Hungarian violinist Eduard Reményi, who offered Brahms a job as his accompanist on a tour featuring both serious works and gypsy music. Along the route Brahms managed to meet some of the leading musicians of the day—including Liszt, Joachim, and Robert and Clara Schumann. He became particularly close lifelong friends with the Schumanns, who enthusiastically championed his piano compositions.

In his 20's he took many jobs briefly, among them, conducting and teaching in Lippe-Detmold and Vienna. But he gave them up and declined others, believing that he composed best when there were no entangling alliances to hamper him. Perhaps for the same reason he never married. "It is as hard to marry as to write an opera," he once said, and never did do either. A painstaking composer, he worked over and over on his pieces before publishing them (his first symphony took him nearly twenty years). He wrote four symphonies, two piano concertos, one violin concerto, one double concerto for violin and cello, a Requiem, plus a number of songs, piano pieces, and chamber works—most of which have become part of the standard concert repertory. He died at the age of sixty-four of an ailment aggravated when he caught cold after an arduous 40-hour journey to attend the funeral of Clara Schumann.

Symphony No. 1 in C minor

The majesty and expressive lyricism of Brahms' themes, and particularly the way they ebb and flow in surging waves of sound, make this one of the most powerful of all symphonies. Brahms, though a well-known composer of piano and chamber works, delayed writing his first symphony until he was in his 40's—declaring at one point: "I shall never finish a symphony. You have no idea how it feels to hear behind you the tramp of a giant like Beethoven." When this symphony was finally completed and performed, one prominent admirer promptly hailed it as "the Tenth Symphony"—linking its Classical form, its grandeur, its dramatic tensions, and its depth of emotional feeling to Beethoven's nine symphonies. The work has long been one of the cornerstones of the concert repertory.

Recommended Recordings

★ Karajan, Berlin Philharmonic (Deutsche Grammophon stereo disc 138924; cassette 923-023; cartridge 88-924)

Haitink, Amsterdam Concertgebouw Orchestra (Philips stereo disc 6500519; cassette 7300247)

Szell, Cleveland Orchestra (Columbia stereo 3-LP set D3S-758, included with all four Brahms symphonies)

b Toscanini, NBC Symphony (RCA Victrola disc, included in 4-LP *mono only* set VIC-6400 with all four Brahms symphonies)

Comments

Karajan leads a spacious, dynamic performance which probes the symphony's depths with both poetry and nobility. The dark hues of the Berlin Philharmonic are ideal for this work, and DG's sound engineering (from 1963) is splendid.

Haitink illuminates both the structure and inner tensions of the music without ever losing the symphony's sweep and power in his 1973 release. What Haitink's performance lacks in Karajan's grandeur it makes up in a down-to-earth humanity.

Szell projects a strong rhythmic urgency and avoids any gushiness in the lyrical parts. Warmth in interpretation was never one of Szell's strong points, but there are few who could bring out so much classic grandeur in works like this. His 1967 release is presently available only in a complete set of the Brahms symphonies which manages to squeeze them all onto three discs without muddying the sound quality.

Toscanini's performance was famous in its time for its sense of urgency and strength. In Toscanini's hands, the Brahms First indeed becomes Beethoven's Tenth. The 1951 mono recording sounds strident by today's standards, but the grandeur of the performance still shines through. It is presently available only in a complete set of the four Brahms symphonies as conducted by Toscanini.

Violin Concerto in D

A prominent critic in Brahms' time called this not a concerto *for* but a concerto *against* the violin. Indeed, its technical complexities—especially in the final movement—test the mettle of any virtuoso. But over the years the popularity of the concerto has come to rest more on the sunny warmth of its lyricism, on its tender and caressing melodies, and on the symphonic sweep of its interweaving solo and orchestral parts.

Recommended Recordings

★ Heifetz, Reiner, Chicago Symphony (RCA Red Seal stereo disc LSC-1903; cartridge R8S-5042)

Stern, Ormandy, Philadelphia Orchestra (Columbia stereo disc MS-6153)

Oistrakh, Szell, Cleveland Orchestra (Angel stereo disc S-36033; cassette 4XS-36033)

b Szeryng, Monteux, London Symphony (RCA Victrola stereo disc VICS-1028; cartridge V8S-1028)

Comments

Heifetz has long been in a class by himself—and he has made few recordings as beautiful as this 1955 one. His performance soars lyrically, and the finale is a virtuoso feast. Reiner's accompaniment is full-blooded and dynamic, and the splendid sound engineering comes from a period when RCA and Chicago seemed to have a magic formula. The cartridge version also includes a fine Heifetz performance of the Tchaikovsky Violin Concerto.

Stern gives a warmer performance, richer in its melodic phrasings and, in the finale, almost as exciting as Heifetz. Ormandy's accompaniment is lush and surging, and the 1959 sound engineering holds up beautifully.

The "cultural exchange" meeting of Oistrakh and Szell in 1970 produced a recording outstanding for its vitality and expressiveness, and for its clarity of Classical structure. Oistrakh's singing tone has rarely been so well recorded.

Szeryng's late 1950's version with Monteux is superior to one he made later (around 1962) with Dorati. He brings much poetry and drama to the concerto, and Monteux's accompaniment sings warmly.

Piano Concerto No. 2 in B flat

Starting quietly with a haunting horn theme, this work evolves into one of the most massive and powerful of piano concertos in the Classical form. One 19th-century critic called it really "a symphony with piano obbligato." Instead of the customary three movements of a concerto, it has four—with the additional movement (a stormy "allegro appassionato," a scherzo) inserted between the dramatic first movement and the usual slow (andante) middle movement. Sir Donald Frances Tovey, the English musicologist, has justified this as a master stroke, assuring that the slow movement's "emotion is a reaction after a storm, not after a triumph." Throughout, the concerto is filled with subtle poetry and dramatic force, forthright melody and imposing eloquence.

Recommended Recordings

★ Watts, Bernstein, New York Philharmonic (Columbia stereo disc MS-7134)

Barenboim, Barbirolli, New Philharmonia (Angel stereo disc S-36526)

Richter, Leinsdorf, Chicago Symphony (RCA Red Seal stereo disc LSC-2466)

Serkin, Szell, Cleveland Orchestra (Columbia stereo disc MS-6967)

b Fischer, Furtwängler, Berlin Philharmonic (Turnabout disc 43422, *mono only;* Vox cassette 678-026, *mono only*)

Comments

Watts was just twenty-one when he made this recording in 1968, but it outshines any other in the catalog. His is a compelling and genuinely alive performance, marked not only by impressive technical authority but also by solid musicianship and interpretive understanding—and an ability to communicate it all excitingly. He is ideally matched by Bernstein's impassioned accompaniment.

Another relative youngster, Barenboim was twenty-five at the time of his recording in 1968. It has a breadth and maturity that belies Barenboim's age, plus a flowing lyricism and dramatic strength throughout. Barbirolli's accompaniment is especially good.

Richter's concept is full of grace and poetry, and is swept along by Leinsdorf's compelling accompaniment. The recording was made during Richter's first "cultural exchange" visit to the U.S. in 1960. Despite the hasty setting up of the recording session (complicated by the fact that the originally scheduled conductor, Fritz Reiner, was hospitalized), everything clicked for a memorable performance.

Serkin is occasionally harsh and overpercussive, but he plays the concerto with impressive sweep and intensity. His 1966 recording with Szell is superior in both interpretation and sound engineering to an earlier version with Ormandy.

The Fischer-Furtwängler recording is a historic document of a famous collaboration in wartime (1943) Berlin. The sound is dated but decent enough, and the performance has an eloquence and profundity that is indeed memorable and worthy of reissue, especially at budget-label prices.

For Follow-Up Consideration

Symphony No. 2 in D major, whose character was described at its premiere by Viennese critic Eduard Hanslick (a staunch defender of Brahms and an opponent of Wagner) as "peaceful, tender, vivacious in its golden serenity." RECOMMENDED RECORDING: Monteux, London Symphony (Philips World Series stereo disc WS-9123), a 1963 budget-priced performance of notable warmth and nobility; regrettably, this recording was withdrawn from the active catalog in 1973, although it may still be available in many stores. Alternate recommendation: Szell, Cleveland Orchestra, available only as part of a 3-LP set of all four Brahms' symphonies (Columbia stereo D3S-758), a performance of impressive thrust and polish.

Symphony No. 3 in F which Eduard Hanslick dubbed Brahms' "Eroica," but which Clara Schumann saw instead as a "forest idyll," and British composer Sir Arnold Bax as "the Four Seasons." Whatever the interpretation, Brahms' Third is a work of drama, majesty and intense lyrical beauty. RECOMMENDED RECORDING: Bernstein, New York Philharmonic (Columbia stereo disc MS-6909), a 1966 release outstanding for the "singing" force and vitality with which Bernstein keeps all the interwoven themes moving dynamically. It is coupled with Brahms' *Academic Festival Overture.*

Symphony No. 4 in E minor, the most elegiac of Brahms' symphonies, which German critic Friedrich Herzfeld has likened to "a heavy-hearted ballad [that] leads to fierce outbursts, whose impulsive power sets that scene for . . . monumental tragedy." RECOMMENDED RECORDINGS: Toscanini, NBC Symphony (RCA Victrola, included in 4-disc *mono only* set VIC-6400 with all four Brahms symphonies), a surging, powerful 1952 performance that has yet to be surpassed. Among later stereo performances available singly, the 1970 release by Giulini and the Chicago Symphony (Angel stereo disc S-36040; cassette 4XS-36040) is most attractive for its warmth and inner strength.

Piano Concerto No. 1 in D minor, very different from Brahms' Second Piano Concerto in mood and structure, being more noble, restlessly searching, and introspective. Of its second movement, Brahms wrote to Clara Schumann: "I am making a gentle portrait of you in the form of an adagio." RECOMMENDED RECORDING:

Rubinstein, Leinsdorf, Boston Symphony (RCA Red Seal stereo disc LSC-2917), a 1964 performance which masterfully blends the work's surging drama and lyricism without the frenetic quality of so many other performers.

Double Concerto for Violin and Cello, Brahms' last concerto, a broadly lyrical one, and unusual in its combination of two solo instruments performing against orchestral textures. Its nearest relative is perhaps the Beethoven Triple Concerto for Violin, Cello, and Piano. RECOMMENDED RECORDING: Stern, Rose, Ormandy, Philadelphia Orchestra (Columbia stereo disc MS-7251), a warmly soaring mid-1960's performance by two soloists who work beautifully together. The coupling is a good Stern-Trampler performance of the Mozart Sinfonia Concertante in E flat for Violin, Viola, and Orchestra (K. 364).

A German Requiem (Ein Deutsches Requiem), a serenely majestic work for soprano, baritone, chorus, and orchestra, based on non-liturgical texts and perhaps "heavier" in mood than most Requiems, but deeply moving and eloquent. RECOMMENDED RECORDING: Klemperer, Schwarzkopf, Fischer-Dieskau, Philharmonia Orchestra and Chorus (Angel 2-disc set S-3624), a broadly spacious 1961 release, magnificently sung (in German) by the soloists.

• CAMILLE SAINT-SAENS

Pronounced: san-*sań*. Born October 9, 1835, in Paris. Died December 16, 1921, in Algiers.

SIGNIFICANCE: French composer, pianist, organist, who emphasized elegance, charm, and form in contrast to the German emphasis during the same period on heavier, more emotionally profound styles.

BACKGROUND: Orphaned in his infancy, Saint-Saens was brought up by an aunt who gave him his first piano lessons when he was three years old. By the age of eleven he was giving public piano recitals in Paris. At thirteen he entered the Paris Conservatory, where he won prizes in organ and composition. He went on to enjoy a long and successful career as both pianist and composer, although his first successes as a composer were not in France but in Leipzig and Weimar. Eventually his Liszt-influenced piano concertos and symphonic poems caught on in France, and helped restore purely orchestral music to eminence at a time when opera dominated French music.

In addition to his world tours as a pianist, Saint-Saens taught music and archaeology in Paris for many years—and still managed to compose prolifically, writing three symphonies, five piano concertos, three violin concertos, two cello concertos, about a dozen operas (including *Samson and Delilah*), four symphonic poems (including *Danse Macabre, Phaeton*), church music, songs, piano pieces, and chamber pieces. His works were once so popular and so overplayed that there has been something of a tendency in the past forty years to disdain them unfairly.

Symphony No. 3 in C minor

Nicknamed the "Organ Symphony" because of its extensive part for that instrument, Saint-Saens' Third was dedicated by the composer to the memory of Franz Liszt—and it indeed has a Lisztian mood about it, tempered with a distinctive French elegance and tonal transparency. Saint-Saens also borrows from Liszt the idea of "thematic transformation," whereby a basic theme or motto is used throughout the work but undergoes numerous changes in color and character. The symphony has become a hi-fi/stereo showpiece work for its mixture of orchestra, organ, piano, and percussion sounds in all sorts of combinations.

Recommended Recordings

★ Munch, Boston Symphony, Zamkochian (organ) (RCA Red Seal stereo disc LSC-2341)

Mehta, Los Angeles Philharmonic, Priest (organ) (London stereo disc 6680; cassette M10241)

Prêtre, Paris Conservatory, Duruflé (organ) (Angel stereo disc S-35924; cassette 4XS-35924; cartridge 8XS-35924)

Comments

It was with the Saint-Saens Third that Munch conquered New York and Boston during his first U.S. appearances following World War II, and it remained a Munch specialty for years thereafter. He recorded the work twice in the U.S., in 1948 with the New York Philharmonic (on a now-deleted Columbia mono LP) and in 1959 with the Boston Symphony. The latter remains a brilliant recording, both interpretively and sonically—with a combination of excitement and lyrical beauty that only Munch could achieve in this kind of music.

Mehta's 1971 release has vividly impressive sound engineering, although his performance is more earthbound than Munch's as a whole.

Prêtre's 1963 performance has the most cathedral-like sound—big, spacious, and highly resonant. The organ of Paris' Church of St. Etienne du Mont comes through especially clearly, but Prêtre's performance is not very exciting.

Piano Concerto No. 2 in G minor

Written in seventeen days for a Paris concert in 1868 at which Saint-Saens was to be piano soloist with his friend Anton Rubinstein conducting, this concerto quickly became one of Saint-Saens' most popular and successful works. The speed with which it was written may explain its generally one-sided form—for the piano clearly dominates throughout, with the orchestra merely underlining or embellishing the various themes introduced or developed by the pianist. Those themes are mostly bright, melodic, and immediately appealing.

Recommended Recordings

★ Rubinstein, Ormandy, Philadelphia Orchestra (RCA Red Seal stereo disc LSC-3165; cassette RK-1165; cartridge R8S-1165)

Rubinstein, Wallenstein, Symphony of the Air (RCA Red Seal stereo disc LSC-2234)

Entremont, Ormandy, Philadelphia (Columbia stereo disc MS-6778)

Sokolov, Yarvy, USSR Symphony (Melodiya/Angel stereo disc SR-40074)

Comments

Rubinstein, ever the superb virtuoso, is dashing and debonair in both of his recordings. The 1970 release with Ormandy has the best sound and most sumptuous orchestral accompaniment; it is coupled with a beautiful Rubinstein-Ormandy performance of Falla's *Nights in the Gardens of Spain*. The sound quality of the late 1950's recording with Wallenstein holds up well; this version is coupled with a first-rate Rubinstein performance of Franck's *Symphonic Variations*.

Entremont gives a more angular and percussive performance, technically dazzling if not as lyrically expressive as Rubinstein. Overside on this 1965 release, he performs Saint-Saens' *Piano Concerto No. 4* in much the same way. The stereo engineering is excellent.

Sokolov was eighteen when he recorded his performance two years after winning first prize in the 1966 Moscow Tchaikovsky Competition— in which the U.S.'s Misha Dichter won second prize. Sokolov's is a more restrained performance than either of the above, with interesting emphasis on the work's lyrical qualities. Overside he offers a good performance of Schumann's *Carnaval*.

For Follow-Up Consideration

Piano Concerto No. 4 in C minor, an elegantly lyrical and melodically lively concerto divided (like Saint-Saens' Third Symphony) into two movements, with contrasting sections within each of the movements. RECOMMENDED RECORDING: Casadesus, Bernstein, New York Philharmonic (Columbia stereo disc MS-6377), a dashing, elegant performance dating from 1964, coupled with a fine Casadesus-Bernstein performance of Fauré's *Ballade*.

Piano Concerto No. 5, sometimes called "The Egyptian Concerto" because one of its main themes is based on a Nubian love song that Saint-Saens said he first heard while vacationing at Luxor on the Nile, and also because it is filled with color accents of a decidedly Near-Eastern character. The finale is especially flashy. RECOMMENDED RECORDING: Richter, Kondrashin, Moscow Symphony (Monitor disc 2004, *mono only*), a poorly recorded version of an elegant and spirited performance dating from the 1950's. (*Note:* In recent years Lorin Hollander has performed the concerto as part of his repertory, giving it a rousingly good performance. If he should record it, the performance would certainly deserve looking into.)

Carnival of the Animals, originally composed as a private joke for some of Saint-Saens' friends and not performed publicly until after his death. This delightfully satiric work for two pianos and orchestra has become widely popular over the past half-century for its cosmopolitan blend of fun and appropriately picturesque music. RECOMMENDED RECORDINGS: (1) Ciccolini and Weissenberg (pianists) with Prêtre and

Paris Conservatory Orchestra (Angel stereo disc 36421), a wryly spirited performance from the mid-1960's, coupled with Poulenc's light-hearted ballet suite *Les Animaux Modèles* (Model Animals), or (2) Hambro and Zayde (pianists) with Kostelanetz conducting, and Noel Coward reading special verses written by Ogden Nash (Odyssey Y-32359, *mono only*), a delightful blend of caustic wit and affectionate spoofing, recorded by Columbia in the late 1940's and, after many years as a hard-to-find collector's item, reissued on budget-priced Odyssey in 1974.

• GEORGES BIZET

Pronounced: bee-*zay*. Born October 25, 1838, in Paris. Died June 3, 1875, in Bougival, France.

SIGNIFICANCE: French composer who helped create a more naturalistic form of French opera.

BACKGROUND: Bizet's father, a singing teacher, recognized his son's musical interests early and entered him in the Paris conservatory when the boy was ten years old. Later Bizet studied with the French composer Halévy, whose daughter he married and whose last opera, *Noë*, he completed. His own works met with little success during his short lifetime, and he, therefore, generally lived under financial strain. Just a few weeks after the premiere of his opera *Carmen*, he died of heart disease at the age of thirty-six. Although *Carmen* initially had a mixed reception, it later became one of the world's most popular operas, and set the pattern for a new kind of realistic opera in the late 19th and early 20th centuries.

Carmen

Based loosely on the novel by Prosper Merimée, *Carmen* tells the story of a tempestuous gypsy girl's tragic romance with a young Spanish corporal in 19th-century Seville. Despite the frequently lively, colorful music (for the Changing of the Guard, a bullfight sequence, etc.), there is an underlying sense of foreboding and doom that grows in intensity until the final curtain. The mezzo-soprano title role has become perhaps the most sought-after in that operatic category. However, a number of famous sopranos have also found the role comfortable for their voices and have sung (and recorded) it with success. Bizet's original version of the opera included spoken dialogue in many scenes, but after Bizet's death, Ernest Guiraud, an American-born French composer (1837–1892), composed recitatives (a form of vocal declamation with orchestral accompaniment) to replace the dialogue. It is Guiraud's version that is used in most opera houses and in most recordings.

Recommended Recordings (Complete)

★ Karajan (conductor), Price (Carmen), Corelli (Don José), Freni (Micaela), Merrill

(Escamillo), Vienna Philharmonic Orchestra and Chorus (RCA Red Seal stereo 3-disc set LDS-6199)

Prêtre (conductor), Callas (Carmen), Gedda (Don José), Guiot (Micaela), Massard (Escamillo), Paris Opera Orchestra and Chorus (Angel stereo 3-disc set S-3650X)

Bernstein (conductor), Horne (Carmen), McCracken (Don José), Maliponte (Micaela), Krause (Escamillo), Metropolitan Opera Orchestra and Manhattan Opera Chorus (Deutsche Grammophon stereo 3-disc set 2709043)

Schippers (conductor), Resnick (Carmen), Del Monaco (Don José), Sutherland (Micaela), Krause (Escamillo), Geneva Grand Theatre Chorus, Suisse Romande Orchestra (London stereo 3-disc set OSA-1369)

Recommended Recordings (Highlights)

★ Karajan, Price, Corelli, Freni, etc. as above (RCA Red Seal stereo disc LSC-2843; cassette RK-1036; cartridge R8S-1038)

Prêtre, Callas, Gedda, Guiot, etc. as above (Angel stereo disc S-36312; cassette 4XS-36312; cartridge 8XS-36312)

Schippers, Resnick, Del Monaco, Sutherland, etc. as above (London stereo disc CS-25924; cassette M-31104; cartridge M-69104)

Comments

The Karajan, Prêtre, and Schippers complete recordings all date from the mid-1960's, and use the Guiraud recitatives. The Bernstein recording, released in 1973, uses the original version with spoken dialogue. For most listeners, however, primary interest will involve the singer of the title role rather than which version is used.

Dramatically, Callas is incomparable. She makes each line excitingly "in character," even if she sometimes sacrifices musical sound for dramatic effect. With Price, the excitement is more musical—often breathtakingly so. She sings glowingly, and with a dramatic view of the role that emphasizes Carmen's warmth as well as her heartlessness. Horne is also musically vibrant, although some aspects of her performance seem more contrived than dramatically natural. Resnick performs with exceptional conviction a role she has long sung to great acclaim on both European and American stages (unlike either Price or Callas, and also Horne up to a short time before the recording).

Among the singers of other roles, Corelli is the most ringing Don José, McCracken the most dramatically compelling. Merrill is the most sonorous Escamillo, and Freni the most lyrically appealing Micaela.

In terms of conducting, Schippers is the most exciting. Prêtre is unfussy and straightforward. Karajan and Bernstein are the warmest and most subtle in emphasizing tonal colors and dramatic structure—with Bernstein conveying the strongest sense of impending tragedy throughout.

RCA's sound engineering is brighter than either Angel's or Deutsche Grammophon's; but London's is more consistently breathtaking.

Thus, as with so many opera recordings, listeners will have to weigh the qualities that mean the most to them in deciding on a *Carmen* recording. My own "all-things-weighed" choice leans to the Price-Karajan edition.

All the recordings cited above are sung in French.

Carmen Suites

Bizet himself arranged two orchestral suites of music from his opera *Carmen*. Over the years they have become probably the most popular orchestral arrangement of any opera. In order to create a more dramatic and cohesive orchestral work, Bizet not only changed the orchestration of some parts, but also the sequence in which the arias and musical interludes occur. Suite No. 1 includes the "March of the Toreadors," the Prelude to Act One, the Intermezzo from Act Three, "Aragonaise," and "Seguidilla." Suite No. 2 includes the "March of the Smugglers," "Habañera," "Toreador Song," the Children's Chorus and "Bohemian Dance."

Another (and more controversial) arrangement of music from *Carmen* was made during the 1960's by the Soviet composer Rodion Shchedrin for a ballet starring his wife, the Bolshoi Ballet's Maya Plisetskaya. Shchedrin's version is for strings and—brace yourselves!—forty-seven percussion instruments. It is a wildly unorthodox view of Bizet's score which some criticize as too distorted but others find great fun.

Recommended Recordings (Original Version)

★ b Ansermet, Suisse Romande Orchestra (London Stereo Treasury disc STS-15052)

Munch, New Philharmonia Orchestra of London (London stereo disc 21023; cartridge M-95023)

Bernstein, New York Philharmonic (Columbia stereo disc M-31800; cassette MT-31800; cartridge MA-31800)

b Toscanini, NBC Symphony Orchestra (RCA Victrola disc VIC-1263, *mono only*)

Recommended Recordings (Shchedrin Ballet Version)

★ Rozhdestvensky, Bolshoi Theater Orchestra (Melodiya/Angel stereo disc S-40067; cassette 4XS-40067; cartridge 8XS-40067)

Fiedler, Boston Pops Orchestra (RCA Red Seal stereo disc LSC-3129; cassette RK-1141)

Comments

Ansermet's early 1960's and Munch's 1967 releases are both brimming with spirit and color, and both are stunningly recorded. Both conductors offer a mixture of excerpts from the two original suites, with Ansermet adding one more than Munch (Ansermet's eight sections include the same seven as Munch plus the "March of the Smugglers"). Overside, both conductors perform excerpts from Bizet's *L'Arlésienne*—with Ansermet again one up on Munch, offering six excerpts to the other's five.

Bernstein's vivid, dramatic performance not only includes all eleven sections of the two suites complete, but also in their original sequence. His recording, however, is not as sonically impressive as Ansermet's or Munch's. First released in 1972, it was recorded five years earlier. The coupling is a good Bernstein performance of the two suites from Grieg's *Peer Gynt*.

Toscanini's 1952 performance was for many years the classic version of the orchestral *Carmen.* It remains fascinating for its dramatic color and intensity, despite its mono sound.

As for Shchedrin's ballet version, both the Angel (1968) and RCA (1969) releases are first-class stereo showpieces. Rozhdestvensky's performance is both more subtle and more incisive in various sections, but Fiedler's has lots of sparkle and dash.

Symphony in C

Written when Bizet was seventeen, this symphony was not "discovered" until 1933, sixty-two years after his death. It has since become part of the standard concert repertory, and also the score for one of George Balanchine's most popular ballets, titled *Symphony in C* in the U.S. and *Palais de Cristal* (*Crystal Palace*) in Paris. Much the way Prokofiev's *Classical Symphony* looks back to Mozart and Haydn from a twentieth-century viewpoint, so Bizet's symphony looks back on the Classical style from a nineteenth-century viewpoint. It is exuberantly melodic, rhythmically vibrant, and spontaneously likable.

Recommended Recordings

★ Bernstein, New York Philharmonic (Columbia stereo disc MS-7159)

b Benzi, London Symphony (Philips World Series stereo disc WS-9086)

Ansermet, Suisse Romande Orchestra (London stereo disc CS-6208)

b Beecham, French National Radio Orchestra (Seraphim stereo disc S-60192)

Comments

Bernstein's 1963 recording has a combination of zip and lyrical breadth perfect for the work, and he imaginatively couples it with a jaunty performance of Prokofiev's similarly "retrospective" *Classical Symphony.*

Benzi was under thirty when he recorded his version in the late 1960's, and it is a youthfully sunny, crisp, superbly clean-cut performance, well recorded. It was recently withdrawn from the active catalog, but still may be available in some shops.

Ansermet was nearing eighty when his was recorded (about 1961), and Beecham was over eighty for his (in 1959), but their individual spirits were as youthful as any conductor a quarter their age, and serve as vivid reminders of their conducting and interpretive vigor.

Both Benzi's and Ansermet's performances are coupled with Bizet's appealing suites *Jeux d'Enfants* (*Children's Games*) and *La Jolie Fille de Perth* (*The Young Girl of Perth*), equally well played. Beecham's coupling is the rarely played and quite pleasant *Symphony in G minor* by French composer Édouard Lalo (1823–1892).

For Follow-Up Consideration

L'Arlésienne, two suites from the incidental music Bizet wrote for Daudet's 1872 play, in which he sought to simulate the folk songs and color of the French town of Arles. The first suite was arranged by Bizet himself, the second after his death by

Ernest Guiraud (who also wrote the *Carmen* recitatives). RECOMMENDED RECORDING: Ansermet, Suisse Romande Orchestra (London Stereo Treasury disc STS-15052), a sonically superb budget release offering the complete first suite and two parts of the second, coupled with Ansermet's first-rate performance of the *Carmen* Suite.

• *MODEST MUSSORGSKY*

> Pronounced: moo-*sorg*-skee. Born March 28, 1839, in Karevo, Ukraine. Died March 28, 1881, in St. Petersburg, Russia.

SIGNIFICANCE: Russian composer, a leading opponent of traditional formalism and a supporter of nationalism in music.

BACKGROUND: Mussorgsky was the son of an impoverished noble Russian family. As a youth he studied the piano, but for economic reasons prepared first for an army career, then became a civil servant in St. Petersburg. He continued to compose, however, and became a member of the so-called Russian nationalist Five (with Balakirev, Borodin, Cui, and Rimsky-Korsakov). Their aim: to use Russian folk elements and Russian subjects for their works.

Mussorgsky's life was an almost continual struggle against poverty and alcoholism, and his works are marked by a primarily morbid mood. He died at the age of forty-one in a St. Petersburg military hospital after an epileptic fit.

Following his death, some of his colleagues, seeking to promote his music, encouraged "corrections" to smooth out what they considered its jagged harmonies. Most controversial has been Rimsky-Korsakov's revision of the opera *Boris Godunov*, which is still preferred in many opera houses today (including Moscow's Bolshoi) even though the original version of *Boris*, published in 1928, is considered more strikingly individual by most scholars, especially in the way the music follows natural speech inflections.

Pictures at an Exhibition

Originally a set of ten piano pieces, *Pictures* was written following a memorial exhibition of drawings and watercolors by Mussorgsky's close friend, the painter Victor Hartmann. Two orchestrations of Mussorgsky's piano suite were made in the 1920's, one by Leopold Stokowski (for the Philadelphia Orchestra), the other by Maurice Ravel (on commission from Serge Koussevitsky for the Boston Symphony Orchestra). The latter has become one of the most popular orchestral showpieces of the hi-fi/stereo age. In either version, *Pictures* is an exceptionally colorful work, successfully capturing the mood of each of the paintings. Among the *Pictures* are: "The Old Castle" (a dreamy serenade by a medieval troubadour before an old Italian castle); "Bydlo" (a Polish ox-cart lumbering down a muddy road); "The Market Place at Limoges" (depicting the lively chatter of French housewives at the market stalls);

"Ballet of the Unhatched Chickens," (a lighthearted interlude full of chirps and twitters); "Catacombs" (a dark and solemn tone picture of the ancient Roman sepulchres); "Samuel Goldenberg and Schmuyle" (contrasting a rich Jew and a Jewish beggar of the Polish ghetto); "The Hut on Fowl's Legs" (an eerie portrait of the legendary Russian witch, Baba Yaga); and "The Great Gate at Kiev" (a majestic finale depicting a procession of medieval nobles entering the ancient capital in splendor).

Recommended Performances (Orchestral Versions)

★ Ansermet, Suisse Romande Orchestra (London stereo disc CS-6177)

Stokowski, New Philharmonia Orchestra (London stereo disc SPC-21006; cassette M-94006)

Ozawa, Chicago Symphony (RCA Red Seal stereo disc LSC-2977; cartridge R8S-1087)

Karajan, Berlin Philharmonic (Deutsche Grammophon stereo disc 139010; cassette 923-018; cartridge 89-010)

Recommended Recordings (Piano Version)

★ Richter (Odyssey stereo disc Y32223)

Horowitz (RCA Red Seal disc LSC-3278, *mono only*)

Comments

Ansermet, using the Ravel orchestration, gives an exceptional performance, bringing out every subtle tonal color, and projecting the contrasting moods of the *Pictures* in all sorts of imaginative ways. His tempo for the final "Great Gate at Kiev" is slower than most other conductors, giving it a much more imposing sense of grandeur. London's sound engineering is excellent, especially in the finale. The coupling of this 1960 release is a stirring Ansermet performance of Liszt's *The Battle of the Huns* (about Attila's battle for the possession of Rome in A.D. 451), whose triumphant final chorale for organ and orchestra again shows off London's sound engineering.

Stokowski, using his own orchestration, is more "Russian-sounding" than Ansermet (or anyone else using Ravel's more "Frenchified" version), but also more distortedly "Stokowskian" in some of his coloristic excesses. Yet there is no denying the marvelous moods and effects Stokowski creates overall, and London's Phase-4 stereo engineering is stunning. Stokowski rounds off this 1967 release with his own atmospheric orchestration of Debussy's piano piece, "The Engulfed Cathedral" ("La Cathédrale Engloutie").

Ozawa, using the Ravel orchestration, offers a spirited, propulsively dramatic performance, excellently engineered. His coupling on this 1968 release is an exceptionally bright, buoyant performance of Britten's delightful *Young Person's Guide to the Orchestra* (also known as *Variations and Fugue on a Theme by Purcell*).

Karajan, using the Ravel orchestration, stresses the work's tonal nuances in a broadly paced and virtuosic performance, beautifully recorded. The coupling on this 1966 release is a similarly virtuoso performance of Ravel's *Bolero*.

Among the piano versions, Richter's Odyssey recording, taken from a "live" 1958 performance in Sofia, Bulgaria, is one of the most exciting recordings this great pianist has ever made. It is full of brilliant interpretive contrasts and poetic insights, and is also impressive in its technical virtuosity. It was this recording (originally released in the U.S. on Columbia) which helped to establish Richter's international reputation two years before his first U.S. appearances. Even with all the audience coughs (Sofia was apparently in the midst of a flu epidemic), the recording is without equal. Its 1973 reissue on Odyssey couples the piano version with a stereo performance of Ravel's orchestration, providing an opportunity to compare the two versions on one disc. Unfortunately, the orchestral interpretation—by Szell and the Cleveland Orchestra—is not in the same league with Richter's, nor is it as interesting as any of the orchestral versions recommended above. But at Odyssey's budget price, the Richter side alone is more than full value.

Horowitz's piano version, dating from the 1940's, remains one of his most famous recordings, and justly so. It is certainly a dazzling display of his technical brilliance and his flair for dramatic music-making. Its 1972 reissue also couples the piano version with Ravel's orchestral one—in a taut, forceful 1953 performance by Toscanini and the NBC Symphony. For all the aging mono sound, the Horowitz and Toscanini "double edition" is musically superior to a 1968 stereo release which has Ashkenazy playing the piano version on one side and a Mehta–Los Angeles Philharmonic version on the other (London stereo disc CS-6559).

Boris Godunov

The only opera that Mussorgsky completed is a stupendous, nationalistic epic based on the tragic life of a Russian czar who reigned between 1598 and 1605. Mussorgsky based his libretto on a Pushkin play. The original version, submitted to the Imperial Opera in St. Petersburg in 1869, was rejected because (among other reasons) it had almost no music for female singers. Mussorgsky rewrote the opera, changing the order of the scenes and adding a romantic episode between a Polish princess and Boris' rival for the throne—and it was finally produced in 1874. Several years after Mussorgsky's death, Rimsky-Korsakov completed and orchestrated another Mussorgsky opera, *Khovantchina*, and its success led Rimsky-Korsakov to decide to edit and reorchestrate *Boris* before its first Moscow production in 1888. In 1892 he made further revisions, and in 1896 and 1908 went even further with his surgery, making major changes in harmonies, modulations, and counterpoint. These reworkings brought the opera new popularity both in and outside Russia. But it also stirred controversy among those preferring Mussorgsky's original version, a controversy that has lasted to today. In the U.S., the original, the Rimsky-Korsakov version, and a Shostakovich version from the 1950's have all been produced at major opera houses at various times. Whatever the version, the opera is best known for its massive choruses and for providing one of the most dramatic bass roles in all opera.

Recommended Recordings (Complete)

★ Karajan (conductor), Ghiaurov (Boris), Vishnevskaya (Marina), Maslennikov (Shuisky), Talvela (Pimen), Vienna Philharmonic, Sofia Radio Chorus & Vienna State Opera Chorus (London stereo 4-disc set OSA-1439)

Cluytens (conductor), Christoff (Boris & Pimen), Lear (Marina), Lanigan (Shuisky), Paris Conservatory Orchestra, Sofia Opera Chorus (Angel stereo 4-disc set S-3633)

Melik-Pashayev (conductor), London (Boris), cast, chorus, and orchestra of the Bolshoi Theatre, Moscow (Columbia stereo 4-disc set M4S-696)

Recommended Recordings (Highlights)

★ Cluytens (conductor), Christoff (Boris & Pimen), etc., as above (Angel disc S-36169)

Melik-Pashayev (conductor), Petrov (Boris), Shulpin (Shuisky), chorus and orchestra of the Bolshoi Theatre, Moscow (Melodiya-Angel stereo disc SR-40049)

Recommended Recordings (Orchestral Synthesis)

Stokowski, Suisse Romande Orchestra (London stereo disc 21032; cassette M-94032; cartridge M-95032)

Comments

All of the vocal albums cited above use a Rimsky-Korsakov edition. In an era when so many conductors (and record producers) favor "original" or "authentic" versions of so many works, it is disappointing that no one has yet committed Mussorgsky's original *Boris* to discs.

Thus, evaluating the available albums narrows down to: (1) the bass singing Boris and (2) the sound engineering.

In the sound category, London's version wins hands down. The 1970 recording is a stunning one—especially in the choral sequences. Both Karajan and London's engineers have seen to it that every nuance, every stirring climax comes through with equal clarity.

As for the Boris interpretations: Christoff offers the most impressively mature characterization overall. Ghiaurov is also outstanding in his combination of vocal strength and dramatic intensity. Russia's Petrov gives a brooding interpretation which some critics have cited as the most "authentically" Russian. London, the most famous American Boris (and the first to sing the role in Moscow), is powerfully dramatic in one of the last recordings he made before illness prematurely cut short his singing career. All but Ghiaurov's recording date from the 1960's.

Stokowski, who introduced the original Mussorgsky version of the opera to the U.S. in 1929, has come up with another of his symphonic arrangements at which "purist" critics usually throw up their hands. Yet many people who enjoy dramatic music played excitingly and colorfully will find this version impressive. Stokowski's "synthesis," arranged in the 1930's, does to Mussorgsky's original what Cecil B. DeMille's film epics did to the Bible—which means part shameless vulgarization, part inspired re-creation. The 1968 sound engineering is spectacular; whatever else you can say about Stokowski, he really understands what recorded sound is all about (or *should* be about). Overside on this release, Stokowski performs Tchaikovsky's *Romeo and Juliet*, and shows that he has his own ideas about how *Romeo* should sound, not hesitating to reshape Tchaikovsky's score to achieve that sound. Taken on its own terms, it's quite gripping and colorful.

For Follow-Up Consideration

A Night on Bald Mountain, a short symphonic poem long popular in its arrangement by Rimsky-Korsakov (used in the Disney film *Fantasia*). RECOMMENDED RECORDING: Bernstein, New York Philharmonic, included as part of at least three different Bernstein LP's: one with Mussorgsky's *Khovantchina* Introduction, Borodin's *Polovetsian Dances*, Glinka's *Russlan and Ludmilla* Overture, and Ippolitov-Ivanov's *Caucasian Sketches* (Columbia stereo disc MS-7014); another with Dukas' *Sorcerer's Apprentice*, Strauss' *Till Eulenspiegel*, and Saint-Saens' *Danse Macabre* (Columbia stereo disc MS-7165); and (my preference among the lot) one with Dukas' *Sorcerer's Apprentice* and Piston's *Incredible Flutist* (Columbia stereo disc MS-6943). The Mussorgsky piece was recorded in 1965.

- ## *PETER ILYICH TCHAIKOVSKY*

   Pronounced: chie-*koff*-skee. Born May 7, 1840, in Votkinsk, Russia. Died November 6, 1893, in St. Petersburg.

SIGNIFICANCE: Russian composer and conductor; the leading nineteenth-century Russian Romantic composer of symphonies and ballets.

BACKGROUND: Tchaikovsky did not take up music seriously until he was twenty-two, originally studying law and entering the government civil service. But in 1863 he gave up his boring job as a clerk in the czar's Ministry of Justice to enter the newly founded St. Petersburg Conservatory. There he was at first considered rather foppish, and his inability to win approval for some of his early works led to a nervous breakdown. He moved to Moscow, where he became a music critic and teacher and continued to compose. A brief, unsuccessful marriage when he was thirty-four led to another nervous collapse.

At about this time his serious financial plight was resolved by a wealthy widow, Madame Nadejda von Meck, who became Tchaikovsky's patroness and gave him a handsome annual allowance, even though they had never met—and probably never did meet. They corresponded extensively over the next thirteen years. Then, for reasons that have never been clear (contrary to the recent fictionalized movie), she abruptly withdrew her support. By this time Tchaikovsky was a world-famous composer.

In 1891 he visited the U.S. to conduct at the opening concert of New York's Carnegie Hall, and then conducted in Baltimore and Philadelphia. Two years later he died suddenly at the age of fifty-three, after drinking unboiled water in cholera-infested St. Petersburg. Controversy has long raged over whether or not he did it deliberately, but most scholars now believe it was accidental.

Piano Concerto No. 1 in B flat minor

The majestic opening of this concerto is probably the best-known theme in all music—at least among Americans. It has been used as the basis for several popular songs, and in innumerable movies and TV shows. The whole concerto is brimful of melody after melody, and also reflects Tchaikovsky's love of color and contrast. Written during one of the happiest periods of his life (when he was in his mid-30's), the concerto is permeated with the joy of living. The piano solo is bold and sometimes florid, and the orchestral accompaniment is full-blooded and dramatic. Tchaikovsky uses two Ukrainian folk songs for major themes, and the finale is full of a Russian folklike, dancing verve. At the concerto's world premiere in Boston in 1875 (by the German pianist-conductor Hans von Bülow) the reaction of the audience was so enthusiastic that the finale had to be repeated. Every four years since 1958—when Van Cliburn won the First Tchaikovsky Piano Competition in Moscow—all of the young first-place winners, and some of the second-placers as well, have dutifully recorded this Tchaikovsky concerto (Ashkenazy, Ogdon, Sokolov, Dichter), swelling the already plentiful number of available versions (at one count there were forty listed in the Schwann catalog, including nearly every top-ranking soloist).

Recommended Recordings

★ Cliburn, Kondrashin, Symphony of the Air (RCA Red Seal stereo disc LSC-2252; cassette RK-1002; cartridge R8S-1002)

Rubinstein, Leinsdorf, Boston Symphony (RCA Red Seal stereo disc LSC-2681)

Friere, Kempe, Munich Philharmonic (Columbia stereo disc MS-7396)

Richter, Karajan, Vienna Symphony (Deutsche Grammophon stereo disc 138822; cassette 923021; cartridge 88-822)

Weissenberg, Karajan, Orchestre de Paris (Angel stereo disc S-36755; cassette 4XS-36755; cartridge 8XS-36755)

Janis, Menges, London Symphony (Mercury stereo disc SRI-75032; cassette MCR4-95002; cartridge MC8-95002)

Dichter, Leinsdorf, Boston Symphony (RCA Red Seal stereo disc LSC-2954)

Ashkenazy, Maazel, London Symphony (London stereo disc CS-6360)

b Gilels, Reiner, Chicago Symphony (RCA Victrola stereo disc VICS-1039; cartridge V8S-1001)

Horowitz, Toscanini, NBC Symphony (RCA Victor LM-2319, *mono only*)

Comments

With so many recordings of this popular concerto, it is harder than usual to narrow the field down to just a few "best."

Cliburn's performance is historic in several ways: first, it was recorded right after his headline-making surprise victory in the First International Tchaikovsky Competition in Moscow in 1958, and with the same conductor and orchestra that joined him for his triumphant homecoming concert at New York's Carnegie Hall. Furthermore, it became the first classical LP ever to sell more than a million copies. Musically, the performance holds up superbly. Cliburn performs the concerto with a grandeur and spaciousness that was outstanding in 1958—and still is. There is also a youthful Romantic freshness to his playing, and Kondrashin's accompaniment combines subtlety and sweep in the right proportions.

Rubinstein was in his 70's when he recorded his stereo performance in 1963, but it has as warm and youthful a Romantic spirit as any in the catalog. It is played in the sweepingly grand and singing manner that has become Rubinstein's trademark, and Leinsdorf's accompaniment is dramatically surging.

Friere gives the most impressive thunder-and-lightning performance since the old Horowitz–Toscanini recording. The young Brazilian's sense of dynamics is exceptional, and he does not overlook poetic subtleties in the score, for all his technical razzle-dazzle. His 1968 release is also something of a bargain in that Columbia's engineers have been able to fit the popular Grieg Piano Concerto on the same disc as well. Kempe's accompaniment is fairly bland.

Richter has recorded the concerto at least three times, but the most memorable is a 1962 version with Karajan. His tempos are slower and the mood uncommonly brooding, yet it is a continually fascinating and convincing performance, with a well-matched accompaniment.

Weissenberg's 1970 release is, next to Richter's, the slowest in tempo and the most poetically moody. Yet it is never dull and has a rare feeling of eloquence and inner pulse. The sound engineering is disappointingly muddy, however.

Janis gives a brilliant performance that also has dramatic breadth, and the sound engineering is especially crisp. Originally released in 1960, it was recoupled in 1966 with Janis' recording of the Rachmaninoff Second Piano Concerto for a most worthwhile "two-for-the-price-of-one" bargain.

Dichter, who brought back to the U.S. one of the 1966 Moscow prizes, brings more zest and warmth to the concerto than Cliburn, if not as much nobility and grandeur. He also shows a rare feeling for the concerto's inner poetry, so that his is not a "fireworks only" performance. Leinsdorf's accompaniment is spirited and pungent.

Ashkenazy also emphasizes much of the concerto's inner poetry, even approaching Richter's brooding quality at times. In the last movement, he and Maazel take off in a bravura sprint that seemingly defies being sustained yet *is* sustained. At other times, however, Maazel's cool and clinical detachment seems ill matched with Ashkenazy's warm, more intense approach. London's stereo engineering (from about 1963) is outstanding.

Among budget-label releases, Gilels' is the most notable—a brilliant, hard-driving, muscular performance, recorded in Chicago during Gilels' first U.S. tour in 1955. The finale is particularly breathtaking.

One historic mono recording deserves praise too, despite its ancient sound: the Horowitz–Toscanini recording, taken from a 1943 Carnegie Hall concert. Author-commentator Martin Bookspan has aptly called it "an astonishing document—a demonic, fire-spewing performance that tears up the turf in its visceral energy and excitement."

Violin Concerto in D major

Like so many works that have won enduring popularity, Tchaikovsky's only violin concerto was not well received when it first appeared. First, Leopold Auer, the celebrated violinist to whom Tchaikovsky had intended to dedicate the score, pronounced it "unplayable." Then at its premiere in Vienna, the leading critic, Eduard Hanslick, denounced it as "vulgar" and "music that stinks in the ear." This was undoubtedly because of the freedom with which Tchaikovsky had moved away from the more Classical forms of Beethoven, Brahms and others. But violinists, critics, and especially audiences have come to view the concerto differently over the years, so that in the early 1970's there were more than twenty different recordings of the concerto in the Schwann catalog—marking it as one of the most popular of all concertos. Its soaring melodies and the variety of its Romantic moods surely account for that popularity.

Recommended Recordings

★ **b** Oistrakh, Ormandy, Philadelphia Orchestra (Odyssey stereo disc Y-30312)

Heifetz, Reiner, Chicago Symphony (RCA Red Seal stereo disc LSC-3304; cassette RK-1284; cartridge R8S-1284).

Zukerman, Dorati, London Symphony (Columbia stereo disc MS-7313; cassette 16-11-0162)

Stern, Ormandy, Philadelphia (Columbia stereo disc MS-6062)

Perlman, Leinsdorf, Boston Symphony (RCA Red Seal stereo disc LSC-3014; cartridge R8S-1093)

Comments

Of the four or five recordings David Oistrakh has made of this concerto, the one he made in the U.S. with Ormandy in 1959 is easily the best—a richly singing, glowing performance, beautifully recorded. Originally released on Columbia, it was reissued on the budget-priced Odyssey label in 1972.

Heifetz's dashingly virtuoso performance is cooler than Oistrakh's in its romantic feeling. His finale is particularly exciting, even though the late 1950's sound tends to be muddy in loud passages. The performance has been released at different times with different couplings; the latest (1972) is with Heifetz's impressive performance of the Mendelssohn Violin Concerto.

Zukerman also offers both the Tchaikovsky and Mendelssohn concertos on his 1969 debut recording. The young Israeli, twenty-one at the time of the recording, displays breathtaking technique and an exhilarating style that stresses Tchaikovsky's lyricism rather than his sentimentality.

Stern is broadly fervent and compelling, with a well-matched accompaniment from Ormandy. His version, dating from the late 1950's, also provides a first-rate performance of the Mendelssohn Violin Concerto.

Perlman, who was twenty-three when his recording was released in 1968, brings extraordinary interpretive depth and understanding to the concerto, though his forceful playing sometimes produces harsher sounds in the microphone than it does in the concert hall. His performance is coupled with Dvořák's beautiful *Romance* (for violin and orchestra), played with enormous warmth and breadth.

Symphony No. 4 in F minor

One of the most forceful and dramatic of Romantic symphonies, Tchaikovsky's Fourth was composed during a period of enormous personal turmoil for him. During this period (1877–78), an unsuccessful marriage drove him to attempting suicide. His brother then took him to Switzerland to rest and recover from what appeared to be almost a complete nervous collapse. As a result, some analysts have speculated on the Fourth Symphony as providing both a cathartic escape and a rehabilitative anchor for Tchaikovsky during a year of severe emotional trauma. Tchaikovsky himself saw his Fourth as a musical expression of "the triumph of sensibility over attacks of fate." "Although there is no actual musical resemblance, the work is modeled after Beethoven's Fifth," he said. A dramatic brass fanfare (sometimes called the "Destiny Fanfare," which Tchaikovsky related to "fear of the unknown") opens the symphony, dominates the first movement, and recurs again in the finale, thus binding the whole symphony together. The first and second movements are filled with contrasts—from profound melancholy to marchlike assertiveness. The third movement is one of the most famous of any symphony—a satirical scherzo for strings played *pizzicato* (plucked with fingers rather than bowed). The fourth movement is defiantly heroic—one of the most swashbuckling, kinetic finales in all music.

Recommended Recordings

★ Karajan, Berlin Philharmonic (Deutsche Grammophon stereo disc 139017; cartridge M89-017)

Mehta, Los Angeles Philharmonic (London stereo disc CS-6553)

Barenboim, New York Philharmonic (Columbia stereo disc MS-30572; cassette MT-30572)

Svetlanov, USSR Symphony (Melodiya/Angel stereo disc S-40043)

b Munch, Boston Symphony (RCA Victrola stereo disc VICS-1100; cartridge V8S-1034)

Comments

Karajan's 1967 DG recording is one of the best stereo showpieces in the catalog. The Berlin Philharmonic plays with dazzling virtuosity, especially for Karajan's fast, all-stops-out finale. Interpretively, Karajan makes the brooding Romantic themes really brood, and the martial-like sections really march along excitingly. The interpretation is almost identical to two Karajan recordings of this symphony for Angel with the same orchestra (S-35885 and S-36884), but the sound is more vivid on the Deutsche Grammophon version.

Mehta offers a rousing, fire-and-thunder performance, with fewer contrasts in mood. London's stereo engineers, working for the first time in Los Angeles (in 1967), provide impressively alive, brilliant sound.

Barenboim's 1971 recording is an exciting one, even with generally slower tempos in the last two movements. His interpretation offers well-conceived dramatic contrasts, and packs considerable punch.

Svetlanov, still in his 30's when this recording was made in 1967, takes the third and fourth movements at a fantastic clip (as most Russian conductors do with this symphony), and brings breadth and probing contrasts to the others. The orchestral playing, however, is not as polished as the others listed.

Munch performs with fervor and dramatic intensity, and the sound of his 1955 recording is still fairly good.

Symphony No. 6 in B minor (Pathétique)

"As far as I am concerned, I am more proud of it than of any other work of mine," wrote Tchaikovsky of his Sixth Symphony. "While composing it I frequently shed tears." Many listeners still do the same—especially those to whom the *Pathétique* has come to be *the* Romantic symphony. Tchaikovsky at first designated it "The Program Symphony (No. 6)," but added that none but he would know the program. The morning after the Moscow premiere, however, he decided the title was unfair because "I do not intend to expound any meaning." He sought instead a title that would convey the symphony's general mood. His brother suggested *Pathétique*, meaning "affecting the emotions," particularly tender or sorrowful emotions. Whatever the original program of the Sixth Symphony was, Tchaikovsky took it to his grave—a week after the premiere he was dead, a victim of cholera. The symphony is, broadly speaking, a mixture of melody and dramatic conflict, of lamentation and defiance. Structurally, it diverges from the traditional symphonic pattern in several ways that were unusual for its time: the first movement is more like a symphonic poem with separate sections; the second movement was one of the first to use a 5/4 rhythm (a rhythm which 20th-century composers have used extensively), and was first mocked as a waltz to be danced by a three-legged man; the third movement has qualities of both a scherzo and a march (different conductors play it with different emphases); and instead of a lively, grand finale, the fourth movement is a melancholy "adagio lamentoso" that ebbs away in desolation.

Recommended Recordings

★ Haitink, Amsterdam Concertgebouw Orchestra (Philips stereo disc 6500081)

b Giulini, Philharmonia Orchestra of London (Seraphim stereo disc S-60031)

  Ormandy, Philadelphia Orchestra (RCA Red Seal stereo disc LSC-3058; cassette RK-1112; cartridge R8S-1112)

  Ormandy, Philadelphia Orchestra (Columbia stereo disc MS-7169 or M-31833; cassette MT-31833; cartridge MA-31833)

  Munch, Boston Symphony (RCA Red Seal stereo disc LSC-2683)

b Monteux, Boston Symphony (RCA Victrola stereo disc VICS-1009; cartridge V8S-1016)

Comments

Haitink's 1971 performance is warm, lyrical, full of dramatic contrasts, and deeply poignant without becoming maudlin.

Giulini's performance is interpretively similar—lyrically expressive and dramatic. Although recorded in 1961 the performance was not released in the U.S. until 1967, and then on the budget Seraphim label (probably because its sound, while quite good, could not qualify by the latest stereo standards of that period).

The first recording Ormandy ever made with the Philadelphia Orchestra back in 1936 was of the *Pathétique* (for RCA), and it became one of the most popular 78-RPM recordings of that era. Ormandy rerecorded it twice for LP during his years at Columbia, and then did so again in 1969 for his return to the RCA label. Both the RCA and Columbia recordings are virtuoso performances, somewhat on the gushy side but always tremendously moving. The sound is brightest on the 1969 RCA version, but the 1960 Columbia is also excellent.

Munch and Monteux both get glowing performances out of the Boston Symphony. Munch's performance is more impetuous and passionate, while Monteux brings out a more relaxed kind of lyrical warmth. Although recorded nearly seven years apart, (Munch's is the later—from 1962), the recorded sound is comparable, with emphasis on the tonal brilliance of the Boston Symphony.

Romeo and Juliet (Overture-Fantasia)

Of the many musical works based on Shakespeare's story, Tchaikovsky's orchestral portrait is the most popular and the most frequently performed. Tchaikovsky does not follow the order of the play, but instead seeks to recreate in music the basic atmosphere of Shakespeare's romantic tragedy. After a solemn introduction (Friar Laurence meditating on the plight of the lovers), the work divides itself between two main themes—a "Battle Theme" representing the struggle for power between the Capulet and Montague families, and a "Love Theme" representing the two young lovers—and the interplay of those themes. Although originally planned in the traditional 19th-century overture form (introduction, development, coda), Tchaikovsky reworked the score so extensively between the time of its first performance in 1870 and its publication in 1881 that he finally called it an "overture-fantasia" (the term "fantasia" being meant to symbolize a work of freer form).

Recommended Recordings

★ Abbado, Boston Symphony (Deutsche Grammophon stereo disc 2530137; cassette 3300184; cartridge 89435)

b Munch, Boston Symphony (RCA Victrola stereo disc VICS-1197)

Bernstein, New York Philharmonic (Columbia stereo disc MS-6014)

Karajan, Vienna Philharmonic (London stereo disc CS-6209)

Karajan, Berlin Philharmonic (Deutsche Grammophon stereo disc 139029; cassette 923-045; cartridge 89-029)

Stokowski, Suisse Romande Orchestra (London stereo disc SPC-21032; cassette M-94032; cartridge M-95032)

Comments

Abbado's 1971 recording is supercharged—both in its interpretation and its sound engineering. Abbado and the Bostonians really let go with a blazingly intense, tonally lush, and vigorous performance. Overside, performers and sound engineers both similarly let out all the stops for Scriabin's *Poem of Ecstasy.*

Munch's performance is also supercharged and vibrant, and the Bostonians again play with exceptional warmth and intensity. The mid-1950's recording is coupled with a vivid Munch performance of Tchaikovsky's *Francesca da Rimini.* A 1961 Munch rerecording is also available (RCA Red Seal stereo disc LSC-2565; cartridge R8S-1018), coupled with a lively *Till Eulenspiegel* by Strauss, but the sound is not that much better.

Bernstein gives an impassioned, exciting performance. The sound engineering, dating from the late 1950's, is no match for Abbado's, but it is still satisfactory. The coupling is Bernstein's colorful reading of Stravinsky's *Firebird* Suite.

Both Karajan recordings are outstanding for their combination of tenderness and excitement. The sound of the Vienna recording (1960) is more brilliant, while that of the Berlin (1966) is more mellow. The Vienna edition is coupled with a richly dramatic Karajan performance of Strauss' *Don Juan.* The Berlin edition is coupled with juicy performances of Tchaikovsky's *Marche Slav* and *1812 Overture,* the latter featuring the Don Cossack Chorus singing (in Russian) the introductory hymn.

Stokowski openly tampers with Tchaikovsky's orchestration in his 1968 performance for London's show-off "Phase-4" stereo series. Purists will undoubtedly shudder, yet the effect is stunning—a colorful, exciting, and dramatic performance, with spectacular sound engineering. Overside, Stokowski offers his own even more radically reworked "symphonic synthesis" of Mussorgsky's *Boris Godunov.*

For Follow-Up Consideration

Symphony No. 5 in E minor, along with the Fourth and Sixth among the most popular symphonies in the concert repertory, and similar to them in its mixture of haunting melody and swashbuckling rhythms, is perhaps the most optimistic (even heroic) in overall mood. RECOMMENDED RECORDING: Bernstein, New York Philharmonic (Columbia stereo disc MS-6312), a warm-blooded, robust performance dating from the early 1960's by a conductor who is not afraid to wear the symphony's Romantic sentiments on his sleeve.

Symphony No. 1 in G minor ("Winter Dreams"), a work that has begun to come into its own in recent years as a long-neglected example of Tchaikovsky's distinctive gift for orchestral color and melodic expressiveness—or, as critic-editor James Lyons has written, "Tchaikovsky was Tchaikovsky right from the beginning." RECOMMENDED RECORDING: Thomas, Boston Symphony (Deutsche Grammophon stereo disc 2530078; cassette 3300-107), a 1970 performance full of drama, tension, warmth, and excitement, led by a conductor who was then the same age (twenty-five) as Tchaikovsky was when he wrote the symphony.

The Nutcracker, that perennial holiday favorite, containing some of Tchaikovsky's most delightfully unpretentious music. It exists in several versions: (1) the complete ballet, (2) the familiar *Nutcracker Suite*, containing most of the short dances from Act 2 of the ballet, and (3) the less-familiar *Nutcracker Suite No. 2*, containing several other dances, the "Snow Journey" scene from Act 1, and the grand finale. RECOMMENDED RECORDINGS: Dorati, London Symphony—either in a 2-disc album of the complete ballet (Mercury stereo 2-disc set SR-2-9013) or in a single-disc version of *both* suites (Mercury SR-90528), a spirited, colorful, sonically superb 1962 performance. An excellent budget-priced version of excerpts from both Acts 1 and 2, including most of the familiar dances, is also available (Monitor stereo disc MCS-2104), played with verve and style by the Bolshoi Theatre Orchestra under Rozhdestvensky, with decent enough sound, though no match sonically for the Dorati-Mercury version.

Swan Lake, probably the most popular of all ballets, filled with some of Tchaikovsky's most haunting and colorful music. The complete four-act score is seldom performed outside the ballet theatre. In programming excerpts from *Swan Lake* for concert programs or recordings, few conductors choose the same set of excerpts, so record buyers are advised to check the contents of highlights albums for their favorite sections. RECOMMENDED RECORDINGS: *Complete*—Rozhdestvensky, Moscow Radio Symphony (Melodiya/Angel stereo 3-disc set S-4106), an alternately mellow and stirring performance dating from the late 1960's. *Highlights*—Fistoulari, Amsterdam Concertgebouw Orchestra (London stereo disc CS-6218), a spirited and elegant 1960 performance, with impressive sound.

Sleeping Beauty, a romantic ballet based on Perrault's famous fairy tale and containing some of Tchaikovsky's most romantic music, colorfully orchestrated. RECOMMENDED RECORDING: *Complete*—Ansermet, Suisse Romande Orchestra (London stereo 3-disc set CSA-2304), a lyrically elegant and balletic performance, dating from the late 1950's but with still-splendid sound. *Highlights*—Ormandy, Philadelphia Orchestra (RCA Red Seal quadrasonic disc ARD1-0030; cartridge ART1-0030), a lush, warmly expressive performance released in 1973.

1812 Overture, an unabashed rouser commemorating the Russian defeat of Napoleon in 1812, written for a Moscow Exhibition in 1882 and calling for a large orchestra, a military band, all sorts of bells and chimes, and cannon shots. In recent years it has become a hi-fi/stereo showpiece, with each new recording attempting to outdo the last one in sonic gaudiness. RECOMMENDED RECORDING: Buketoff, New Philharmonia Orchestra, Cathedral Choir and Children's Choir of St. Ambrose, Central Band of the Royal Air Force, Guns of the Royal Horse Artillery, etc. (RCA Red Seal stereo disc LSC-3051; cassette RK-1115; cartridge R8S-1115), a knockout of a 1968 performance musically and sonically, effectively interpolating more choral sections (sung in Russian) than most other recordings; overside are several fascinating and rarely heard Rachmaninoff choral pieces. (A cartridge edition in quadrasonic sound was released in 1973 as RQ8-1115.)

• *ANTONIN DVOŘÁK*

Pronounced: d'-*vor*-zhahk. Born September 8, 1841, in Mühlhausen, Bohemia. Died May 1, 1904, in Prague.

SIGNIFICANCE: Bohemian (Czech) composer, violist, teacher; a strong champion of nationalism in music (basing music on native folk elements).

BACKGROUND: The son of an innkeeper, Dvořák earned his livelihood as a violist in the Prague National Theatre before turning seriously to composing in his 30's. At 32 he submitted two symphonies for a competition, and won a stipend from the Austrian government. Brahms was one of the judges for the stipend's renewal, and became a lifelong friend and champion of Dvořák thereafter. A set of colorful, folkish *Slavonic Dances* won Dvořák his first popular success. He became a professor at the Prague Conservatory in 1891, and a year later was invited to head the National Conservatory in New York.

His arrival in New York was greeted at the ship's pier by a three hundred-voice chorus and an orchestra of eighty-seven. For the next three years his New York home became a popular rendezvous for leading musicians. Dvořák provoked controversy, however, by seeking to influence U.S. composers to use Negro folk themes in their works, composing his own *From the New World* Symphony, and his String Quartet No. 6, the "American," in such a manner. After three years in New York, he returned to Prague. On his sixtieth birthday he was made a member of the Austrian House of Lords, the first musician to be so honored.

For many years there was confusion about the numbering of Dvořák's symphonies, since they had been numbered as published instead of in the sequence composed (for example, the sixth symphony Dvořák composed was the first to be published, and thus became known as No. 1). Since 1960, however, there has been general agreement among record companies and concert managers to renumber them in sequence of composition. Occasionally, the old numbers still crop up. The usual practice today is to list the old number parenthetically—example: Symphony No. 9 (old No. 5).

Symphony No. 9 (old No. 5) in E minor—From the New World

Though once regarded as the first successful symphony to employ "American" themes, Dvořák's *New World* is now generally regarded as reflecting as much of Dvořák's native Bohemia (today part of Czechoslovakia) as America—or, perhaps more precisely, to have a mixture of both Bohemian and American elements. Although some critics have found a resemblance between the second theme of the first movement and the Negro spiritual "Swing Low, Sweet Chariot," Dvořák denied using any specific

Negro or Indian folk material. He did, however, tell one writer that in composing the *Largo* (the second movement), he had part of Longfellow's *Hiawatha* in mind—although, again, he denied using actual Indian melodies. Later, words were adapted to a portion of the *Largo*, and the song, "Goin' Home," has since become accepted throughout the world as an "American folk classic." Some critics have found in Dvořák's *New World* Symphony a musical portrait of the tensions and conflicts of American culture and life in the late 19th century—basically European-rooted but with qualities adapted from indigenous New World elements.

Recommended Recordings

★ Bernstein, New York Philharmonic (Columbia stereo disc MS-6393)

Kertesz, London Symphony (London stereo disc CS-6527)

b Toscanini, NBC Symphony (RCA Victrola disc VIC-1249, *mono only;* cartridge V8S-1009)

Szell, Cleveland Orchestra (in Columbia 3-disc set D3S-814 or 2-disc set MG-30371).

Fiedler, Boston Symphony (RCA Red Seal stereo disc LSC-3134; cassette RK-1160; cartridge R8S-1160; also quadrasonic cartridge RQ8-1160)

Comments

Bernstein's performance, dating from about 1962, is spirited and dramatic, and especially moving in the breadth of the *Largo*. Bernstein is also one of the few conductors to honor the repeat of the exposition of the first movement.

Kertesz's London Symphony recording (from 1966) is warm and vibrant, with a particularly exciting final movement. There's also a very worthwhile bonus: a first-rate performance of Dvořák's highly dramatic *Othello* Overture. The sound engineering is excellent, and is superior to that of an earlier (1963) Kertesz-Vienna Philharmonic version reissued in 1971 on the London Stereo Treasury series (STS-15101).

Toscanini's 1953 recording may be showing its age, but the sound is still acceptable (especially at budget-label prices), and it may well be the best-engineered of all Toscanini recordings. The performance is outstanding—full of vitality and strength, and with marvelous rhythmic articulation in the final movements. It is coupled with a taut 1947 Toscanini performance of Schumann's *Manfred* Overture.

Szell's performance is similar in many ways to Toscanini's, and has the advantage of excellent stereo engineering. However, the 1960 recording is available only as part of multiple sets. One, a 3-disc set, also includes crisp, buoyant Szell performances of Dvořák's Seventh (old No. 2) and Eighth (old No. 4) Symphonies. The other, a 2-disc set, is a special Szell memorial tribute released in 1971 that also includes his polished performances of Beethoven's Symphony No. 5 and Schubert's Symphony No. 8 ("Unfinished").

Fiedler's 1970 release is his only major recording with the full Boston Symphony Orchestra, and stems from a concert commemorating his seventy-fifth birthday. He leads a warm, spirited performance, rounding off the album with a rousing Dvořák *Carnival* Overture. (A cartridge edition in quadrasonic sound was released in 1973.)

Cello Concerto in B minor

This greatest of all cello concertos was composed by Dvořák during the last of his three years in the United States as head of a New York conservatory. But the flavor is clearly Czech, and Dvořák admitted being homesick for his native land during that last year in the U.S. The inspiration for the concerto came partly from a concert Dvořák attended of the New York Philharmonic in 1894 at which Victor Herbert was soloist in his own Second Cello Concerto. (Before he became world famous as a composer of operettas, Herbert had been a widely acclaimed cellist.) The concerto is filled with eloquent, bittersweet melody—some of it darkly mysterious and melancholy, some of it strong, robust, and energetic. Brahms is reported to have said of it: "Why on earth did I not know that it is possible to write a cello concerto like this?"

Recommended Recordings

★ Rostropovich, Karajan, Berlin Philharmonic (Deutsche Grammophon stereo disc 139044; cassette 923-098; cartridge 89-044)

Fournier, Szell, Berlin Philharmonic (Deutsche Grammophon stereo disc 138755; cassette 923-060)

Starker, Dorati, London Symphony (Mercury stereo disc 90303; cassette MCR4-90303; cartridge MC8-90303)

DuPré, Barenboim, Chicago Symphony (Angel stereo disc S-36046)

Casals, Szell, Czech Philharmonic (Angel disc COLH-30, *mono only*)

Comments

Rostropovich is in a class by himself among present-day cellists. His 1969 release superbly communicates the warmth, glow, excitement, passion, and poetry of this concerto. Karajan's accompaniment lacks the special thrust Szell provided in a live Cleveland concert performance the author heard just a few weeks before this recording was released, but it is still a finely etched accompaniment. Overside, Rostropovich rounds off the album with an elegant, virtuoso performance of Tchaikovsky's *Rococo Variations.* (*Note:* There are several other Rostropovich performances available on budget labels, one made in Prague in the 1950's and another in Moscow at an indeterminate date; none of them is well recorded by today's standards, especially in comparison with the Deutsche Grammophon release.)

Fournier has the distinct advantage of Szell's accompaniment, and gives a truly inspired performance—intense and soaring. The sound engineering of this 1962 release remains first-rate.

Starker's 1961 recording is also outstanding—dramatic, intense, and richly expressive. Dorati is in uncommonly good form for the accompaniment. Starker rounds off side 2 with a superbly poetic version of Bruch's *Kol Nidrei.*

DuPré's 1971 release is exceptionally ardent in mood—almost too much so in some sections, where she seems to be straining to wrench the last iota of feeling out of every phrase. But there is no denying the warmth and electricity of her playing, and of Barenboim's orchestral accompaniment.

Casals' mono performance dates from the 1930's, and remains a recording classic despite its faded sound. Casals was at the peak of his form, collaborating with Szell on a truly beautiful, eloquent performance. The Angel edition has been withdrawn from the active catalog, but reportedly may be reissued on the Seraphim label.

For Follow-Up Consideration

Slavonic Dances, among the most popular of all orchestral dances, composed in two sets (Op. 46 in 1878, and Op. 72 in 1886–87) and based on Czech dance forms. RECOMMENDED RECORDING: Szell, Cleveland Orchestra (Columbia stereo disc MS-7208; cartridge 18-11-0098), vividly spirited and beautifully played in a recording dating from the mid-1960's.

Symphony No. 8 (old No. 4), an alternately pensive and spirited but always freshly melodic symphony that some critics have said reflects the Bohemian countryside. RECOMMENDED RECORDING: Kertesz, London Symphony Orchestra (London stereo disc CS-6358), a warmly lyrical, dramatic performance dating from 1963, coupled with a jaunty Kertesz performance of Dvořák's delightful *Scherzo Capriccioso*.

• EDVARD GRIEG

Pronounced: *greeg*. Born June 15, 1843, in Bergen, Norway. Died September 4, 1907, in Bergen.

SIGNIFICANCE: Norwegian composer and pianist, whose Romantic music mainly reflects a sturdy Norse spirit.

BACKGROUND: Grieg's family was of Scottish origins, and his father was the British consul in Bergen at the time of Grieg's birth. Grieg began piano lessons at the age of six, and as a teenager studied in Leipzig and Copenhagen. He became a close friend of the composer Rikard Nordraak, and under his influence became committed to writing music that would be recognized as Norwegian nationalist music.

He wrote music on Norwegian literary themes (for Ibsen's *Peer Gynt*, Bjørnson's *Sigurd Jorsalfar*), various Norwegian folk song arrangements, plus many songs and piano works. He settled mainly in Bergen, and spent most of his life plagued by poor health. When his health permitted, he toured as a pianist, particularly as accompanist to his wife Nina, who sang his songs.

Piano Concerto in A minor

This melodic, rhapsodic concerto is modeled in many ways after Schumann's (also in A minor). Written when Grieg was twenty-five, it has long been one of the most popular of all piano concertos, and has been the source of several pop songs in the 1940's and 1960's. The concerto has also provided the finale for the popular musical play *Song of Norway* (a Broadway hit in the 1940's and still a summer musical tent favorite) as well as the 1970 biographical film also called *Song of Norway*.

Recommended Recordings

★ **b** Baekkelund, Grüner-Hegge, Oslo Philharmonic (RCA Victrola stereo disc VICS-1067; cartridge V8S-1026)

Rubinstein, Wallenstein, unnamed orchestra (RCA Red Seal stereo disc LSC-2566; cartridges R8S-5009 and R8S-1011)

Cliburn, Ormandy, Philadelphia Orchestra (RCA Red Seal stereo disc LSC-3065; cassette RK-1113; cartridge R8S-1113)

Friere, Kempe, Munich Philharmonic (Columbia stereo disc MS-7396)

b Lipatti, Galliera, London Philharmonia (Odyssey disc 32160141, *mono only*)

Comments

Norway's Baekkelund plays with sweep and poetry, and is well recorded in this 1964 release. Overside is a stylish performance of excerpts from *Peer Gynt.*

Rubinstein blends a broadly Romantic feeling with his great virtuosity, giving an engaging performance (his third recorded version, and his second with Wallenstein). At the time of its original release in 1962, the album cover quoted Rubinstein as saying unabashedly that "this is the most perfect recording I have made." Overside Rubinstein offers a solo recital program of popular piano pieces by Liszt, Schumann, Falla, Prokofiev, and Villa-Lobos.

Cliburn underplays the flamboyance of the work while Ormandy overemphasizes all sorts of brilliant orchestral colors in their 1968 release. Overside they do much the same with Liszt's Piano Concerto No. 1.

Friere blends breadth, elegance, and technical deftness in his 1968 recording. Overside is a volatile performance of the Tchaikovsky Piano Concerto No. 1. Kempe's orchestral accompaniments, however, are bland.

Lipatti's pre-1950 performance is dated sonically, but it remains one of uncommon sensitivity and Romantic feeling—and deserves being kept in the active catalog, especially at budget-label prices and in its present coupling with Lipatti's matchless performance of the Schumann Piano Concerto.

Peer Gynt Suites

Grieg's incidental music for Ibsen's 1876 poetic drama about a legendary Norwegian rogue has become a popular concert work through two orchestral suites Grieg drew from the original. Suite No. 1 contains the best-known sections: "Dawn," "The Death of Ase," "Anitra's Dance," and "In the Hall of the Mountain King." Suite No. 2 includes "Ingrid's Lament," "Arabian Dance," "The Return of Peer Gynt," and "Solvejg's Song." The music is by turns brooding, vigorous, dramatic, and colorful. "Solvejg's Song" is for soprano and orchestra, but is most often performed by orchestra alone in concert performances. Similarly, "In the Hall of the Mountain

King" and the "Arabian Dance" both have brief choral sections which are usually omitted in concert performances and most recordings.

Recommended Recordings

★ Barbirolli, Hallé Orchestra, Ambrosian Singers (Angel stereo disc S-36803)

b Grünner-Hegge, Oslo Philharmonic (RCA Victrola stereo disc VICS-1067; cartridge V8S-1026)

Bernstein, New York Philharmonic (Columbia stereo disc M-31800; cassette MT-31800; cartridge MA-31800)

Ormandy, Philadelphia Orchestra (Columbia stereo disc MS-6196)

Comments

Barbirolli's 1971 release not only includes both suites complete but also all the choral sections, and features soprano Sheila Armstrong in a lovely account of "Solvejg's Song." Barbirolli's interpretation is warm and engaging, and the inclusion of the choral sections makes his "In the Hall of the Mountain King" especially vivid. He rounds off the disc with spirited performances of four of Grieg's Norwegian Dances.

Grünner-Hegge performs all of Suite No. 1 (orchestra only) and two parts of Suite No. 2 ("Arabian Dance" and "Solvejg's Song," again orchestra only) with marvelous nuances, taut rhythms, and dramatic feeling, and the mid-1960's engineering is very good. The excellent Baekkelund performance of the Grieg Piano Concerto overside makes this an outstanding budget selection.

Bernstein's 1972 release offers Suites No. 1 and 2 complete (without chorus or soprano soloist). "In the Hall of the Mountain King" is heavy-handed, but Bernstein brings off the other sections colorfully and gracefully. Overside is a vivid account of Bizet's orchestral suites from *Carmen*.

Ormandy offers just Suite No. 1 (orchestra only) in a tonally lush, brightly recorded performance from the late 1950's. He rounds off the disc with whipped-cream readings of Alfven's *Swedish Rhapsody* and Sibelius' *Valse Triste*, plus a stirring *Finlandia* in which the Mormon Tabernacle Choir joins in the finale.

For Follow-Up Consideration

Songs of Norway, one of the last albums made by the great Norwegian soprano Kirsten Flagstad, including five lovely Grieg songs sung in their original Norwegian (London stereo disc OS-25103). It was recorded in 1959.

• *NIKOLAI RIMSKY-KORSAKOV*

Pronounced: *rim*-skee-*kor*-suh-koff. Born March 18, 1844, in Novgorod, Russia. Died June 21, 1908, near St. Petersburg.

SIGNIFICANCE: Russian composer, conductor, teacher, perhaps best known as the most exotic, colorful orchestrator of his day (he wrote a book on orchestration that has remained a classic text—and has particularly influenced the composers of Hollywood movie scores).

BACKGROUND: Though he began studying piano at the age of six and wrote his first composition at nine, Rimsky-Korsakov's aristocratic family insisted that he undertake a career as a Russian naval officer. He continued to study music in his spare time, especially after a meeting with composer-conductor Mily Balakirev convinced him he had talent. In 1865 Balakirev introduced Rimsky-Korsakov's First Symphony (partly written at sea) at a St. Petersburg concert. Eight years later, after he had composed several other works, including an opera, he resigned from the navy to devote himself fully to music.

Despite his lack of formal music education, he became a professor at the St. Petersburg Conservatory—sometimes teaching lessons to himself first to keep one jump ahead of his pupils. He learned to play many instruments in order to improve his understanding of orchestration and conducting. He turned out more than a dozen operas, mostly based on Russian stories or legends, and various orchestral works that made his name synonymous with rich orchestration.

In 1905 he was dismissed from his professorship after he had spoken out against the czar's use of armed force to suppress student political gatherings. In reaction, other prominent faculty members, including Glazunov and Liadov, also resigned. Rimsky-Korsakov was later reinstated, when Glazunov became the Conservatory's director. Three years later Rimsky-Korsakov's opera *Le Coq d' Or* (*The Golden Cock*) was banned by the czar's censors as a thinly veiled satire on imperial despotism. Many believe the censorship controversy triggered the sudden heart attack which caused the composer's death in 1908.

Scheherazade

Although he was known as a man of fastidious habits and an ultramethodical mind, Rimsky-Korsakov wrote some of the most fanciful, extravagant music of any 19th-century composer—and none more fanciful and extravagant than *Scheherazade*. Its melodic charm and rich colors have kept it a concert favorite for nearly a century (in 1974 there were more than twenty different recordings available). *Scheherazade* was composed in 1888 and inspired by the tales of the *Arabian Nights*. The composer wrote this foreword to his score: "The Sultan Schariar, convinced of the faithlessness of all women, vowed to put each of his wives to death after the first night of marriage. But the Sultana Scheherazade saved her life by entertaining him with tales which she told for a thousand and one nights. Pricked by curiosity, the Sultan postponed his wife's execution from day to day, and finally gave up his bloodthirsty plan altogether." Rimsky-Korsakov's work is in four movements, with the following subtitles: (1) "The Sea and Sinbad's Ship"; (2) "The Tale of the Kalandar Prince"; (3) "The Young Prince and Princess"; (4) "Festival at Baghdad and Shipwreck on the Rock Surmounted by the Bronze Warrior." However, Rimsky-Korsakov provided no program beyond the titles, saying: "I meant these hints only to direct the hearer's fancy on the path that my own fancy had traveled . . . and to carry away the impression that it is beyond doubt an Oriental narrative of varied fairy-tale wonders." The musical connecting link is a violin theme representing the storyteller Scheherazade, heard in each of the movements and emerging triumphant at the end.

Recommended Recordings

★ Stokowski, London Symphony (London stereo disc 21005; cassette M-94005; cartridge M-95005)

Ansermet, Suisse Romande Orchestra (London stereo disc CS-6212; cassette M-10076; cartridge M-67076)

Karajan, Berlin Philharmonic (Deutsche Grammophon stereo disc 139022; cassette 923-027; cartridge 89-022)

Ormandy, Philadelphia Orchestra (RCA quadrasonic disc ARD1-0028; cassette ARK1-0028; cartridge ARS1-0028)

Ormandy, Philadelphia Orchestra (Columbia stereo disc MS-6365)

Ozawa, Chicago Symphony (Angel stereo disc S-36034; cassette 4XS-36034; cartridge 8XS-36034)

Comments

Stokowski has always had a special magic with this work, recording it four times over the past 45 years. His 1964 London stereo version is spellbinding both musically and sonically. Stokowski really knows how to make the most of *Scheherazade*'s coloristic effects and melodies, plus something few other conductors see in the score: its wit and good fun.

Ansermet's more subtly shaded yet dramatic 1961 reading is also a sonic knockout—in fact, during the early 1960's it was considered by many critics to be *the* best symphonic example of what stereo engineering could achieve, and has not often been surpassed since then. Moreover, London includes an exciting bonus: a vivid Ansermet performance of Borodin's "Polovetsian Dances" (from the opera *Prince Igor*), including the choral sections omitted in most other recordings of the dances.

Karajan's 1967 performance emerges with warm, rich colors, a lavish Romantic mood, and, in the proper places, intense excitement. And the climax of the shipwreck scene is surely the most sweepingly dramatic on records. Excellent sound.

It was inevitable that *Scheherazade* should be one of the first quadrasonic showpiece albums, and Ormandy and the Philadelphia Orchestra have made it just that in their 1973 release for RCA. It's a sumptuously lush performance, interpretively less interesting in its details than Stokowski's, Ansermet's, or Karajan's, but certainly never dull and often stunning in its virtuosity. If you don't have quadrasonic playback equipment, the recording still sounds impressive on a conventional stereo system—though no more so than the Stokowski, Ansermet, Karajan, or Ozawa recordings, or even Ormandy's 1962 recording for Columbia. The latter is basically similar in interpretation to the newer RCA version. Purists, incidentally, may object to a minor cut Ormandy makes in the third movement.

Ozawa's 1970 release is colorful, spirited, and superbly played by the Chicago

Symphony. Ozawa (like Ansermet) not only provides a coupling but makes it a rip-roaring performance of Borodin's "Polovetsian Dances" (without the chorus, however).

For Follow-Up Consideration

Russian Easter Overture, a colorful musical evocation of the Easter celebrations of the Russian Orthodox Church, which the composer said was designed to show the "transition from the gloomy and mysterious evening of Passion Saturday to the joyous pagan-religious merrymaking on the morn of Easter Sunday." RECOMMENDED RECORDING: Stokowski, Chicago Symphony Orchestra (RCA Red Seal stereo disc LSC-3067; cartridge R8S-1122), a fervent, rich-sounding 1968 performance—Stokowski's third recording of the work and easily his best; it is coupled with a sonically superb performance of Khachaturian's rambling Third Symphony.

● *GIACOMO PUCCINI*

Pronounced: poo-*chee*-nee. Born December 22, 1858, in Lucca, Italy. Died November 29, 1924, in Brussels.

SIGNIFICANCE: Italian opera composer, one of the most fluent melodists of all opera, and an advocate of dramatic realism (*verismo*) and intimacy in opera production (in contrast to the heroic, mythological, or historical "grand" style of earlier opera).

BACKGROUND: The son of a poor family of locally eminent church musicians, Puccini studied in Milan and wrote his first operas for production there. In 1884, after the premiere of his one-act *Le Villi*, one of Milan's best-known critics wrote: "We seem to have before us not a young student, but . . . the composer for whom Italy has long been waiting." It was nine years, however, before Puccini produced his first widely recognized success, *Manon Lescaut*.

There followed over the next dozen years *La Bohème* (1896), *Tosca* (1900), and *Madama Butterfly* (1904)—not all of them well received at first, but all eventually winning international fame and popularity for Puccini. While in the U.S. in 1907 for the Metropolitan Opera's first production of *Madama Butterfly*, he accepted the Met's commission to write an opera on an American subject. The result was *La Fanciulla del West* (*Girl of the Golden West*)—the first operatic "western." (At the premiere in 1910, Toscanini conducted and Enrico Caruso and Emmy Destinn headed the cast.)

Puccini's later operas—*La Rondine, Suor Angelica, Il Tabarro*, and *Gianni Schicchi*— failed to win the popular success of his earlier works, and he died before completing the last scene of *Turandot*, his most ambitious blending of orchestral, choral, and solo vocal writing. He worked almost exclusively in opera, and once declared: "The only music I can or will make is that of small things . . . so long as they are true and full of passion and humanity and touch the heart."

La Bohème

One of the four or five most popular of all operas, *La Bohème* (pronunced boh-*aim* and translated as "The Bohemian Life") is based on a French novel by Henri Murger about student artist life on the Left Bank in Paris in the 1830's—the days of cobblestone streets and cold, candlelit garrets. The story involves a penniless group of young artists, and ranges from their gay camaraderie and "seventh heaven" romances to heartbreak and despair—"a sentimental romantic comedy with a sad ending," as one annotator has called it. To some critics, the characters are Puccini's most sharply etched and well rounded, and his music some of the most warmly melodic and appealing in all opera. In *Puccini: A Biography*, George R. Marek goes further: "Puccini accomplished something in the opera. He combined his gift for writing good tunes with a new ability to set weekday conversations to music." To those who criticized the opera for its sentimentality, Puccini replied: "It is said that sentimentality is a sign of weakness. However, I find weakness beautiful."

Recommended Recordings (Complete Opera)

★ Karajan (conductor), Freni (Mimi), Pavarotti (Rodolfo), Harwood (Musetta), Panerai (Marcello), Ghiaurov (Colline), Berlin Philharmonic Orchestra, Berlin Deutsche Opera Chorus (London stereo 2-disc set OSA-1299)

Schippers (conductor), Freni (Mimi), Gedda (Rodolfo), Adani (Musetta), Sereni (Marcello), Mazzoli (Colline), Rome Opera Orchestra & Chorus (Angel stereo 2-disc set S-3643)

Serafin (conductor), Tebaldi (Mimi), Bergonzi (Rodolfo), D'Angelo (Musetta), Bastianini (Marcello), Siepi (Colline), Santa Cecilia (Rome) Orchestra & Chorus (London stereo 2-disc set OSA-1208)

b Beecham (conductor), De los Angeles (Mimi), Bjoerling (Rodolfo), Amara (Musetta), Merrill (Marcello), Tozzi (Colline), RCA Orchestra and Chorus (Seraphim stereo 2-disc set 6000, *mono only*)

b Toscanini (conductor), Albanese (Mimi), Peerce (Rodolfo), McKnight (Musetta), Valentino (Marcello), NBC Symphony and Chorus (RCA Victrola 2-disc set VICS-6019)

Recommended Recordings (Highlights)

★ Schippers, Freni, Gedda, etc., as above (Angel stereo disc S-36199; cassette 4XS-36199; cartridge 8XS-36199)

Serafin, Tebaldi, Bergonzi, etc., as above (London stereo disc CS-25201)

Leinsdorf (conductor), Moffo (Mimi), Tucker (Roldolfo), Costa (Musetta), Merrill (Marcello), Tozzi (Colline), Rome Opera Orchestra & Chorus (RCA Red Seal stereo disc LSC-2655; cassette RK-1077; cartridge R8S-1077; also quadrasonic cartridge RQ8-1077)

Comments

Karajan leads a sonically luxurious, romantically caressing performance that some critics have labeled more Viennese *schmaltz* than Italian *verismo*. Be that as it may, his 1973 recording is a beautiful one—especially for the fresh and youthful, ardent yet tender sound of Pavarotti and Freni as the ill-fated lovers. And while pacing the performance broadly enough for his singers to make the most of Puccini's melodies, Karajan and London's stereo engineers bring out more orchestral nuances than any previous *Bohème* has done. There are weaknesses: Act Two is a bit leaden, and Harwood is only fair as Musetta. But overall, the pluses of Pavarotti, Freni, Karajan, and London's sound are strong ones.

Freni is also the Mimi for Schippers' 1964 recording, and she sings the role almost as affectingly. Schippers leads a brisker performance than Karajan, yet a warmly lyrical one that emphasizes the opera's youthful spirit and romantic fervor. Gedda starts out unevenly, but is splendid in the last two acts. Adani, however, is not a very interesting Musetta. If you don't want too gushy a *Bohème* but a basically good one overall, then this one's for you.

Serafin's 1960 recording is more leisurely paced than Schippers' but not as much as Karajan's. Tebaldi and Bergonzi engage in some voluptuously creamy singing, and D'Angelo is a delightful Musetta. The sound engineering is overly resonant as far as the singers are concerned (almost as if they were at the other end of the hall from the orchestra), but still very clear and lush. (*Note:* An earlier Tebaldi mono recording, still available on Richmond, is no match for the 1960 version sonically, although Tebaldi's singing is quite beautiful.)

Beecham's mono-only recording from the mid-1950's has long been a favorite of many critics for its lyrical beauty and lack of gushiness, and for the memorable singing of Bjoerling and De los Angeles. The mono sound remains satisfactory enough, especially at budget-label prices.

Toscanini's 1946 recording is taken from two "live" performances (two acts at a time) that he broadcast for the fiftieth anniversary of the opera's premiere (which he, at twenty-seven, had conducted). It is an exciting performance by some standards, a horror by others. Musically the performance is supercharged, with especially poignant singing by Albanese. But there is an additional singer whom neither Puccini nor the broadcast engineers had planned on: Toscanini himself—who hums, sings, and groans along audibly throughout the performance. Although originally released in mono only, the recording was "electronically rechanneled" for stereo in its 1968 Victrola rerelease—a process that has somewhat improved the "dead" acoustics of the original.

The Leinsdorf-Moffo-Tucker highlights are from a 1962 recording of the complete opera in which Moffo projects Mimi's changing moods uncommonly well both vocally and dramatically, and with Tucker probably the most passionate Rodolfo on records. A quadrasonic cartridge version of these excerpts was released in 1973.

Tosca

Puccini saw Sarah Bernhardt act the title role of Sardou's melodramatic play *Tosca* five years before he set it to music. In between, there were a series of intrigues involving Puccini, his librettist, and his publishers before the rights could be cleared—and in the process Puccini earned the undying enmity of another composer, Alberto Franchetti, who had originally owned the rights. (Verdi was also reportedly interested in the rights at this same time.) Puccini and his librettists turned Sardou's play into one of the most taut and exciting operas ever written, with a title role that has become a favorite of almost every prima donna—which is not surprising, since the title character is a temperamental prima donna! The music is colorful and often beautiful, even though the opera was considered brutal in its time because of its depiction of police torture, an attempted rape, and an onstage execution, among other things. The action takes place in Rome in June of 1800, and is based on historic events during Napoleon's fight to control the Italian states. A Roman prima donna (Floria Tosca) and her lover, a painter with republican sympathies, become involved in the political skulduggery of the despotic chief of Rome's police (Baron Scarpia), and it all ends most melodramatically.

Recommended Recordings (Complete Opera)

★ Karajan (conductor), Price (Tosca), Di Stefano (Mario), Taddei (Scarpia) Vienna Philharmonic & Vienna Opera Chorus (London stereo 2-disc set 1284; cartridge D-31170)

DeSabata (conductor), Callas (Tosca), Di Stefano (Mario), Gobbi (Scarpia), La Scala Milan Orchestra & Chorus (Angel 2-disc set 3508, *mono only*)

Prêtre (conductor), Callas (Tosca), Bergonzi (Mario), Gobbi (Scarpia), Paris Conservatory Orchestra & Paris Opera Chorus (Angel stereo 2-disc set S-3655)

b Leinsdorf (conductor), Milanov (Tosca), Bjoerling (Mario), Warren (Scarpia), Rome Opera Orchestra & Chorus (RCA Victrola stereo 2-disc set VICS-6000; cartridge V8S-1022)

Recommended Recordings (Highlights)

★ Karajan, Price, Di Stefano, Taddei, etc., as above (London stereo disc OS-25218)

Prêtre, Callas, Bergonzi, Gobbi, etc., as above (Angel stereo disc S-36326; cassette 4XS-36326; cartridge 8XS-36326)

Comments

Tosca is the role which marked Leontyne Price's nationwide opera debut in 1955 with the NBC Opera, and her 1962 recording combines vocal beauty with the special Price warmth and intensity. Di Stefano and Taddei are both very good when they don't push their top range. Karajan's pacing is broad and dramatic, and the sound engineering is excellent. (This performance was originally released on RCA Red Seal, but was transferred to London in 1970 under a contractual arrangement involving the producer.)

Callas' two recordings date from 1953 and 1965. The earlier one (3508) finds her voice in much better shape, and her dramatic use of it peerless. Gobbi's earlier Scarpia has rarely been equaled for its sinister power, Di Stefano is excellent, and DeSabata's conducting has excitement and flair. The 1965 stereo version has much better sound, but the intervening years had not been kind to Callas' voice—it is more shrill, wobbly, and sometimes piercingly unattractive. Yet in a role like this, Callas can still carry a listener along by the sheer drama and excitement of her performance. Gobbi is almost as good as he was earlier, Bergonzi is splendid, and Prêtre conducts with drive and dramatic tension.

It is a shame that Milanov could not have recorded her Tosca a few years earlier than she did in 1956, for she projects the role with tremendous flair, although not always with the vocal beauty and consistency of tone of earlier days. Bjoerling, too, strains a bit, but he still sings with notable lyric beauty. Warren is exceptional in the way he conveys a simultaneously suave and sinister characterization, and in the way he really *sings* a role which many others just snarl or declaim. Leinsdorf's pacing is taut and dramatic, and the sound engineering holds up well.

For Follow-Up Consideration

Madama Butterfly, a tragic, sentimental, and exotic work which has become one of the most popular of all operas. It is also a great lyric *prima donna's* opera, for the tenor disappears in the first act and returns only briefly in the last. Adapted from an American play by David Belasco (in turn based on a reportedly true story by John Luther Long), the opera is set in Japan in 1900, and tells the story of a Japanese girl who marries an American Navy lieutenant with tragic results. Although Puccini used several authentic Japanese themes and coloristic effects in the opera, the work is essentially Italian in mood and musical approach. RECOMMENDED RECORDING: Leinsdorf (conductor), Price (Butterfly), Tucker (Pinkerton), Elias (Suzuki), Maero (Sharpless), RCA Italiana Opera Orchestra and Chorus (*complete*—RCA Red Seal stereo 3-disc set LSC-6160; *highlights*—RCA Red Seal stereo disc LSC-2840; cassette RK-1048; cartridge R8S-1048 and RQ8-1048), one of the all-time great opera recordings (1962), with Price at her overwhelming best in the title role, soaring with intense emotion and vocal beauty throughout. Leinsdorf leads a consistently exciting, deeply touching performance. (A quadrasonic cartridge of highlights only was released in 1973.)

Turandot, Puccini's uncompleted last opera, almost his masterpiece. It is his most ambitious blending of orchestral, choral, and solo vocal lines, and more advanced than any of his previous works in harmony, even introducing polyharmony. The title role is regarded as one of the most devilishly difficult in opera (one of the reasons it is not performed too often). The story takes place in China during legendary times, and concerns a cold-blooded princess who has promised to marry any man of noble blood who can solve three special riddles—and who meets her match in the son of a dethroned Tartar king. Puccini finished the opera up to the last two scenes in Act III; those two were completed by Franco Alfano from Puccini's sketches. RECOMMENDED RECORDING: Leinsdorf (conductor), Nilsson (Turandot), Bjoerling (Calaf), Tebaldi (Liu), Tozzi (Timur), Rome Opera Orchestra & Chorus (*complete*—RCA stereo Red Seal LSC-6149; *highlights*—RCA Red Seal disc LSC-2539), a 1959 release that has yet to be topped (even by a later Nilsson–Corelli recording for Angel), a throbbingly exciting, superbly sung performance all the way.

All of the recordings listed above are sung in the original Italian.

• *GUSTAV MAHLER*

Pronounced: *mah*-ler. Born July 7, 1860, in Kalischt, Bohemia. Died May 18, 1911, in Vienna.

SIGNIFICANCE: Bohemian composer and conductor, last of the great Romantic symphonists; a composer of massive, intensely expressive and profound orchestral music and song cycles.

BACKGROUND: Mahler, the son of a poor Jewish innkeeper, studied music in Prague and Vienna (winning both piano and composition prizes at the Vienna Conservatory). In his thirties he became one of Europe's most famous conductors—first in Prague, then in Budapest and Hamburg. In 1900 he became director of the Vienna State Opera, and set standards of performance over the next six years that were the talk of Europe. But he grew increasingly unpopular with many of his colleagues—partly through anti-Semitism and partly because of his dictatorial working habits—and he was forced to resign. The following year, the New York Philharmonic named him its music director at what was, to that time, the highest salary ever paid a symphony conductor anywhere: $30,000 a year. But his tenure in New York was to be brief because of illness.

Throughout most of his life, Mahler led a full conducting schedule during the winter months, but reserved the summer for composing. He gave most of his works a literary or philosophical theme in the Romantic tradition. But he also foreshadowed more modern directions by his use of "progressive tonality" (beginning a movement in one key and leading it toward an ending in another key) and some of the devices of serial music. He sometimes combined instrumental, choral, and solo vocal parts in works of enormous scope ("A symphony is like the world—it must embrace everything," he once said).

During the first half of the 20th century, Mahler's music was rarely performed, except by such disciples as conductor Bruno Walter. "My time will come," Mahler had said—and indeed it did, in the 1950's and 1960's. Impassioned championing by Leonard Bernstein, Dimitri Mitropoulos, and a few others played a big role. So, too, did the coming of the hi-fi/stereo age—for Mahler's massive, often sonically overwhelming symphonies pulled out all the stops not only for an orchestra but for recording engineers as well. Says critic-essayist Herbert Reid: "He does not spare today's generation of listeners [from] . . . stretching their emotional range." And author David Hall adds: "The circumstances of war, of overdeveloped technology and underdeveloped humanity . . . have posed hard-core questions of faith in human destiny that Mahler, as a solitary individual, tried to answer."

Symphony No. 1 in D ("Titan")

From his very first symphony, composed when he was in his twenties, Mahler sought to expand the limits of symphonic form. Originally, he subtitled the First Symphony

"Titan"—after a novel by Jean-Paul (Johann Paul Friedrich Richter) "for whose emotional abundance, boundless fantasy, and grotesque humor [Mahler] felt a deep affinity," to quote Bruno Walter. Mahler also gave descriptive titles to each of its five movements: (1) "Spring without End," (2) "Blumine" ("Flowers"), (3) "Under Full Sail," (4) "The Hunter's Funeral Procession," and (5) "From Inferno to Paradiso." Later he withdrew all the titles except the fourth, and dropped the "Blumine" movement from the published score (reportedly at his publisher's urging, and reluctantly). However, he continued to defend the use of subtitles as guides to the general atmosphere of a work, saying: "During the first period, when my style may still seem strange and new, the listener gets some word maps and milestones on the journey . . . but such an explanation cannot offer more." Mahler's First is a large-scale symphony of dramatic contrasts. It is full of trumpet calls and marching rhythms. It has quiet, lyrical pastoral moments and catchy peasant dances (one movement uses the folk song "Frère Jacques" or "Bruder Martin"). It has moments of grotesque black humor ("The Hunter's Funeral Procession" refers to an engraving by Jacques Callot showing a procession of dancing animals escorting the body of a dead hunter to the grave). And in its awesome finale all the major previous themes recur—including the "Blumine," which some conductors say justifies restoring the dropped movement—before the movement's own theme finally emerges in blazing glory.

Recommended Recordings

★ Ormandy, Philadelphia Orchestra (RCA Red Seal stereo disc LSC-3107; cassette RK-1133; cartridge R8S-1133)

b Walter, Columbia Symphony Orchestra (Odyssey stereo disc Y-30047)

Haitink, Amsterdam Concertgebouw Orchestra (Philips stereo disc 6500-342)

Kubelik, Bavarian Radio Symphony (Deutsche Grammophon stereo disc 139331; cassette 923070; cartridge 89-331)

b Brieff, New Haven Symphony (Odyssey stereo disc 32160286)

Comments

Ormandy's 1969 performance pulsates with drama, excitement, interpretive depth, breadth, and tonal grandeur. It includes the long-lost and recently rediscovered "Blumine" movement—a sentimental morsel which the Philadelphians play sweetly. The sound is impressively spacious throughout, and the finale is especially eloquent.

Bruno Walter's performance of the traditional four-movement version was recorded in Los Angeles a year before his death in 1962, and is one of his most powerful recorded legacies. The performance has depth, warmth, sparkle, and grandeur, and the sound engineering is excellent.

Haitink's 1973 release (traditional four movements) is impressive for the spaciousness and vividness of Haitink's interpretation, and for the beautifully lucid, deeply felt playing of the Concertgebouw Orchestra. Haitink leads a much more forceful performance for this recording than he did for an earlier one of the First in 1963 (Philips 900017).

Kubelik stresses the more lyrical side of the four-movement version in his 1968 release, achieving strength and nobility without the open emotional intensity of Walter, Ormandy, or Haitink.

Brieff's is the only other five-movement version besides Ormandy's—in fact, it was the first, in 1968. The New Haven Symphony gives a good performance, well paced, dramatic, and compelling, but only moderately well recorded.

Symphony No. 2 in C minor ("Resurrection")

If Mahler had written no other work, his Second Symphony (completed in 1894, when he was thirty-four) would certainly place him among the great composers. It is a monumental, mystical, heavens-storming work about the meaning of life. To quote annotator William Mann, it "takes the form of a funeral address, dwelling on sorrow and the transitory nature of existence, the hope of better things, the happy memory of past joys, the hectic chaos of competition, and then . . . innocent childish faith which moves mountains and allows the believer to survive, yes to float through, the ultimate ordeal of the Last Judgment." Nearly an hour and a half long, the symphony requires not only a large orchestra but also a chorus, two vocal soloists, an organ, and an offstage brass band. The first three movements are purely orchestral. The first is an alternately stormy and lyrical dirge (to quote Mahler: "We are standing beside the coffin of one dearly loved . . . [and ask] is it all a hollow dream, or does our life have meaning?"). The second is a gentle Ländler, a triple-time folk dance of Austria. The third is an ironic, desparing scherzo ("A recollection of the world's vulgarities," said Mahler, and its "spirit of negation"). The fourth movement is a hushed and haunting song for mezzo-soprano, "*Urlicht*" ("Primal Light")—taken from Mahler's earlier song cycle *Des Knaben Wunderhorn* (The Youth's Magic Horn), based on German folk poetry. The fifth movement is an apocalyptic portrait of the Day of Judgment, climaxed by a choral setting of the "Resurrection Ode" by the 18th-century German poet Klopstock (extended by Mahler with words of his own)—ending jubilantly as "an overwhelming Love shines," to quote Mahler, "we know and are."

Recommended Recordings

★ Bernstein, Tourel, Venora, New York Philharmonic, Collegiate Chorale (Columbia stereo 2-disc set M2S-695)

Haitink, Ameling, Heynis, Amsterdam Concertgebouw Orchestra, Netherlands Radio Chorus (Philips stereo 2-disc set 802884/5)

b Abravanel, Sills, Kopleff, Utah Symphony, University of Utah Civic Chorale (Vanguard-Cardinal stereo 2-disc set C-10003/4)

b Walter, Forrester, Cundari, New York Philharmonic, Westminster Choir (Odyssey stereo 2-disc set Y2-30848)

Solti, Harper, Watts, London Symphony Orchestra and Chorus (London stereo 2-disc set 2217; cassette D-10187)

Comments

Bernstein's performance is one of his most memorable. The symphony obviously means much to Bernstein personally, for he conducted it at one of his first Tanglewood concerts in the 1940's, chose to play it in a Rome concert on Easter Sunday of the 1950

Holy Year, picked it for his John F. Kennedy memorial concert on CBS-TV two days after the President's assassination in 1963, led it at the historic Mount Scopus concert of the Israel Philharmonic in 1967 following the liberation of all of Jerusalem, and chose it for his record-breaking 1000th concert with the New York Philharmonic in 1971. Over the years, moreover, Bernstein has learned to communicate the depths of this symphony with more drama, poetry, ironic bite, and spiritual vigor than any other conductor. And in the finale he blends the massive orchestral forces with the organ, soloists, and chorus in an ever-building, almost time-suspending climax whose emotional impact is staggering. The sound engineers have matched Bernstein's obvious dedication with a recording (dating from 1964) of admirable clarity and definition.

Haitink's 1969 release is outstanding in every respect—a compelling, penetrating, powerful achievement. It does not have the open-hearted passion of Bernstein's, but it has its own magical poetry, depth of feeling, and dramatic excitement. The playing of the Amsterdam orchestra is first-rate, and the sound engineering is excellent—especially for the tremendous finale.

Abravanel's 1967 release is also outstanding—not the least for being on a budget label. He brings power, poignance, sweep, bite, and eloquence to his performance, and the sound engineering is first-rate. The soloists are especially good.

Bruno Walter's performance was once the touchstone for this work, but others have since come to speak just as eloquently for it—and to have the advantage of better sound engineering than Walter had in the late 1950's. Yet Walter's performance has a special warmth, nobility, and strength that still shine through beautifully.

Solti's 1967 recording plays down the emotional excesses of the score, and stresses the dramatic conflict and lyrical elements of the work. The sound engineering is excellent.

Das Lied von der Erde (*The Song of the Earth*)

To many, Mahler's song cycles are the essence of Mahler, and *The Song of the Earth* his supreme achievement. Bruno Walter once went so far as to call it the greatest work in all music. Subtitled "A Symphony for Tenor, Contralto (or Baritone), and Orchestra," it is a profoundly moving song cycle based on old Chinese poems about youth, natural beauty, loneliness, life, and death. Mahler began the work shortly after the death of one of his daughters, and after learning that he himself had an incurable heart ailment. Musicologist and Mahler expert Deryck Cooke has written: "He found himself face-to-face with death as an existential reality—as the imminent cessation of his own life. If his earlier works had been full of *images* of immortality, this one is permeated with the bitter *taste* of mortality." This is not to imply that the work is filled with despair. On the contrary, it is a loving testament to the mysteries of life—ending with the words: "The dear earth everywhere blossoms in spring and grows green again/Everywhere and eternally the distance shines bright and blue/Forever . . . forever . . . forever. . . ." In contrast to the massive power of most of Mahler's symphonies, the orchestral texture of *The Song of the Earth* is blended as subtly and sensitively as Chinese watercolors.

Recommended Recordings

★ Bernstein, Fischer-Dieskau, King, Vienna Philharmonic (London stereo disc OS-26005)

b Walter, Ferrier, Patzak, Vienna Philharmonic (Richmond disc R-23182, *mono only*)

b Walter, Miller, Haefliger, Columbia Symphony (Odyssey stereo disc Y-30043)

Klemperer, Ludwig, Wunderlich, New Philharmonia (Angel stereo 2-disc set S-3704)

Solti, Minton, Kollo, Chicago Symphony (London stereo disc 26292)

Comments

Bernstein's 1966 recording brings to the music a unified flow, intensity, depth, and power that almost stretch the limits of emotional endurance. Bernstein uses a baritone rather than a contralto (Mahler made it optional)—and since his baritone is the remarkable Fischer-Dieskau, even those who (like this writer) prefer a contralto sound in this music must admit that rarely will we ever hear an account of the lyrics so meaningfully complete as this one. Fischer-Dieskau is infinitely more subtle and expressive than he was in an earlier recording with Kletski (Angel 2-disc set S-3607). Tenor King sings with fervor if little subtlety. The recorded sound is splendid.

Bruno Walter gave the world premiere of this work six months after Mahler's death in 1911, and made three recordings (in 1936 with Thorborg and Kullmann, in 1952 with Ferrier and Patzak, and in 1960 with Miller and Haefliger). The 1952 version is particularly outstanding for the matchless nobility and tenderness of Ferrier's singing. Originally available in a 2-disc album (London 4212), it was reissued on a single, budget-priced disc in 1973. Its mono sound holds up better than some other companies' later stereo.

Walter's 1960 stereo recording, originally on Columbia and transferred to that company's budget label in 1972, has the best sound of his three versions. Haefliger is splendid, and Miller sings with sincerity and feeling, if not with the sublimity of Ferrier.

Klemperer's 1966 release is thoughtful and probing, though occasionally ponderous. Ludwig sings the finest contralto version of the score since Ferrier, and Wunderlich's performance is excitingly ardent. The fourth side of this 2-LP edition contains five other Mahler songs beautifully sung by Ludwig.

Solti's performance is more emotionally restrained than Bernstein's or Walter's, but more dramatically forceful than Klemperer's. Minton sings beautifully and compellingly, but Kollo is disappointing. The sound engineering of this 1973 release is outstanding.

For Follow-Up Consideration

Symphony No. 3 in D minor, a profoundly moving work which opens with one of the most mammoth marches in all music, then settles down to more serene but deeply poignant sections, including one for mezzo-soprano and chorus. RECOMMENDED RECORDING: Bernstein, Lipton, New York Philharmonic, Schola Cantorum, etc. (Columbia stereo 2-disc set M2S-675), an intensely moving 1961 performance, one of the finest Bernstein has put on records.

Symphony No. 4 in G major, Mahler's shortest symphony, and one of his most melodically appealing. The final movement is a song for soprano and orchestra depicting a child's view of paradise. RECOMMENDED RECORDING: Bernstein, Grist, New York Philharmonic (Columbia stereo disc MS-6152), a glowingly warm 1960 recording with an especially beautiful final movement.

Symphony No. 5 in C sharp minor, a large-scale mixture of songful melodies, marches, waltzes, and an *adagietto* (fourth movement) that must be one of the most beautiful movements any symphony can claim, and which was used in the film *Death in Venice*. RECOMMENDED RECORDING: Haitink, Amsterdam Concertgebouw (Philips stereo 2-disc set 6700-048), a tremendously forceful, deeply probing performance, with a searingly intense, almost time-suspending performance of the *adagietto* movement. The coupling on this 1972 release is an equally splendid Haitink performance of the only fully completed movement from Mahler's Tenth Symphony (in F sharp).

Symphony No. 6 in A minor, which Mahler called his "Tragic" Symphony; a somber and dramatically profound work, which Bruno Walter described as "reeking of the bitter cup of life." RECOMMENDED RECORDING: Solti, Chicago Symphony (London 2-disc set 2227), a tremendously compelling, surging 1970 performance, with some of the best sound any company has ever put on records with an American orchestra. Solti uses the Mahler Society's 1963 Critical Edition, which reverses the second and third movements (based on evidence that that's the way Mahler wanted it, contrary to his publisher). The coupling is a restrained yet eloquent performance of the *Songs of the Wayfarer* by Australian contralto Yvonne Minton with Solti and the Chicago Symphony.

Symphony No. 8 in E flat, the so-called "Symphony of a Thousand" because of the huge number of instrumentalists, vocal soloists, and choristers required; part one is less interesting than part two, a deeply moving setting of the closing scene of Goethe's *Faust*. RECOMMENDED RECORDING: Bernstein, London Symphony Orchestra, choruses, eight soloists (Columbia stereo 2-disc set M2S-751), a 1966 release which, like Bernstein's recording of Mahler's Second, is overwhelming in its emotional intensity and dramatic impact.

Symphony No. 9 in D, a long, brooding, but powerfully expressive, purely orchestral work which some critics call the sphinx among Mahler's symphonies, an enigma poised between Romantic and modern styles. RECOMMENDED RECORDING: Walter, Columbia Symphony Orchestra (Odyssey stereo 2-disc set Y-30308), a profoundly moving 1962 performance that ranks among Walter's all-time finest.

Des Knaben Wunderhorn (*The Youth's Magic Horn*), a setting of songs from German folk poetry (sometimes light, sometimes somber, sometimes macabre) for soprano, baritone, and orchestra. RECOMMENDED RECORDING: Szell, Schwarzkopf, Fischer-Dieskau, London Symphony Orchestra (Angel stereo disc S-36547; cassette 4XS-36547; cartridge 8XS-36547), a 1968 performance of rare style and poetic profundity by two of the greatest *lieder* singers of our time.

Lieder eines Fahrenden Gesellen (*Songs of a Wayfarer*), a set of bittersweet, folkloric songs for contralto (or baritone) and orchestra, written when Mahler was twenty-three. RECOMMENDED RECORDINGS: *With a contralto*—Baker, Barbirolli, Hallé Orchestra (Angel stereo disc S-36465), a 1969 release noteworthy for its poetic insight and beauty of musical line; the coupling is a deeply moving *Kindertotenlieder* (*Songs for Dead Children*). *With a baritone*—Prey, Haitink, Amsterdam Concertgebouw Orchestra (Philips stereo disc 6500-100), a searchingly expressive, beautifully sung performance, released in 1972, and coupled with a strong, dignified *Kindertotenlieder.*

• CLAUDE DEBUSSY

Pronounced: deh-bew-*see*. Born August 22, 1862, in St. Germain-en-Laye, France. Died March 26, 1918, in Paris.

SIGNIFICANCE: French composer and critic, father of Impressionistic music, which creates or reflects a mood or image rather than relating a dramatic sequence. Impressionism takes its name from its kinship with Impressionist painting and poetry of the late 19th and early 20th century.

BACKGROUND: The poverty of Debussy's parents led them to turn over their children to a well-to-do aunt when things got particularly difficult. And it was she who started Debussy on his musical studies. At the age of eleven, he successfully passed the exams for admission to the Paris Conservatory. As a student he experimented with revolutionary harmonies and progressions despite the opposition of his professors. Increasingly, he rebelled against the emotional excesses of German Romanticism, and sought to develop a more subtle, more original style.

His first significant effort was the sensitive orchestral prelude *The Afternoon of the Faun* (1894). It was followed by the *Nocturnes for Orchestra, La Mer* (*The Sea*), *Jeux* (*Games*), *The Martyrdom of St. Sebastian*, and *Images for Orchestra.* In his only opera, *Pelléas and Mélisande* (1902), he completely broke away from 19th-century traditions by supplanting arias with recitatives more closely resembling speech (using the unique sounds of the French language) and by using the orchestra to create an Impressionistic atmosphere. Debussy also wrote many piano pieces, some of which have been orchestrated by others—such as the popular "Clair de Lune" ("Moonlight"). Debussy suffered from cancer during the last ten years of his life, with its intense pain complicated by the harsh living conditions during World War I and his financial problems.

Prélude à l'Après-Midi d'un Faune (Prelude to the Afternoon of a Faun)

Despite its brevity (nine and a half minutes), this sensuously beautiful, perfectly sculptured work laid the foundations of Impressionistic orchestral music. Inspired by Malarmè's poem *L'Après-Midi d'un Faune* (*The Afternoon of a Faun*), the piece evokes the delicate atmosphere of the dreams of a faun on a hot summer afternoon. Its premiere in 1894, when Debussy was thirty-two, was an instant success. Says composer-conductor Pierre Boulez: "Just as modern poetry is rooted in certain poems of Baudelaire, one is justified in saying that modern music awakens with the premiere of *The Afternoon of a Faun.*"

Recommended Recordings

★ Boulez, New Philharmonia of London (Columbia stereo disc MS-7361)

   Munch, Boston Symphony (RCA Red Seal stereo disc LSC-2668; cartridge R8S-5043)

b Munch, Boston Symphony (RCA Victrola stereo disc VICS-1323; cartridge V8S-1033)

   Thomas, Boston Symphony (Deutsche Grammophon stereo disc 2530145; cassette 3300187; cartridge 89438)

Comments

The Boulez performance, from 1966, is plastic and sensuous. It is part of a superb Debussy album (with *La Mer* and *Jeux*) that boosted Boulez's growing reputation as a conductor prior to his appointment to succeed Bernstein as music director of the New York Philharmonic in 1971.

Munch's two recordings are both beautifully evocative and poetic. The 1962 version (on RCA Red Seal) has better sound, and is coupled with excellent Munch performances of *Printemps* (Springtime) and two of Debussy's *Nocturnes* ("*Nuages*" and "*Fetes*"—"Clouds" and "Festivals"). The cartridge also contains *La Mer*, as well as early 1960's performances of Ravel's *La Valse, Bolero,* and *Pavane for a Dead Princess.* Munch's earlier version, on RCA's budget-priced Victrola, dates from the mid-1950's and is coupled with exhilarating performances of Ravel's *La Valse* and *Bolero,* and Ibert's *Escales (Ports of Call).*

Thomas, a former assistant to Boulez, leads Munch's former orchestra in his 1971 release. It interestingly blends the clarity of Boulez's approach with the intensity and tonal warmth of Munch, and the orchestral sound is beautifully mellow. It is coupled with a vividly atmospheric performance of Debussy's complete *Images for Orchestra (Gigues, Rondes de Printemps,* and *Iberia).*

Nocturnes for Orchestra

Following the success of the *Prelude to the Afternoon of a Faun,* Debussy wrote this longer work evoking the mood or atmosphere of three scenes: (1) "*Nuages*" ("Clouds"), reflecting the "slow, solemn motion of clouds, fading away in gray tones tinged with white," to quote the composer; 2) "*Fêtes*" ("Festivals"), with restless, flashing rhythms including those of a passing procession; and (3) "*Sirènes*" ("Sirens," after the ancient Greek myths), depicting a glistening sea in the moonlight, with waves splashing against the rocks from which the Sirens sing their seductive melody. In the final section, Debussy employs a small women's chorus in addition to the orchestra; because of this the first two sections are frequently performed independently.

Recommended Recordings

★ Ansermet, Suisse Romande Orchestra (complete) (London stereo disc CS-6023)

   Boulez, New Philharmonia (complete) (Columbia stereo disc M-30483)

b Monteux, Boston Symphony (complete) (RCA Victrola stereo disc VICS-1027)

b Stokowski, London Symphony (complete) (Seraphim stereo disc S-60104)

Comments

Ansermet weaves the most subtle of tone colors throughout the complete work, giving a sensuously beautiful and atmospheric performance. It is coupled with a similarly beautiful performance of the rarely played complete ballet score of Ravel's *Ma Mère l'Oye* (*Mother Goose*). The 1959 sound engineering holds up splendidly.

Boulez's 1968 recording is magical in its combination of orchestral clarity and haunting mood. The *"Fêtes"* section, in particular, has a rhythmic cleanness and instrumental unity rarely heard in this section of the work. Overside on this all-Debussy set (entitled "Boulez Conducts Debussy, Vol. 3"), Boulez offers an unusually spacious *Printemps* (*Springtime*), and a fine account of the sportive Rhapsody for Clarinet and Orchestra, with De Peyer as clarinet soloist.

Monteux's performance is less sensual than Ansermet's and less refined than Boulez's, but he leads an orchestra capable of more marvelously rich tone colors. Overside, Monteux leads a lively and colorful *Firebird* Suite (Stravinsky). The mid-1950's sonics hold up well. (*Note:* A later Monteux–London Symphony performance on London CS-6248 is not as interesting, nor is it complete—omitting *"Sirènes"*).

Stokowski paints a haunting sonic picture, with an especially atmospheric *"Sirènes"* section. The coupling is a colorful Stokowski performance of Ravel's *Rapsodie Espagnole*. The sound engineering, from about 1960, is good.

La Mer (The Sea)

The late English composer-conductor Constant Lambert described *La Mer* (in his book *Music Ho!*) as "a landscape without figures, or rather a seascape without ships." It is just the sea—with its shimmery surface and restless currents, as one might impressionistically feel it while gazing out alone over open waters. Some critics have called *La Mer* a symphonic poem or even the first great Impressionist symphony. Debussy called the work merely "three symphonic sketches," and gave subtitles to its three parts: "From Dawn to Noon on the Sea," "Play of the Waves," and "Dialogue between the Wind and the Sea." The subtitles are meant only as clues to the atmosphere of the music, not to describe a specific scene—although Erik Satie once joshingly told Debussy that he particularly liked the passage in the first movement "at about a quarter to twelve."

Recommended Recordings

★ b Munch, Boston Symphony (RCA Victrola stereo disc VICS-1041; cartridge V8S-1040)

   Boulez, New Philharmonia (Columbia stereo disc MS-7361)

Ansermet, Suisse Romande Orchestra (London stereo disc CS-6437)

Ormandy, Philadelphia Orchestra (RCA Red Seal quadrasonic disc ARD1-0029; cassette ARK1-0029; cartridge ARS1-0029)

Comments

Munch's performance has excitement, mystery, brilliant colors, and a relentless surge. The Boston Symphony Orchestra plays radiantly, and the mid-1950's sound engineering is still adequately bright, if occasionally strident. Overside, Munch offers an exuberant performance of Ravel's *Rapsodie Espagnole*.

Boulez illuminates the tonal textures and rhythmic pulse of the score with rare skill. His 1966 performance may not be quite as exciting as Munch's, but it is more subtly dynamic and prismatic. It is coupled with a beautiful *Afternoon of a Faun* and a brilliant *Jeux*.

Ansermet made three recordings of *La Mer*. His third and best (from about 1964) is a glittering performance, filled with marvelous coloristic details and subtle nuances. Overside, Ansermet offers two rarely recorded Debussy works: the dark and eerie ballet score *Khamma* (orchestrated for Debussy by Charles Koechlin), and the sportive *Rhapsody for Clarinet and Orchestra* with Robert Gugholz as the excellent soloist.

Ormandy's 1973 release is the first quadrasonic *La Mer*, and for those with quadrasonic playback equipment the recording really puts you in the middle of the sea, surrounded by all sorts of tonal waves. Others will find Ormandy's performance more polished than penetrating, more effect than substance. Overside is a lushly played but interpretively bland account of Ravel's Suite No. 2 from *Daphnis and Chloé* and Debussy's *Afternoon of a Faun*.

For Follow-Up Consideration

Jeux (Games), written for a Diaghilev ballet about a three-cornered flirtation between a boy and two girls on a tennis court, and increasingly viewed by critics as one of Debussy's most inventive scores. RECOMMENDED RECORDING: Boulez, New Philharmonia Orchestra (Columbia stereo disc MS-7361), a beautifully lucid, teasingly sensuous 1967 performance, coupled with Boulez's outstanding versions of *La Mer* and *Afternoon of a Faun*.

The Martyrdom of St. Sebastian, incidental music for D'Annunzio's mystery play of 1911, and a score of quiet eloquence and mystical tenderness. RECOMMENDED RECORDING: Munch, Curtin, Kopleff, Akos, Boston Symphony, New England Conservatory Chorus (RCA Victrola stereo disc VICS-1404), a deeply moving, hauntingly beautiful performance, dating from the mid-1950's and still unequaled—even though RCA deleted Munch's eloquently-spoken narration when it transferred the performance to its budget-priced Victrola label in the mid-1960's.

Pelléas and Mélisande, the most important Impressionist opera, written to a text by Maeterlinck about two ill-fated lovers. RECOMMENDED RECORDING: Boulez, Shirley, Soederstroem, Minton, Royal Opera House Orchestra and Chorus of Covent Garden (Columbia stereo 3-disc set M3-30119), released in 1970, a masterfully spun, flesh-and-blood performance, in contrast to the "overrefined" approach this opera is usually given.

Piano Music. RECOMMENDED RECORDING: *Vasary Plays Debussy* (Deutsche Grammophon stereo disc 139458), including *Suite Bergamasque* (of which *"Clair de Lune"* is a part), *"L'Isle Joyeuse," "Masques," "Le Plus Que Lente," Tarantelle Styrienne,* and two *Arabesques*; a 1970 release that has much to recommend, both for the representative Debussy piano pieces it includes in one album and the quality of Vasary's playing. Excellent sound engineering.

• RICHARD STRAUSS

Pronounced: *shtrows.* Born June 11, 1864, in Munich, Germany. Died September 8, 1949, in Garmisch, (West) Germany.

SIGNIFICANCE: German conductor and composer of late Romantic symphonic poems and operas (no relation to Johann Strauss, the Viennese waltz king).

BACKGROUND: As a student, Strauss became a fierce disciple of Wagner, even though his father, a celebrated horn player, had organized bitter intrigues against Wagner and his music. Three years after leaving the University of Munich in 1882, Strauss became assistant to the well-known conductor Hans von Bülow, and eventually became chief conductor at Weimar, Berlin, and Munich.

Between 1887 and 1898, Strauss wrote a series of symphonic poems (sometimes called tone poems) that were strikingly original in their use of large orchestral forces—*Macbeth, Don Juan, Death and Transfiguration, Till Eulenspiegel's Merry Pranks, Thus Spake Zarathustra, Don Quixote,* and *A Hero's Life.* He turned primarily to opera after 1900, first with a series of heavily scored works on texts that were considered shocking in their time (*Salome, Elektra*), then with more subtle works that combined the tonal colors of Romanticism with more Classical elegance and simplicity (*Der Rosenkavalier, Ariadne auf Naxos, Arabella*). He also wrote some of the finest *lieder* since Schubert.

In his later years, controversy followed his acceptance of an official music post under the Nazi regime of Adolf Hitler in 1933, even though he resigned it in 1935 because the Nazis opposed his continuing to work on an opera with a libretto by Stefan Zweig, who was Jewish. He lived in virtual retirement in Bavaria during World War II, and died a few years after the war.

Till Eulenspiegels Lustige Streiche (Till Eulenspiegel's Merry Pranks)

The character of Till Eulenspiegel is as familiar to German children as Robin Hood is to English-speaking children. But Till's origins seem to be much more in doubt. Some say there really was a Till Eulenspiegel, and that he was Flemish (others say German) and that he lived in the 14th or 15th century. Stories about him began to appear in 15th-century German folk literature, and were frequently related to the growing peasant rebellion against the authority of church and state. Till even appears in 16th-century English literature as Tyl Owlglass (*Eulenspiegel*, in German, means owl's mirror). Whatever his origins, Till is now the legendary prototype of the gaily rebellious imp, prankster, or rapscallion—boldly and continually upsetting the respectable life of the conformist "Establishment." Strauss' musical characterization of Till is lusty and colorful, witty and lively. The fifteen-minute work, composed in 1895, calls for unusually large orchestral forces. Before its premiere, Strauss withdrew the literary program he had prepared. However, he did confide to one conductor that various episodes depict Till upsetting a marketplace, assuming the disguise of a monk and giving a mock sermon, trying to make love to a girl who isn't interested, twitting a group of pompous professors, being arrested and brought to trial for flouting authority, then thumbing his nose at his executioners in the belief that they are merely playing a joke on him—followed by a sudden strangled squeak and a deadly drum roll as Till plunges through the gallows' trap door. But the work does not end grimly, for suddenly Till's spirit reappears, defiantly demonstrating his immortality.

Recommended Recordings

★ b Leinsdorf, Philharmonia Orchestra (Seraphim stereo disc S-60097)

Munch, Boston Symphony (RCA Red Seal stereo disc LSC-2565; cartridge R8S-1018)

Böhm, Berlin Philharmonic (Deutsche Grammophon stereo disc 138866; cassette 923-120; cartridge 88-866)

b Toscanini, NBC Symphony (RCA Victrola disc VIC-1267, *mono only*)

Comments

Leinsdorf's performance has snap, sparkle, and a robust quality which has not often marked Leinsdorf's recorded work. The 1961 sound remains bright and spacious. The piece is coupled with a lush performance of the "Dance of the Seven Veils" from *Salome*, and Leinsdorf's own arrangement of a suite from one of Strauss' most beautiful operas, *Die Frau öhne Schätten* (*The Woman without a Shadow*).

Till has long been a specialty of the Boston Symphony Orchestra, and the orchestra's virtuosity shines through somewhat muddy sound engineering in Munch's lively, beguiling romp, dating from the early 1960's. It is coupled with a vibrant Munch performance of Tchaikovsky's *Romeo and Juliet*.

Böhm brings zest and ardor, if not always a light touch to his version, recorded in 1963. It is coupled with first-rate Böhm performances of Strauss' "Dance of the Seven Veils" from *Salome*, the *Festival Prelude*, and *Don Juan*.

Toscanini's mono-only 1952 performance was for many years one of his most highly acclaimed. Despite the dated sonics, its electricity and pungency remain impressive. It is coupled with an ardent *Don Juan* and a spirited performance of Dukas' *Sorcerer's Apprentice*.

Also Sprach Zarathustra (Thus Spake Zarathustra)

Zarathustra has become enormously popular in recent years—partly because of its use in the film *2001: A Space Odyssey*, and partly because of its reputation as a hi-fi soundbuster. Its opening is one of the most dramatic in all music, and just the sort to show off the qualities of a stereo system—with the lowest C of the organ laying down a solid bass while trumpets and kettledrums herald ever-building sonorities that soon explode in an awesome climax. Critic Herbert Reid says of the opening: "The world has been created, and we go on from there." As to the quality of the music that follows, most critics feel that banalities jostle with moments of great beauty and cleverness. The title is taken from the book of the same name by the 19th-century German philosopher Nietzsche. Strauss' tone poem (written in 1896) is not a literal setting of the book, but a loose, symbolic tribute to Nietzsche's ideas. Said Strauss: "I meant to convey musically an idea of the development of the human race from its origin, through the various phases of evolution, religious as well as scientific, up to Nietzsche's idea of the superman." This last point aroused considerable controversy for many years, particularly because of widespread associations of Nietzsche's superman theories with Hitler's Nazis. Writes George C. Marek, for many years head of RCA Victor's classical division, in a 1967 biography of Strauss: "Nietzsche has been widely misunderstood by Hitler's intellectual stooges on purpose. His superman is not a mindless and bigoted warrior armed to the teeth. He is a being who, through breeding, education, hard thinking, and harder egotism, rises above mediocrity and conformity. . . . [But] Nietzsche is not a lucid writer, and *Zarathustra* is probably the least lucid of his works." Moreover, in Strauss' version the superman arrives too late, as the bells toll midnight and the world runs out of time. The work ends softly and enigmatically on an unresolved chord, indicating that for all of Zarathustra's philosophy, life will always remain a mystery.

Recommended Recordings

★ Steinberg, Boston Symphony (Deutsche Grammophon stereo disc 2530160; cassette 3300185; cartridge 89436)

Mehta, Los Angeles Philharmonic (London stereo disc CS-6609; cassette M-10209)

Bernstein, New York Philharmonic (Columbia stereo disc M-30443; cassette MT-30443; also quadrasonic disc MQ-30443; cartridge MAQ-30443)

Reiner, Chicago Symphony (RCA Red Seal stereo disc LSC-2609; cassette RK-1168; cartridge R8S-1168)

b Reiner, Chicago Symphony (RCA Victrola stereo disc VICS-1265; cartridge V8S-1007)

Comments

Both Steinberg's 1971 and Mehta's 1968 recordings are sensational sonically, especially in the clarity and impact of the opening section. Thereafter, it's difficult to decide which one is better interpretively. Steinberg's performance is much more propulsive and exuberant, and the Boston Symphony's tonal colors are more impressive than the Los Angeles Philharmonic's. Mehta, however, gives a taut, dramatic interpretation throughout, with some details more sharply etched than Steinberg's. It's a difficult choice, but in the final analysis I would give Steinberg the edge.

Bernstein's 1971 release is exceptionally expansive and warmly intense throughout. The Philharmonic gives its all, and the sound engineering is first-rate. The only reservation sound buffs might have is that the organ sound in the opening section is not as rich and resonant as in either Steinberg's or Mehta's versions.

Reiner's two versions date from 1954 (now on Victrola) and 1962 (on RCA Red Seal), and were for many years *the* stereo showcase albums of the '50's and '60's respectively. The 1962 recording is superior in detail rather than basic substance. Reiner's performance in both editions is surgingly powerful and eloquent.

Der Rosenkavalier (The Cavalier of the Rose)

Strauss' great opera is not an easy work at first hearing. To be sure, it contains two of the most beautiful duets and one of the most beautiful trios ever written for female voices, and its waltz sequences have long been a concert favorite. But there are also many lengthy scenes which may seem less appealing at first, yet whose dramatic and musical subtleties grow with familiarity. Strauss called *Der Rosenkavalier* "a comedy for music"—but it is a comedy of rare maturity and psychological depth. In some ways *Rosenkavalier* blends the farce style of Viennese operetta with refined orchestral grand opera. The plot involves the complications of love among the nobility of mid-18th-century Vienna, but much more significant is the way the characters emerge (through both text and music) as human beings.

Recommended Recordings (Complete)

★ Solti (conductor), Crespin (Marschallin), Donath (Sophie), Minton (Octavian), Jungwirth (Ochs), Vienna Philharmonic (London stereo 4-disc set OSA-1435; cassette 131165)

Karajan (conductor), Schwarzkopf (Marschallin), Stitch-Randall (Sophie), Ludwig (Octavian), Edelmann (Ochs), Philharmonia Orchestra (Angel stereo 4-disc set S-3563)

Bernstein (conductor), Ludwig (Marschallin), Popp (Sophie), Jones (Octavian), Berry (Ochs), Vienna Philharmonic (Columbia stereo 4-disc set M4X-30652; cassette MTX-30652)

b Kleiber (conductor), Reining (Marschallin), Gueden (Sophie), Jurinac (Octavian), Weber (Ochs), Vienna Philharmonic (Richmond 4-disc set, 64001, *mono only*)

Recommended Recordings (Highlights)

★ Solti, Crespin, Donath, Minton, Jungwirth, etc. as above (London stereo disc OS-26200; cassette M-311207)

Karajan, Schwarzkopf, Ludwig, Stitch-Randall, Edelmann, etc. as above (Angel stereo disc S-35645)

Neuhaus (conductor), Della Casa (Marschallin and Octavian), Rothenberger (Octavian and Sophie), Dresden State Orchestra (Angel stereo disc S-36436)

b Heger (conductor), Lehmann (Marschallin), Schumann (Sophie), Olszewska (Octavian), Mayr (Ochs), Vienna Philharmonic (Seraphim 3-disc set 6041, *mono only*)

Comments

Solti leads a warm, vibrant, richly alive performance, recorded in 1968. Crespin has never been better, and Donath and Minton make genuinely exciting disc debuts. The sound engineering is especially impressive.

Karajan's recording, dating from the late 1950's, is also a superb one—beautifully molded by the conductor, and radiantly sung by Schwarzkopf in an interpretation of the Marschallin without peer in recent years. Ludwig, Stitch-Randall, and Edelmann are all first-rate.

Bernstein's 1971 release finds the conductor in topnotch form, but not so all his singers. Christa Ludwig, though not as effective a Marschallin as she is an Octavian (in Karajan's recording), is still generally impressive in many scenes. Berry and Popp are especially good, and Bernstein gives the waltz sequences an irresistible lilt.

Kleiber's 1954 recording remains a mono classic—exceptionally expressive and moving, and with Gueden and Jurinac at their prime. The sound remains most acceptable, especially at Richmond's budget price.

The Della Casa-Rothenberger release of 1968 has Rothenberger singing Octavian to Della Casa's Act I Marschallin (on side 1), then Della Casa switching to Octavian while Rothenberger becomes the Act II and Act III Sophie (on side 2)—an interesting switch which Della Casa pulls off best. Her refined, sumptuous singing (especially in Act I) is the highlight of these fifty minutes of beautifully recorded excerpts.

The sound is ancient and cramped on the Heger recording from the 1930's, and the opera is not complete, but it features one of the all-time great singers of the role of the Marschallin: Lotte Lehmann. Her perception and authority remain unique. Seraphim is to be commended for keeping this version available, especially at budget prices.

All of the performances listed above are sung in German (with English translations included).

For Follow-Up Consideration

Don Juan, the tone poem which first brought world fame to Strauss at the age of twenty-four; a vibrant, expressive, colorful study which looks on Don Juan less as a rake than as an idealist seeking the perfect woman. RECOMMENDED RECORDING: Böhm, Berlin Philharmonic (Deutsche Grammophon stereo disc 138866; cassette 923-120; cartridge 88-866), a spirited, ardent account released in 1964 for the centennial of Strauss' birth; it is coupled with Böhm's zesty performance of *Till Eulenspiegel* and the "Dance of the Seven Veils" from *Salome*.

A Hero's Life (*Ein Heldenleben*), an alternately boisterous and beautifully lyrical tone poem which most critics have interpreted as symbolically autobiographical, but which Strauss said was about "an average man whose heroism lies in his triumph over the inward battles of life." RECOMMENDED RECORDING: Haitink, Amsterdam Concertgebouw Orchestra (Philips stereo disc 6500048; cassette 7300061), a luminous, expansive, dramatic, beautifully played 1970 performance.

Four Last Songs, written a year before Strauss' death and among the most distinctively beautiful songs ever written; each treats the approach of death through various metaphors. RECOMMENDED RECORDING: Schwarzkopf, Szell, Berlin Radio Symphony Orchestra (Angel stereo disc S-36347; cartridge 8XS-36347), a tremendously moving, peerless interpretation by a soprano closely identified with the songs for the past twenty-five years; overside on this 1967 release Schwarzkopf sings five other Strauss songs with orchestra.

Salome, a high-voltage opera based on Oscar Wilde's morbid and long-controversial version of the Biblical story of Salome and John the Baptist. RECOMMENDED RECORDING: Solti (conductor), Nilsson (Salome), Wächter (Jokanaan), Hoffman (Herodias), Vienna Philharmonic (London stereo 2-disc set OSA-1218), a supercharged 1962 recording sonically and interpretively, with Nilsson soaring awesomely and magnificently over Strauss' blazing orchestration. *Note*: The final scene alone is available singly (London stereo disc OS-25991), coupled with the final scene from the Nilsson–Solti *Götterdämmerung*, thus combining on one disc two outstanding versions of two of opera's greatest scenes.

Die Frau öhne Schatten (*The Woman without a Shadow*), a long, allegorical opera with a complicated plot, but with some of Strauss' most resplendent, lushly scored, surgingly dramatic music. RECOMMENDED RECORDING: Böhm (conductor), Rysanek (Empress), Hopf (Emperor), Goltz (Barak's Wife), Schoeffler (Barak), Vienna Philharmonic (Richmond stereo 4-disc set 64503), a budget-priced 1970 reissue of one of Böhm's finest recordings, originally released in 1957; a surging, ardent performance despite uneven singing in a few roles.

All of the vocal works listed are sung in German.

• JEAN SIBELIUS

Pronounced: sih-*bay*-lee-us. Born December 8, 1865, in Tavastehus, Finland. Died September 20, 1957, in Jarvenpää, Finland.

SIGNIFICANCE: Finnish composer, who wrote in a restrained, frequently austere form of late Romanticism, often on nationalistic Finnish subjects.

BACKGROUND: Sibelius started out to be a lawyer, but switched to music in his early 20's, going to Berlin and Vienna to study. He returned to Finland at a time of ruthless suppression of that country by czarist Russia, and took as his mission to write music in the cause of Finnish liberation.

He became a Finnish national hero with such works as *Kullervo*, *En Saga*, *The Swan of Tuonela*, *Lemminkäinen*, *Tapiola*, and particularly *Finlandia*—which became the national anthem after Finland won independence. His seven symphonies, written between 1898 and 1924, reflect the development of Sibelius' style from one that was ardently melodic to a more ruggedly austere one.

During the last thirty-two years of his life he wrote no works for publication, a situation some critics interpreted as evidence that Western tonal music had reached a dead end which even a master like Sibelius could not resolve.

Symphony No. 2 in D major

Though Sibelius' music has often been compared to huge icebergs or granite blocks, the Second Symphony, written in Italy in 1901, is a sunny, boldly tempestuous work. Sibelius declared that none of his symphonies were programmatic, yet some commentators have persisted in attempting descriptions of the First and Second Symphonies, the two most Romantic of Sibelius' works. George Schneevoight, Sibelius' close friend and among the first to conduct his music, said that the first movement depicted the quiet, pastoral life of the Finns; the second, the timid dawn of patriotic feeling, tempered by thoughts of brutal czarist repression; the third, the awakening of national hope; and the fourth, an apotheosis of hope and the dream of triumph of Finnish nationalism. Critic Paul Rosenfeld related the music more to nature than to politics: "It is blood brother to the wind and silence, to the lowering cliffs and the spray, to the harsh crying of sea-birds and the breath of fog. . . . The musical ideas . . . recall the ruggedness and hardiness and starkness of things that persist in the Finnish winter. . . ."

Recommended Recordings

★ Ormandy, Philadelphia Orchestra (RCA Red Seal quadrasonic disc ARD1-0018; cassette ARK1-0018; cartridge ARS1-0018)

b Ormandy, Philadelphia Orchestra (Odyssey stereo disc Y-30046)

Karajan, Philharmonia Orchestra (Angel stereo disc S-35891)

Maazel, Vienna Philharmonic Orchestra (London stereo disc CS-6408)

Szell, Amsterdam Concertgebouw Orchestra (Philips stereo disc 835306; cassette PCR4-900-092; cartridge PC8-900-092)

Comments

Ormandy, long one of the foremost Sibelius interpreters, gives an unabashedly Romantic performance that stresses the work's melodic force and dramatic majesty. His 1973 RCA release is available only on a quadrasonic disc (playable with a minimum of sonic loss on stereo equipment). The Philadelphians' lush tone and Ormandy's dramatic interpretation also come through the 1957 sonics of the budget-priced Odyssey release surprisingly well, too.

Karajan's 1961 release is broadly spacious and poetic, and the most Romantic next to Ormandy in overall mood. The sound is also notably spacious.

Maazel's 1965 performance is heroic and tightly-knit. He builds the symphony's massive sonorities solidly, at times almost overwhelmingly. London's engineers provide excellent sound.

Szell's 1965 performance is less Romantic and more intellectualized, but filled with surging strength and incisiveness.

Violin Concerto in D minor

Like Beethoven, Brahms, Mendelssohn, and Tchaikovsky before him, Sibelius wrote only one violin concerto—but that one is unlike any other in the repertory. Moreover, Sibelius, unlike the others mentioned, was himself a violinist as a young man, giving it up at the age of twenty-five to concentrate on composing. Thirteen years later (1903) he wrote his violin concerto, and he revised it in 1905. It is one of the most difficult violin concertos. Yet it does not show off a violinist's technique as much as it challenges his ability to spin out a deeply lyrical, richly colored line—more mysterious and introspective in mood than the outgoing warmth and glitter of most nineteenth-century concertos.

Recommended Recordings

★ Perlman, Leinsdorf, Boston Symphony (RCA Red Seal stereo disc LSC-2962)

Heifetz, Hendl, Chicago Symphony (RCA Red Seal stereo disc LSC-2435 or LSC-4010)

b Ricci, Fjeldstad, London Symphony (London stereo disc STS-15054)

Ferras, Karajan, Berlin Philharmonic (Deutsche Grammophon stereo disc 138961; cassette 923077)

Comments

Perlman was twenty-one when he made his recording in 1966, and it is a remarkable testament to his early talent—a broadly songful, darkly searching, alternately strong and sensitive performance. Leinsdorf's accompaniment could not be better. The coupling is an electric Perlman–Leinsdorf performance of Prokofiev's Second Violin Concerto. Excellent sound.

Heifetz's late 1930's 78-rpm recording with Beecham was for many years the critical standard for this concerto, and his 1960 stereo remake with Hendl is outstanding for its jewel-like brilliance and clarity—despite somewhat too-closely-miked violin sound. When originally released (as LSC-2435) there was no "filler" or coupling, but in 1972 the performance was "repackaged" (as LSC-4010) with Heifetz's exciting performance of the Prokofiev Violin Concerto No. 2 overside.

Ricci's late 1950's recording remains impressive for its intensity and for what one reviewer has called its "craggy momentum." It is coupled with a fine Ricci performance of Tchaikovsky's *Sérénade Mélancholique*.

Ferras gives a lush and glowing performance, more broadly paced than most of the others, yet sometimes more boldly forceful too. Karajan rounds off the 1965 release with a stirring performance of *Finlandia*. The sound engineering is excellent.

For Follow-Up Consideration

Finlandia, a tone poem in tribute to Sibelius' homeland but *not*, as is commonly thought, using any Finnish folk themes. RECOMMENDED RECORDING: Ormandy, Philadelphia Orchestra, with the Mormon Tabernacle Choir (Columbia stereo disc MS-6196); Ormandy's full-blooded performance is made even more dramatic by the addition of the chorus (singing in English) in the finale. The disc also includes Sibelius' "Valse Triste," Alfven's *Swedish Rhapsody*, and Grieg's *Peer Gynt* Suite No. 1, all in lush Ormandy 1959 performances.

Symphony No. 1 in E minor, a sweepingly dramatic, eloquently melodic symphony. RECOMMENDED RECORDING: Barbirolli, Hallé Orchestra (Angel stereo disc S-36489), an early 1960's performance of uncommon breadth and strength.

Symphony No. 5 in E-flat major, which critic Olin Downes once called "a work of firm serenity and immense contained strength"; the finale is one of Sibelius' most nobly eloquent. RECOMMENDED RECORDING: Karajan, Berlin Philharmonic (Deutsche Grammophon stereo disc 138973; cassette 923-039), a beautifully spacious, dramatic performance from 1965; the coupling on the disc is Sibelius' *Tapiola* and on the cassette *Finlandia*, both in majestic Karajan interpretations.

• *ALEXANDER SCRIABIN*

Pronounced: skree-*ah*-bin. Born January 6, 1872, in Moscow. Died April 27, 1915, in Moscow.

SIGNIFICANCE: Russian pianist and composer of colorful, sensuous works, often expressing complex mystical concepts about man and the cosmos. He was the first composer to design colored "light shows" to accompany his music.

BACKGROUND: Scriabin's mother, a pianist who had studied at the St. Petersburg Conservatory, died when he was still an infant. Since his father was a lawyer in the consular service and frequently traveled, Scriabin was raised by his grandmother and an aunt who pampered and spoiled him. Partly because of his devotion to his mother's memory, he became obsessed with the piano as a youth. He worked so intensively at it that the muscles of his right hand became temporarily paralyzed. This kind of excessive zeal for things he believed in was to characterize much of his life—and to make him admired by some as a musical Messiah. Boris Pasternak, for example, almost abandoned literature to become a musician under his influence. Others regarded Scriabin as a neurotic charlatan.

Scriabin's early works were influenced by Chopin, Liszt, and Wagner. His later works grew increasingly complex as he sought to make his music express various mystical concepts. And in seeking to expand the impact of his music, he developed a color keyboard for projecting lights on a screen while his music was being performed (a device that was the forerunner of today's psychedelic light shows).

In 1912 he began work on a gargantuan project to create a work that would sum up the history of man from the dawn of time to the final, inevitable cataclysm, and which would use not only sound and sight but also smell. He wanted this work, to be called *Mysterium*, to be performed only in India in a special temple to be built for that purpose. When World War I broke out, he became convinced that this *was* the cataclysm and that his *Mysterium* was a divine project. His sudden death in 1915 (from gangrene which developed from an untreated carbuncle) left the work unfinished, with very little of its music actually sketched out.

In the years following his death, Scriabin's works were rarely performed outside Russia. But just as the 1950's were the years in which Mahler was rediscovered, so the late 1960's brought about a new interest in Scriabin. To some, his ideas seem perfectly in tune with today—not only because of his use of light shows, but also because his music is so highstrung and impulsive, full of "cosmic fire, pure hallucinogenics promising rainbow Nirvana" (to quote author Henry Miller).

Symphony No. 4 (Poem of Ecstasy)

Scored for a very large orchestra, this is lushly colorful, late Romantic music that builds sweepingly to what is probably the loudest final chord in all music (all instruments playing full blast)—which has made the *Poem of Ecstasy* something of a showpiece work in the hi-fi/stereo age. Some critics interpret the work as basically about the joy of artistic creation. Some others regard it as a broader view of love's role in both creation and procreation. And one Scriabin biographer, Faubion Bowers, concludes that "behind this distillation of Scriabin's world-view there was something blunt—sex." Whatever the interpretation, it is worth noting that Scriabin declined to have his text of the poem on which he based the work printed together with the score. "Conductors can always be apprised that there is such a text, but in general I would prefer for them to approach it first as pure music," Scriabin declared.

Recommended Recordings

★ Abbado, Boston Symphony (Deutsche Grammophon stereo disc 2530137; cassette 3300184; cartridge 89435)

Ormandy, Philadelphia Orchestra (RCA Red Seal stereo disc LSC-3214; cartridge R8S-1193)

Mehta, Los Angeles Philharmonic (London stereo disc CS-6552)

Comments

Not many orchestras can execute this work as spectacularly as either the Boston Symphony or the Philadelphia Orchestra, and both have outstanding versions released in 1971. Trying to decide between them is difficult indeed. Both recordings, in their own ways, are testaments to the unique qualities of two of America's greatest orchestras.

The Boston performance is crisper, more brilliant, more surging—and Abbado's interpretation is more intensely driving. Overside is an intense, exciting performance of Tchaikovsky's *Romeo and Juliet*. Sonically, the Deutsche Grammophon version has an edge over its competitors.

The Philadelphians play with the mellow glow, tonal richness, and warmth that is theirs alone, and Ormandy's pacing is more lushly prismatic. Overside, Ormandy offers more Scriabin—the glimmering *Prometheus: Poem of Fire* (Symphony No. 5) for orchestra, piano, and chorus. Sonically, the album is only a shade less spectacular than Abbado's.

Mehta's orchestra is no match for either the Bostonians or Philadelphians, but he nonetheless comes through with a searingly dramatic, constantly surging performance that can hold its own interpretively against either Abbado or Ormandy. London's 1967 sound engineering is exceptionally good. Overside is a ripely romantic performance of Schoenberg's early *Transfigured Night* (*Verklärte Nacht*).

For Follow-Up Consideration

Piano Music. Hilde Somer, who has given Scriabin recitals complete with light shows throughout the U.S., has a special feeling for the poetic spirit and tone colors of his piano music. In two albums (Mercury stereo discs SR-90525 and SR-90500; cassettes MCR4-90525 and MCR4-90500; cartridges MC8-90525 and MC8-90500) she offers an excellent cross-section of short pieces as well as two sonatas, Nos. 7 and 9, subtitled "White Mass" and "Black Mass" respectively. Ruth Laredo has also recorded several fine albums of Scriabin sonatas (Connoisseur Society stereo discs CS-2032 and CS-2034), which are brilliant in the exotic moods she weaves and excitingly virtuoistic. For a sampling, I'd recommend Somer's 90525 and Laredo's 2034, which include no duplications.

Symphony No. 2 in C minor, the most interesting of Scriabin's first three symphonies; a five-movement work from 1903, at its best in two hauntingly lovely *andantes*. RECOMMENDED RECORDING: Svetlanov, U.S.S.R. Symphony Orchestra (Melodiya/Angel disc S-40118), a warmly flowing, fervid 1970 performance, very well recorded.

• *SERGEI RACHMANINOFF*

Pronounced: rahkh-*mahn*-in-ahff. Born April 1, 1873, in Novgorod, Russia. Died March 28, 1943, in Beverly Hills, California.

SIGNIFICANCE: Russian composer, pianist, conductor; one of the last great Romantics, combining a gift for beautiful—though often melancholy—melody with a unique understanding of tone color.

BACKGROUND: Rachmaninoff showed musical talent at an early age, as well as an intense dislike for practicing. He entered the Moscow Conservatory at the age of twelve, and won a number of prizes as both pianist and composer during his teens. By twenty, he had written the Prelude in C-sharp minor, which rapidly became one of the most popular of all piano works. Several years later the first performances of his First Symphony and First Piano Concerto fared badly, and he went into years of deep depression, convinced he had no real talent. Partly through the controversial efforts of a hypnotist, he regained his confidence, composing a Second Piano Concerto which was an enormous success.

He reentered the concert field, and became one of the great piano virtuosos of the first half of the 20th century. He also conducted widely, including a year as conductor for Moscow's Bolshoi Theatre. Following the Communist Revolution in 1917, Rachmaninoff went into exile, eventually becoming a U.S. citizen. A man of deep emotions, he endured the dual ironies of being a Russia-loving aristocrat forced to live in exile because he could not accept life in Russia under the Communist system, and of being a conservative composer in an age when music was developing in radically new directions with which he was not in sympathy. After 1920 he composed fewer and fewer works (the major ones on commission from the Philadelphia Orchestra) which, in general, looked back nostalgically at a world that *was*. He was one of the first composers to record most of his works as either conductor or piano soloist.

Piano Concerto No. 2 in C minor

Its use in numerous movies and TV shows has made this concerto one of the most widely familiar of all concertos. Several popular songs based on its themes have also become pop "standards" over the years. The concerto is richly melodic, alternating between a strongly heroic mood and a more melancholy tenderness. Its contrasting movements show how uniquely Rachmaninoff understood the modern piano's potential for tonal color. The orchestration is also brilliant, indicating that Rachmaninoff viewed a piano concerto as essentially a symphony led by or dominated by the piano soloist.

Recommended Recordings

★ Ashkenazy, Kondrashin, Moscow Philharmonic (London stereo disc CS-6390)

Rubinstein, Ormandy, Philadelphia Orchestra (RCA Red Seal quadrasonic disc ARD1-0031; cassette ARK1-0031; cartridge ARS1-0031)

Davis, Lewis, Royal Philharmonic Orchestra (London stereo disc SPC-21057)

Richter, Wislocki, Warsaw Philharmonic (Deutsche Grammophon stereo disc 138076; cassette 923-059; cartridge 88-076)

Rachmaninoff, Stokowski, Philadelphia Orchestra (included in RCA Red Seal 3-disc set ARM-0296, *mono only*)

Comments

Ashkenazy's first recording dates from 1963 (when he was twenty-six), shortly after he had quietly left the Soviet Union—or, more accurately, refused to return and settled in his wife's homeland, Iceland. Whatever his political problems with Moscow, Ashkenazy's rapport with the musicians of the Moscow Philharmonic is clearly evident in this recording, made while the orchestra was in London on a Western European tour. It is a compelling, deeply felt performance, exciting and beautifully poetic by turns. Kondrashin conducts a first-rate accompaniment, and London's stereo engineering is superb. A later (1971) Ashkenazy recording of the concerto, with Previn conducting (included in London stereo 3-disc set CSA-2311), is somehow less exciting overall, though it has many of the same admirable qualities as the earlier one.

Rubinstein has recorded the concerto at least three times, and his latest (1972) is its first quadrasonic edition. This is a lyrically surging, dynamic interpretation, with a particularly beautiful accompaniment by Ormandy's Philadelphians.

Davis' 1971 release has exceptionally good stereo engineering (it is one of London's showpiece "Phase-4 Stereo Concert Series"), as well as being uncommonly majestic in Davis' approach and exciting for his technical command.

Richter gives the most brooding, melancholic performance, but exquisite in its poetry and beautifully expressive. His Warsaw-made recording won the Grand Prix du Disque in Paris in 1961, and is sonically excellent. (*Note:* this recording should not be confused with several earlier, Russian-made Richter recordings of the concerto that are sonically inferior.)

Rachmaninoff's own recording, dating from 1929, has more than historic worth, for the performance remains one of the most expressive in the catalog, and the sonics are better than many recordings made twenty years later. Its latest reissue (1973) is in Volume Five of *The Complete Rachmaninoff*, together with Philadelphia recordings of all his other piano concertos, released for the centennial of his birth.

Piano Concerto No. 3 in D minor

This concerto was written for Rachmaninoff's first U.S. tour in 1909, during which one of the New York performances was conducted by Gustav Mahler (whose accompaniment Rachmaninoff warmly described as "perfection"). For many years the Third Concerto languished in the shadow of the more immediately popular Second—even though many critics from the start considered the Third superior. Recently, however, the Third has become one of the most popular of all piano concertos, thanks mainly to Van Cliburn, who played it in the Moscow competition of 1958 that turned him into an American hero. Technically one of the most demanding of modern concertos (the sort that separates the champs from the pretenders), it is full of surging melodies, a ceaseless rhythmic drive, and vivid tonal colors.

Recommended Recordings

★ Cliburn, Kondrashin, Symphony of the Air (RCA Red Seal stereo disc LSC-2355; cartridge R8S-5011)

Weissenberg, Prêtre, Chicago Symphony (RCA Red Seal stereo disc LSC-3040)

b Janis, Munch, Boston Symphony (RCA Victrola stereo disc VICS-1032; cartridge V8S-1038)

b Horowitz, Coates, London Symphony (Seraphim disc 60063, *mono only*)

Comments

Cliburn's recording is taken from the "home-coming" concert he gave in New York's Carnegie Hall on May 19, 1958, following his return to the U.S. in triumph as winner of the First Moscow Tchaikovsky competition. Soviet conductor Kiril Kondrashin flew in at Cliburn's request to conduct the concert with what was then left of the former (and once great) NBC Symphony Orchestra. The result: a performance of exceptional musical excitement. Cliburn plays the Third with a sweep and grandeur that is just right, building toward a brilliant and increasingly electric final movement.

Weissenberg's performance too is charged with excitement and astounding technical skill, and has the advantage of more recent (1968) stereo engineering. Weissenberg also brings more breathtaking speed to certain passages. But Prêtre's accompaniment is not as well matched with Weissenberg as Kondrashin's is with Cliburn.

Janis has recorded the concerto twice, and the better recording is on the Victrola budget label, with Munch and the Boston Symphony. Janis plays with sweep, fire, and dazzling technique, and the late 1950's sound engineering is better than on Cliburn's, but not up to that on Weissenberg's.

The Horowitz mono recording dates from the early 1930's (when he was about the same age as Cliburn at the time of *his* recording). Though sonically ancient, it reveals the young Horowitz's superhuman technique, and helps explain why he remained for more than twenty years unchallenged as this concerto's great interpreter.

(*Note:* Rachmaninoff's own 1940 mono recording, available in a 3-disc RCA set ARM3-0296 with his other concertos, is disappointingly perfunctory. It is also a "cut" performance, apparently to accommodate 78-rpm timings of the day.)

Rhapsody on a Theme of Paganini

Rachmaninoff's last major work for piano and orchestra, composed in 1934, takes as its theme the last of *24 Caprices* by the Italian violinist-composer Niccolo Paganini (1782–1840)—the same theme which Schumann, Brahms, and Liszt also used for solo piano works. Rachmaninoff uses it for a set of twenty-four colorful variations, divided into three general sections (corresponding to the three movements of a conventional piano concerto). In some of the variations, he combines Paganini's lighthearted theme with the ominous "Dies Irae" ("Day of Wrath") motif of the Catholic Mass for the Dead—a theme Rachmaninoff also used in his Third Symphony, his *Symphonic Dances*, and his tone poem *Isle of the Dead*. For the 18th variation, Rachmaninoff inverts (turns upside down) the original Paganini theme and develops it into the lush melody for which the work is best known (the 18th variation is sometimes played separately at pops concerts). In 1937 Rachmaninoff suggested the outline for a ballet to the great Russian choreographer Fokine, based on the legend that Paganini had sold his soul to the devil in return for the perfection of his art and for success as a lover. The variations with the "Dies Irae" theme were to represent episodes with the devil, and variations 11 to 18 were to be love episodes. The ballet enjoyed popularity in the early 1940's. Today, however, the work's fame rests on its concert performances by virtuoso pianists.

Recommended Recordings

★ Cliburn, Ormandy, Philadelphia Orchestra (RCA Red Seal stereo disc LSC-3179; cassette RK-1199; cartridge R8S-1199)

Rubinstein, Reiner, Chicago Symphony (RCA Red Seal stereo disc LSC-2430)

Graffman, Bernstein, New York Philharmonic (Columbia stereo disc MS-6634)

b Katchen, Boult, London Philharmonic (Everest stereo disc 3280)

Comments

Cliburn's 1970 recording is one of the best he has ever made, full of marvelous detail and clear articulation, but without ever sacrificing the work's overall flow and vitality. Overside, Cliburn offers a sweepingly grand performance of the Liszt Concerto No. 2.

Rubinstein plays with more virtuoso fervor, but the late 1950's recorded sound must take a back seat to the more recent Cliburn. Still, Rubinstein's version is *very* good, and overside he offers a marvelously evocative performance of Falla's beautiful *Nights in the Gardens of Spain.*

Graffman's mid-1960's recording is technically brilliant, with a steely kind of rhythmic force. Bernstein's accompaniment is vigorous and full-blooded. Overside, Graffman and Bernstein offer an assertive, vivid Rachmaninoff Piano Concerto No. 2.

Katchen's 1954 mono performance, originally released on the London label, remains a first-rate and spirited one by the late pianist, recorded when he was 27. Overside is a splendid Katchen performance of Dohnanyi's delightful (and lamentably ignored) *Variations on a Nursery Tune.* The original mono sound has been electronically rechanneled to achieve a stereo effect, and the result is not necessarily an improvement.

For Follow-Up Consideration

Piano Concerto No. 1, similar in its basic mood and melodic feeling to his Second and Third Concertos. RECOMMENDED RECORDING: Janis, Kondrashin, Moscow Philharmonic (Philips stereo disc SR1-75019; cassette MCR4-90300; cartridge MC8-90300), a surging, exciting 1962 performance which includes, overside, a brilliant performance of Prokofiev's Third Piano Concerto. This recording, incidentally, marked the first time the Russians allowed an American company to make a recording in Moscow using American equipment, and the sound engineering is indeed excellent.

Symphonic Dances, Rachmaninoff's last orchestral work, and his finest; a richly melodic, colorful work whose three sections were once subtitled "Youth," "Maturity," and "Decline," then "Morning," "Noon," and "Night," before Rachmaninoff abandoned all the subtitles. RECOMMENDED RECORDINGS: Johanos, Dallas Symphony (Vox/Turnabout stereo disc 34145), a crisp and lilting but dryly recorded 1967 budget-label performance; or Kondrashin, Moscow Philharmonic (Melodiya/Angel stereo disc S-40093), a more brooding, more spacious-sounding 1969 recording.

Symphony No. 2 in E minor, a lushly melodic, unabashedly Romantic work, for many years Rachmaninoff's most popular orchestral piece. RECOMMENDED RECORDING: Ormandy, Philadelphia Orchestra (Columbia stereo disc MS-6110), a luxuriantly warm and colorful performance, dating from 1959.

Preludes for Solo Piano, twenty-four brief but expressive pieces which beautifully show the pianist-composer's sense of musical colors. RECOMMENDED RECORDING: Weissenberg (RCA Red Seal stereo 2-disc set LSC-7069), a 1970 release full of marvelous tonal subtleties, though emotionally restrained.

• *ARNOLD SCHOENBERG*

Pronounced: *she(r)n*-berg. Born September 13, 1874, in Vienna. Died July 13, 1951, in Los Angeles, California.

SIGNIFICANCE: Austrian composer and teacher, whose theories of pan-tonal and 12-tone music made him one of the most influential composers of this century.

BACKGROUND: Schoenberg grew up in a Vienna waltzing to Johann Strauss while still dwelling on the days of Schubert and Beethoven. He started to study the violin and cello, and when his father died Schoenberg went to work at the age of sixteen orchestrating operettas to help support his family. But his chief love was chamber music, and on his own time he began to write chamber works that would have the emotionalism of Wagner's operas. After turning to teaching in the early 1900's, first in Vienna and then in Berlin, Schoenberg became convinced that the tonality and key structure on which Western music was based had become exhausted. He set out to devise a new vocabulary and grammar for music which would liberate melody and harmony from what he felt was the tyranny of traditional modes.

He became the father of "pan-tonal" music—more familiarly known, despite Schoenberg's objections, as atonal music—music without a specific key relationship for its notes. The difference lies in the focus of the words: pan-tonal means using *all* tones, while atonal implies that *no* tone is a focal point or key note. In 1912 Schoenberg created a sensation with his pan-tonal song cycle *Pierrot Lunaire*, which also introduced *Sprechstimme* (literally, speaking voice), a vocal line that is half sung, half spoken.

Schoenberg was also the innovator of 12-tone (or dodecaphonic) music, in which the seven white and five black notes of a piano octave (the thirteenth note makes the octave) are subjected to an ordered relationship as equals, unlike the major–minor key system of traditional music.

His theories aroused enormous controversy in Europe and the U.S., revolutionizing the direction of 20th-century music. Driven out of Germany and Austria by the Nazis because he was a Jew, Schoenberg came to the U.S., teaching primarily at the University of California at Los Angeles until his death. His works have only recently begun to become concert standards, but his influence on composers of the past thirty years has been significant.

Five Pieces for Orchestra

This is one of Schoenberg's most important early explorations of pan-tonality (it is not yet into his 12-tone theories). A set of brief, self-contained, highly expressive pieces, it is concerned with individual instrumental color rather than massive orchestral sound. Written in 1909 and revised in 1949, (primarily to reduce the orchestral requirements), the pieces are designed to express inner emotional states—not a surprising purpose for an avant-garde work written in Vienna at a time when Sigmund Freud was a leading figure. A program note for the work's London premiere in 1912 stated: "This music seeks to express all that dwells in us subconsciously like a dream . . . [and] is built upon none of the lines that are familiar to us. . . . [But it] has a rhythm, as the blood has its pulsating rhythm, as all life in us has a rhythm; [it] has a tonality, but only as the sea or the storm has its tonality; [it] has harmonies, though we cannot grasp or analyze them nor can we trace its themes." Not unexpectedly, such a work merely baffled most audiences for many years. But since the 1960's it has become increasingly appreciated for its tight concentration of expressive thought, even by average listeners unequipped to recognize its structural properties. The titles of the five pieces are: (1) "Premonitions"; (2) "Yesteryears"; (3) "Summer Morning by a Lake—Colors" (originally this piece was called "The Changing Chord"); (4) "Peripeteia" (meaning the sudden reversal of a dramatic action); and (5) "The Obligatory Recitative."

Recommended Recordings

★ Craft, Columbia Symphony (Columbia Special Products stereo disc CMS-6103)

   Dorati, London Symphony (Mercury stereo disc SR-90316)

b Wand, Gurzenich Orchestra of Cologne (Nonesuch stereo disc 71192)

Comments

Craft's 1960 recording is pungent and vivid, and is coupled with excellent performances of Webern's *Five Movements for String Quartet* and Berg's *Altenberg Songs*, splendidly sung by Bethany Beardslee—a most interesting coupling of representative works of these three allied composers. A later Craft recording (from about 1965) is included in an all-Schoenberg album (Columbia stereo 2-disc set M2S-709) recorded with the Cleveland Orchestra and the CBC Symphony of Canada; it has superior sonics and an equally fine performance and may be preferred by those less concerned with economy or the more diverse couplings of the 1960 release.

   Dorati's 1962 release is intense and colorful, and is coupled with two of the finest works by Webern and Berg, the *Five Pieces for Orchestra* and *Three Pieces for Orchestra*, respectively. The sound engineering is very good. This recording has recently been withdrawn from the active catalog, but still may be available in some shops.

   Günther Wand's 1968 release offers a sensitive, penetrating performance, but the dynamic range of the sound is only fair. It is coupled with Webern's fascinating *Cantata No. 1* and Stravinsky's neo-Baroque *Dumbarton Oaks* Concerto.

For Follow-Up Consideration

Verklärte Nacht (*Transfigured Night*) Op. 4, an early tone poem for string orchestra (originally written as a sextet for violins, violas, and cellos) whose mood and musical vocabulary are directly descended from Wagner's *Tristan und Isolde* in its restless Romanticism. The work describes two lovers whose happiness transforms a bleak winter night into a thing of beauty. The score has been used for many years for the popular ballet *Pillar of Fire*. RECOMMENDED RECORDING: Mehta, Los Angeles Philharmonic (London stereo disc CS-6552), an intense, ripely romantic 1967 performance, coupled with an equally tense performance of Scriabin's *Poem of Ecstasy.*

Variations for Orchestra, Schoenberg's first orchestral work (1928) to be composed strictly within the 12-tone scheme. Says critic Alfred Frankenstein: "It is a colossal virtuoso study in instrumentation. . . . Since the 12-tone philosophy is essentially one of variation, the use of the episodic variation form [in this work] exposes its essential logic with the utmost clarity and precision; the music is wonderfully lithe and energetic too." RECOMMENDED RECORDINGS: Craft, unnamed orchestra (Columbia stereo disc ML-5244), recorded in California in the late 1950's; or Craft, CBC Symphony of Toronto (Columbia stereo 2-disc set M2S-694), dating from about 1963 and part of the 2-disc Volume Two of "The Music of Arnold Schoenberg"; the first is coupled with several short 12-tone vocal works, the second with discerning Craft performances of Schoenberg's symphonic poem *Pelléas and Mélisande* (composed a year after Debussy's opera), the string orchestra version of *Transfigured Night,* and *Three Little Orchestra Pieces.*

Pierrot Lunaire (*Moonstruck Pierrot*), a setting of twenty-one Symbolist poems by Albert Giraud for voice and eight instruments, composed in 1912 and one of the most controversial of revolutionary landmarks in 20th-century music. The poems are basically decadent and macabre (one describes Pierrot smoking his tobacco out of a human skull). One critic has called the piece "German Expressionism at its most paranoid, half-mad best." This was the first work to use *Sprechstimme,* which has become a basic device of much avant-garde music ever since. RECOMMENDED RECORDING: Pilarczyk, Boulez, Domaine Musical Ensemble of Paris (Everest stereo disc 3171), a mid-1960's recording that has been widely praised for the clarity of Boulez's conducting and his emphasis on the text's ironic aspects, but which has also been criticized by others for the liberties Boulez takes with tempos indicated by the composer.

• CHARLES IVES

Born October 20, 1874, in Danbury, Connecticut. Died May 19, 1954, in New York City.

SIGNIFICANCE: American composer and insurance executive who wrote some of the most ruggedly individualistic music of the early 20th century—full of challenging harmonies, advanced ideas, and occasionally wild humor.

BACKGROUND: Ives lived most of his life in western Connecticut. He studied music at Yale, but when he realized that he could not support his wife except by writing the kind of music he did not believe in, he went into the insurance business in 1898, eventually becoming one of New York's most successful insurance executives. In his spare time between 1900 and 1920, he continued to write music, and occasionally paid musicians to come to his Connecticut house to play it. When they had difficulty getting through his complex instrumentation, he despaired of ever having his work publicly performed, but refused to alter it. After 1920 he lived in precarious health in virtual isolation, and composed little. It was not until 1946 (when he was 71) that he heard any of his orchestral music played in public.

When he won the Pulitzer Prize in 1947 for his Third Symphony (written in 1904) he scorned the award as coming too late to interest him. In the 1950's Leonard Bernstein and others began to play Ives' music regularly. By the 1960's, Ives was widely recognized as perhaps the greatest American composer to date, and by 1970 all his major works had been recorded. Some of them antedate Schoenberg, Stravinsky, Bartók, and others in musical ideas, including experimentation with multiple rhythms, polytonality, note clusters, and tone rows. He also mixed hymn tunes, patriotic songs, college songs, ragtime, etc., into a jigsaw of sound patterns, sometimes seriously, sometimes for humorous effect. As Leonard Bernstein has said: "We have suddenly discovered our musical Mark Twain, Emerson, and Lincoln all rolled into one."

Holidays Symphony

Subtitled "Recollections of a Boy's Holidays in a Connecticut Town," this is really a suite of related pieces rather than a symphony in the formal sense. Its four parts were written between 1904 and 1913, and were placed together by Ives in a folder marked "4 New England Holidays" with a note that "these movements may be played as separate pieces . . . [or] lumped together as a symphony." The pieces are kaleidoscopic views of four American holidays and the four different seasons in which they occur. They mix melody with dissonance, seriousness with wild humor, and snatches of familiar tunes with some of the most challenging and thickest harmony in American music—sometimes simultaneously. The first movement, "Washington's Birthday" (1909), evokes the mood of Whittier's "Snowbound" with its feeling of cold and solitude, broken for a brief spell by a barn dance. The second movement "Decoration Day" (1912), describes the gathering of flowers for the day's memorial ceremony and a town parade. The third, "Fourth of July" (1912–1913), is (to quote Ives) "a boy's Fourth—no historical orations, with a patriotism nearer kin to nature than jingoism"; it explodes in a cacophonous finale of firecrackers. The fourth, "Thanksgiving and/or Forefathers' Day" (1904), is based on two earlier organ pieces by Ives, culminating in a short choral setting of the Forefathers' Day Hymn found in many Protestant hymnals; it represents (according to Ives) "the sternness and strength and austerity of the Puritan character."

Recommended Recordings

★ **b** Johanos, Dallas Symphony (Turnabout stereo disc 34146)
Bernstein, New York Philharmonic (Columbia stereo disc MS-7147)

Comments

Both Johanos' and Bernstein's performances, dating from the mid-1960's, are excellent. Bernstein brings a natural flair to both the serious and sportive parts of the score, has

206 • *Discovering Music*

the more resonant recording, and the more virtuoso orchestra. Johanos is more incisive and less puffy in a number of places, brings a greater clarity of detail without ever losing dramatic thrust, and also lets Ives' raucous humor spring up more crisply from the polytextural mix.

Three Places in New England

One of the most profoundly moving inquiries into Americana by any U.S. composer, these three short symphonic pieces were written between 1903 and 1914, yet never performed until 1931 (and then not very often until the late 1950's). They are stream-of-consciousness reflections about the history of places in New England known to Ives. The first movement, " 'St. Gaudens' in Boston Common—Col. Shaw and His Colored Regiment," is a sombre meditation on the Civil War (in which Shaw's regiment served), with songs of that war quoted in various, often distorted guises. The second movement, "Putnam's Camp, Redding, Connecticut" is a wild and raucous vision (during a Fourth of July celebration) of Gen. Israel Putnam's Revolutionary army on the march; it is based in part on the *1776* overture Ives sketched for an opera about John André and Benedict Arnold (from a play by Ives' uncle, Judge Lyman Brewster), and weaves several Revolutionary period songs into its complex texture, plus some of later vintage ("The Battle Cry of Freedom," "Massa's in de Cold, Cold Ground," Sousa's *"Semper Fidelis,"* etc.). The third movement, "The Housatonic at Stockbridge," is an enigmatic scene by the Housatonic River in the Berkshires, beginning with misty orchestral hues and then building to a climax of overpoweringly melancholy intensity which unexpectedly returns to the original mood and then ends abruptly.

Recommended Stereo Recordings

★ Thomas, Boston Symphony (Deutsche Grammophon stereo disc 2530048; cassette 3300-017)

Ormandy, Philadelphia Orchestra (Columbia stereo disc MS-7015, MS-6684, or MS-7111)

Comments

Thomas, in his first recording with the Boston Symphony in 1970, offers a vivid, gripping performance, beautifully recorded (among Deutsche Grammophon's first in Boston). It is coupled with another outstanding and infrequently played American work, Ruggles' *Sun-Treader*—inspired by Robert Browning's tribute to Shelley—which Thomas gives a strong, compelling reading.

Ormandy's 1964 performance is more intense and lush than Thomas's, and is also beautifully recorded. It is available in several couplings: 7111 has Ormandy's performance of Ives' Symphony No. 1; 7015 includes Ives' *Robert Browning* Overture (played by Stokowski) and the "Washington's Birthday" movement from the *Holidays* Symphony (played by Bernstein); 6684 offers Ormandy performances of two Copland pieces, the *Lincoln Portrait* (with Adlai Stevenson as narrator) and the *Fanfare for the Common Man.*

For Follow-Up Consideration

The Four Symphonies, packaged in one reduced-price 3-LP album (Columbia stereo set D3S-783), performed by Ormandy–Philadelphia (First Symphony), Bernstein–New York Philharmonic (Second and Third), and Stokowski–American Symphony (Fourth); all of these mid-1960's performances are better than their competitors on other labels, and the album includes an informative booklet about Ives and the works.

American Scenes, American Poets, a collection of some of the songs Ives wrote about the American scene as he saw it, ten of them set to poems by Thoreau, Holmes, Whittier, Whitman, and others; beautifully recorded in 1969 by Lear (soprano), Stewart (baritone), and Mandel (piano), (Columbia stereo disc M-30229).

Calcium Light Night, a 1969 album of twenty fascinating short pieces for chamber orchestra, edited and conducted by Gunther Schuller (Columbia stereo disc MS-7318). One piece, "The New River" is an astonishingly prophetic (for 1912) lament about what industrial pollution was doing to Connecticut's Housatonic River.

Music for Chorus, a collection of short choral pieces that show much the same adventurousness and originality as Ives' orchestral music, as well as combining folk, pop, and strictly cornball elements with more solemn ones (Columbia stereo disc MS-6921); well performed by the Ithaca College Concert Choir, the Texas Boys Choir of Fort Worth, the Gregg Smith Singers, and Columbia Chamber Orchestra (1966).

● *MAURICE RAVEL*

Pronounced: rah-*vell*. Born March 7, 1875, in Ciboure, France. Died December 28, 1937, in Paris.

SIGNIFICANCE: French composer, pianist, conductor; a master of Impressionistic orchestration and piano sonorities, whose music is usually marked by elegance, wit, and extraordinary virtuosity.

BACKGROUND: Although he was raised in Paris, Ravel made much of his partly Basque ancestry and the influence of Spanish music on his development. At fourteen he entered the Paris Conservatory, where he was greatly influenced by Erik Satie. With a series of piano works (including *Miroirs*, 1905, *Rapsodie Espagnole*, 1907, and *Daphnis and Chloé*, 1912), Ravel became, next to Debussy, the most popular French composer in the years just before World War I.

The war affected him deeply, and in 1920 he wrote *La Valse*, interpreted by many as a musical depiction of the collapse of the old European social order with the war. He visited the U.S. in the 1920's, and became fascinated by the jazz he heard, incorporating jazz elements into his last two piano concertos and a few other works. In 1928 his *Bolero*, written for the dancer Ida Rubinstein, quickly became one of the most popular orchestral scores of the era; six different recordings appeared within a year, it was played frequently on radio, and its title was bought for a 1932 Hollywood movie.

In 1932 Ravel was injured in an automobile accident, and it led in subsequent years to his losing his powers of coordination. He died following brain surgery in 1937.

La Valse

One of the century's great orchestral showpieces, *La Valse* begins as a nostalgic daydream and ends as a snarling, chaotic nightmare. Some see in it a musical portrait of the collapse of the 19th century's social and political structure following World War I. Others see it as a broader symbolic dissection of modern life generally. Still others see it in more personal terms, as a portrait of the folly of "waltzing" through life's corruptions. The orchestral version is the best known, but there is also a piano version which Ravel himself wrote.

Recommended Recordings (Orchestral Version)

★ Bernstein, New York Philharmonic (Columbia stereo disc MS-6011)

Ansermet, Suisse Romande Orchestra (London stereo disc CS-6367)

b Munch, Boston Symphony Orchestra (RCA Victrola stereo disc VICS-1323; cartridge R8S-5043)

Maazel, New Philharmonia Orchestra (Angel stereo disc S-36916; cassette 4XS-36916; cartridge 8XS-36916)

Recommended Recordings (Piano Version)

★ Laredo (Connoisseur Society stereo disc S-2005)

Comments

Bernstein's performance (from the late 1950's) is interpretively peerless—dynamic, dramatic, lilting, sentimental, incisive, frightening, all in the right spots.

Ansermet, once the most probing interpreter of this work, had developed some idiosyncrasies about certain sections by the time of his last recording of the work (around 1964). Still it is a brilliant, masterful interpretation overall, especially in its orchestral clarity. An earlier Ansermet recording (with the Paris Conservatory Orchestra) is still available on Everest disc 3283; although the interpretation is more subtly cogent, the dated mono sound (from the late 1940's) has not been much improved by Everest's electronically rechanneled stereo.

Munch took *La Valse* at an uncommonly fast tempo which inevitably blurred many of the subtleties in the score—but there can be no denying the breathtaking excitement of the performance. His 1956 recording (reissued in 1968 on the budget-priced Victrola label) is better than his later 1962 recording (presently RCA Red Seal LSC-2664) and has less muddy sound than the later version.

Maazel's 1972 release swirls with drama and has many fascinating coloristic touches, although the sound engineering of the finale is disappointingly fuzzy.

Among the piano versions, Laredo's 1968 release is the only outstanding one—and outstanding it is: rhythmically vibrant, continually pulsating, and with all sorts of clean, subtle detail.

In terms of couplings (*La Valse* is only about fifteen minutes long), no one of the above recordings really stands out. Bernstein includes a superbly played Ravel *Rapsodie Espagnole* but also a blaringly superficial *Bolero*. Ansermet, Munch, and Maazel also include Ravel's *Bolero*, none in particularly distinguished performances, plus other short French works of varying qualities.

Daphnis and Chloé

The second of the two suites Ravel extracted from his 1912 ballet score has become one of the most popular works in the concert repertory. It is among the century's most sumptuous examples of orchestral color and virtuosity, alternating between subtle elegance and glittering fireworks. The ballet from which the suites are taken is loosely based on an ancient Greek legend about a young girl abducted by pirates and rescued by a young Greek shepherd.

Recommended Recordings (Complete Ballet)

★ Munch, Boston Symphony Orchestra, New England Conservatory Chorus (RCA Red Seal stereo disc LSC-2568)

Bernstein, New York Philharmonic, Schola Cantorum Chorus (Columbia stereo disc MS-6260)

Ansermet, Suisse Romande Orchestra, Radio Lausanne Chorus (London stereo disc CS-6456)

Recommended Recordings (Suite No. 2)

★ b Munch, Boston Symphony Orchestra, New England Conservatory Chorus (RCA Victrola stereo disc VICS-1674; cartridge V8S-1050)

Haitink, Amsterdam Concertgebouw Orchestra (Philips stereo disc 6500-311)

Bernstein, New York Philharmonic, Schola Cantorum Chorus (Columbia stereo disc MS-6754)

Ormandy, Philadelphia Orchestra, Mendelssohn Club Chorus (RCA Red Seal quadrasonic disc ARD1-0029; cassette ARK1-0029; cartridge ARS1-0029)

Comments

Daphnis was one of the great specialties of Charles Munch, and he made two stunning recordings of the complete score with the Boston Symphony and New England Conservatory Chorus—one in 1955, the other in 1961. The latter is the best sonically, and is available on the RCA Red Seal label. In 1967, RCA "edited" the parts of the earlier recording that correspond to the two suites Ravel drew from the ballet, and they make up the edition available on the Victrola budget label. Both of Munch's performances remain significantly superior to another recording of the Second Suite by the Boston Symphony, as led by Abbado in 1970 (Deutsche Grammophon stereo disc 2530038).

Bernstein's suite is similarly "edited" from his complete 1961 recording. Bernstein's performance, in both complete and suite versions, has less tonal glow than Munch's, but it is still an exciting one, with emphasis on the pulsating qualities of the score, and with the fastest final dance on records.

Ansermet's complete 1966 performance is shimmeringly beautiful in its tonal hues, but cooler and more detached in its overall feeling than either Munch's or Bernstein's. An Ansermet performance of the Second Suite was recorded separately around 1961, without the chorus, and is disappointingly lackluster (London Stereo Treasury disc STS-15092) and not recommended.

Haitink offers both the First and Second Suites, without chorus, on his 1972 release. His performance is sonically sumptuous and interpretively vivid, and overside he leads as beautiful a performance of Ravel's complete ballet score *Ma Mere l'Oye* (Mother Goose) as you are ever likely to hear.

Ormandy's 1973 quadrasonic release is resplendent in its tone colors, and meltingly creamy in the "Daybreak" and "Pantomime" sections; however, Ormandy's final dance has more polish than bite. Overside are sonically impressive performances of Debussy's *La Mer* and *Afternoon of a Faun*.

Bolero

What Ravel intended as a technical exercise in a steadily building *crescendo* has become one of the most popular works in all music. The form continues to be adopted and imitated by both classical and popular composers (for example, Shostakovich's Seventh Symphony or Bécaud's hit song "What Now My Love?").

Recommended Recordings

★ Karajan, Berlin Philharmonic (Deutsche Grammophon stereo disc 139010; cassette 923-018; cartridge 89-010)

Dervaux, Paris Orchestre Colonne (Command stereo disc 11007)

Munch, Orchestre de Paris (Angel stereo disc S-36584; cassette 4XS-36584; cartridge 8XS-36584)

b Ravel, Paris Orchestre Lamoureux (Turnabout disc 4256, *mono only*)

Comments

Conductors in America have long been noted for playing the *Bolero* at a faster tempo than is common in Europe. Ravel himself is reported to have been so distressed at Toscanini's tempo at a New York concert in the 1930's that he walked out. The tempo difference is strikingly demonstrated by the four recordings Charles Munch made of the *Bolero* between 1947 and 1968. His two Boston Symphony versions (from about 1956 and 1962 respectively) are much faster than either of the recordings he made with Paris orchestras in 1947 (on a London mono disc now deleted from the catalog) or just before his death in 1968. Could it have been the pace of American life rubbing off on the conductor?

Karajan and Dervaux play *Bolero* at the tempo Ravel specified—a little over fifteen minutes. Karajan's orchestra and sound engineering are the most resplendent, creating an orchestral showpiece of the first rank. The coupling on Karajan's mid-1960's release is a virtuoso performance of the Mussorgsky-Ravel *Pictures at an Exhibition.* Dervaux's 1963 release also has impressive sound, and is coupled with an exhilarating performance of Ravel's *Rapsodie Espagnole.*

Munch's last recording, with the Orchestre de Paris, is the slowest *Bolero* of all at seventeen minutes—perhaps a bit *too* slow. But it is also uncommonly sensuous and certainly preferable to the two Boston versions he made for RCA (Red Seal LSC-2664 or Victrola VICS-1323).

Ravel's own recording, made in 1928, is strictly of historic interest. But its reissue on the Turnabout budget label is recommended to students and collectors, if only for the composer's own word on that debatable tempo.

For Follow-Up Consideration

Piano Concerto for Left Hand (in D major), written for an Austrian pianist who lost his right hand in World War I. A relatively brief concerto, it has been interpreted by some as an attempt by Ravel to depict musically the forces of war and peace battling for control of man's destiny. In the concerto, a theme resembling the nursery tune "Three Blind Mice" is pitted against a sinister march. RECOMMENDED RECORDING: Entremont, Boulez, Cleveland Orchestra (Columbia stereo disc M-31426; cassette MT-31426), a vibrant, penetrating, rhythmically biting 1970 performance. Overside, Entremont is much less impressive with Ravel's Piano Concerto in G.

Piano Concerto in G, an exuberant, vivacious, jazz-influenced concerto with a dashing finale that makes fantastic demands on the soloist. RECOMMENDED RECORDING: Weissenberg, Ozawa, Orchestre de Paris (Angel stereo disc S-36785), a blithe and spirited 1971 performance that shows off Weissenberg's exceptional technique as well as his interpretive elegance, even if the orchestral playing is occasionally imprecise. Overside is a performance of Prokofiev's Piano Concerto No. 3 that starts off excitingly but loses its momentum by the last movement.

L'Enfant et les Sortilèges (*The Child and the Sorcerers*), a one-act operatic fairy tale that is a sophisticated, witty, and satiric musical fantasy. It has sections of shimmering Impressionistic beauty, a wry fox-trot sung to fractured English lyrics, and a wildly comic duet for two singers impersonating meowing cats. RECOMMENDED RECORDING: Ansermet, Suisse Romande Orchestra, Geneva Choir, and vocal soloists (London/ Richmond stereo disc SR-33086)—one of the true gems on the budget-priced Richmond label, dating originally from the late 1950's but with excellent sound engineering.

• *BELA BARTÓK*

Pronounced: *bar*-tock. Born March 25, 1881, in Nagyszentmiklos, Hungary. Died September 26, 1945, in New York City.

SIGNIFICANCE: Hungarian composer and pianist, whose music varies from darkly full-blooded to austere, sometimes with harsh dissonances, sometimes with simple folklike melody.

BACKGROUND: Bartók made his debut as a pianist in Hungary at the age of ten. As a teenager he studied at the Royal Academy of Music in Budapest, later becoming a professor there. A pioneer collector of authentic Hungarian folk songs (he proved that the "Hungarian Rhapsodies" of Liszt were based on gypsy songs), he spent more than eight years collecting, writing down, and making phonograph recordings of them. His own original orchestral music, operas, and ballet scores (*The Miraculous Mandarin, The Wooden Prince, Bluebeard's Castle*, etc.) met with generally hostile receptions at first.

Bartók lived most of his life in or near poverty, and spent his last years in the U.S. after fleeing the Nazi takeover of Hungary. He worked for a time in Columbia University's music library until failing health (leukemia) prevented him from working regularly. Although it was generally believed that he died because of neglect, ASCAP (the American Society of Composers, Authors, & Publishers) had assured him medical care, which Bartók agreed to accept only as an advance against future royalties. Despite his rapidly deteriorating health, he worked until the last on his Third Piano Concerto, leaving only the final seventeen bars unfinished. They were completed from his sketches by his pupil Tibor Serly.

Concerto for Orchestra

In 1943, while Bartók was hospitalized in New York with leukemia, two Hungarian compatriots, violinist Joseph Szigeti and conductor Fritz Reiner, set in motion an effort to help him. The effort resulted in a commission from Serge Koussevitzky, then conductor of the Boston Symphony Orchestra, for $1,000 for orchestral work. The commission so buoyed Bartók's spirits that he was able to leave the hospital to go to Asheville, N.C., where he started work on the Concerto for Orchestra. On December 1, 1944, Bartók went to Boston for the premiere, of which he wrote: "The performance was excellent. Koussevitzky is very enthusiastic about the piece, and says it is 'the best orchestral piece of the last twenty-five years.'" Koussevitzky's judgment has long since been confirmed. In fact, few contemporary works of the past thirty years have been admired more enthusiastically by both critics and audiences. Bartók treats the instruments in a colorful, soloistic manner, contrasting groups of instruments against the full body of the orchestra. Bartók provided this broad outline for the premiere: "The general mood of the work represents, apart from the jesting second movement, a gradual transition from the sternness of the first movement and the lugubrious death song of the third to the life-assertion of the last one." The fourth movement,

"Interrupted Intermezzo," is a gentle interlude interrupted by raucous references to themes from Lehár's operetta *The Merry Widow* and from Shostakovich's Seventh (*Leningrad*) Symphony, which Bartók had heard on a Toscanini broadcast while working on the concerto.

Recommended Recordings

★ Ormandy, Philadelphia Orchestra (Columbia stereo disc MS-6626)

b Reiner, Chicago Symphony (RCA Victrola stereo disc VICS-1110; cartridge V8S-1036)

Bernstein, New York Philharmonic (Columbia stereo disc MS-6140)

Haitink, Amsterdam Concertgebouw (Philips stereo disc 900233; cassette 18172CAA)

Ozawa, Chicago Symphony (Angel stereo disc S-36035; cassette 4XS-36035)

Boulez, New York Philharmonic (Columbia quadrasonic disc MQ-32132; cartridge MAQ-32132; also stereo disc M-32132; cassette MT-32132; cartridge MA-32132)

Comments

Since Bartók's *Concerto* is a work that tests the mettle of any virtuoso ensemble, the Philadelphia Orchestra has an automatic head start over most orchestras. But it is the breathtaking incisiveness of Ormandy's 1963 interpretation along with the drive and intensity of the performance, as well as its dazzling coloristic effects, that makes this version so outstanding. The sound engineering is excellent.

Reiner not only played a role in making the Concerto possible, but was also the first to record it (on a long-deleted Columbia mono disc with the Pittsburgh Symphony). His second recording, in 1956, remains a glowing one, interpretively alive and dramatically trenchant. The sonics, which were excellent in the mid-1950's, have been surpassed by later versions but are still impressive.

Bernstein's 1959 performance is exciting and colorful. Author-commentator Martin Bookspan has said of this version that "the conductor lays on some of the Hungarian goulash elements with a rather lavish hand"—but Bookspan has justly continued to rank it high in his annual "Basic Repertoire" listings for *Stereo Review* magazine.

Haitink and Ozawa both lead first-rate performances with superbly virtuoistic orchestras, and each is very well recorded (1968 and 1969 respectively). Haitink's is the more lyrical interpretation, Ozawa's the more exuberant.

Boulez's 1972 recording, the first quadrasonic edition of the Concerto, has won widespread praise for its sound engineering and for the unusual clarity of the orchestral playing. But the interpretation is dramatically blander than the others listed.

Music for Strings, Percussion and Celesta

Considered by many to be the greatest of Bartók's works and one of his most original, this 1936 composition seems to have anticipated the stereo age. It is scored for double string orchestra—one group on each side of the stage—with piano, celesta, harp, xylophone, timpani, and various percussion instruments between them. Bartók uses the instruments in unusual ways to explore new sonorities—sometimes for mysterious effects, sometimes for aggressive, sharp accents. The first movement has been described by Pierre Boulez as "a fugue unfolding fanwise to a maximum intensity and then folding back to its initial mystery." The second movement is rhythmically vibrant and jocose, with some of the most arresting combinations of percussive and pizzicato sounds in any orchestral work. The third is a quiet and eerie example of what Boulez calls Bartók's "night music." The finale is violent and dancelike in its rhymthic urgency.

Recommended Recordings

★ Boulez, BBC Symphony (Columbia stereo disc MS-7206)

  Bernstein, New York Philharmonic (Columbia stereo disc MS-6956)

b Reiner, Chicago Symphony (RCA Victrola stereo disc VICS-1620)

  Haitink, Amsterdam Concertgebouw (Philips stereo disc 6500015; cassette 7300-017)

Comments

Boulez's 1968 recording projects the work's striking rhythms with exceptional thrust and vitality, and his finale has a marvelous Hungarian Rhapsody-like flair. The mood of mystery he creates in the first and third movements is also outstanding. The stereo separation is particularly good. The coupling is a Boulez performance of Stravinsky's *Firebird Suite* (the early 1910 version that omits the Lullaby and Finale).

Bernstein's performance has thrust and drama, and surges with tension—not to mention some hair-raising tempos. Originally released in 1962 (coupled with a Hindemith work), it was reissued in 1967 with a new Bartók coupling: the brittle Concerto for Two Pianos and Percussion, with Gold and Fizdale as the excellent soloists. Excellent stereo separation.

Reiner leads a dynamic performance, exciting in the fast movements and eerie in the slow ones. The 1959 sound is good, but the stereo separation is below par. The coupling is a colorful Reiner performance of Bartók's *Five Hungarian Sketches*.

Haitink's 1968 recording is most subtly colored and atmospheric in the slow movements, and has marvelous rhythmic clarity in other parts. It is coupled with a vivacious performance of Kodály's *Háry János* Suite. The sound engineering is unusually clear, although the stereo separation of the specific instrumental groups is not.

For Follow-Up Consideration

Piano Concerto No. 2, a slashingly rhythmic, darkly surging concerto written in the early 1930's. RECOMMENDED RECORDING: Weissenberg, Ormandy, Philadelphia Orchestra (RCA Red Seal stereo disc LSC-3159; cassette RK-1156; cartridge R8S-1156), a 1970 release that is one of the most impressive technical displays any pianist has yet put on records.

Piano Concerto No. 3, Bartók's last work and one of his most unashamedly Neoromantic in mood; he worked on it virtually to the day he died. RECOMMENDED RECORDING: Katchen, Kertész, London Symphony (London stereo disc CS-6487;

cassette M10196), a warm and exhilarating performance from the mid-1960's, coupled with a somewhat languid performance of Ravel's Piano Concerto in G.

Bluebeard's Castle, Bartók's only opera, dating from 1911; a short two-character work based on the legend of the much-married Bluebeard, but recast as a symbolic rather than a literal horror story. It is not an "easy" work on first hearing, but it has many fascinating scenes and remains one of Bartók's most volcanically powerful scores. RECOMMENDED RECORDING: Kertész, Ludwig, Berry, London Symphony (London stereo 2-disc set OSA-1158), a taut, full-blooded 1965 performance sung in the original Hungarian.

• IGOR STRAVINSKY

Pronounced: strah-*vin*-skee. Born June 17, 1882, in Oranienbaum, Russia. Died April 6, 1971, in New York City.

SIGNIFICANCE: Russian-born composer and conductor, a dynamic innovator in a number of different styles, and one of the most influential composers of the 20th century.

BACKGROUND: After studying with Rimsky-Korsakov in St. Petersburg, Stravinsky went to Paris in 1908 to work with Diaghilev's Ballet Russe. There he created a sensation with the *Firebird* in 1910 and *Petrushka* in 1911. *Firebird* blended elements of Impressionism with more colorful, folklike Russian elements; *Petrushka* was more strikingly original in its rhythms and harmonies. His third work for Diaghilev, the massively savage and howling *Le Sacre du Printemps* (*The Rite of Spring*) was so electrifyingly unorthodox that it caused a riot at its Paris premiere in 1913—but promptly established itself as a landmark of orchestration, rhythm, and polytonality.

The ever-unpredictable Stravinsky then switched directions in the 1920's and 1930's, moving toward a more austere Neoclassicism (*Oedipus Rex, Apollo, Symphony of Psalms*). In the 1950's he stunned the music world by embracing serialism, the system to which his music had been the major "alternative" for nearly forty years. His last works (*Agon, Canticum Sacrum, Requiem Canticles*) were highly original explorations of new approaches to serial composition. When Stravinsky died in 1971, young conductor Michael Tilson Thomas, who had worked closely with Stravinsky in California in the late 1960's, said: "The world has lost its oldest and youngest composer." The composer Nicholas Nabokov has written: "Despite his many twists and turns, Stravinsky became the unquestioned leader of Western music [in our time]. . . . Today Stravinsky and Schoenberg remain the lonely founding fathers of the strangely eccentric and highly anarchic state of modern music."

The Firebird

Few pieces of 20th-century music have become so widely popular as Stravinsky's *Firebird*, composed when Stravinsky was twenty-seven. A ballet based on Russian folktales about the Firebird and the evil magician Katschei had been commissioned from the Russian composer Liadov in 1909 by the great ballet impresario Diaghilev. However, Diaghilev became dissatisfied with Liadov's progress and turned to the young Stravinsky, whose short orchestral works had impressed him. Although Stravinsky later admitted that "the *Firebird* did not attract me as a subject," he accepted the offer and produced the score in less than six months. It was an immediate success, and launched Stravinsky's international career. Critics hailed its brilliant colors and ingenious instrumental combinations. Stravinsky himself remained its severest critic: "I was more proud of some of the orchestration than of the music itself," he later wrote. "The *Firebird* belongs to the style of its time. It is more vigorous than most of the 'composed' folk music of the period, but it is also not very original. These are all good conditions for a success," he said. Stravinsky twice revised parts of the score—first in 1919 in arranging a concert suite from the complete score, and again in 1945 (partly for copyright reasons, and different only in small details).

Recommended Recordings (Complete Score)

★ Ansermet, New Philharmonia (London stereo 2-disc set FBD-S-1)

Ozawa, Orchestre de Paris (Angel stereo disc S-36910)

Stravinsky, Columbia Symphony (Columbia stereo disc MS-6328)

Recommended Recordings (Suite)

★ Stokowski, London Symphony (London stereo disc SPC-21026; cassette M94026)

Giulini, Chicago Symphony (Angel stereo disc S-36039; cassette 4XS-36039; cartridge 8XS-36039)

Stravinsky, Columbia Symphony (Columbia stereo disc MS-7011)

Boulez, BBC Symphony (Columbia stereo disc MS-7206)

Comments

Ansermet's 1968 recording of the complete score, his last before his death that same year, is a beautiful achievement—different in many ways (particularly in dramatic accents and in the more lush playing of London's New Philharmonia Orchestra) from an earlier, mid-1950's recording with his regular Suisse Romande Orchestra (London CS-6017). Ansermet creates a gossamerlike mood of mystery and fantasy throughout, and his slowly paced finale has never sounded so regal. The sound engineering is electrifying in its clarity. *Note:* It is the earlier Suisse Romande recording—almost as good interpretively, but less well executed—that is included in the 3-LP set called "Ernest Ansermet & Igor Stravinsky: A Legendary Partnership" (London CSA-2308) along with the complete *Petrushka*, the *Rite of Spring*, and *Le Baiser de la Fée* (*The Fairy's Kiss*), plus a free "bonus" record on which Ansermet gives a very erudite talk (in English) on some of his musical theories.

Ozawa's 1972 recording accents more primary colors than Ansermet's, and there is also more of a feeling of rhythmic urgency to the earlier sections. The sound engineering is exceptionally good.

Stravinsky's 1961 recording of the complete score is taken at a faster pace than Ansermet's, and has more dramatic punch, if less sensitivity or sense of mystery. The same performance is included in a 3-LP set (Columbia stereo D3S-705) together with the complete *Petrushka* and *Rite of Spring*. Stravinsky's 1967 recording of the 1945 Suite has much the same qualities as his complete version, and includes the most familiar—and best—parts of the ballet. It is coupled with an abridged *Petrushka* Suite.

Stokowski probably did as much as any conductor to popularize *The Firebird* over the past fifty years. He was the first to record it, and has re-recorded it at least four times. His latest version (1967) is a highly individualistic and brilliantly colorful version of the 1919 suite, superbly engineered. It is coupled with dramatic performances of Tchaikovsky's *March Slav* and Mussorgsky's *A Night on Bald Mountain*.

Giulini's 1970 recording of the 1919 suite is a splendid one in the way it blends a feeling of mystery and drama, and the Chicagoans play it superbly. Overside, Giulini offers a marvelously subtle and poignant *Petrushka* Suite.

Boulez's 1970 performance is excellent in its mood and rhythmic detail—as far as it goes, for he uses the original 1910 suite which does not include the Lullaby and Finale, two of the most popular sections of the later suites. It is coupled with a superb performance of Bartók's *Music for Strings, Percussion, and Celesta*.

Petrushka

Close to *The Firebird* in popularity, but much more original, is *Petrushka* (1911)—sometimes spelled *Petrouchka* (the French transliteration of Stravinsky's title as used at the Paris premiere). The ballet is set in czarist St. Petersburg in 1830, during the Shrovetide Fair just preceding Lent. A puppeteer has set up a booth for performances by three of his life-size puppets which he has, through magic, imbued with human feelings. To tell the ballet's tragicomic story, Stravinsky used an intriguingly mechanical kind of rhythm, a colorful orchestration, and a number of catchy Russian folk themes. But most significant and controversial were Stravinsky's harmonic innovations. He boldly combined chords of the most distant keys to create a new *bitonality* (sometimes, but not always accurately, called *polytonality*). He also varied time signatures and even used different ones simultaneously. For all such technical inventiveness, the music is immediately appealing to the listener. The music from *Petrushka* exists in several forms: the original 1911 score, a revised 1947 edition (in which Stravinsky thinned down some of the orchestration and made other alterations), a suite of dances (mainly the carnival scenes) from the complete score, and a 1921 piano transcription of three scenes.

Recommended Recordings

★ Ansermet, Suisse Romande Orchestra (London stereo disc CS-6009)
  Boulez, New York Philharmonic (Columbia stereo disc M-31076; cassette MT-31076; cartridge MA-31076; also quadrasonic disc MQ-31076; cartridge MAQ-31076)
  Stravinsky, Columbia Symphony (Columbia stereo disc MS-6332)

Giulini, Chicago Symphony (Angel stereo disc S-36039; casette 4XS-36039; cartridge 8XS-36039), *suite only*

Monteux, Boston Symphony (RCA Red Seal stereo disc LSC-2376)

Comments

Ansermet's international reputation in the years following World War II owed as much to a 1947 *Petrushka* recording as to anything else. That recording also made history by introducing to the U.S. the "ffrr" high fidelity technique of London Records (then known as English Decca), virtually setting off the whole postwar hi-fi boom. Ansermet twice re-recorded the score, each time setting new high fidelity or stereo standards in the process. His last version (CS-6009), made in the mid-1960's, is a stunning achievement all around. Using the original 1911 version of the score, Ansermet brings out all sorts of rhythmic and coloristic subtleties that other conductors rarely even hint at (particularly in his use of percussion instruments). And his rhythmic pulse is unerring, whatever the score's complexities. Sonically, the recording is one of the best any company has ever made. *Note:* The same performance is also available in the 3-LP set (London CSA-2308) "Ernest Ansermet & Igor Stravinsky," discussed in the comments on *Firebird* above.

Boulez's 1972 recording, his first as music director of the New York Philharmonic, also uses the 1911 version. He performs it with more bite than Ansermet, and at brisker tempos (closer to Stravinsky's own). And the clarity of detail in the performance is outstanding. It is available in both stereo and quadrasonic editions.

Stravinsky, using the 1947 revision, conducts a lively, jaunty performance, with many wonderful touches, both humorous and dramatic. Critic Alfred Frankenstein (writing in *High Fidelity*) said of this 1960 recording: "Stravinsky seems to see—or hear—the whole of this score as if it were played on a vast concertina as big as the pit of an opera house. The feeling of squeeze-box music for a popular fair dominates everything." A Stravinsky-led *Petrushka* Suite (Columbia stereo disc MS-7011) is taken from the same 1960 complete recording, with the concert ending Stravinsky wrote for the Suite edited in to replace the final scene; the Suite is coupled with a Stravinsky-led performance of the *Firebird* Suite. Sound on all of these is very good.

Giulini's 1970 recording of the 1947 suite is a marvelously subtle and poignant creation, played without the hardness so many other conductors mistake for "punch." It is coupled with an excellent *Firebird* Suite.

Monteux's 1960 recording, using the 1911 score which he premiered, is rhythmically vibrant and colorful, and he brings a particular depth of feeling to the scene in Petrushka's room.

Le Sacre du Printemps (The Rite of Spring)

Few musical works of this (or any) century have created quite the sensation Stravinsky's *Rite* did at its premiere in 1913—or have changed the direction of subsequent orchestral music so significantly. Pierre Boulez has called the *Rite* "the cornerstone of modern music" and "a manifesto work." Coming at a time when

Romantic and Impressionistic music had made rhythm subordinate to form, expression, or mood, the *Rite* boldly asserted the preeminence of rhythm and rhythmic impulse. It did so with a work designed to depict the celebration of primitive, pagan rites in old Russia. Its barbaric, almost convulsive power, its rhythmic invention, tension, and decibel intensity were unlike anything Western music had ever known before. Inevitably, some critics at first attacked it as "a blasphemous attempt to destroy music as an art" or as "the precise exploitation of violence." But over the years, understanding of the *Rite's* freshness and inventiveness has grown—while the electric excitement of the work rarely fails to affect audiences. The Paris premiere of 1913 ended in a near-riot with half the audience scrambling for the exits. In contrast, in 1965 the largest audience ever known to attend a single symphony concert to that time—estimated at 75,000 people—turned out in New York's Central Park to hear Leonard Bernstein lead Stravinsky's *Rite* and Beethoven's *Eroica*. The ballet for which Stravinsky wrote his score is divided into two parts: (1) "The Adoration of the Earth," which depicts the gradual emergence of spring and the celebration of the new season through pagan ceremonies and dances; (2) "The Sacrifice," which depicts the selection of the chosen virgin whose sacrifice will fertilize the earth, and finally her frenetic dance of death.

Recommended Recordings

★ Bernstein, London Symphony (Columbia quadrasonic disc M-31520; cassette MT-31520; cartridge MA-31520)

Boulez, Cleveland Orchestra (Columbia stereo disc MS-7293; cassette 16-11-0154)

Thomas, Boston Symphony (Deutsche Grammophon stereo disc 2530252)

Stravinsky, Columbia Symphony (Columbia stereo disc MS-6319)

Frühbeck de Burgos, New Philharmonia (Angel stereo disc S-36427, cassette 4XS-36427; cartridge 8XS-36427)

Comments

Bernstein's 1972 recording has enormous force and excitement. It is, in fact, one of his all-time best recordings—packed with the kind of kinetic drama, rhythmic drive, and sheer gut power few others ever achieve with this score. Available in both quadrasonic and stereo versions, it is sonically outstanding as well—and definitely superior to an earlier (1958) Bernstein recording with the New York Philharmonic (Columbia MS-6010 or D2S-749).

Boulez brings astonishing clarity and definition to his 1969 Cleveland recording. His is a more clinically intellectual view of the score, but without ever sacrificing the work's rhythmic pulse, energy, or tension. The sound engineering is excellent. *Note:* This version is infinitely superior to an earlier Boulez recording made with the French National Orchestra (Nonesuch stereo disc 71093) in both orchestral execution and sound engineering.

Thomas' 1972 performance is close to Bernstein's in its dramatic urgency and rhythmic bite, and has even more of an aura of mystery in its quieter sections. The sound engineering, while excellent, is not quite as impressive as Columbia's for either Bernstein or Boulez. However, Thomas' recording has an interesting bonus: a short, rarely-heard choral work *Svesdolikia* (The King of the Stars), written just before the *Rite of Spring* as an experiment in complex harmony, and well sung by the Men's Choir of the New England Conservatory of Music under Thomas' direction. Thomas, together with Canadian pianist Ralph Grierson, has also recorded Stravinsky's own piano version (four-hand) of the *Rite* (Angel stereo disc S-36024; cassette 4XS-36024; cartridge 8XS-36024), a 1969 release. It is an interesting curio, not only for the excellent playing of the two young pianists, but also as a documentary view of how Stravinsky himself (composing at the piano) must have first "heard" his history-making score. The orchestral colors may be lacking, but the rhythmic pulse is there.

Stravinsky's own recording is a vivid performance recorded in the early 1960's. It is tauter and leaner-sounding than most other performances (except Boulez's). It is available singly or in a 3-LP album (Columbia D3S-705) which also contains excellent performances of the complete *Firebird* and *Petrushka*.

Frühbeck de Burgos, a master at projecting almost any work's rhythmic pulse, gives an exciting, strongly animated performance (from about 1966), with excellent sound.

For Follow-Up Consideration

Symphony of Psalms, a deeply eloquent work for chorus (singing in Latin) and orchestra based on Biblical psalms, written a year after Stravinsky's reconversion to the Russian Orthodox Church in 1928. RECOMMENDED RECORDINGS: Ansermet, Suisse Romande Orchestra and Geneva Choir (London stereo disc CS-6219), or Shaw, RCA Victor Symphony and Robert Shaw Chorale (RCA Red Seal stereo disc LSC-2822). Ansermet premiered the score in 1930, and his 1962 stereo release is a superbly spacious and moving one, coupled with a spirited performance of Stravinsky's *Les Noces*. Shaw's 1965 release is equally exceptional in every respect, and is coupled with an outstanding performance of Poulenc's joyously beautiful *Gloria* (1960).

Symphony in Three Movements, composed in 1945 and, according to the composer, reflecting some of his feelings about World War II. RECOMMENDED RECORDING: Stravinsky, Columbia Symphony Orchestra (Columbia stereo disc MS-6331), a rhythmically vital 1961 performance, coupled with an excellent performance overside of Stravinsky's rather dry Violin Concerto, with Stern as soloist and Bernstein conducting.

Concerto in D for String Orchestra, a gripping, rhythmically vibrant, yet lyrical orchestral work, composed in 1946 and fairly well known as the score for Jerome Robbins' ballet *The Cage* (for the New York City Ballet repertory). RECOMMENDED RECORDING: Colin Davis, English Chamber Orchestra (London/L'Oiseau-Lyre stereo disc 60050), one of Davis' first (1962) major recordings and still one of his best, coupled with Stravinsky's good-humored *Danses Concertantes* (1941) and the neo-Baroque *Dumbarton Oaks* Concerto (1938).

Agon, a dry, terse, but fascinating ballet score written for George Balanchine and the

New York City Ballet in 1957; its seventeen relatively short movements combine Neoclassical tonality, chromaticism, and modified serial procedures. RECOMMENDED RECORDING: Stravinsky, Los Angeles Festival Symphony (Columbia stereo disc CMS-6022), a crisply definitive performance from the late 1950's, coupled with Stravinsky's serialist *Canticum Sacrum.*

• ANTON VON WEBERN

Pronounced: *vay*-burn. Born December 3, 1883, in Vienna, Austria. Died September 15, 1945, in Mittersill, near Salzburg.

SIGNIFICANCE: Austrian composer and conductor, who distilled the essence of 12-tone music in works of remarkable sensitivity, transparency, economy, and precision.

BACKGROUND: After studying composition and musicology at the University of Vienna, Webern earned his living by conducting in small opera houses and theatres in Austria. He met Arnold Schoenberg in 1904, and studied privately with him for the next six years. Later he founded—with Schoenberg—the Society for Private Musical Performances in Vienna, which first presented many of the works of the Schoenberg school.

After 1924, Webern composed only in the 12-tone idiom. But, in contrast to Schoenberg and Berg, he composed in a more tightly-knit, more economical style. He became active as a conductor of modern works in Germany and Austria, and in 1929 served as a guest conductor with the British Broadcasting Company (BBC) in London. During World War II, he lived quietly in Austria in what some commentators have called an "inner exile." Just a few months after the war's end, he was accidentally killed by a soldier on patrol duty at night in the American occupation zone while out walking near his son-in-law's home.

Five Pieces for Orchestra

These short, spare pieces are like miniature jewels. Composed between 1911 and 1913, they are impressive examples of the sensitivity, economy, and kaleidoscopic coloring of Webern's writing. The work is scored for a fairly small orchestra and includes such unconventional instruments as guitar and mandolin. The shortest of the five pieces is about thirty seconds, the longest about a minute and a half.

Recommended Recordings

★ Boulez, London Symphony (Columbia stereo disc OS-3320)
   Craft, Columbia Symphony (Columbia stereo disc CMS-6103)

Comments

Boulez's performance is beautifully transparent and sensitive. It is included in an album along with Berio's *Visage* and a part of Mahler's Fourth Symphony (led by

Bernstein) as used in the 1969 French film *La Prisonnière*, although it is also scheduled to be included in an all-Webern album that Boulez completed recording in 1973.

Craft's mid-1960's performance is also a fine one, perceptive and clear. It is coupled with an excellent performance of Schoenberg's *Five Pieces for Orchestra* and Berg's *Altenberg Songs*, splendidly sung by Bethany Beardslee.

For Follow-Up Consideration

Six Pieces for Orchestra, similar in many ways to the *Five Pieces* in their economy, sensitivity, and prismatic coloring. RECOMMENDED RECORDING: At this writing there are, shockingly, no recordings listed in the Schwann catalog—of an influential work written in 1909! However, a 1972 Boulez recording with the London Symphony was awaiting release on Columbia, and, on the basis of a performance I heard Boulez conduct of the work in a concert with the Cleveland Orchestra, it should be highly recommendable.

Im Sommerwind, a short, lushly Romantic, almost Richard Straussian tone picture written just before Webern met Schoenberg in 1904 and therefore interesting in comparison with his later works. RECOMMENDED RECORDING: Ormandy, Philadelphia Orchestra (Columbia stereo disc MS-7041), coupled with a later, more terse, 12-tone Webern work, *Three Pieces for Orchestra* (1911), Schoenberg's *Theme and Variations*, and the orchestral suite from Berg's opera *Lulu*.

• ALBAN BERG

Pronounced: *bairg*. Born February 7, 1885, in Vienna, Austria. Died December 24, 1935, in Vienna.

SIGNIFICANCE: Austrian composer, a pioneer in the development of serial music.

BACKGROUND: Although Berg pursued musical interests as a youth in Vienna, he had no formal musical training until he was nineteen. After meeting Schoenberg, he gave up his position as a minor government official to study with him in Vienna and Berlin. He became one of Schoenberg's chief disciples in developing the principles of 12-tone (dodecaphonic) composition.

Berg's opera *Wozzeck*, written between 1914 and 1922 (partly while Berg, despite poor health, served in the Austrian army) is considered a modern milestone—a powerfully dramatic, atonal opera blending realism, irony, and sentimentality in a strikingly original way. An exacting craftsman, Berg's output was small, and he died (of blood poisoning following a bee sting) before finishing his second opera, *Lulu*. The latter is nonetheless widely considered another modern masterpiece even in its incomplete form.

Three Pieces for Orchestra

In comparing the music of Schoenberg, Webern, and Berg, some commentators have described Berg as the most openly dramatic and accessible. And the *Three Pieces* of 1914–15 certainly qualify as openly dramatic and accessible to the average listener. Dedicated to Schoenberg, they were intended for his fortieth birthday, but were not completed until the following year—and then not given a complete performance for another fifteen years. Today they are widely recognized among this century's finest works. Scored for large orchestra, the *Three Pieces* are basically dark in color—Berg was partial to low sonorities, rarely using instruments in their upper registers. Their mood varies from brooding to violently explosive. The first movement, *"Präludium"* ("Prelude") is murkily mysterious; the second, *"Reigen"* ("Round Dances"), plays gloomily with faded waltz rhythms; the third, *"Marsch"* ("March"), is a big, dramatic, violently anguished processional which is almost harrowing in its intensity. This music, particularly the third movement, is recommended as an introduction to Berg's operatic masterpiece, *Wozzeck*—whose dramatic force has much in common with the *Three Pieces*.

Recommended Recordings

★ Boulez, BBC Symphony Orchestra (Columbia stereo disc MS-7179)
  Abbado, London Symphony (Deutsche Grammophon stereo disc 2530146)

Comments

Boulez's 1969 release is dramatically forceful and remarkably clear in texture, bringing out all sorts of subtleties that other performances don't even hint at. It is coupled with two other worthwhile Berg works—the five *Altenberg Songs*, expressively sung by Halina Lukomska, and the Chamber Concerto (for Piano, Violin, and 13 Winds), with Barenboim as pianist.

Abbado's 1971 release is a bit on the overdramatic side, but it is harrowingly effective and sonically impressive. It is coupled with an intensely feverish account of the suite from *Lulu*, and a moving performance of the five *Altenberg Songs* sung by Margaret Price.

Wozzeck

To many critics, this is the most important opera of the 20th century, and it is the first primarily atonal opera to win a place in the world's great opera houses. Its acceptance was slow, however. Premiered in Berlin in 1925 (under conductor Erich Kleiber), *Wozzeck* promptly divided audiences into fanatic admirers and fanatic antagonists, with the latter in the majority. Yet over the next ten years it was heard more than 150 times in 28 different cities—mostly in Germany, until the Nazis banned it in 1936. Leopold Stokowski introduced *Wozzeck* to the U.S. in 1931 in Philadelphia; and Dimitri Mitropoulos was an active U.S. champion of it in the 1940's and '50's. *Wozzeck* entered the repertory of the New York City Opera in 1952, and of the Metropolitan

Opera in 1965. Today it is increasingly admired for its integration of musical structure and dramatic thought, and for its compassionate view of a Kafkaesque humanity.

Berg based his opera on the play of the revolutionary young German dramatist Georg Büchner, who died in 1837 at the age of twenty-five. Büchner's *Wozzeck* tells the tragic story of a desperately poor, persecuted, simple soldier, and the events leading to the murder of his mistress. Just as Büchner was many decades ahead of his time in his scientific understanding of human behavior and in his denunciation of Europe's social order, so Berg was many decades ahead of his time in his musical version. The entire score is organized in abstract musical forms—yet, as annotator Theodor W. Adorno has written, "the music and words are so artfully linked that it is impossible to tell where one begins and the other ends." Large sections of *Wozzeck*'s three acts (fifteen scenes, reduced from Büchner's twenty-six) are written in a chamber music style, with Berg using full orchestral resources sparingly to heighten specific points of the drama. Says noted musicologist Ernest Newman: "It is music drawn from [the character] of Wozzeck's poor, worried, inarticulate, chaotic soul. . . . The orchestra is just a bundle of nerves; at first sight it seems to consist only of confused strands, but it is actually a living organism. . . . Even the noise proves to be expression, and the naturalism style. . . . The work is full of what lies behind and beneath our ordinary waking life."

Recommended Recordings (Complete)

★ Böhm (conductor), Fischer-Dieskau (Wozzeck), Lear (Marie), Wunderlich (Andres), Berlin Deutsche Opera Orchestra and Chorus (Deutsche Grammophon stereo 2-disc set 2707023)

Boulez (conductor), Berry (Wozzeck), Strauss (Marie), Van Vrooman (Andres), Paris National Opera Orchestra and Chorus (Columbia stereo 2-disc set M2-30852)

Recommended Recordings (Excerpts)

★ Leinsdorf (conductor), Curtin (Marie), Boston Symphony (included in RCA Red Seal stereo 2-disc set LSC-7031)

Kegel (conductor), Kühse (Marie), Leipzig Radio Symphony (included in Vanguard stereo 2-disc set C-10011/2)

Comments

Both the Böhm and Boulez complete recordings, dating from the mid-1960's, are outstanding for the conductors' penetrating understanding and execution of this complex score, and are very well recorded. Böhm conducted the score in Germany before the Nazi ban, and has been a faithful advocate ever since. Boulez was responsible for the Paris Opera's belated but highly-acclaimed 1963 premiere, and is among the foremost champions of Berg's music generally.

Surprisingly (considering their approach to other music), it is Böhm who stresses the work's form more consistently, although Boulez is more subtle in some of the orchestral parts. Böhm's cast is outstanding—especially Fischer-Dieskau in the title role and Lear as Marie. Berry has many interesting moments as Wozzeck in the Boulez recording, but he is sometimes guilty of overacting and of distorted vocal mannerisms.

Both sets of excerpts listed above are included as the fourth side of 2-LP recordings of Mahler's Symphony No. 5 (Mahler's widow was instrumental in getting *Wozzeck* published, and the opera is dedicated to her). Phyllis Curtin sings Marie's arias beautifully, if a bit too elegantly for the character, and Leinsdorf's performance is gripping and forceful. Hanne-Lore Kühse is Marie in the East German set of excerpts, and she uses her big, bright voice unusually expressively. The accompanying performances of Mahler's Fifth by Leinsdorf and Neumann, however, are only fair. The RCA was released in 1964, the Vanguard in 1967.

All of the listed performances are sung in German.

For Follow-Up Consideration

Violin Concerto, one of the most expressive of 12-tone works, an elegiac concerto which turned out to be Berg's last completed work. RECOMMENDED RECORDING: Stern, Bernstein, New York Philharmonic (Columbia stereo disc MS-6373), a deeply moving, forceful performance from the late 1950's, coupled with Bartók's Rhapsody for Violin and Orchestra.

Lulu Suite, an orchestral suite of five movements which Berg arranged in 1934 from his opera *Lulu* (partly, perhaps, to stir public anticipation for the opera itself, which he planned to finish soon). This is complex, atonal music similar in many ways to *Wozzeck*. RECOMMENDED RECORDING: Ormandy, Philadelphia Orchestra (Columbia stereo disc MS-7041), played with great sweep and fervor, and coupled with several interesting, rarely recorded works by Webern and Schoenberg.

• SERGE PROKOFIEV

Pronounced: pro-*kaw*-fee-ef. Born April 23, 1891, in Sonzowka, Russia. Died March 7, 1953, in Moscow.

SIGNIFICANCE: Russian composer and pianist, one of the most lyrical, frequently witty, and rhythmically vibrant of the early 20th-century "modernists."

BACKGROUND: Prokofiev began composing when he was five, and tried to write his first opera at nine after having seen one. As a teenager he studied at the St. Petersburg Conservatory with Rimsky-Korsakov and Liadov, stirring controversy there by his experimentations with unconventional, often violent tonalities. Between 1914 and 1921 he wrote several scores for Diaghilev's Ballet Russe. One, the barbaric, dissonant *Scythian Suite* (clearly influenced by Stravinsky's *Rite of Spring*) caused a scandal and won considerable sympathy for Prokofiev when a famous critic wrote a review violently attacking the music even though he had not heard it (the work had been withdrawn at the last moment, unknown to the critic).

Prokofiev left Russia after the Communist Revolution, traveled for a while in the U.S., then settled in Paris. In 1934 he decided to return to Russia permanently. Over the following years he had his ups and downs with the Soviet authorities, who sometimes praised him as the greatest modern Russian composer and at other times denounced him bitterly for writing in "decadent" Western styles. After World War II he suffered a series of strokes which seriously curtailed his activity, though he continued to compose and extensively revise earlier works up to his death in 1953.

Romeo and Juliet

Composed in 1935 as a full-length ballet score, Prokofiev's *Romeo and Juliet* was at first rejected by the Leningrad Ballet as "undanceable" music (the same charge once made about Tchaikovsky's *Swan Lake*). Since a 1947 Bolshoi production in Moscow, however, it has gone on to become one of the most internationally popular ballets of the 20th century in different Russian, English, Danish, and German productions. Two of them have been turned into films, one with Ulanova, the other with Fonteyn and Nureyev. It has also become an increasingly popular orchestral score in the concert hall. The music is colorful and lyrical, the duel sequences are exciting, the depiction of the Verona aristocracy is grandly sumptuous and bitingly sardonic, and the romantic tragedy of Shakespeare's lovers is eloquently conveyed. In the late 1930's Prokofiev, despairing of a production of the complete ballet, arranged some of the music into a series of concert suites. He did not just lift sections straight from the ballet, but rather reworked them. These suites are the basis for most of the recordings of this music, although it has become common for conductors to select different movements from the suites and to perform them in various sequences.

Recommended Recordings (Complete Ballet)

★ Previn, London Symphony Orchestra (Angel stereo 3-disc set SC-3802)
Maazel, Cleveland Orchestra (London stereo 3-disc CSA-2312)

Recommended Recordings (Highlights or Suites)

★ Leinsdorf, Boston Symphony Orchestra (RCA Red Seal stereo disc LSC-2994; cartridge R8S-1088)
Ansermet, Suisse Romande Orchestra (London stereo disc CS-6240)
Skrowaczewski, Minneapolis Symphony (Mercury stereo disc SR-90315)
b Prokofiev, Moscow Philharmonic (Turnabout disc 4160, *mono only*)

Comments

With recordings, it's sometimes either feast or famine. Until 1973 there had been no complete recordings of this Prokofiev score (the closest had been a poorly recorded, Russian-made, 2-disc mono set released in the U.S. briefly in the mid-1950's by Colosseum). When the gap was finally filled, it was with two simultaneous releases— both outstanding for their stereo engineering and for the quality of the performances. It's difficult to choose between them. Previn is perhaps a bit jauntier in the street scenes, and brings many marvelously subtle touches to the romantic ones. Maazel's lyrical intensity is impressive, and he zips through the livelier sections with great exuberance. Angel's sound has a slight edge over London's overall.

Leinsdorf is the only conductor named above to record excerpts from the original ballet itself—not the reworked suites Prokofiev made for concert performance. His arrangement offers a greater amount of the music (eighteen movements) than do the suites, and he performs it all with marvelous color, sweep, and lyrical intensity in this 1968 release.

Ansermet chooses ten movements from Suites No. 1 and 2, performing them with tremendous thrust and color, and London's sound engineering (from about 1960) is exceptionally vivid.

Skrowaczewski's 1962 recording offers the complete Suite No. 1 and all but one section of Suite No. 2 (fourteen movements in all), played with exceptional vividness, sparkle, and rhythmic tautness. This recording has recently been withdrawn from the active catalog, but may still be available in some shops.

The recording of the Suite No. 2 conducted by the composer is of historic interest only, for the sound (apparently from the late 1940's) is primitive.

Classical Symphony

Actually Prokofiev's Symphony No. 1, this brief symphony was written in 1917 "as Mozart or Haydn might have written a symphony if they lived in our day," to quote the composer. It is high-spirited, frequently whimsical, and dissonant, yet a lyrically elegant work of Classical simplicity and clarity.

Recommended Recordings

★ Bernstein, New York Philharmonic (Columbia stereo disc MS-7159)

 Ansermet, Suisse Romande Orchestra (London stereo disc CS-6223)

 Abbado, London Symphony (London stereo disc CS-6679)

 Rozhdestvensky, Moscow Radio Symphony (Melodiya/Angel stereo disc S-40061)

Comments

Bernstein is marvelously jaunty and dynamic in a 1968 performance that wisely does not rush the first movement and therefore makes the tempo of the finale that much more effective. Overside, Bernstein pursues the theme of a young composer "commenting on" earlier Classical forms with an exceptionally good performance of Bizet's Symphony in C.

Ansermet's early 1960's performance has an even more leisurely beginning, bringing out a wealth of superb detail all the way through to a crisp and lively finale. His coupling includes some well-played short pieces by Glinka and Borodin.

Abbado also doesn't rush the first movement, and offers a sparklingly clean-lined, well-proportioned performance throughout. Overside on his 1970 release is a first-rate performance of Prokofiev's frenzied and brooding Third Symphony, based on themes from his long-neglected 1925 opera, *The Flaming Angel*.

Rozhdestvensky's late 1960's performance is stylish and vibrant, and it is coupled with his spirited account of Prokofiev's nostalgically lyrical Symphony No. 7.

Symphony No. 5

Prokofiev called this work, written in 1944, "a symphony on the greatness of the human spirit." Many inner meanings have been read into the work, based on Prokofiev's ups and downs with Soviet officialdom. For example, some say its vigorously marching rhythms symbolize the Soviet state and its promises, while its broodingly melancholic melodies reflect the harshness of the system on individual human existence. Others say the work reflects a more basic, non-political conflict between men and machines in our century. One could go on and on, but what counts most is that the music itself is exciting and moving—one of the monumental symphonic statements of the 20th century.

Recommended Recordings

★ Karajan, Berlin Philharmonic (Deutsche Grammophon stereo disc 139040; cassette 923-084; cartridge 89-040)

Bernstein, New York Philharmonic (Columbia stereo disc MS-7005)

Leinsdorf, Boston Symphony (RCA Red Seal stereo disc LSC-2707)

Comments

Karajan, in his 1968 recording, builds the first movement to an overwhelming climax, and then goes on to mold each movement dramatically and sharply into a perfect whole.

Bernstein also builds the first movement overpoweringly, and gives the second and fourth movements exceptional thrust in this mid-1960's recording. But he gives the third movement an almost Mahler-like profundity which some may find too heavy-handed.

Leinsdorf's 1963 recording brings structural clarity, rhythmic drive, and brilliant tonal balances to one of the cornerstones of his outstanding Prokofiev series for RCA.

Piano Concerto No. 3 in C major

A bold, intricate, percussive, yet witty modern concerto, this work was first performed by the composer himself as soloist with the Chicago Symphony Orchestra in 1921—during the period when Prokofiev lived in the U.S. following the Russian Revolution. It has gone on to become one of the most popular of all modern piano concertos.

Recommended Recordings

★ Argerich, Abbado, Berlin Philharmonic (Deutsche Grammophon stereo disc 139349; cassette 923-040)

Janis, Kondrashin, Moscow Philharmonic (Philips stereo disc SR1-75019; cassette MCR4-90300; cartridge MC8-90300)

Browning, Leinsdorf, Boston Symphony (RCA Red Seal stereo disc LSC-3019)

Graffman, Szell, Cleveland (Columbia stereo disc MS-6925)

Prokofiev, Coppola, London Symphony (Angel disc COLH34, *mono only*)

Comments

Argerich tosses off the most difficult passages deftly and spiritedly, and also understands that underneath all the dissonance Prokofiev was one of this century's most lyrical composers. She is matched every bar of the way in this 1967 recording by Abbado's incisive accompaniment.

Janis' 1962 recording marked the first time an American pianist was recorded with a Russian orchestra in Moscow by U.S. technicians using U.S. equipment. Musically, it is a brilliant, exhilarating performance, with a dynamic accompaniment by Kondrashin.

Browning and Leinsdorf have collaborated on two outstanding versions. A deleted earlier one (once Capitol SP8545, and dating from 1962) was crisper, the later Boston recording (1968) more subtly vibrant.

Graffman has also recorded the concerto twice, once in the late '50's, with Jorda and the San Francisco Symphony (still available as RCA Victrola stereo disc VICS-1105), and then a decade later with Szell. The later edition is much superior in both Graffman's steely, propulsive playing, and in Szell's pungent accompaniment.

Prokofiev's own 1932 recording is dated sonically, but it still shows off the composer's impressive strengths as a pianist, as well as providing a definitive interpretation. It has recently been deleted from the active catalog, but may still be available in some stores.

In terms of couplings, both Browning and Graffman offer other Prokofiev piano concertos overside—Graffman a rousing performance of the First Concerto plus the Piano Sonata No. 3, and Browning the unusual Fourth Concerto for Left Hand Alone (with themes Prokofiev reused later in his ballet *Romeo and Juliet*). Janis offers a sweepingly expressive, brilliant account of Rachmaninoff's First Piano Concerto. Argerich offers Ravel's Piano Concerto in G in an amiable performance. The Prokofiev reissue is filled out with seventeen short piano pieces recorded by the composer in 1935.

Peter and the Wolf

Although this piece was designed as a musical fairy tale for children, its humor, charm, and vitality have long kept it an adult favorite, too. Its narration has been assayed in English over the years by such diverse personalities as Mrs. Franklin D. Roosevelt, Boris Karloff, Sean Connery, Wilfred Pickles, Lorne Green, Warren Rich, Mrs. Edward (Ted) Kennedy, Mia Farrow, and many others.

Recommended Recordings

★ Bernstein, New York Philharmonic (Columbia stereo disc MS-6193; cassette 16-11-0030; cartridge 18-11-0030)

Henderson, Lillie, London Symphony (London stereo disc CS-6187)

Stokowski, Keeshan, Stadium Symphony of New York (Everest stereo disc 3043)

Comments

Bernstein both narrates and conducts with warmth, good humor, and marvelous spirit. Overside he offers a good performance of Tchaikovsky's *Nutcracker Suite* in this 1960 release.

Beatrice Lillie blends a sense of irreverent camp with just enough straightforward charm to make her 1960 version a special delight, and Skitch Henderson's conducting is crisp and stylish. Overside Lillie reads Ogden Nash's wry lines for Saint-Saens' *Carnival of the Animals*, with Katchen and Graffman as the superstar duo-pianists.

Stokowski offers a unique two-for-the-money deal, with TV's Bob Keeshan handling the narration on one side, and with Prokofiev's music alone without any narration on the reverse side—an edition with many advantages for those who tire of narrations after a few times. The Stadium Symphony, incidentally, is essentially the New York Philharmonic in its late 1950's summer guise.

For Follow-Up Consideration

Lieutenant Kijé, a light and bubbly orchestral suite which Prokofiev drew from his music for the 1934 Soviet film *The Czar Sleeps*—a satire about government bureaucracy in which a group of army officers invents adventures for a nonexistent Lt. Kijé to cover up a typographical error ("kijé" is roughly the Russian equivalent for "whatchamacallit"). RECOMMENDED RECORDING: Leinsdorf, Boston Symphony (RCA Red Seal stereo disc LSC-3061), a wry and frisky 1967 performance in which Leinsdorf includes the rarely heard baritone solos, sung in Russian with just the right mock seriousness by David Clatworthy. Overside is a propulsive Leinsdorf performance of Prokofiev's thunderous Second Symphony.

Alexander Nevsky, a colorful, frequently exciting, massively scored cantata for orchestra, chorus, and mezzo-soprano, based on the music Prokofiev wrote for the 1938 Eisenstein film epic *Alexander Nevsky*, the highly propagandistic but visually classic account of the Teutonic invasion of Russia in 1240. RECOMMENDED RECORDING: Schippers, Chookasian, New York Philharmonic, Westminster Choir (Odyssey stereo disc Y-31014), a rousing 1961 performance (originally on Columbia, reissued on Odyssey in 1972), bursting with drama, especially in the slashing rhythms of the climactic "Battle on the Ice."

Symphony No. 6 in E-flat minor, considered by many critics to be Prokofiev's finest symphony, although less immediately appealing than the Fifth. If the Fifth is about "the spirit of man," then the Sixth is about "the spirit of the artist." Its complex second movement, in particular, has been interpreted as reflecting Prokofiev's mixed emotions about artistic creativity under the Soviet system. RECOMMENDED RECORDING: Leinsdorf, Boston Symphony (RCA Red Seal stereo disc LSC-2834), a 1965 performance that is searingly intense and rightly austere where it should be, and beautifully delicate in the subtler parts of the finale.

Violin Concerto No. 2 in G minor, an alternately vivacious and pensive, beautifully lyrical, modern concerto. RECOMMENDED RECORDING: Heifetz, Munch, Boston Symphony (RCA Red Seal stereo disc LSC-4010; cartridge R8S-1083), a brilliant performance dating from the mid-1950's, coupled with an outstanding Heifetz–Hendl performance of the Sibelius Violin Concerto.

Piano Concerto No. 2, an exciting, lyrical, capricious, and occasionally sarcastic concerto, with many dizzying technical demands for the soloist. RECOMMENDED RECORDING: Browning, Leinsdorf, Boston Symphony (RCA Red Seal stereo disc LSC-2897), a 1965 performance that abounds in driving energy, yet which also lets the piece sing mellowly. It is coupled with an equally outstanding Browning–Leinsdorf performance of Prokofiev's First Piano Concerto.

• GEORGE GERSHWIN

Pronounced: *gur*-shwin. Born September 26, 1898, in Brooklyn, N.Y. Died July 12, 1937, in Hollywood, California.

SIGNIFICANCE: American composer and pianist, one of the first and most successful in combining American popular melody and jazz elements in symphonic forms.

BACKGROUND: Gershwin began studying music as a teenager in his native New York City. Almost from the beginning, he talked of blending American popular music with classical music. He published his first popular song at eighteen, and soon afterward began contributing to a long series of successful Broadway shows. In 1922 he wrote a one-act "jazz opera," *Blue Monday*, which was to be incorporated in one of George White's popular *Scandals* but was dropped after the first performance because it was considered too morbid for a Broadway revue. It was seen, however, by bandleader Paul Whiteman, who commissioned Gershwin to write an extended symphonic jazz work for concert performance. The result was *Rhapsody in Blue* (1924), which was a triumphant success.

Gershwin continued to write concert works in a jazz vein (Piano Concerto in F, *An American in Paris*, *Cuban Overture*) while also writing songs for Broadway shows and Hollywood films. His most ambitious serious effort, the "Negro folk opera" *Porgy and Bess* (1935), had a mixed reception from both critics and the public, and did not achieve success until revivals after his death. In 1937, while working in Hollywood, he developed a brain tumor and died a few months before his thirty-ninth birthday. In the years since then, his popularity on Broadway and in the concert hall has remained undimmed.

Rhapsody in Blue

This first notable (and still the most popular) jazz-oriented concert work was written at the last minute for a 1924 concert of American music—during a period when

Gershwin, then twenty-five, was also working on the score for a Broadway show called *Sweet Little Devil*. Paul Whiteman had approached Gershwin the preceding year about writing a jazz concerto. But in the press of all his activities, Gershwin had virtually forgotten about the project until a newspaper ad in January of 1924 announced the concert five weeks away. Because of the shortness of the time left, Gershwin and Whiteman agreed that Gershwin would provide just the piano score, and that the Whiteman band's chief arranger, Ferde Grofé (who later wrote the popular *Grand Canyon Suite*), would handle the details of the orchestration.

About the *Rhapsody*, Gershwin later said: "I had no set plan, no structure. The *Rhapsody*, you see, began as a purpose, not a plan. I worked out a few themes, but just at this time I had to appear in Boston for the premiere of *Sweet Little Devil*. It was on the train [from New York to Boston], with its steely rhythms, its rattly-bang (I frequently hear music in the very heart of noise) that I suddenly heard—even saw on paper—the complete construction of the *Rhapsody* from beginning to end. . . . I heard it as a sort of musical kaleidoscope of America—of our vast melting-pot, of our incomparable national pep, our blues, our metropolitan madness. By the time I reached Boston I had the definite plot of the piece, as distinguished from its actual substance."

Even so, by the night of the first performance, Gershwin had still not worked out all the piano passages, and therefore improvised whole sections on the spot. Whiteman took cues from Gershwin in order to bring in the orchestra in the right places. The *Rhapsody* was the sensation of the concert. In fact, "few musical compositions of our time have enjoyed the instantaneous triumph of this Gershwin work," writes author-critic David Ewen. "It soon became the most famous piece of serious music by an American, and earned fabulous royalties," he continues. "It was performed by jazz bands and symphony orchestras, by solo pianists, two-piano teams, and piano ensembles; by solo harmonicas, harmonica bands, and mandolin orchestras; by tap dancers and ballet dancers; by choral groups. It was featured in stage shows and in an early talkie. It lent its principal theme to a novel, and furnished the signature for Paul Whiteman's radio shows."

Today, concert performances of the *Rhapsody* usually use one of two versions: the original 1924 Whiteman band arrangement by Grofé, or an expanded version arranged several years later by Grofé for symphony orchestra (different primarily in the orchestral accompaniment). Because of the frequent use of other abbreviated arrangements by pop and jazz orchestras, the second Grofé arrangement is sometimes advertised as the "uncut" version.

Recommended Recordings

★ Bernstein, Columbia Symphony Orchestra (Columbia stereo disc MS-6091 or MS-7518; cassette 16-11-0130; cartridge 18-11-0130)

Wild, Fiedler, Boston Pops Orchestra (RCA Red Seal stereo disc LSC-2367 or LSC-2746)

Haas, De Waart, Monte Carlo Opera Orchestra (Philips stereo disc 6500118; cassette 7300096; cartridge 7750027)

Levant, Ormandy, Philadelphia Orchestra (Columbia stereo disc CS-8641)

Gershwin, Whiteman Orchestra (RCA Victor disc LPV555, *mono only*)

Comments

Bernstein's marvelously relaxed and colorful 1958 performance, with Bernstein as both conductor and piano soloist, has an intuitive sense of the *Rhapsody's* jazz moods and syncopated rhythms. It is available in several editions: one is coupled with a breezy Bernstein performance of *An American in Paris* (MS-6091); the other is part of a 1969 album called *Gershwin's Greatest Hits* (MS-7518), which also includes Ormandy's heavier-handed *An American in Paris*, three piano preludes played by Oscar Levant, part of the *Porgy and Bess Suite* (Ormandy conducting), and the finale of the Concerto in F (Previn).

Wild's keyboard work is technically more deft, but "cooler" in its jazz impulse than Bernstein's. His late 1950's performance is available with two different Boston Pops couplings: one offers a bright and lively *An American in Paris* (LSC-2367), the other a group of rhapsodies by Liszt, Enesco, and Chabrier, all colorfully led by Fiedler (LSC-2746).

Since the *Rhapsody* has been identified for so long with American performers, it may surprise some to hear how jauntily it's performed by German pianist Werner Haas and young Dutch conductor Edo de Waart (the latter a former Bernstein assistant). Their 1971 recorded sound is also first-rate. The coupling is a similarly fresh and appealing Gershwin Concerto in F and the *Variations on "I Got Rhythm."*

Levant's spirited and stylish performance dates from the mid-1940's (the original mono sound has been electronically rechanneled for stereo release). It retains considerable sparkle within its restricted sonic range, and has long been considered interpretively authoritative because of Levant's close friendship with Gershwin. It is coupled with a Levant–Kostelanetz performance of the Concerto in F dating from the same period and about which the same general comments hold.

The sonically ancient Gershwin-Whiteman performance of the original version, recorded in 1927, is mainly of historic interest, and is included in Volume 1 of an RCA "Vintage Series" collection of Paul Whiteman pop recordings dating from 1920 to 1934. It should not be confused with another truncated Gershwin performance on Movietone 1009.

Piano Concerto in F

A year after the success of the *Rhapsody in Blue*, Gershwin sought to blend jazz elements in a larger symphonic form, and the result was this concerto, which many consider his finest "serious" work. Gershwin wrote that the first movement "is in sonata form—but." The second movement is a melodic, bluesy *andante*. The finale is a breezy rondo reusing some of the material from the first two movements.

Recommended Recordings

★ Wild, Fiedler, Boston Pops Orchestra (RCA Red Seal stereo disc LSC-2586)

Entremont, Ormandy, Philadelphia Orchestra (Columbia stereo disc MS-7013; cartridge 18-11-0064)

Haas, De Waart, Monte Carlo Opera Orchestra (Philips stereo disc 6500118; cassette 7300096; cartridge 7750027)

Levant, Kostelanetz, New York Philharmonic (Columbia stereo disc CS-8641)

Comments

Wild takes off like a whirlwind, and the Boston Pops keeps up with him all the way for a razzle-dazzle performance recorded in 1961. Overside, Wild and Fiedler are equally brilliant in Gershwin's appealing and inventive *Variations on "I Got Rhythm."*

Entremont's late 1960's performance is lively and colorful. It is coupled with a brittle and less appealing performance of the *Rhapsody in Blue.*

The jaunty Haas–De Waart performance of 1971 proves that Gershwin is no longer the exclusive province of American musicians. The coupling is a first-rate performance of the *Rhapsody in Blue* and the *Variations on "I Got Rhythm."*

Levant's spirited performance dates from the mid-1940's (the original mono sound has been electronically rechanneled for its stereo reissue), and is coupled with a similarly stylish if sonically dated performance of the *Rhapsody in Blue.*

Porgy and Bess

The book for this 1935 "Negro folk opera" has long divided critics—and civil rights partisans who feel it reflects outdated white stereotypes of black Americans. But Gershwin's score has been universally hailed as one of his most inspired—in fact, some consider it the best American opera yet written. The story, laid in Catfish Row, a waterfront tenement section of Charleston, South Carolina, is of a crippled black beggar's love for the woman of a stevedore whom he subsequently kills.

Recommended Recordings (Vocal Versions)

★ Henderson (conductor), Price (Bess), Warfield (Porgy), RCA Orchestra and DePaur Chorus (RCA Red Seal stereo disc LSC-2679; cartridge R8S-1065—*highlights only*)

b Engel (conductor), Williams (Bess), Winter (Porgy), Johnson Chorus (Odyssey 3-disc set 32360018—*complete*)

Recommended Recording (Symphonic Synthesis)

★ Fiedler, Boston Pops Orchestra (RCA Red Seal stereo disc LSC-3130; cassette RK-1143; cartridge R8S-1143)

Comments

The original production of *Porgy* in 1935 lost money, and though a 1942 revival did better, the opera really didn't win worldwide acclaim until a 1952 production starring Leontyne Price and William Warfield, which first toured Vienna, Berlin, London, Paris, and later the U.S. Still, it was not until 1963 that Warfield and Price recorded the title roles—and then they only recorded highlights, not the complete score. But what a superb performance they give under Skitch Henderson's spirited conducting. The cast credits on the label and jacket are not very clear, but Price sings the arias of Serena and Clara as well as Bess.

The 1951 Williams–Winter recording is complete (it was the first, and is still the only complete one). It is generally excellent if not always as vocally exciting as the Price–Warfield version. For its recent transfer to the Odyssey budget label the original mono recording has been electronically rechanneled for stereo.

In 1942 the well-known Broadway and radio conductor-arranger Robert Russell Bennett was commissioned by Fritz Reiner (then conductor of the Pittsburgh Symphony) to make a symphonic arrangement of the music from Gershwin's opera. It has since become a popular concert standard, and today completely overshadows a less colorful 1936 orchestral suite Gershwin himself adapted from the opera and called *Catfish Row*. Fiedler's late 1960's performance is jaunty and warmly lyrical. The recording is coupled with Shostakovich's satiric incidental music for a 1931 Soviet production of *Hamlet* and Glazunov's *Carnaval* Overture. (*Note:* A shorter set of orchestral excerpts from *Porgy* has also been recorded by Fiedler and the Boston Pops, and should not be confused with this complete version of the Bennett arrangement.)

For Follow-Up Consideration

An American in Paris, a warmly melodic and amiable "orchestral rhapsody" (as Gershwin called it) about Paris in the 1920's, scored for large orchestra plus four automobile horns, and orchestrated by Gershwin himself (unlike the *Rhapsody in Blue*). RECOMMENDED RECORDING: Bernstein, New York Philharmonic (Columbia stereo disc MS-6091), a dashing, colorful performance from the late 1950's, coupled with the *Rhapsody in Blue*.

• *AARON COPLAND*

Pronounced: *kope*-land. Born November 14, 1900, in Brooklyn, N.Y. Now living in New York.

SIGNIFICANCE: American composer, conductor, teacher, writer. His best-known works evoke an American folk spirit; much of his music is also abstract, austere, and complex.

BACKGROUND: Copland has written that he was born in Brooklyn, N.Y., "on a street that can only be described as drab, that had none of the garish color of the ghetto, none of the charm of an old New England thoroughfare, or even the rawness of a pioneer street. . . . I mention it because it was there that I spent the first twenty years of my life. Also, because I am filled with wonder each time I realize that a musician was born on that street." He became serious about music at the age of fifteen, studying first in New York and then in Paris, where he became the first American composition student of the noted teacher and organist Nadia Boulanger.

In 1929 he won a competition sponsored by RCA Victor for a symphonic work—his winning entry being a jazz-influenced *Dance Symphony*. Three ballet scores written between 1938 and 1944 (*Billy the Kid, Rodeo*, and *Appalachian Spring*) established his reputation. He has written several highly praised books on music (*What to Listen for in Music, Our New Music*), and for many years headed the composition department at the Berkshire Music Center in Tanglewood, Mass. In recent years he has been involved in a series of nationally syndicated educational TV and radio programs about music.

A Lincoln Portrait

This short, eloquent tribute in words and music was commissioned in 1942 by conductor André Kostelanetz for his CBS radio series. Says Copland of the work: "No composer could possibly hope to match in musical terms the stature of so eminent a figure as Lincoln. Secretly I hoped to avoid the difficulty by doing a portrait in which the sitter himself might speak. With the voice of Lincoln to help me, I was ready to risk the impossible. The letters and speeches of Lincoln supplied the text. It was a comparatively simple matter to choose a few excerpts that seemed particularly apposite to our own situation today. I avoided the temptation to use only well-known passages, permitting myself the luxury of quoting only once from a world-famous speech [the Gettysburg Address]. The order and arrangement of the selections are my own." The work is divided into three general sections. The somber opening, according to Copland, is meant "to suggest something of the mysterious sense of fatality that surrounds Lincoln's personality . . . [and] also something of his gentleness and simplicity of spirit." The lively middle section gives a flavor of the time in which he lived, and quotes from two songs of the period, "Camptown Races" and "Springfield Mountain" (also known as "The Pesky Sarpent"). The concluding section uses a speaker quoting Lincoln's words, building to a simple, forceful conclusion.

Recommended Recordings

★ Sandburg, Kostelanetz, New York Philharmonic (Columbia Special Projects disc 91A-02007)

Fonda, Copland, London Symphony (Columbia stereo disc M-30649; cassette MT-30649; cartridge MA-30649)

Stevenson, Ormandy, Philadelphia Orchestra (Columbia stereo disc MS-6684)

Peck, Mehta, Los Angeles Philharmonic (London stereo disc CS-6613)

Comments

The late Carl Sandburg, probably the nation's foremost authority on Lincoln, reads Lincoln's words eloquently—if without the polish of others—in his 1960 recording. Kostelanetz's accompaniment is obviously deeply felt. Overside, Kostelanetz leads William Schuman's *New England Triptych* (based on early American hymns and marching tunes) and Barber's lovely "Intermezzo" from *Vanessa.*

Copland himself conducts an excellent 1970 recording in which Henry Fonda (who played Lincoln in a 1939 movie) reads the text with dignity and appropriate understatement. Overside, Copland conducts a dramatic performance of his *Appalachian Spring* and *Fanfare for the Common Man.*

The Adlai Stevenson recording was released in 1965 as part of the one hundredth anniversary commemoration of Lincoln's death. The late statesman reads Lincoln's words simply and movingly. Overside Ormandy offers a superb performance of *Fanfare for the Common Man* and Ives' *Three Places in New England.*

Gregory Peck's 1969 reading is quietly forceful, and Mehta leads a cogent orchestral performance. Overside, Mehta offers two interesting but uneven works by William Kraft, *Configurations*: a Concerto for Four Percussion Soloists and Orchestra, and *Contextures: Riots—Decade '60*, in which juxtaposed musical textures (some played by jazz soloists) are used to express conflicts within the fabric of U.S. society in the 1960's caused by racial tensions and the Vietnam war.

Billy the Kid

Written in 1938 for the American Ballet Caravan (a forerunner of the New York City Ballet) on commission from Lincoln Kirstein, *Billy* is a musical evocation of the old American West. It is interesting to note that the Eastern-born and city-bred Copland had little interest in "cowboy music" until commissioned to do the ballet. References to such songs as "The Old Chisholm Trail," "Old Paint," and "Git Along, Little Dogies" are worked into the essentially light, catchy score. The action of the ballet involves key moments in the life of Billy the Kid—from his childhood to the family murder that made him an outlaw to his capture and death in a shoot-out. About two-thirds of the ballet score has been adapted by Copland into a concert suite, whose section titles describe the musical mood: "The Open Prairie," "Street in a Frontier Town," "The Card Game," "Gun Fight," and "Celebration after Billy's Capture."

Recommended Recordings

★ Bernstein, New York Philharmonic (Columbia stereo disc MS-6175 or 2-disc set MG-30071; cassette MGT-30071)

   Dorati, London Symphony (Mercury stereo disc 90246)

b Johanos, Dallas Symphony (Vox Turnabout stereo disc 34169; cartridge 678.005)

   Copland, London Symphony (Columbia stereo disc M-30114; cassette MT-30114)

Comments

Bernstein gives an idiomatic and spirited performance, dating from the early 1960's and well recorded. It is available in two editions: one (MS-6175) on a single LP coupled with a lively account of Copland's similar *Rodeo* ballet suite, the other (MG-30071) a reduced-price 2-disc *Copland Album* including Copland's most popular ballet scores (*Rodeo*, *Appalachian Spring*, and *El Salon Mexico*), issued in 1970 to commemorate the composer's seventieth birthday.

Dorati gives a vivid, colorful performance of music he often led as a ballet conductor in the 1940's. His early '60's recording is coupled with a forceful performance of Copland's *Appalachian Spring.*

Johanos is splendid in the lyrical sections of the suite and in the crisply percussive "Gun Fight," but in the livelier dances he is disappointingly square compared to

Bernstein or Dorati. Overside, Johanos' 1967 recording offers a taut *Rodeo* and *Fanfare for the Common Man.*

Copland's 1970 recording finds the composer a much more expressive conductor of the *Rodeo* overside than of *Billy*, which is well recorded but doesn't have the verve of Bernstein or Dorati.

For Follow-Up Consideration

El Salon Mexico, a rhythmically catchy tone picture of a Mexican dance hall in the early 1930's. RECOMMENDED RECORDING: Bernstein, New York Philharmonic (Columbia stereo disc MS-6355 or 2-disc set MG-30071), a warmly vivacious early 1960's performance coupled (MS-6355) with Copland's *Appalachian Spring* or (in the 2-LP album) with *Appalachian Spring*, *Rodeo*, and *Billy the Kid.*

Appalachian Spring, one of Copland's most sensitively austere and mature scores, written for a 1944 Martha Graham ballet about a pioneer celebration of spring in a newly built farmhouse in Pennsylvania in the early 1800's. RECOMMENDED RECORDINGS: Copland, Boston Symphony (RCA Red Seal stereo disc LSC-2401), a moving, expressive performance dating from the late 1950's and coupled with a composer-led performance of the orchestral suite from his 1954 opera *The Tender Land*; or Copland, London Symphony (Columbia stereo disc M-30649; cassette MT-30649; cartridge MA-30649), a later (1970) recording and therefore sonically superior, just as expressive interpretively if not as colorfully played by the orchestra, and coupled with *Fanfare for the Common Man* and *A Lincoln Portrait.*

Piano Variations, a complex, partly 12-tone work written in 1930, representative of the composer's more abstract scores, and called by the late composer William Flanagan (writing in *Stereo Review*), "a work of prime significance in the composer's musical development . . . [with] stature as a sort of granitic masterwork." RECOMMENDED RECORDING: Masselos (Odyssey stereo disc 32160040), a first-rate performance by a pianist who specializes in this kind of contemporary music, and coupled on this budget-priced release with Copland's partly 12-tone 1957 *Piano Fantasy.*

• DMITRI SHOSTAKOVICH

Pronounced: shoss-tah-*koh*-vitch. Born September 25, 1906, in St. Petersburg, Russia. Now living in Leningrad.

SIGNIFICANCE: Russian composer and pianist, the leading Soviet symphonist to date, whose best works are marked by rhythmic drive, intensely lyrical expressiveness, and colorful harmonies.

BACKGROUND: Shostakovich began studying music at the age of nine in St. Petersburg (now Leningrad). His formative years were deeply affected by the turbulence of the Communist revolution in Russia. The death of his father intensified his family's poverty, and Shostakovich's own suffering from tuberculosis interrupted his education several times.

He wrote his first symphony as a graduation exercise from the Leningrad Conservatory in 1926, and its tart originality won him fame over the next few years, not only in Russia but also in Europe and the United States. But his next three symphonies and two operas (*The Nose* and *Lady Macbeth of Mzensk*) were attacked by Soviet officials as "crude, vulgar, decadent," and full of "foreign modernisms." This marked just the beginning of a long series of conflicts Shostakovich has since experienced with Soviet officialdom. At times Shostakovich has sought to adapt to a role as Soviet musical spokesman, while at other times he has boldly continued to assert his own individuality.

He has been one of the most prolific symphony composers of this century—fifteen so far. Three of his most famous (the Seventh, Eighth, and Ninth) were written during World War II, when Shostakovich endured the long, bitter Nazi siege of Leningrad (and sometimes doubled as a fire-fighter); the symphonic trilogy reflects his feelings about the war, from despair to victorious joy. In recent years he has collaborated on several occasions with the popular but controversial young Soviet poet Yevtushenko, although one of their works (the Symphony No. 13) protesting Soviet anti-Semitism was banned in Russia after its first performance.

Symphony No. 1 in F minor

Written when Shostakovich was still a teenaged Leningrad student, this symphony remains one of his most original and immediately attractive scores. It is traditional in form, but is filled with brash and novel harmonies, sharp-edged humor, and, in the third movement, a dark and meditative lyricism.

Recommended Recordings

★ Weller, Suisse Romande Orchestra (London stereo disc CS-6787)

   Kondrashin, Moscow Philharmonic (Melodiya/Angel stereo disc S-40236)

   Bernstein, New York Philharmonic (Columbia stereo disc M-31307)

Comments

None of the presently available recordings really does this work full justice. All three of those listed above are much better at conveying the work's solemn moments than its jauntier, more light-hearted ones.

Weller comes closest to catching the roguish spirit of the first movement. He zips perkily through the second, and is dramatically expressive in the two final movements. Overside on this well-engineered 1973 release, he gives a bright and airy performance of the Shostakovich Ninth Symphony.

Kondrashin's 1973 release is heavier-handed than his earlier mono version (still available in Vanguard 2-disc album 6030/1 with the Shostakovich Eighth). But the new one is much better recorded, with many more coloristic details, and the lyrical third movement has rarely been so affectingly played. Overside, Kondrashin leads a gripping performance of Shostakovich's long-neglected Second Symphony, an unusually original (for 1927) musical depiction of chaos and anarchy out of which order is eventually pulled; it ends up with one of those full-throated choral finales that Russian composers seem to be addicted to.

After a somewhat ponderous first movement, Bernstein dashes through the second at a tremendous clip, then settles down for a deeply moving account of the last two movements. His 1972 release also includes the Shostakovich Ninth overside, in a much stodgier performance than Weller's.

Symphony No. 5 in D minor

Since its premiere in 1937, this has been one of the most widely popular of 20th-century symphonies. It marked a significant change in Shostakovich's style, from brashly satiric and clever to suggesting a wider and deeper range of emotions. The Fifth is a big, bold, epic symphony—strikingly dramatic, rhythmically vigorous, occasionally humorous, and, in the slow movement, coolly lyrical.

Recommended Recordings

★ M. Shostakovich, USSR Symphony (Melodiya/Angel SR-40163)

Bernstein, New York Philharmonic (Columbia stereo disc MS-6115)

Previn, London Symphony (RCA Red Seal stereo disc LSC-2866)

Comments

The composer's son, Maksim, leads a performance of exceptional eloquence and dramatic force, excellently engineered for this 1973 release.

Bernstein is intense and expressive, and the New York Philharmonic gives the work its "biggest-sounding" performance, dating from the late 1950's. This is, incidentally, one of the works Bernstein and the New York Philharmonic played to great acclaim on their 1959 Soviet tour.

Previn's 1965 release combines tension with poetic restraint in an effective way. It remains one of the best recordings he has made.

Symphony No. 10 in E minor

Probably Shostakovich's most mature symphony, the Tenth is a deeply expressive, generally dark-hued work that has been compared to the sketches of Goya, yet also contains sections of songlike and dancelike affirmation. It has also been widely interpreted as depicting the lonely man fighting against oppression (a view the composer has publicly rejected). The rhythmically supercharged second movement is a dazzling test of the virtuosity of any orchestra.

Recommended Recordings

★ Karajan, Berlin Philharmonic (Deutsche Grammophon stereo disc 139020)

Svetlanov, USSR Symphony (Melodiya/Angel stereo disc S-40025)

b Mitropoulos, New York Philharmonic (Odyssey stereo disc 32160123, *mono only*)

Comments

Karajan's 1966 performance is stunning in its darkly dramatic fervor, its vivid rhythmic propulsion, and the attention to detail and tonal balances.

Svetlanov's performance from the late 1960's is interpretively forceful, even if his orchestra is not a match for the Berliners.

Mitropoulos' 1955 recording is one of the best he ever made, filled with the kind of power and intensity he was noted for. The Philharmonic plays brilliantly (especially in the whirlwind second movement), but the mono sound shows its age.

For Follow-Up Consideration

Concerto in C minor for Piano, Trumpet, and String Orchestra, a generally bright and lighthearted concerto written in the early 1930's and scored for string orchestra with a prominent trumpet part in the spirited finale. RECOMMENDED RECORDING: Shostakovich, Cluytens, Paris Conservatory Orchestra (Seraphim 60161, *mono only*), one of the composer's few recordings as a pianist, and one of his best, dating from a Paris visit in the late 1950's and reissued on the budget-priced Seraphim label in 1971, coupled with his delightfully easy-going Piano Concerto No. 2 and *Fantastic Dances.*

Symphony No. 7, subtitled "Leningrad" and the first of a trilogy of symphonies Shostakovich wrote during World War II. A mammoth, often sprawling, epic work, it depicts the impact of the Nazi siege of Leningrad on its people. It is best known for its overwhelming first movement, which begins with an insidiously insistent little martial theme (representing the Nazis), which grows bigger and bolder until it consumes everything around it with terrifying force. The structure is not unlike Ravel's *Bolero*, the content more like a *Danse Macabre*. RECOMMENDED RECORDING: Bernstein, New York Philharmonic (Columbia stereo 2-disc set M2S-722), a tautly dramatic, monumentally eloquent 1962 recording.

Symphony No. 9, the last of the World War II trilogy, and—unlike the mammoth Seventh and Eighth—a brief (twenty-two minutes), lightly scored, generally easy-going work. Said Shostakovich in 1945: "It's a merry little piece. Musicians will love to play it and critics will delight in blasting it." He was right, especially with regard to Soviet critics. But in recent years the work has begun to earn more of the respect it deserves as a warm and unpretentious tribute to the survival of the human spirit. RECOMMENDED RECORDING: Kondrashin, Moscow Philharmonic (Melodiya/Angel stereo disc S-40000; cassette 4XS-40000), a joyously buoyant and well-recorded performance from the late 1960's. The coupling is *The Execution of Stepan Razin*, an interesting if uneven collaboration between Shostakovich and the poet Yevtushenko—their subject being the execution of a 17th-century Cossack chief for leading an uprising against the czar, and the legend of how his severed head continued to laugh its defiance of the czar from the execution block. It is one of the better examples of works on Soviet patriotic or propaganda themes that Shostakovich has written.

Symphony No. 13, an intense, darkly scored hybrid of symphony and cantata, written in 1962 to five poems by the outspoken young poet Yevtushenko—and banned in the Soviet Union after its first performances because of controversy about its text. One part, "Babi Yar," is a protest against Soviet anti-Semitism; another, "Humor," attacks the hypocrisy of "czars, kings" and other "rulers"; and the final "A Career" salutes Galileo, Leo Tolstoi, and other "men of genius" who had to assert themselves against false charges from the state. RECOMMENDED RECORDING: Krause (baritone), Ormandy, Philadelphia Orchestra, Mendelssohn Club Male Chorus (RCA Red Seal stereo disc LSC-3162; cartridge R8S-1151), a deeply compelling 1970 performance, beautifully recorded.

• OLIVIER MESSIAEN

Pronounced: mess-ee-*yahn*. Born December 10, 1908, in Avignon, France. Now living in Paris.

SIGNIFICANCE: French composer, organist, teacher, who once described his complex, mystical, often exotic musical language as "like a rainbow of rhythms and harmonies"; a pioneer in blending both early and late Western music with Indian and Oriental ideas, and in recreating musically the nonhuman (bird and animal) noises of the animate world.

BACKGROUND: The son of French poetess Cécile Sauvage, Messiaen spent his childhood at Grenoble, near the French Alps, and says he still prefers to compose in mountain territories. He entered the Paris Conservatory at the age of eleven, winning first prizes in five different areas of study before his graduation in 1930. He became organist at Trinity Church in Paris in 1931, holding the post for more than 40 years and writing for it some of the most original and important organ music of this century.

In 1936 he co-founded a Paris musical group, La Jeune France (Young France), to play "young, free works as much estranged from trite revolutionism as from trite academicism." While fighting with French forces in World War II, he was captured by the Nazis and imprisoned for two years. Since the war, he has combined composing with teaching, primarily at the Paris Conservatory.

A Roman Catholic, he has said that music should communicate "lofty sentiments . . . and, in particular, the loftiest of all: religious sentiments." As critic Philip Ramey has commented: "True music to him is an act of faith." Yet his music is usually considered more sensuous, exotic, and iridescent than other, more traditional Catholic models. French critic André Hodier has described Messiaen's music as, paradoxically, "a voluptuous, ingrown world of subtle thrills."

L'Ascension (The Ascension)

Subtitled "Four Symphonic Meditations for Orchestra," this was originally composed as an organ work in 1934 and was later orchestrated. The first three movements are for full orchestra, the fourth for strings alone. It remains one of Messiaen's most profoundly moving works. Each of the four meditations bears a Biblical quotation, and the work as a whole is meant to depict mystical feelings about the ascension of Jesus rather than being a musical depiction of the event.

Recommended Recording

★ Stokowski, London Symphony Orchestra (London stereo disc SR-21060; cassette M-94060; cartridge M-95060)

Comments

The 1972 Stokowski release at long last replaces a deleted Stokowski mono recording from the late 1940's—and proves that over the years Stokowski has lost none of his ability to communicate the nobility, eloquence, and strength of this score. It is beautifully engineered (as part of London's Phase-4 stereo series), and is coupled with a stunning Stokowski performance of Ives' *Orchestral Set No. 2.*

Et Exspecto Resurrectionem Mortuorum
(And I Await the Resurrection of the Dead)

Partly inspired by the works of St. Thomas Aquinas and written in 1964 to a commission by André Malraux (the noted author and DeGaulle's culture minister), this is a shatteringly moving and mystical sound picture of man's last days on earth. Scored for a large orchestra of woodwinds, brass, and percussion, the work embraces many of the compositional techniques which have made Messiaen's work so distinctive—including the use of religious plainsong, Oriental harmonies, birdsong, and irregular rhythms.

Recommended Recordings

★ Boulez, Domaine Musicale Orchestra, Strasbourg Percussion Ensemble (Columbia stereo disc MS-7356)

Baudo, Orchestre de Paris (Angel stereo disc S-36559)

Haitink, Amsterdam Concertgebouw (Philips stereo disc 6500086)

Comments

The Boulez performance of 1967 is brilliantly and subtly etched, the Baudo of 1968 and the Haitink of 1971 only slightly less so. However, it is arguable whether any recording can ever fully capture its gigantic, ear-shattering final climax for gongs and full orchestra.

Boulez offers overside a similarly complex Messiaen work of 1963, *Couleurs de la Cité Celeste* (*Colors of the Heavenly City*), which combines the birdsong of different countries with Greek and Hindu rhythms and various "sound-colors" (warm and cool) to symbolize a Biblical text taken from the Book of Revelation.

Baudo fills out his disc with one of Messiaen's most appealing early works, *Les Offrandes Oubliées* (*Forgotten Offerings*), a profoundly affecting tone poem on the theme: "You love us, gentle Jesus—we had forgotten it."

Haitink's coupling is *November Steps* by the Japanese composer Tori Takemitsu (born in 1930)—a 1967 work counterposing not only Western and Oriental musical ideas, but also Western and Japanese solo instruments. It is not an easy work on first hearing, but adventurous listeners will find many fascinating moments in it.

Turangalîla

This mammoth, ten-movement symphony (pronounced too-rahn-gah-*lee*-lah) was commissioned by Serge Koussevitzky and the Boston Symphony Orchestra, and was introduced by that orchestra in 1949 under Leonard Bernstein's direction. Since then it has been much talked about, but seldom performed. Its title is a Sanskrit word symbolizing (at one and the same time) love, joy, time, rhythm, life, and death. The symphony itself is an exotic hymn to transcendental love as part of the game of life and death, and key sections use a theme from Wagner's *Tristan und Isolde*. The composer has also related the feeling of his music to the paintings of the French artist Chagall. The symphony makes extensive use of the Ondes Martenot (an electronic wave generator) and a solo piano.

Recommended Recordings

★ Ozawa, Yvonne Loriod (piano), Jeanne Loriod (Ondes Martenot), Toronto Symphony Orchestra (RCA Red Seal stereo 2-disc set LSC-7051)

Comments

Ozawa's performance is an overwhelming experience. Recorded in 1968 under the composer's supervision and with his wife as piano soloist, it brilliantly combines a feeling of Oriental mysteriousness with colorful Western expressionism, the twin elements that dominate so much of Messiaen's work. The composer's extensive notes help make the album one of the most important releases of contemporary music of the past decade. The final side of the 2-LP album includes a Japanese work counterposing Oriental and Western musical ideas, Takemitsu's *November Steps*, which Ozawa premiered in November, 1967.

For Follow-Up Consideration

Trois Petites Liturgies de la Présence Divine (*Three Little Liturgies of the Divine Presence*), an eloquent and exotic 1944 work for a chorus of sopranos and an unusual combination of cymbals, gongs, piano, Ondes Martenot, and strings. In it, Messiaen probes God's presence within us, God's presence in Himself, and God's presence in all things. RECOMMENDED RECORDING: Bernstein, New York Philharmonic, Women's Chorus of the Choral Art Society (Columbia stereo disc MS-6582), a vividly poetic performance recorded in 1961 but not released until 1964, and then sugar-coated in an album entitled *Bernstein Plays Two Modern French Masterpieces*—the other piece being Roussel's rhythmically vigorous Symphony No. 3 in G minor of 1930.

Oiseaux Exotiques (*Exotic Birds*), an "ornithological fantasy" of 1956 containing (according to the composer) forty different birdcalls combined with involved rhythmic patterns and unusual sonorities achieved by piling layer upon layer of sound. RECOMMENDED RECORDING: Loriod, Neumann, Czech Philharmonic (Vox/Candide stereo disc 31002), one of the more interesting albums to come out of Czech dabbling with new Western music during the "liberal spring" of 1968, with Messiaen's wife as piano soloist and Messiaen himself acting as "artistic director."

• *SAMUEL BARBER*

> Pronounced: *bar*-ber. Born March 9, 1910, in West Chester, Pa. Now living in Mt. Kisco, New York.

SIGNIFICANCE: American composer, a conservative by contemporary standards, who emphasizes fluent melodic writing and expressive Neoromantic feeling.

BACKGROUND: Barber began to study the piano at the age of six, and a year later attempted his first composition. At twelve he was organist for a local church. At fourteen he entered the Curtis Institute of Music in Philadelphia, later studying also in Rome. In 1932, at twenty-two, Koussevitzky and the Boston Symphony Orchestra introduced his first orchestral work, *The School for Scandal* overture. Within four years he had won two Pulitzer Prizes—he was the first composer to do so—and the American Prix de Rome, and had his First Symphony (1936) honored as the first American work ever performed at the Salzburg Festival in Austria.

Since then he has written several ballet scores (*Medea*, *Souvenirs*), a violin concerto, a piano concerto, several works for voice and orchestra, and two operas: *Vanessa* (1958) and *Antony and Cleopatra* (1966). He long shared his home and studios near New York City with the composer Gian-Carlo Menotti, who wrote the libretto for *Vanessa*.

Knoxville: Summer of 1915

Based on a poem fragment by James Agee (used as the prologue of Agee's Pulitzer Prize-winning novel *A Death in the Family*), this is a deeply moving, lyrical, and warmly homespun work for soprano and orchestra. Composed in 1947, it is a nostalgically Romantic look at a bygone era of American life.

Recommended Recordings

★ Price, Schippers, London's New Philharmonia Orchestra (RCA Red Seal stereo disc LSC-3062)

b Steber, Strickland, Dumbarton Oaks Chamber Orchestra (Odyssey stereo disc 32160230)

Comments

Price is vocally glorious and profoundly touching in her dramatic shadings, and Schippers leads an ardent orchestral accompaniment, beautifully recorded in 1968. Overside, Price and Schippers offer two of the best arias from Barber's much-maligned *Antony and Cleopatra*, which was commissioned for the opening of the new Metropolitan Opera House at Lincoln Center in 1966, and may have been more the victim of staging excesses than of musical shortcomings during that unsuccessful production.

Steber commissioned *Knoxville* in the first place, and it remains one of her finest recordings. Her voice may not be as naturally sumptuous as Price's, but she sings the work with great feeling and style. Recorded in 1950, the original mono sound has been electronically "enhanced" for stereo in the Odyssey reissue. Overside is another collector's item—one of Price's first recordings, made in 1954, of Barber's fascinating *Hermit Songs*, based on 8th- to 13th-century poems of anonymous Irish monks, with Barber himself accompanying at the piano.

Adagio for Strings

One of Barber's earliest works, this is still among his finest and most frequently performed. Actually, it is an orchestrated version of the adagio movement of Barber's String Quartet No. 1, written in 1936. The lyrical adagio begins quietly, builds to a grippingly intense climax, then subsides tenderly to its original mood.

Recommended Recordings

★ Schippers, New York Philharmonic (Columbia stereo disc CBS3211005)
Ormandy, Philadelphia Orchestra (Columbia stereo disc MS-6224)
Bernstein, New York Philharmonic (Columbia stereo disc M-30573; cassette MT-30573; cartridge MA-30573)

Comments

Schippers leads an intense, vivid performance, recorded in the mid-1960's. Ormandy's 1957 performance is more tonally suave as well as intense. Bernstein's 1971 performance is surprisingly restrained, almost elegiac.

Schippers' has the advantage of being coupled with three of Barber's best other works (*Medea's Meditation and Dance of Vengeance*, the *Second Essay for Orchestra*, and *Overture to The School for Scandal*).

Ormandy's performance is coupled with a varying array of lushly played pieces: Tchaikovsky's *Serenade in C for Strings*, Vaughan Williams' *Fantasia on "Greensleeves,"* and Borodin's *Nocturne for String Orchestra*.

Bernstein's performance is part of an album called "Nocturne, Music for Quiet Listening," and includes Ravel's *Pavane for a Dead Princess*, Vaughan Williams' *Fantasia on "Greensleeves,"* Offenbach's "Barcarolle" from *Tales of Hoffmann*, Humperdinck's "Children's Prayer" from *Hansel and Gretel*, plus short works by Grieg and Bizet.

For Follow-Up Consideration

Piano Concerto, the 1963 Pulitzer Prize-winner and one of the most widely performed contemporary concertos in many decades (more than forty performances in the U.S., Western Europe, and the Soviet Union between 1963 and 1965 alone). It is by turns splashy and technically complex, then disarmingly touching and songful. RECOMMENDED RECORDING: Browning, Szell, Cleveland Orchestra (Columbia stereo disc MS-6638), a virtuoso performance by the pianist for whom the concerto was written. The coupling is another recent American work, William Schuman's darkly moving *Song of Orpheus*, with Leonard Rose as cello soloist under Szell.

Symphony No. 1, one of Barber's first international successes (1936) and still a warmly appealing example of his lyrically surging writing. RECOMMENDED RECORDING: Hanson, Eastman-Rochester Orchestra (Mercury stereo disc SRI-75012), originally a mono recording of the mid-1950's but electronically rechanneled for this 1974 stereo re-release, and coupled with good Hanson performances of Barber's *Medea* Suite (the original 1947 version), the *Adagio for Strings*, and the *School for Scandal* Overture.

Medea's Dance of Vengeance, rescored (for large orchestra) in 1955 from part of a ballet Barber wrote in 1946 for Martha Graham on the Medea legend; it was originally titled *Medea's Meditation and Dance of Vengeance*, but in 1973 Barber asked that the shorter title be used for future performances; the work begins with a muted and mysterious episode, building to a rhythmically biting, frenzied dance. RECOMMENDED RECORDING: Schippers, New York Philharmonic (Columbia stereo disc 3211005), a splendidly taut, dramatic performance, coupled with excellent performances of the *Adagio for Strings*, the *Second Essay for Orchestra*, and the *Overture to The School for Scandal*.

• *PIERRE BOULEZ*

Pronounced: boo-*lezz*. Born March 26, 1925, in Montbrison, France. Now living in London and New York.

SIGNIFICANCE: French composer, conductor, and staunch exponent of serial music; his own tightly constructed, rhythmically mobile works reflect his special liking for Debussy and Webern.

BACKGROUND: Boulez was born in the south of France, and went to Paris to study in 1943, primarily with Olivier Messiaen at the Paris Conservatory. In 1948 he began a decade as music director of the famous Jean-Louis Barrault–Madeleine Renaud theatre company. In 1954, Barrault let him use his theatre on off-days to organize concerts of new music, and the resulting "Domaine Musicale" (Musical Domain) concerts became the center of new music in Paris for many years. During this period Boulez had a series of stormy encounters with French government officials, who kept his music off French radio.

In 1966 Boulez became conductor of the Southwest German Radio Orchestra at Baden-Baden, an orchestra noted for its performances of contemporary music. In 1968 he became associate conductor of the Cleveland Orchestra under George Szell, and in 1969 its principal guest conductor. In 1971 he became conductor of the BBC Symphony in London (succeeding Colin Davis) and music director of the New York Philharmonic (succeeding Leonard Bernstein).

A man of enormous intellectual energy, Boulez has been an outspoken champion of the 12-tone music of Webern, Berg, and Schoenberg as the major "classics" of our century. He has steadfastly used his position as a conductor to promote their music and those of other composers, only rarely performing his own works.

Le Marteau sans Maître (The Hammer without a Master)

Stravinsky, when asked in 1957 which work of the younger generation most impressed him, cited Boulez's *Marteau* as the "only important work of this new age of search." He added, "It will be a considerable time before the value of *Le Marteau sans Maître* is recognized. Meanwhile, I shall not explain my admiration for it but adapt Gertrude Stein's answer when asked why she liked Picasso's paintings: 'I like to look at them'—I like to listen to Boulez."

Le Marteau, written in 1954 and revised in 1957, is a complex work in nine movements (lasting about twenty-eight minutes altogether) based on three short Surrealistic French poems by René Char. Four of the movements are set for contralto and an instrumental group, and five for the instruments alone. Only six instruments are used: guitar, vibraphone, alto flute, viola, xylorimba (which combines the qualities of a xylophone and marimba), and percussion. Words and music are placed in an extremely involved mutual relationship, with related vocal and instrumental sections not necessarily succeeding one another, but instead being woven crisscross into the work's overall fabric. The voice is used especially daringly, with many wide vocal leaps, sometimes on the same syllable. The overall listening effect of the music is not unlike a stream-of-consciousness exploration of a huge underground cavern. Composer-critic Eric Salzman has called *Le Marteau* "the musical classic of today's European avant-garde."

Recommended Recordings

★ Minton, Boulez, Ensemble Musique Vivante (Columbia stereo disc M-32160; quadrasonic disc MQ-32160; quadrasonic cartridge MAQ-32160)

b Deroubaix, Boulez, six instrumentalists (Vox/Turnabout stereo disc 34081; cassette 673028)

b MacKay, Craft, six instrumentalists (Odyssey stereo disc 32160154)

Comments

Boulez's own two recordings reveal how even composers can change their minds about interpreting their own compositions. His 1973 Columbia performance is slower than the one on Turnabout from the mid-1960's, and a number of instrumental details are accented differently. Beyond that, it's a toss-up. The sound engineering is superior on the Columbia set, and Minton's voice is more attractive (though not necessarily more convincing) than Deroubaix's. However, the alto flutist (Gazzelloni) on Turnabout is more effective than his counterpart on Columbia. If price is the primary consideration, the Turnabout set is a fine introduction to this score. If slicker sound and Boulez's latest refinements are the criteria, then it's Columbia. The brief Boulez *Livre pour Cordes* which Columbia also includes is an attractive, Webernesque dividend.

Craft's 1958 performance is good, but not as well recorded as either of Boulez's. It is coupled with Stockhausen's *Zeitmasse* No. 5, an unusual experiment in the time values of rhythm.

Pli selon Pli (Fold on Fold)

If *Le Marteau sans Maître* established Boulez's international reputation as a significant composer, then *Pli selon Pli* (premiered in 1960) solidified that reputation. It is a complex, hour-long set of five pieces for soprano and orchestra, inspired by the work of the French poet Stéphane Mallarmé (1842–1898). According to Boulez: "The title is taken from a Mallarmé poem not used in my musical transposition; it [instead] indicates the meaning and direction of the work. In this poem the author describes the way in which the dissolving mist gradually reveals the stones of the city of Bruges. In the same way, as the five pieces unfold, they reveal, fold by fold, a portrait of Mallarmé." The "folds" are basically layers of delicate, sensuous sounds—making unusually subtle use of a wide range of percussion instruments (xylophones, vibraphones, several kinds of bells, etc.). The first and fifth pieces—*"Don"* (Gift) and *"Tombeau"* (Tomb)—are primarily instrumental, with lines from the Mallarmé poems of their titles intervening only as brief vocal quotations. The three central pieces, titled "Improvisations sur Mallarmé I, II, et III" ("Improvisations on Mallarmé I, II, and III"), use three longer Mallarmé sonnets—with the vocal line more central to the musical development, and with more modest instrumental forces than the opening and closing pieces. Boulez has made an interesting comment on the relationship between an understanding of the Mallarmé poems he has used and his musical "transposition" (he declines to use the word "setting" in the conventional sense): "My idea is not to be restricted to immediate understanding, which is only *one* of the forms (the least rich, perhaps?) of the transmutation of the poem. It strikes me as too restrictive to limit oneself to a kind of 'reading in/with music'; from the point of view of simple understanding, this will never replace a reading *without* music, which remains the best way of being informed as to the contents of a poem. . . . In my transposition, or transmutation, of Mallarmé, I take for granted that the direct sense of the poem has been acquired by reading it. I can therefore play on a variable degree of immediate understanding. This play, moreover, tends to give prominence sometimes to the musical and sometimes to the poetic text."

Recommended Recording

★ Boulez (conductor), Lukomska (soprano), Bergmann (piano), Stingl (guitar), D'Alton (mandolin), BBC symphony (Columbia stereo disc M-30296)

Comments

The composer's own 1969 recording is exceptionally clear in the way it delineates the subtlest colors and shifting timbres of the instrumental part. Polish soprano Lukomska's warm, pleasant voice handles the difficult vocal part with impressive agility.

For Follow-Up Consideration

Le Soleil des Eaux ("The River in the Sun"), a short (eight-minute) work for chamber orchestra, chorus, and three vocal soloists that might be called the first "ecological cantata" of the post-World War II era. The score was adapted in the mid-1950's from some of the music Boulez wrote for a 1948 poetic radio drama by René Char, and its second movement deals with man's misuse of nature, with direct warnings of man's annihilation because of such misuse. Musically, the score is a kind of synthesis of 12-tone techniques with Boulez's then-developing "layers of sound" style. RECOMMENDED RECORDING: Boulez, BBC Symphony Orchestra and Chorus (Angel stereo disc S-36295), a well-recorded 1966 release coupled with two fascinating works, one by Boulez's teacher Messiaen (his rhythmically complex *Chronochromie*), the other by the late Charles Koechlin (his colorful *Bandar-Log*, based on Kipling's *Jungle Books*), both conducted by Dorati.

• *HANS WERNER HENZE*

Pronounced: *hen*-tseh. Born July 1, 1926, in Gütersloh, Germany. Now living near Rome, Italy.

SIGNIFICANCE: German composer and conductor, one of the most provocative and imaginative post-World War II composers, blending Neoromanticism, Neoclassicism, and serial techniques in dramatically forceful instrumental, vocal, and operatic works.

BACKGROUND: Henze grew up in Germany under the Nazi regime, and served briefly as a teenager in the German army toward the end of the war. His revulsion over the Nazi experience has had a profound effect on his strong political and moral views ever since. After the war, he studied in Heidelberg and Paris, and was strongly influenced first by Stravinsky's Neoclassicism, then by Schoenberg's 12-tone music. His first works sought to reconcile what were then regarded as irreconcilable schools of music. In the early 1950's he won increasing attention for a number of ballet scores and a violin concerto, and served a year as ballet conductor at the Hessian State Theatre, Wiesbaden.

But his increasing dislike of the economic, social, and cultural forces dominating

Germany led him to move in 1953 to Italy, where he now lives. A number of his major operatic and vocal works since then (*The Young Lord, Moralities, The Bassarids, Essay on Pigs, El Cimarron*) have had themes with thinly disguised social or political meanings. He has become increasingly outspoken in his defense of "music of commitment," which in the late 1960's and early '70's meant to him mainly radical leftist commitment.

His works are not easy to classify, combining as they do many different elements. But always a basic impression is of an earnest artist seeking to make these elements his own, seeking to make them say something personal and significant in terms of a changed world *he* did not change. More than most contemporary composers—who often seek to establish their identities in a rapidly changing world by contriving new and usually empty technical devices—Henze builds stoutly on the traditions and substance of the past by showing them (as Henze himself has put it) "in new lights and from fresh angles." To quote Henze further: "Ancient forms appear to me as classical ideals of beauty, no longer attainable, but visible from a great distance, arousing memories like dreams. But the way to them is the most difficult and most impossible thing. However, to me it seems the only folly worth living for."

Moralitäten (Moralities)

Written to a text by poet W. H. Auden, *Moralities* was composed for the 1968 Cincinnati Music Festival—and, says Henze, with high school, college, or opera studio performances in mind. Based on three of Aesop's fables, Auden's text has obvious implications for today's world. The first piece is about anarchy, the second about modernism, and the third about "the speedy forgetting of a society which believes it has escaped yet again." The music, for chorus and small orchestra, is itself generally bright and rhythmically vibrant, sometimes humorous and even jazzy.

Recommended Recording

★ Henze, Leipzig Gewandhaus Orchestra, Dresden Kreuzchor (Deutsche Grammophon stereo disc 139374; cassette 923-094)

Comments

The only recording, made under the composer's direction in 1968, has excellent stereo engineering. Overside is Henze's *Musen Siziliens* (*Sicilian Muses*) (1966), based on several of Virgil's Eclogues, also sung by the Dresden Kreuzchor, with the Dresden State Orchestra and the American duo-pianist team of Joseph Rollino and Paul Sheftel. Henze says the inspiration for this piece came from hearing the Rolling Stones perform in Rome in 1966, and that he believes "serious" music should be brought into closer contact with contemporary pop music. How he has achieved this through *Sicilian Muses* will probably escape the average listener (and most Stones' fans), though some music students will find a key in Henze's jacket-note description of "simple formulae circling around single notes and tonal clusters."

El Cimarrón

The biography of Esteban Montejo, the 104-year-old former Cimarrón (a runaway slave) who was discovered in a small Cuban village in 1963 by ethnologist Miguel Barnet, forms the basis for this highly dramatic "recital for four musicians." Composed in 1970 it is one of Henze's finest works to date. Montejo's story is gripping enough on its own—a harrowing indictment of man's inhumanity to man. Henze's music gives it heightened impact and a meaningful new dimension—doing so with a minimum of musical forces strikingly used: a baritone singer-narrator, a guitarist, a flutist, and a percussionist.

Recommended Stereo Recording

★ Henze (conductor), Pearson (baritone), Brouwer (guitar), Zoller (flute), Yamash'ta (percussion) (Deutsche Grammophon stereo 2-disc set 2707050)

Comments

The American baritone, Cuban guitarist, German flutist, and Japanese percussionist who made this 1970 recording under Henze's direction give a strong virtuoso performance, vividly recorded. The percussionist is particularly outstanding.

Violin Concerto

Written when Henze was twenty-two, this concerto is a large-scale, four-movement work that combines 12-tone concepts with warmly expressive, even folklike melody. It is easily the most interesting violin concerto since those of Berg and Stravinsky, written in the early 1930's. Eclectic as it may be in form, it reveals that even in his youth Henze was a master of instrumental color and rhythmic pulse.

Recommended Recording

★ Schneiderhan, Henze, Bavarian Radio Orchestra (Munich) (Deutsche Grammophon stereo disc 139382; cassette 9723-103)

b Lautenbacher, Gruber, Radio Luxembourg Orchestra (Candide stereo disc 31061)

Comments

Schneiderhan, who has played the concerto often in concert, plunges into it with enormous verve, and gives its lyrical third movement an especially soaring performance. Henze leads the intense, vivid accompaniment of this 1968 recording. Overside, cellist Siegfried Palm (with Henze again conducting) performs Henze's *Ode to the West Wind*, a 1954 setting of Shelley's poem (the one ending with "If Winter comes, can Spring be far behind?"). There are traces of Webern and Stravinsky in the *Ode's* subtle, intricate sonic layers, but Henze's underlying Romantic temperament gives the work its own identity and flavor.

Lautenbacher plays the concerto with impressive fluency, but the orchestral accompaniment is not as good as Henze's own. Overside on this 1972 recording, Ms.

Lautenbacher makes a persuasive case for the more aggressively rhythmic Violin Concerto (1950) of another contemporary German composer, Bernd Alois Zimmermann (1918–1970).

For Follow-Up Consideration

Symphonies No. 1 to 5, available in one 2-LP album conducted by the composer leading the Berlin Philharmonic (Deutsche Grammophon stereo 2-disc set 2707029); or just Symphonies 1, 3, and 5, available on one cassette (Deutsche Grammophon 923-114). Written between 1947 and 1962, these five symphonies are quite different from each other in form and mood. Some parts are darkly brooding, other parts are rhythmically vibrant and occasionally jazzy, and some are as intensely and openly emotional as anything since Mahler or Berg. Of his first five symphonies, Henze has written: "The theatre is clearly evident in [these] pieces, although the characteristics of certain symphonic traditions are kept. This is chamber music on a large scale, directed outward and heightened."

The Young Lord (Der Junge Lord), a two-act "comic opera" about an ape who fools a 19th-century German town into thinking he's a man. This 1965 opera is black comedy indeed—and Henze approaches the text in a style that is more barbed and ironic than "comic." RECOMMENDED RECORDING: Dohnanyi (conductor), Mathis, Otto, Driscoll, Grobe, etc. (West) Berlin Deutsche Oper Orchestra and Chorus (Deutsche Grammophon stereo 3-disc set 2709027), recorded in 1967. (*Note:* This is not the sound track of the film version of the Berlin production, with virtually the same cast, released in the U.S. in 1970.)

• *KARLHEINZ STOCKHAUSEN*

Pronounced: *shtawck*-how-zen. Born August 22, 1928, in Mödrath, Germany. Now living in Cologne, West Germany.

SIGNIFICANCE: German composer and teacher, one of the foremost contemporary experimenters in electronic music, aleatoric, or "chance," music, and a proponent of the notion of music as sound moving in space.

BACKGROUND: Orphaned during the Nazi period in Germany during World War II ("My father was killed . . . my mother was taken to a hospital with depressions and later killed by the state as a useless member of society . . . [and] I was sent to a state school"), Stockhausen was drawn as a teenager to both music and religion. "Of my own choice, I became a practicing Catholic when I was seventeen or eighteen," he has said.

Musically, he aligned himself with the most radical postwar trends at the Cologne High School for Music and at Cologne University. Later he studied at the Acoustical Sciences Department of Bonn University and with Messiaen in Paris. "By 1951 I was very much aware that I was part of a completely new epoch."

A key part of that new epoch to him was electronic music. In 1952 he was the first to make music of synthetic electronic sounds. In 1953 he became "permanent collaborator" at the Electronic Music Studio of the West German Radio at Cologne, and has been its music director since 1962. Meanwhile, he has taught at Darmstadt's International Summer School for New Music, at the Basel (Switzerland) Conservatory, and the University of Pennsylvania. His experiments with electronic sounds and with the spatial relationships of music have kept him in the forefront of avant-garde music since the 1950's, and have won him worldwide fame (or notoriety, depending on the viewpont), especially among young people.

In a 1971 *New York Times* interview, Stockhausen spoke of the composer as a spiritual guide for the new generation: "Young people . . . sense the fantastic catastrophes that will come in this century. They also feel that we have reached the beginning of a new age. They don't believe anymore in the old systems, and they are right. These systems can't go on the way they are. . . . What I am trying to do is to produce . . . music that brings us to essentials . . . and that is going to be badly needed during the time of shocks and disasters that is going to come. I'm trying to produce models that herald the stage after destruction. . . . An example, let's say: like the musician in Negro tribes, in American Indian tribes, or as it still is in India or Bali—what he does is always part of a spiritual activity. He makes the sounds the others can fly on, on which they can act together in this sacred act of making contact with the divine. . . . That visionary force in [a composer's] music should prepare people for what is coming. And if he doesn't have that, well, then he is just an entertainer."

Kontakte (Contacts)

This 1960 work remains one of the best introductions to Stockhausen and electronic music in general. It involves "contacts" between electronic and instrumental sound groups (piano and percussion).

Recommended Recording

★ Electronic Studios of the West German Radio, Cologne (Deutsche Grammophon stereo disc 138811; cassette 925-0661)

Comments

The only recorded version of this work to date, made under the composer's supervision in the early 1960's, is coupled with the composer's earlier (1955–56) *Song of the Adolescents* (*Der Gesang der Jünglinge*), which combines electronic sounds with sung ones. The program notes on the jacket explain each work in excellent detail.

Gruppen (Groupings)

Dating from 1955–57, this work for three chamber orchestras (109 players in all) uses conventional instruments subdivided in unconventional ways to reflect "alternation, isolation, fusion, rotation, etc." (to quote the composer) in various spatial relationships. At times the three orchestras play in different tempos, at times in a common rhythm. They call to each other, answer each other, and echo each other. According to the composer, "the hearer finds himself in the middle of many spaces which together then form a new 'time-space.' "

Recommended Recording

★ Stockhausen, Gielen, Maderna, Cologne Radio Orchestra (Deutsche Grammophon stereo disc 137002; cassette 921-022; cartridge 87-002)

Comments

The only recording of *Gruppen* to date can be considered definitive since it was made under the composer's direction and approved by him for release. Overside is a second "space" work called *Carré*, for four orchestras and four choirs, which fuses orchestra and voice in a phonetically conceived text. Though very avant-garde, it is an intriguing work, more concerned with sustaining a communicative mood than some of Stockhausen's other works.

For Follow-Up Consideration

Hymnen (*Anthems*), the much-talked-about work Stockhausen directed at a 1971 concert of the New York Philharmonic (at which he used an alternate version of the work that combines live instrumentalists, orchestra, and electronic music instead of the original all-electronic version he had recorded earlier). This two-hour-long, spatially complex work uses snatches of the American, British, French, Russian, Swiss, West German, and several African national anthems as its basis. These anthems are then transformed and integrated into electronic music along with the gibberish of shortwave broadcasts, people shouting and talking, bird sounds, and so on. Its purpose is "to achieve something more than a primitive collage, to evoke a unity in which hate is abolished as a result of meditation among all mutually hostile forces" and "to establish many-faceted interrelationships among the various anthems as well as among new abstract sound shapes," to quote the composer. The effect is something like listening in to all sorts of sounds coming from earth on the receiver of a spaceship circling the earth at enormous speed. RECOMMENDED RECORDING: Electronic Studios of the West German Radio, Cologne (Deutsche Grammophone stereo 2-disc set 139421/122), recorded in 1968 under the composer's direction.

Opus 1970, a "soundpiece" for piano, electric viola, tam-tam, shortwave radio, filters, and potentiometers, in which sound fragments are transmitted to the players by radio shortwaves, and then "spread, condensed, differently colored, transposed, modulated, multiplied, and synchronized" against a prerecorded tape reproducing fragments of music by Beethoven. Stockhausen's intention was "to hear familiar, old, preformed musical material with new ears." RECOMMENDED RECORDING: Stockhausen, Kontarsky, Fritsch, Boié, Gehlhaar (Deutsche Grammophon stereo disc 139461), released for the Beethoven Bicentennial in 1970.

• *KRZYSZTOF PENDERECKI*

Pronounced: pen-der-*ret*-skee. Born November 25, 1933, in Krakow, Poland. Now living in Berlin.

SIGNIFICANCE: Polish composer, one of the few avant-garde composers under forty to win worldwide recognition in the 1960's; his vivid, adventurous music mixes infinite modern complexity and subtlety with an almost medieval simplicity and directness.

BACKGROUND: Penderecki began his study of music in Krakow during years of turmoil and confusion for Poland—first the upheavals of World War II and then the establishment of a Communist government after the war. Like a number of other Poles in the arts, Penderecki experimented privately with avant-garde ideas, often without knowledge of similar Western experiments. After 1956, some Communist restrictions on the arts were eased for a while, including cultural exchanges with the West, and Polish avant-garde music came out more into the open.

In 1959, Penderecki anonymously entered three works in the Competition of Young Polish Composers, and won three first prizes. Two years later his *Threnody for the Victims of Hiroshima* was honored by UNESCO's International Tribune of Composers, and became one of the most talked-about pieces of new music. Since then, Penderecki has written a number of major works with religious themes, including a *Stabat Mater* (1963), a *St. Luke Passion* (1966), and a *Dies Irae* (1967) subtitled "Auschwitz Oratorio" (in memory of those killed in the Nazi extermination camp at Auschwitz). When questioned about his writing religious works in a Communist country, Penderecki told *Musical America's* Bernard Jacobson in 1968: "I am a Catholic . . . and I am concerned with these things in an essentially moral and social way, not in either a political or a sectarian religious way."

Threnody for the Victims of Hiroshima

Few works in recent years have had the impact on listeners that the *Hiroshima Threnody* has had. This ten-minute piece is a searing, violent cataclysm of modern orchestral sound that uses tone clusters, unusually high string registers, and special percussion techniques to depict the horrors of the atomic bombing of Hiroshima. Scored for an orchestra of fifty-two strings, it creates a unique web of intense sound colors and an overpowering sense of energy.

Recommended Recordings

★ Rowicki, Warsaw Philharmonic (Philips stereo disc PHS-900141, also in 2-LP set 802771/2)

b Maderna, Rome Symphony (RCA Victrola stereo disc VICS-1239; cartridge V8S-1013)

Comments

Rowicki's scorchingly intense performance was first released in 1967 as part of a *Contemporary Polish Music* album (the first Philips album listed above), which also includes unusually interesting works by Baird (b. 1928), Bacewicz (b.1913), and Serocki (b.1922). In 1968 the same performance was also included in a 2-LP album (the second listing above) with Penderecki's widely acclaimed *St. Luke Passion*. Moreover, Philips—in an enlightened move that other companies might follow for similarly offbeat releases—has made the 2-LP set available for the price of one LP. The sound engineering is very good.

Maderna's 1967 performance is also excellent, but the sound engineering is not as spacious or resonant as it is on the Rowicki recording. Still, at RCA's budget-label prices, this version has much to recommend since it is coupled with three other works involving today's avant-garde explorations into multiple worlds of sound: Stockhausen's *Kontra-Punkte* (1952), one of his pre-electronic scores; Belgian composer Pousseur's *Rimes*, in which he intriguingly "rhymes" electronic sounds with instrumental ones; and Massachusetts-born Earle Brown's *Available Forms I* (1961), an aleatoric work involving "chance" selections in the score by conductor and players. The liner notes do a good job of explaining what most of this is all about, and anyone seriously interested in where contemporary music is going should find it fascinating.

For Follow-Up Consideration

Capriccio for Violin and Orchestra, an eerily striking and expressive 1967 work that sounds something like a violin concerto being contorted through the sound system of a spaceship in flight. RECOMMENDED RECORDING: Zukofsky, Foss, Buffalo Philharmonic (Nonesuch stereo disc 71201), a 1968 release in which the then twenty-five-year-old Zukofsky performs with astonishing virtuosity in a piece few violinists would even attempt. The coupling is Penderecki's short electroniclike *De Natura Sonoris* (On the Nature of Sound), plus two complex but fascinating works by the contemporary Rumanian Xenakis (b.1922), *Akrata* and *Pithoprakta*, which involve mathematically logical "clouds" of sound, among other things.

The Passion According to St. Luke, widely hailed as one of the most significant religious works of the 20th century. This eighty-minute oratorio (composed in 1965) freely mingles traditional (Gregorian chant, Baroque counterpoint) and avant-garde elements (tone clusters, choral hissing, and instrumental whacking) in remarkably expressive, dramatic, and emotionally intense ways. RECOMMENDED RECORDING: Czyz, Woytowicz, Hiolski, Ladysz, Herdegen, Krakow Philharmonia and Choir (Philips stereo 2-disc set 802771/2), a recording made shortly after the premiere in Krakow's St. Catherine's Church under the composer's supervision, with the final band of the last side given over to the searing *Hiroshima Threnody* as led by Rowicki.

Utrenja, a large-scale, eighty-minute choral and orchestral work (*Utrenja* is an Old Slavonic word for the Eastern Orthodox Church's morning prayer) that interprets the burial and resurrection of Christ in contemporary sounds—and contemporary they indeed are, including singing, talking, yelling, shrieking, murmuring, etc., in massed dissonances, microtones, and just about every other sound the human voice and orchestral instruments are capable of reproducing; the effect is staggeringly powerful. RECOMMENDED RECORDING: Markowski, Woytowicz, Pustelak, Lagger, Ladysz, Warsaw Philharmonic Orchestra and Choir (Philips stereo 2-disc set 6700065), a dramatically compelling and sonically exciting 1974 release of the complete score. An earlier 1971 recording by Ormandy and the Philadelphia Orchestra (RCA Red Seal stereo disc LSC-3180) includes only Part One, but it is a gripping performance which may be preferred by newcomers who need to take modern works in smaller doses.

Postscripts and Postludes

There are, of course, many other composers of interest besides the fifty discussed in the preceding pages. Some have written works which have become popular showpieces of the hi-fi/stereo age. Some have been overshadowed by other composers writing in similar styles. Some have only recently begun to win or rewin renown for the individual qualities of their works. Here are brief notes and recording recommendations on an additional group of such composers.

• *VINCENZO BELLINI*

> Pronounced: bell-*lee*nee. Born November 3, 1801, in Catania, Sicily. Died September 23, 1835, in Puteaux, France.

The lyrical, patrician operas he wrote before his untimely death at age thirty-three have recently begun to find favor again after decades of neglect (partly because of their *bel canto* vocal demands).

Norma, Bellini's masterpiece, based on a French tragedy about a Druid priestess in ancient Gaul and a virgin of the temple who loved the same Roman soldier; the title role has long been considered one of the most challenging in the entire operatic repertory.

Recommended recordings: *Complete opera*—Cillario (conductor), Caballé (Norma), Cossotto (Adalgisa), Domingo (Pollione), others, Ambrosian Opera Chorus, London Philharmonic Orchestra (RCA Red Seal stereo 3-disc set LSC-6202), a 1972 release notable for the stylistic grace and subtle beauty of Caballé's singing of the title role, and for the radiant ensemble work between Caballé and Cossotto. *Highlights only*—Bonynge (conductor), Sutherland (Norma), Horne (Adalgisa), Alexander (Pollione), London Symphony Orchestra (London disc OS-26168; cassette M-31171), recommended in the absence of a highlights edition of the Caballé album. Sutherland and Horne are heard in two *Norma* duets on one side, singing them beautifully if somewhat less subtly and more coolly than Caballé and Cossotto; overside Sutherland and Horne offer two arias from Rossini's *Semiramide*. The duets are taken from complete recordings of *Norma* and *Semiramide* originally released in 1965 and 1969 respectively.

• LEONARD BERNSTEIN

Pronounced: *burn*-stine. Born August 25, 1918, in Lawrence, Massachusetts. Now living in New York City.

In addition to being one of the most popular conductors of his generation, he has composed three symphonies, several ballets, four Broadway musicals (the most famous, *West Side Story*, was also an award-winning film), a controversial Mass, and other works notable for their melodic vigor, jazz influences, and unabashed theatricality.

Chichester Psalms, written in 1965 for England's Chichester Festival; an eloquently simple, disarmingly melodic, compellingly rhythmic, and deeply moving work for chorus and orchestra. The text, sung in Hebrew, is taken from six Old Testament Psalms (2, 23, 100, 108, 131, 133) concerning war and peace.

Recommended recording: Bernstein, New York Philharmonic, Camerata Singers (Columbia stereo disc MS-6792), a superbly animated 1966 recording, definitively led by the composer; the coupling is an earlier but still pungent Bernstein ballet score, *Facsimile*.

• ALEXANDER BORODIN

Pronounced: *bohr*-oh-deen. Born November 12, 1834, in St. Petersburg, Russia. Died February 20, 1887, in St. Petersburg.

A member of the so-called Russian nationalist Five (together with Mussorgsky and Rimsky-Korsakov), Borodin was a part-time composer whose principal career was as a chemistry professor. He completed two symphonies and two string quartets, but his second opera, *Prince Igor*, remained unfinished at his death even though he had been working on it for twenty-five years (it was completed by Rimsky-Korsakov and Glazunov).

"Polovetsian Dances" from *Prince Igor*, a set of vigorously exciting and colorful dances representing the revels of a Tartar camp in the second act of Borodin's uncompleted opera; long popular as a concert work (and hi-fi showpiece) on its own; its principal themes have also been used in the popular musical play *Kismet*.

Recommended recording: Ansermet, Suisse Romande Orchestra and Radio Lausanne Choir (London stereo disc CS-6212; cassette M-10076; cartridge M-67076), a vivid, rousing, superbly engineered 1960 release which includes the choral sections omitted on most other recordings; the coupling is an outstanding Ansermet performance of Rimsky-Korsakov's *Scheherazade*.

• BENJAMIN BRITTEN

Pronounced: *brit*-ten. Born November 23, 1913, in Lowestoft, England. Now living in Aldeburgh, England.

Considered by many critics to be the greatest English composer since Henry Purcell (1659–1695); a prolific composer of orchestral works, concertos, song cycles, and, particularly, operas (many of the latter based on well-known literary themes, such as Herman Melville's *Billy Budd*, Henry James' *The Turn of the Screw*, and Thomas Mann's *Death in Venice*).

The Young Person's Guide to the Orchestra, also known as *Variations and Fugue on a Theme by Purcell*, written for a 1945 documentary film explaining the various instruments of a symphony orchestra; a marvelously inventive score, sometimes light and frolicsome, at other points expressively lyrical and dramatic.

Recommended recordings: (1) *with narration*, Previn (conductor and narrator), London Symphony Orchestra (Angel stereo disc S-36962), a 1973 release in which Previn delivers the narration uncloyingly and unpatronizingly, and with the LSO instrumentalists in fine form; overside both Previn (as conductor) and his wife Mia Farrow (as narrator) are less ingratiating in a perfunctory performance of Prokofiev's *Peter and the Wolf*. (2) *without narration*, Ozawa, Chicago Symphony Orchestra (RCA Red Seal stereo disc LSC-2977; cartridge R8S-1087), an exceptionally bright and spirited 1967 performance, superbly played by the Chicagoans; the coupling is a first-rate Ozawa–Chicago performance of the Mussorgsky-Ravel *Pictures at an Exhibition*.

• JOHN CAGE

Pronounced: *kayj*. Born September 5, 1912, in Los Angeles, California. Now living in New York City.

One of the most trail-blazing and influential of American avant-garde composers, especially in the electronic and aleatoric areas; many of his works reflect Oriental influences as well as impulses toward the absurd and the grotesque.

Concerto for Prepared Piano and Orchestra, a 1951 work for the so-called prepared piano (which Cage introduced in 1938)—a piano with pieces of metal, rubber, and other materials fitted between the strings, giving the piano a distorted, almost exotic sound; the concerto is essentially reflective in mood, with passages of unusual delicacy.

Recommended recording: Foss, Buffalo Philharmonic Orchestra (Nonesuch stereo disc 71202; cassette N5-71202), a well-recorded 1968 budget-label release, making this an especially attractive Cage "sampler"; overside Foss conducts one of his own works, *Baroque Variations*, in which he uses themes by Handel, Scarlatti, and Bach to explore interesting new sonic perceptions.

- ## *GAETANO DONIZETTI*

    Pronounced: doh-nee-*zet*-tee. Born November 29, 1797, in Bergamo, Italy. Died April 8, 1848, in Bergamo.

Probably the most prolific of Italian opera composers (he wrote between sixty-five and seventy operas), and the leading Italian opera figure between Rossini and Verdi.

Lucrezia Borgia, an opera based on Victor Hugo's highly fictionalized account of an episode in the life of the much-maligned daughter of Pope Alexander VI in 16th-century Italy. Although less widely known than Donizetti's *Lucia di Lammermoor* (long popular for its dramatic "Mad Scene") and some of his comic operas (*Don Pasquale, The Daughter of the Regiment*), *Lucrezia Borgia* (1833) is in many ways superior in the sustained impact of its musical substance and its abundance of singable melodies, as well as its historical significance in moving 19th-century Italian opera toward greater emotional realism.

Recommended recording: Perlea (conductor), Caballé (Lucrezia), Verrett (Orsini), Kraus (Gennaro), others, RCA Italiana Opera Orchestra and Chorus (*complete*—RCA Red Seal stereo 3-disc set LSC-6176; *highlights*—RCA Red Seal stereo disc LSC-3038, cartridge R8S-1106), a superbly sung 1966 recording in which Caballé recreates the role which made her an overnight star in 1965; although there are several minor cuts made in the score, this recording restores two long-lost cabalettas for the title role, found by the RCA producer in the archives of a European publishing firm.

- ## *MANUEL DE FALLA*

    Pronounced: *fye*-yah. Born November 23, 1876, in Cadiz, Spain. Died November 14, 1946, in Córdoba, Argentina.

Spain's most internationally renowned composer in this century, noted at first for his Impressionistic, folk-influenced ballets and vocal scores, and later for more neoclassical works.

The Three-Cornered Hat, a 1919 ballet score which one critic has described as treating the orchestra "like a gigantic Spanish guitar." A rhythmically vibrant, elegant, and colorful work, it uses elements of Spanish folk music in an Impressionistic manner. Although a set of three dances from the ballet has long been popular concert fare, the complete score has only recently come into its own as a concert work (partly through LP recordings).

Recommended recording: Frühbeck de Burgos, Philharmonia Orchestra (Angel stereo disc S-36235), a crisply vivid, subtly detailed 1964 performance, in which the two brief soprano chants are sung by Victoria de los Angeles. The opening section, with its choral "olés" and its strongly accented castinet and percussion beats, makes an unusually effective stereo showpiece. In this respect, another recording—by Ansermet and the Suisse Romande Orchestra, with Teresa Berganza as vocal solist (London stereo disc CS-6224)—has an equally impressive opening section sonically, but the rest of Ansermet's performance is not quite as exciting as Frühbeck's.

• PAUL HINDEMITH

> Pronounced: *hin*-deh-mith. Born November 16, 1895, in Hanau, Germany. Died December 28, 1963, in Frankfurt, Germany.

Distinguished as a violinist, violist, conductor, teacher, and theoretician as well as a composer in Germany in the years following World War I. In 1934 the Nazis banned his music (partly because his wife's family was "non-Aryan," partly because of the anti-authoritarian theme of his opera *Mathis der Maler*). He spent the rest of his life teaching, successively, in Turkey, the U.S., and Switzerland. Much of his music has been called "Gebrauchsmusik"—"workaday" or "utility" music—because it was composed for a specific function in schools, cabarets, movies, etc.

Symphonic Metamorphoses (*on Themes of Carl Maria von Weber*), composed in the U.S. in 1943 and the most popular of Hindemith's "American" works; based mainly on themes from some virtually forgotten piano music by Weber (1786–1826), its four movements are in essence a witty, sophisticated set of variations, masterly transforming Weber's themes into massive, modern orchestral textures.

Recommended recording: Bernstein, New York Philharmonic (Columbia stereo disc MS-7426), a rhythmically propulsive and ebullient performance by Bernstein, who makes more of the jazz-like syncopations in parts of the score than do other conductors. His coupling for this 1970 release is Hindemith's more sombre but expressive Symphony in E flat, also composed in the U.S. (in 1940) and considered by some critics to be an extended *danse macabre* reflecting the state of the world at the beginning of World War II.

• GUSTAV HOLST

> Pronounced: *hohlst*. Born September 21, 1874, in Cheltenham, England. Died May 25, 1934, in London.

English composer of Swedish descent, best-known for his orchestral suite *The Planets*, and one of the most influential English music teachers of his generation.

The Planets, a colorful, Impressionistic orchestral suite about space—written between 1914 and 1917, long before movie composers made clichés of some of Holst's ideas. The seven sections bear descriptive astrological titles, such as "Mars, the Bringer of War," "Venus, the Bringer of Peace," "Mercury, the Winged Messenger," "Neptune, the Mystic."

Recommended recording: Haitink, London Philharmonic Orchestra, John Alldis Choir (Philips stereo disc 6500072; cassette 7300058), a 1971 release that is interpretively superior to the competing versions of Bernstein, Boult, Hermann, Karajan, Mehta, Steinberg, and Stokowski, and sonically superior to all except Hermann (London Phase-4) and Steinberg (DG)—but not really that much below those two, either. Haitink brings out each of the sections' varying moods with telling effect, particularly the sinister undercurrent of "Mars" and the eerie mysticism of "Neptune."

• GYÖRGY LIGETI

Pronounced: *lig*-git-tee. Born May 28, 1923, in Dioseoeszentmarton, in Rumanian Transylvania. Now living in Western Europe.

One of the better-known of contemporary avant-garde musicians, particularly after several of his works were used (without his permission) in the film *2001: A Space Odyssey*.

Lontano, a 1960 work which explores music as a series of weblike sound complexes, with constantly unfolding and varying layers of tone colors and contours.

Recommended recording: Bour, Southwest German Radio Orchestra of Baden-Baden (Heliodor/Wergo stereo disc 2549011), a first-rate performance, coupled with two other Ligeti works, including *Requiem* (for soprano, mezzo-soprano, two choirs, and orchestra), a part of which was used in the film *2001: A Space Odyssey*. *Note:* A brief part of both *Lontano* and *Requiem* are included in an album called *Space 2001: Vol. 2* (MGM stereo disc S-4722) in the same German Radio performances, but are not complete.

• GIAN-CARLO MENOTTI

Pronounced: meh-*not*-tee. Born July 7, 1911, in Cadigliano, Italy. Now living in the U.S.

Best-known as a composer of several operas which have been produced successfully on Broadway, in films, and on television. Since 1958 he has been closely identified with the Spoleto Festival in Italy, which he founded.

Amahl and the Night Visitors, an hour-long opera commissioned by the NBC television network for a Christmas Eve production in 1951, and frequently produced since then both on TV and on stage throughout the United States. It tells an essentially sentimental fable about a crippled shepherd boy's encounter with the Three Wise Men on their way to Bethlehem. Although less intensely melodramatic than some of Menotti's other operas (*The Consul*, *The Medium*, *The Saint of Bleeker Street*), it shares with them an overall musical conservatism, lyrical simplicity, and emotional directness.

Recommended recording: Schippers (conductor), Kuhlmann (Mother), Allen (Amahl), others, NBC Orchestra and Chorus (RCA Victrola disc VIC-1512, *mono only*), originally released in 1952 (as RCA LM-1701) and reissued in 1971 on RCA's budget-priced label; the sound holds up surprisingly well on this original cast recording—which, combined with Schippers' animated conducting and Kuhlmann's luminous singing, make this preferable to a later, full-price stereo version recorded in the mid-1960's by a later TV cast (on RCA Red Seal stereo disc LSC-2762).

• CARL ORFF

Pronounced: *orf.* Born July 10, 1895, in Munich, Germany. Now living in West Germany.

Advocate of an essentially neo-primitive musical style—going back to old legends and medieval literature for the texts of his operas and cantatas, and writing music that dispenses with counterpoint and traditional lyricism in favor of a kind of straightforward rhythmic declamation, often accompanied by large percussive forces.

Carmina Burana, written in the 1930's and based mostly on the drinking songs and love poems of defrocked medieval monks. Its hedonistic text, sung in Latin, may be in questionable taste (if not downright offensive to some)—but there is no denying the impact and appeal of its directly physical music, or the fact that it has become one of the most popular works of the past twenty years. It is full of blazing brass and biting percussive effects, full-blooded choral sections, and alternately lusty and tender sections for soprano, tenor, baritone, and orchestra.

Recommended recording: Ozawa, Mandac, Kolk, Milnes, Boston Symphony Orchestra, New England Conservatory Chorus (RCA Red Seal stereo disc LSC-3161; cartridge R8S-1161), a rousing 1969 performance, electric in its excitement and rhythmic pulse, superbly sung, and with excellent sound engineering.

• FRANCIS POULENC

Pronounced: *poo*-lank. Born January 7, 1899, in Paris, France. Died January 30, 1963, in Paris.

Perhaps the best-known of "Les Six" (The Six), a group of prominent French composers in the 1920's (with Honegger, Milhaud, Auric, Durey, Tailleferre) who sought to move French music away from both 19th-century Romanticism and early 20th-century Impressionism to a more Neoclassical style; at first known mainly for his urbane, witty piano and orchestral works, but later for his lyrical songs and eloquent religious works.

Gloria (for Soprano, Chorus, and Orchestra), an elegantly joyous 1961 work composed on the premise that a work dedicated to the glory of God should be gay, moving, and beautiful. There are even a few traces of jazz syncopation here and there, though the basic mood is warmly lyrical.

Recommended recording: Shaw (conductor), Endich (soprano), Robert Shaw Chorale and Orchestra (RCA Red Seal stereo disc LSC-2822), a beautifully sung 1965 performance by the tragically short-lived Miss Endich. The coupling is a broadly spacious yet stirring Shaw performance of Stravinsky's *Symphony of Psalms*.

• OTTORINO RESPIGHI

Pronounced: res-*pee*-ghee. Born July 9, 1879, in Bologna, Italy. Died April 18, 1936, in Rome.

Best-known in the U.S. for a series of lush orchestral tone poems about Rome, but equally well-known in Italy for works based on old Classical structures (including a piano concerto in the Mixolydian mode and a violin concerto based on Gregorian chant).

The Pines of Rome, one of a trilogy of colorful tone poems about Rome that Respighi wrote between 1917 and 1928. Its four sections depict: (1) noisy children playing in the pine groves of the historic Villa Borghese; (2) the deserted, pine-shadowed entrance to an ancient Roman catacomb; (3) a moonlit night among the pines of the Janiculum Hill's gardens; and (4) ancient Roman soldiers marching up the pine-lined Appian Way to enter the Capitoline Hill triumphantly. The last section, building steadily from soft percussion and winds to trumpet flourishes and then to blaringly full orchestral sounds, is a popular stereo showpiece.

Recommended recording: Munch, New Philharmonia Orchestra (London stereo disc SPC-21024; cassette M-94024; cartridge M-95024); a 1966 recording that combines London's spectacular Phase-4 stereo technique with a sweepingly colorful, dramatically charged, tonally resplendent Munch performance. Munch is also one of the few conductors to pace the final Appian Way march to match the gait of foot-soldiers (a few other recordings sound more like armored tanks rolling down the road). Munch's coupling is an equally lush, beautifully engineered performance of Respighi's *Fountains of Rome*.

• GEORGE ROCHBERG

Pronounced: *rock*-berg. Born July 5, 1918, in Paterson, New Jersey. Now living in Montclair, New Jersey.

Arguably the most outstanding American composer of the post-World War II era; winner of probably more major awards than any other contemporary composer (including the Gershwin Memorial Award, 1952, a Koussevitzky Foundation Award, 1957, the Naumburg Recording Award, 1961, and the Pulitzer Prize, 1973). Until 1965 he accepted "the historical inevitability of the 12-tone language," but since then he has moved away from serialism as "too confining" and has sought to integrate a wider range of styles, "denying neither the past nor the future." In this respect, some critics consider him especially influential in expanding the language and direction of present-day American composition.

Tableaux, a set of "sound pictures" for soprano, small chorus, and chamber orchestra; composed in 1968, and based on "The Silver Talons of Piero Kostrov," a surrealistic story written by the composer's teenage son (who died in 1964). Most of its twelve sections are of a shimmering, silvery beauty typical of Rochberg, full of mystery and expressive images—and sonically intriguing even when one isn't sure of the relationship of the words to the musical atmosphere.

Recommended recording: Wernick (conductor), DeGaetani (soprano), Penn Contemporary Players (Vox/Turnabout stereo disc TVS-34492), a well-recorded 1973 budget-label release by a group of young professionals and University of Pennsylvania musicians with an impressive flair for the contemporary idiom; soprano Jan DeGaetani is especially outstanding. The coupling is that rarity of rarities: a work by a woman composer. *O the Chimneys* by Israel's Shulamit Ran is a set of five poems for soprano and chamber ensemble, based on a group of apocalyptic verses by Nelly Sachs about the horrors of being a Jew in Nazi Germany. The fifth poem, depicting the end of the world, augments the chamber orchestra with a pretaped assemblage of electronic and percussive sounds—and the effect is as harrowing as anything since Penderecki's *Threnody for the Victims of Hiroshima*. Gloria Davy is the excellent soloist in the Ran work.

• GIOACCHINO ROSSINI

Pronounced: roh-*see*-nee. Born February 29, 1792, in Pesaro, Italy. Died November 13, 1868, in Passy, France.

One of the most successful Italian opera composers of the early 19th century; his first opera was produced when he was eighteen years old, and he was a popular idol by twenty-one. He wrote thirty-eight operas before he "retired" at age thirty-seven for reasons that have long been debated. He was one of the first opera composers to write out cadenzas instead of allowing singers to improvise them.

Rossini Overtures. In Rossini's case, it is primarily the overtures to his major operas which have remained popular rather than the operas themselves—and many leading conductors love to play them and record them. The reason is not hard to understand, for the overtures are brimming with rhythmic vitality and a wealth of melody, and are frequently well-laced with delightful humor.

Recommended recordings: (1) Toscanini, NBC Symphony Orchestra (RCA Victrola disc VIC-1274, *mono only*), a group of five overtures (*William Tell, The Barber of Seville, Il Signor Bruschino, La Gazza Ladra, Semiramide*) plus a brief, catchy dance from *William Tell*—all played to the hilt by the conductor who had a unique flair for this music; recorded between 1945 and 1953, the sonic quality is limited by today's standards but not disturbingly so. (2) Reiner, Chicago Symphony Orchestra (RCA Red Seal stereo disc LSC-2318), a group of six overtures (*William Tell, The Barber of Seville, Il Signor Bruschino, La Gazza Ladra, Cenerentola,* and *La Scala di Seta*); a better-sounding stereo set from the late 1950's, with Reiner bringing out more of the charm and humor if less of the rhythmic bite and verve than Toscanini.

● *ERIK SATIE*

Pronounced: sah-*tee*. Born May 17, 1866, in Honfleur, France. Died July 1, 1925, in Paris.

French pianist and composer, a pioneer in a modern style of ultra-cool harmonic simplicity that militantly rejected Romantic emotionalism in music. He gave his spare, neoclassical pieces eccentric titles (*Three Pieces in the Shape of a Pear, Flabby Preludes for a Dog, Desiccrated Embryos,* etc.), and experimented in the 1920's with the use of movies in combination with live performances of song and dance—a forerunner of today's mixed media. Though dismissed by some critics as a musical dilettante, he had a profound influence on Ravel and a number of other prominent French composers of this century.

Gymnopedies, a set of three stately, limpid pieces which Satie wrote for the piano in 1888. Debussy thought so highly of them that he orchestrated two (Nos. 1 and 3), even though he couldn't always find the time or energy to orchestrate his own music. The title is a word coined by Satie, but it is derived from a Greek word for the dances and gymnastics performed in honor of fallen warriors. During the late 1960's the Gymnopedie No. 3 was used in a pop recording by the group Blood, Sweat and Tears and sparked something of a Satie boomlet, especially on high school and college campuses.

Recommended recordings: *Piano version*—Ciccolini (Angel stereo disc S-36482; cassette 4XS-36482; cartridge 8XS-36482), a beautifully played performance, included in the first of six excellent albums Ciccolini has made over the past decade of Satie's complete piano music. *Orchestral version*—Previn, London Symphony Orchestra (RCA Red Seal stereo disc LSC-2945; cartridge R8S-1183), an especially beautiful and hauntingly mellow performance of the two Debussy orchestrations, highlighted by the splendid oboe of John de Lancie (regularly of the Philadelphia Orchestra); this 1967 release is rounded out with short works by two other 20th-century French composers influenced by Satie, Jacques Ibert (*Symphonie Concertante for Oboe and Strings*) and Jean Francaix (*The Flower Clock*), with De Lancie again the soloist. (*Note:* the label of the RCA disc erroneously lists the Gymnopedies as Numbers 1 and 2, whereas they are actually Numbers 1 and 3, as correctly noted in the same album's liner notes.)

• *RALPH VAUGHAN WILLIAMS*

Pronounced: vawn *will*-yims. Born October 12, 1872, in Down Ampney, England. Died August 26, 1958, in London.

One of the last dedicated symphonists of this century, and also a composer of many fine vocal works. His music has been described by some critics as late Romantic with a "typically English" restraint, but some also stress its mixture of nobility, serenity, and power. In both his vocal and orchestral works, Vaughan Williams was strongly influenced by his own extensive research into early English folk music.

Symphony No. 2 (*"A London Symphony"*), a stoutly melodic musical evocation of London, painting a series of tonal impressions of the city from the bustle of Piccadilly to the misty Thames River at dawn, from the pageantry of Westminster to the barrel organs and Cockney street cries of the East End. The introduction echoes the notes of Big Ben's famous chimes, and later sections use two English songs, "Sweet Lavender" and "We'll All Go Down to the Strand." Begun in 1912 and first performed in 1914, the symphony was revised in 1920 and again in the mid-1930's; however, in 1951 when Vaughan Williams revised all of his six symphonies to that year, he wrote: "The 'London Symphony' is past mending—though with all its faults I love it still; indeed it is my favorite."

Recommended recording: Barbirolli, Hallé Orchestra (Angel stereo disc S-36478; cassette 4XS-36478; cartridge 8XS-36478), a warmly lyrical, spirited, deeply expressive performance dating from the mid-1960's.

• *HEITOR VILLA-LOBOS*

Pronounced: *veel*-lah *loh*-bohs. Born March 5, 1887, in Rio de Janeiro, Brazil. Died November 17, 1959, in Rio de Janeiro.

Internationally the best-known South American composer, noted for his boldly rhythmic, frequently sensuous but sometimes primitively vehement music, much of it strongly influenced by Brazilian folk music.

Bachianas Brasilieras No. 5, the fifth in a series of suites that Villa-Lobos wrote in the 1930's attempting a fusion of the spirit of Bach with Brazilian folk materials. The fifth is in two movements (Aria, Danza), is scored for soprano and eight celli (with optional additional celli and double basses), and is set to two poems—one by Ruth Correa that evokes a mood of midnight moonlight, the other by Manuel Bandeira about songbirds of the woods.

Recommended recordings: (1) Moffo, Stokowski, American Symphony Orchestra (RCA Red Seal stereo disc LSC-2795), a sensuously beautiful, hauntingly limpid performance in excellent stereo; the coupling for this 1965 release is a lush Moffo–Stokowski performance of Canteloube's folk-derived *Songs of the Auvergne*, plus Rachmaninoff's wordless *Vocalise.* (2) Sayão, Villa-Lobos, cello ensemble including Leonard Rose (Columbia disc ML-5231, *mono only*), with the outstanding Brazilian soprano Bidu Sayão in a now-classic performance of the first part of the work (Aria) under the composer's direction, dating from the mid-1940's but still sonically acceptable; the same excerpt is included in two different Sayão albums, with the one listed above containing a rare group of Brazilian folk songs, plus five Puccini arias with which Sayão was closely identified during her Metropolitan Opera career.

• KURT WEILL

Pronounced: *vhile.* Born March 2, 1900, in Dessau, Germany. Died April 3, 1950, in New York City.

Together with poet-dramatist Bertolt Brecht, he was a major force in revolutionizing German opera and musical theatre after World War I, especially in its incorporation of elements of jazz and popular music (*The Three-Penny Opera, Mahagonny,* etc.). After coming to the U.S. in 1935 he composed almost exclusively for Broadway shows and for films, although some critics consider several of these works (particularly *Street Scene*) serious, innovative, modern operas.

The Seven Deadly Sins (Die Sieben Todsünden), the last Weill-Brecht collaboration (1933), a stinging satire on the corruption the average man must endure (and even contribute to) in order to survive in modern "civilization." Weill's music for this ballet-opera is alternately jazzy and traditional, as it traces the travels of two sisters (one sung, the other danced) to seven American cities to try to get enough money to build their family a "little home down by the Mississippi"—only to find in each city that they can fight sins only with bigger sins. The score is one of Weill's best and most typical—harmonically lean, rhythmically vibrant, melodically bittersweet, alternately caustic and tender, and, overall, always cutting into the text's bitter, cynical surface with a feeling of deep humanity

Recommended recording: Kegel, May, Schreier, Rotzsch, Leib, Polster, Leipzig Radio Symphony Orchestra (Deutsche Grammophon stereo disc 139308; cassette 923-092), a dramatically pungent, vivid performance sung in the original German (an English translation is provided)—particularly notable for the deep-throated gusto, warmth, and dramatic intensity of Gisela May in the leading role. The album was first released in the U.S. in 1969, but was recorded two or three years before then; the stereo sound is excellent.

PART THREE

Major Music-Makers on Discs and Tapes

Major Music-Makers on Discs and Tapes

Have you ever heard a piece of music and then gone to buy a recording of it—only to open up the record catalog and be overwhelmed by a long list of names with which you weren't familiar? How do you choose?

There's no foolproof system, of course. But knowing who the major conductors and soloists are, something about their background, and what types of music they're usually best at, can at least provide a start.

That is the purpose of this section. It is not a complete "Who's Who" of the concert world by any means. It includes most of the established recording artists plus some of today's most promising newcomers.

(Pronunciations are for the closest approximation of the Anglicized version of each name.)

CLAUDIO ABBADO
(pronounced: ah-*bah*-doh)

Conductor. Born June 26, 1933, in Milan, Italy. He studied at the Verdi conservatory in Milan and at the Vienna Academy in the 1950's. He won first prize in a conducting competition at Tanglewood (Massachusetts) in 1958, and was an assistant to Bernstein with the New York Philharmonic in 1963. During the past decade he has been increasingly acclaimed as one of the finest conductors of his generation, a particularly forceful and incisive interpreter of both 19th- and early 20th-century works. In 1971 he was named music director of the Vienna Philharmonic Orchestra.

Recommended recordings: Tchaikovsky *Romeo and Juliet* and Scriabin *Poem of Ecstasy* (Deutsche Grammophon stereo disc 2530137). Prokofiev: Symphony No. 1 ("Classical") and 3 (London stereo disc CS-6679).

MAURICE ABRAVANEL
(pronounced: ah-brah-vah-*nell*)

Conductor. Born January 6, 1903, in Salonica, Greece. He was educated in Switzerland, and began his conducting career in Lausanne. In the 1920's he was with the Berlin Opera. He came to the U.S. in 1926, and was for many years one of the leading conductors of Broadway musicals, including Kurt Weill's *Lady in the Dark* and *Street Scene*, Marc Blitzstein's *Regina*, and the Vernon Duke-Igor Stravinsky *Seven Lively Arts*. For a number of years he was also music director of the Sydney (Australia) Orchestral Society. Since 1947 he has been conductor of the Utah Symphony Orchestra. He is most closely identified with Romantic and early 20th-century music.

54

Licia Albanese

52

Claudio Abbado

57

Marian Anderson

53

Maurice Abravanel

55

Karel Ancerl

58

Ernest Ansermet

56

Geza Anda

61

Vladimir Ashkenazy

59

Martha Argerich

64 °

Daniel Barenboim

60

Martina Arroyo

62

Janet Baker

65

Serge Baudo

63

Sir John Barbirolli

Recommended recordings: Gottschalk *A Night in the Tropics* and *Grand Tarantelle* (Vanguard stereo disc S-275). Mahler Symphony No. 2 (with Sills, Kopleff) (Vanguard stereo 2-disc set C-10003/3).

LICIA ALBANESE

(pronounced: ahl-bah-*nay*-zeh)

Soprano. Born July 22, 1913, in Bari, Italy. She made her operatic debut at Milan's La Scala in 1934, substituting for an indisposed singer in Puccini's *Madame Butterfly*. The same opera was also her debut vehicle at New York's Metropolitan Opera in 1940. She remained at the Met for 25 seasons as one of its most popular stars, best-known for her Puccini heroines (Butterfly, Tosca, Mimi in *La Bohème*, Manon Lescaut). She became an American citizen in 1945 after marrying a New York stockbroker. In the 1930's she was the first woman to broadcast over the Vatican radio.

Recommended recordings: Puccini *Manon Lescaut* (RCA Victrola 2-disc set VIC-6027, *mono only*), with Bjoerling, Merrill. Puccini *La Bohème*, excerpts (RCA Victrola disc VIC-1604, *mono only*), Toscanini conducting.

KAREL ANCERL

(pronounced: *ahn*-chayrl)

Conductor. Born April 11, 1908, in Tucapy, Czechoslovakia. Died July 3, 1973, in Toronto, Canada. From 1933 to 1939 he was a conductor for the Czechoslovak Radio, until the Nazis sent him to a concentration camp. After World War II he conducted at the Prague Opera (1946–49), and in 1950 became principal conductor of the Czech Philharmonic. At the time of the Soviet-led invasion of Czechoslovakia in 1968 he was conducting in the U.S. at Tanglewood, and decided to remain in the West. In 1969 he succeeded Seiji Ozawa as conductor of the Toronto Symphony Orchestra, holding that post until his death. He was best-known as an unusually expressive conductor of Romantic Slavic works and early 20th-century works.

Recommended recordings: Martinu Symphony No. 5 (Everest stereo disc 3329). Smetana *Ma Vlast* (Crossroads stereo disc 22160050, recently deleted).

GEZA ANDA

(pronounced: *ahn*-dah)

Pianist and occasional conductor. Born November 19, 1921, in Budapest, Hungary. He studied at the Budapest Academy of Music, winning its coveted Franz Liszt Prize and making his professional debut at the age of 18. He has lived in Switzerland since 1942, and became a Swiss citizen in 1955. He is best known for his performances of Classical and early Romantic works, and in the 1960's became the first pianist to record all of Mozart's piano concertos as both pianist and conductor.

Recommended recording: Mozart Piano Concerto No. 21 (Deutsche Grammophon stereo disc 138783; cassette 923052; cartridge 88-783).

MARIAN ANDERSON

Contralto. Born February 17, 1902, in Philadelphia, Pennsylvania. One of the first

American blacks to overcome long-standing obstacles to a major concert career. She first gained prominence in the 1920's as winner of a contest to appear with the New York Philharmonic. She left the U.S. from 1930 to 1935, scoring numerous triumphs in Europe. In 1939 the D.A.R. refused to allow her, because of her color, to give a concert at Constitution Hall in Washington, D.C., whereupon the President's wife, Eleanor Roosevelt, and others arranged a concert for her on the steps of the Lincoln Memorial—and it became one of the most famous concerts in Washington's history. In 1955 she became the first black to sing a major role (Ulrica in Verdi's *Un Ballo in Maschera*) at the Metropolitan Opera. She retired from active concertizing in 1965. She was noted for her deeply expressive singing of Brahms, Schubert, and Schumann, and for her eloquent interpretations of Negro spirituals.

Recommended recordings: Treasury of Immortal Performances—Marian Anderson (RCA disc LM-2712, *mono only*). *He's Got the Whole World in His Hands* (RCA stereo disc LCS-2592), an album of spirituals.

ERNEST ANSERMET
(pronounced: *ahn*-sayr-may)

Conductor. Born November 11, 1883, in Vevey, Switzerland. Died February 20, 1969, in Geneva. A mathematics professor who turned to conducting in 1914, he was for many years principal conductor of Diaghilev's Ballet Russe de Monte Carlo, premiering numerous works by Stravinsky, Ravel, Prokofiev, and others. In 1918 he founded l'Orchestre de la Suisse Romande at Geneva, Switzerland, and remained its conductor for 49 years—raising it to major international status through outstanding recordings following World War II. In the late 1940's he was a frequent guest-conductor of the NBC Symphony Orchestra at Toscanini's invitation, and subsequently conducted the orchestras of Boston, Philadelphia, New York, and Chicago. He was considered one of the century's masters of tonal subtlety, particularly in Impressionistic and Neoclassical works.

Recommended recordings: Stravinsky *Petrushka* (London stereo disc CS-6009). Ravel *L'Enfant et les Sortileges* (London/Richmond stereo disc 33086).

MARTHA ARGERICH
(pronounced: *ahr*-geh-ritch)

Pianist. Born June 5, 1941, in Buenos Aires, Argentina. Following study in Europe with Friedrich Gulda, Mme. Dinu Lipatti, and others, she won first prize at the 1965 International Chopin Competition in Warsaw. Her subsequent career has been marked by major critical acclaim as a dynamic pianist with a special affinity for works with a strong rhythmic pulse.

Recommended recording: Prokofiev Piano Concerto No. 3 (Deutsche Grammophon stereo disc 139349; cassette 923-040).

MARTINA ARROYO
(pronounced: ah-*roy*-yo)

Soprano. Born February 2, 1940, in New York City. After study in New York, she won the Metropolitan Opera Auditions in 1958 at the age of eighteen, and made her debut the following season as the offstage Celestial Voice in Verdi's *Don Carlo*. She continued to sing minor roles at the Met for the next six years, while singing major ones at the Vienna State Opera, the Berlin Deutsche Oper, and the Zurich Opera. In 1965 she substituted on short notice for Birgit Nilsson in the title role of *Aïda* at the Met—to enormous acclaim. She has since been one of the Met's principal singers, noted for her impressively large, clear voice. She is also an active recitalist, particularly in modern works.

Recommended recordings: Verdi *La Forza del Destino* (Angel 4-disc stereo set S-3765; cassette 4X3S-3765). Verdi *Requiem* (Columbia stereo 2-disc set M2-30060).

VLADIMIR ASHKENAZY
(pronounced: ash-keh-*nah*-zee)

Pianist. Born July 6, 1937, in Gorky, Russia. He studied at the Moscow Conservatory, and in 1950 won the Queen Elisabeth of Belgium Competition. In 1964 he was co-winner of the Tchaikovsky International Competition in Moscow. Since his marriage in 1961 to an Icelandic girl, he has maintained his residence in Reykjavik and London, declining to return to the Soviet Union but remaining a Soviet citizen. One of the most outstanding of the post-World War II generation of pianists, he is considered a particularly penetrating and poetic interpreter of Mozart, Beethoven, Rachmaninoff, and Prokofiev.

Recommended recordings: Rachmaninoff Piano Concerto No. 2 (London stereo disc CS-6390). Prokofiev Piano Sonatas Nos. 7, 8 (London stereo disc CS-6573).

JANET BAKER

Mezzo-soprano. Born August 21, 1933, in Yorkshire, England. She grew up in the cathedral city of York and was active from an early age in church and school choirs. In 1956 she won the Kathleen Ferrier Prize, and used it to study at the Mozarteum in Salzburg. In the early 1960's she became one of England's most-acclaimed oratorio and concert singers, and in 1966 made her operatic debut at London's Covent Garden (in Britten's *A Midsummer Night's Dream*). She also made her U.S. concert debut in 1966, and today ranks as one of the outstanding interpreters of both English oratorios and German lieder.

Recommended recordings: Mahler and Elgar Songs (Angel stereo disc S-36796). Handel Cantatas Nos. 1, 13 (Angel stereo disc S-36569).

SIR JOHN BARBIROLLI
(pronounced: bahr-bih-*roh*-lee)

Conductor. Born December 2, 1899, in London, England. Died in Manchester, England, July 28, 1970. Originally a cellist, then a conductor—first of his own Barbirolli Chamber Orchestra in 1925, then of the Scottish National Orchestra. In 1936 he succeeded Toscanini as conductor of the New York Philharmonic, but his tenure was not generally successful with either critics or subscribers. After World War II he built Manchester's Hallé Orchestra into one of England's finest, and re-established his international reputation as a warm, tasteful interpreter of 19th- and early 20th-century works. For several years in the 1960's he was also music director of the Houston Symphony Orchestra. He was knighted in 1949 by King George VI.

Recommended recordings: Vaughan Williams Symphony No. 2 ("A London Symphony") (Angel stereo disc S-36478; cassette 4XS-36478; cartridge 8XS-36478). Sibelius Symphony No. 1 (Angel stereo disc S-36489).

DANIEL BARENBOIM

(pronounced: *baa*-ren-boym)

Pianist and conductor. Born November 15, 1942, in Buenos Aires, Argentina. When he was 10, he moved with his parents to Israel and he is now an Israeli citizen. He became internationally known as a pianist while still in his teens, after winning the Alfredo Cassella competition in Naples in 1956. Meanwhile, he studied conducting. In 1968 he made a much-acclaimed, short-notice substitution for Istvan Kertesz as conductor of the touring London Symphony Orchestra in a series of New York concerts. Since then, he has divided his time between the piano and the podium. He is usually at his best in the Classical and Romantic repertory, where his intense interpretations are often marked by uncommonly broad pacing. He is married to the young British cellist Jacqueline du Pré.

Recommended recordings: *As pianist*—Brahms Piano Concerto No. 2 (Angel stereo disc S-36526). *As conductor*—Mozart Symphony Nos. 35 ("Haffner"), 38 ("Prague") (Angel stereo disc S-36512).

SERGE BAUDO

(pronounced: *bow*-doh)

Conductor. Born July 16, 1927, in Marseilles, France. He served four years as resident conductor of the Paris Opera before becoming Second Conductor (under Charles Munch) of the Orchestre de Paris upon its founding in 1968. He has also been music director of the Aix-en-Provence Music Festival in France for more than ten years, and has conducted opera at Milan's La Scala, the Vienna State Opera, and New York's Metropolitan Opera.

Recommended recordings: Messiaen *Les Offrandes Oubliées* and *Et Exspecto Resurrectionem Mortuorum* (Angel stereo disc S-36559). Honegger Symphony Nos. 2 and 3 (Crossroads stereo disc 22160010, recently deleted).

DAVID BEAN

Pianist. Born December 12, 1928, in Rochester, New York. He was graduated from Oberlin College with a degree in economics, but also studied music there and at Juilliard in New York. His New York recital debut was in 1957. Since 1960 he has been Artist-in-Residence at Miami University at Oxford, Ohio, combining teaching with his concert tours. He is an adventurous pianist with a strong rhythmic drive, at his best in 19th- and 20th-century works which explore the color and sonority of the piano.

Recommended recordings: David Bean Plays Scriabin, Liszt, and Ginastera (Westminster stereo disc WST-17161). Busoni *Six Elegies* and Villa-Lobos *Rudepoêma* (RCA Victrola stereo disc VICS-1379).

SIR THOMAS BEECHAM
(pronounced: *bee*-chum)

Conductor. Born April 29, 1879, in St. Helens, Lancashire, England. Died March 8, 1961, in London. For many years he was Britain's best-known and most popular conductor. The son of a wealthy patent-medicine manufacturer, the Oxford-educated Beecham first organized his own orchestra, the New Symphony, with family funds in 1906. In 1911 he became music director of opera at London's Covent Garden, introducing many new and long-neglected works. In 1932 he founded the London Philharmonic Orchestra, and in 1947 the Royal Philharmonic Orchestra—and recorded extensively with both. A highly individualistic, colorful conductor of Classical and Romantic works, he was particularly noted as a champion of Delius and Sibelius, and for his orchestral arrangements of Handel. His wit and temper were famous in his time, and he was outspoken off the podium as well as on it.

Recommended recordings: Music of Delius (Seraphim stereo disc S-60185). Handel *Love in Bath* (Seraphim stereo disc S-60039).

EDUARD VAN BEINUM
(pronounced: van *by*-num)

Conductor. Born September 3, 1901, in Arnheim, Holland. Died April 13, 1959, in Holland. In the 1930's he was second conductor (under Mengelberg) of the Amsterdam Concertgebouw Orchestra, but he withdrew from active musical life during the Nazi occupation of his country. After the war, when Mengelberg was sent into lifetime exile for his wartime collaboration with the Nazis, Beinum became music director of the Concertgebouw Orchestra and significantly rebuilt its international reputation. For a number of years in the 1950's he was also principal conductor of the London Philharmonic Orchestra. In 1956 he was named music director of the Los Angeles Philharmonic, but the appointment never took effect because of illness.

Recommended recording: Elgar Cello Concerto (Everest disc 3141, *mono only*). Regrettably, most of Beinum's best Philips and London recordings of the 1950's have been deleted from the present catalogs.

ROBERTO BENZI
(pronounced: *ben*-zee)

Conductor. Born December 12, 1937, in Bayonne, France. The son of an Italian music professor, he began his musical studies in Paris at the age of four and made his debut as a conductor in Bayonne at eleven. As a teenager he conducted extensively in Europe and also worked in French films, at the same time continuing his musical studies. He made his debut at the Paris Opera in 1959. His U.S. debut came in 1972 with the Philadelphia Orchestra, and in 1974 he became music director of the newly formed symphony orchestra of Bordeaux, France. He is considered one of Europe's most dashing and talented young conductors, and is married to the French soprano Jane Rhodes.

66

David Bean

67

Sir Thomas Beecham

68

Eduard van Beinum

69

Roberto Benzi

70

Leonard Bernstein

Jussi Bjoerling

71

72

Karl Böhm

73

Pierre Boulez

74

John Browning

Recommended recording: Bizet Symphony in C and *Jeux d'Enfants* (Philips stereo disc PHC-9086).

LEONARD BERNSTEIN
(pronounced: *burn*-styne)

Conductor, pianist, composer. Born August 25, 1918, in Lawrence, Massachusetts. In the early 1940's he studied with Boston Symphony director Serge Koussevitzky, and was assistant to Artur Rodzinski, conductor of the New York Philharmonic. In 1943 he made a dramatic, last-minute substitution conducting the Philharmonic when Bruno Walter became ill. Soon after, he was hailed as a composer for his ballet *Fancy Free*, his "Jeremiah" Symphony, and the hit Broadway musical *On the Town*. In 1957 he composed *West Side Story*, the landmark musical (later an award-winning film) conceived as part opera and part ballet, with strong jazz influences. In 1959 he began a ten-year directorship of the New York Philharmonic, and in 1970 was named its Laureate Conductor for life. His concert, movie, Broadway, and TV activities have made him one of the best-known and most popular American musicians in history. As a conductor, he is noted for his highly dramatic, openly emotional approach to Romantic and modern works.

Recommended recordings: Mahler Symphony No. 2 (Columbia stereo 2-disc set M2S-695). Bernstein Conducts Bernstein, including *Fancy Free*, *West Side Story* Suites (Columbia stereo 2-disc set MG-32174; cassette MGT-32174).

JUSSI BJOERLING
(pronounced: *byehr*-ling)

Tenor. Born February 2, 1911, in Stora Tuna, Sweden. Died September 9, 1960, in Silar Oe, near Stockholm. As a boy, he and his two brothers joined their father in the Bjoerling Quartet, which toured Scandinavia and the U.S. singing Scandinavian songs. In 1929 he made his operatic debut almost immediately upon graduation from the Royal Opera School in Stockholm. In the early 1930's he sang at the major European opera houses, and made his U.S. debut with the Chicago Opera in 1937. The following year he joined New York's Metropolitan Opera, and became one of its leading tenors throughout the 1940's and 1950's. His beautifully lyrical, elegant, always tasteful interpretations of Italian opera roles (particularly Verdi and Puccini) are considered among the century's finest.

Recommended recordings: The Art of Jussi Bjoerling (Seraphim disc 60168, *mono only*). The Incomparable Bjoerling (RCA Red Seal stereo disc LSC-2570).

KARL BÖHM
(pronounced: boehm)

Conductor. Born August 28, 1894, in Graz, Austria. His early career was in opera in Austria and Germany, as principal conductor of the Graz Opera (1924), Darmstadt (1927), and Hamburg (1931). In 1933 he began a long association with the Dresden Opera. After World War II he served for a period as music director of the Vienna State Opera. In recent years he has been particularly active at the Metropolitan Opera in New York, with the New York Philharmonic and Berlin Philharmonic, and with the

Salzburg Festival. He ranks today as one of the foremost masters of German Classical and Romantic works, especially those of Mozart, Schubert, and Richard Strauss.

Recommended recordings: Mozart Symphony Nos. 40, 41 (Deutsche Grammophon stereo disc 138815; cassette 923-056; cartridge 88-815). Strauss *Don Juan, Till Eulenspiegel* and other works (Deutsche Grammophon stereo disc 138866; cassette 923-120; cartridge 88-866).

PIERRE BOULEZ
(pronounced: boo-*lezz*)

Conductor and composer. Born March 26, 1925, in Montbrison in southern France. In 1948 he became music director of the Jean-Louis Barrault-Madeleine Renaud theatre company in Paris. In 1954 Barrault agreed to let him use the theatre on off-days to present concerts of avant-garde music, and his subsequent Domaine Musicale concerts became both well-known and controversial. A series of disputes with the French government led him to move to Germany, where in 1966 he became conductor of the Southwest German Radio Orchestra at Baden-Baden. In 1968 he became an associate of George Szell with the Cleveland Orchestra, and in 1971 music director of both the New York Philharmonic and the BBC Symphony Orchestra in London. As a conductor he is considered one of the most exacting orchestral technicians of our time, but his unusually analytical, intellectual and unemotional interpretations have divided both critics and audiences. He is usually at his best in complex 20th-century works, especially serial works. (For more about Boulez the composer, see Section Two).

Recommended recordings: Boulez Conducts Debussy, Vol. 1—*La Mer, Jeux, The Afternoon of a Faun* (Columbia stereo disc MS-7361). Stravinsky *Le Sacre du Printemps* (Columbia stereo disc MS-7293; cassette 16-11-0154).

JOHN BROWNING

Pianist. Born May 23, 1933, in Denver, Colorado. He studied at Occidental College in California, and then at Juilliard in New York, where he was a student of Josef and Rosina Lhevinne. In 1954 he won the Steinway Centennial Award, in 1955 the Leventritt Award, and in 1956 the Queen Elisabeth of Belgium Competition. In 1962 he introduced the Pulitzer Prize-winning Piano Concerto by Samuel Barber, and has performed it extensively throughout the U.S. In recent years, in addition to performing concertos and solo works, he has also performed with chamber ensembles.

Recommended recordings: Barber Piano Concerto (Columbia stereo disc MS-6638). Prokofiev Piano Concerto No. 1 and 2 (RCA Red Seal stereo disc LSC-2897).

GRACE BUMBRY
(pronounced: *bum*-bree)

Mezzo-soprano. Born January 4, 1937, in St. Louis, Missouri. She first sang in church choirs in St. Louis, then began serious voice study in Boston and New York, including study with retired soprano Lotte Lehmann. In 1958 she won a Marian Anderson scholarship to study in Paris. In 1960 she made her debut at the Paris Opera (as Amneris in Verdi's *Aïda*), and in 1961 became the first Black to sing at Bayreuth (as Venus in Wagner's *Tannhauser*). Her American opera debut was in 1963 with the

77

Maria Callas

75

Grace Bumbry

80

Pablo Casals

76

Montserrat Caballé

78

Guido Cantelli

81

Maria Cebotari

79

Robert Casadesus

Chicago Lyric Opera (again in *Tannhauser*), and two years later she joined the Metropolitan Opera in New York. In 1966 she sang *Carmen* in a Salzburg production led by Herbert von Karajan, and later filmed the opera with Karajan. She is noted for the silken beauty of her voice in most mezzo-soprano and some soprano roles.

Recommended recordings: Verdi *Aïda*, with Price, Domingo (RCA Red Seal 3-disc set LSC-6198; or highlights only on stereo disc LSC-3275; cassette RK-1237; cartridge R8S-1237). Gluck *Orfeo ed Euridice*, with Rothenberger (Angel stereo 2-disc set S-3717).

MONTSERRAT CABALLÉ
(pronounced: kah-bahl-*yay*)

Soprano. Born April 12, 1933, in Barcelona, Spain. She studied at the Liceo Consebfadobi in Barcelona, winning its prestigious Gold Award in 1954. She made her operatic debut in 1957 in Basel, Switzerland (as Mimi in Puccini's *La Bohème*), remaining three years with the Basel company and then two years with the Bremen Opera in West Germany. In 1965 her New York debut with the American Opera Society (in Donizetti's *Lucrezia Borgia*) created a sensation, and led to her Metropolitan Opera debut ten months later. She has since become one of the most popular and most admired singers in both Europe and the U.S., and is particularly noted for her remarkably delicate, floating tones and *pianissimos*. Her husband is Spanish tenor Bernabé Martí.

Recommended recordings: Presenting Montserrat Caballé (RCA Red Seal stereo disc LSC-2862). Verdi Arias (Angel stereo disc S-36830). Zarzuela Love Duets, with Martí (RCA Red Seal stereo disc LSC-3039).

MARIA CALLAS
(pronounced: *kah*-lahs)

Soprano. Born December 3, 1923, in New York City. Of Greek parentage, she was taken to Greece as a teenager and studied at the Athens Conservatory. She made her operatic debut at the age of thirteen at the Athens Royal Opera House (in Mascagni's *Cavalleria Rusticana*). After World War II she studied with Italian opera conductor Tullio Serafin. In 1947 she joined Milan's La Scala Opera, creating sensation after sensation in *Tosca*, *Norma*, *Lucia di Lammermoor*, and *I Puritani*. Her international reputation as a great singing actress of extraordinary vocal range and versatility quickly spread, and she was heard with the Paris Opera, the Vienna State Opera, London's Covent Garden, Chicago's Lyric Theatre, and New York's Metropolitan Opera over the next ten years. Although some critics found her voice limited in natural beauty, most admired the excitement, skill, and intelligence she brought her roles. Various controversies over her private and professional life also kept her one of the most publicized prima donnas of the era. She has not sung regularly since the mid-1960's, but has appeared in a non-singing film version of *Medea* in 1970 and directed an opera for the first time in Italy in 1973.

Recommended recordings: "La Divina" (Angel stereo 2-disc set SCB-3743, including free bonus disc of an hour-long Callas interview). Bizet *Carmen* (Angel stereo 3-disc set

S-3650X; highlights only on stereo disc S-36312; cassette 4XS-36312; cartridge 8XS-36312).

GUIDO CANTELLI
(pronounced: kahn-*tehl*-lee)

Conductor. Born April 27, 1920, in Novara, Italy. Died in a plane crash near Paris, November 24, 1956. Shortly after making his debut as a conductor in Novara in 1941, Cantelli was sent to labor camps in Italy and Germany for refusing to work with the Fascists. He escaped in 1944, but was caught while fighting with the Italian Partisans and was sentenced to be shot. The American liberation of Italy saved his life. In 1945 he became a conductor at Milan's La Scala. There he was heard by Toscanini, who invited him to the U.S. as principal guest conductor of the NBC Symphony Orchestra. At the time of his death, he was considered the most promising young conductor of his generation.

Recommended recordings: Schubert "Unfinished" Symphony and Mendelssohn "Italian" Symphony (Seraphim disc 600062, *mono only*).

ROBERT CASADESUS
(pronounced: kah-sah-*day*-soo)

Pianist. Born April 7, 1899, in Paris, France. Died September 19, 1972, in Paris. He studied at the Paris Conservatory, graduating with first-prize honors in 1913. He was a professor at the conservatories of Genoa (1929–30) and Lausanne (1931–35), and then became head of the piano department of the American Conservatory at Fontainebleau in 1936. Following World War II he toured both Europe and the U.S. extensively, sometimes giving joint piano recitals with his wife, Gaby. He was best known as an elegant, always tasteful interpreter of 18th- and 19th-century composers. He was also a composer of numerous sonatas and several concertos.

Recommended recording: Saint-Saens Piano Concerto No. 4 (Columbia stereo disc MS-6377). Casadesus Piano Concerto (Columbia M-30946).

PABLO CASALS
(pronounced: kah-*sahlz*)

Cellist and conductor. Born December 29, 1876, in Vendrell (near Barcelona, in Catalonia), Spain. Died October 23, 1973, in San Juan, Puerto Rico. He started studying the cello at the age of eleven in Barcelona. In his early 20's, he continued his studies in Paris, living on money he earned playing in dance halls. He made his concert debut in Paris in 1899 playing Bach's Unaccompanied Cello Suites. He soon won almost legendary acclaim throughout Europe and the U.S. for his broad-lined, intensely singing technique. In 1920 he founded the Casals Orchestra in Barcelona, and personally subsidized it for nearly a decade. In 1939 he went into voluntary exile from Spain following the Spanish Civil War, and thereafter severely limited his public appearances. He settled in Puerto Rico in 1957, organizing and directing an annual Festival Casals there—appearing primarily as a conductor and only occasionally as a cellist. In his later years he also composed a number of works, including a *Hymn to the United Nations*.

Recommended recordings: The Art of Pablo Casals (RCA Red Seal disc LM-2699, *mono only*). Dvořák Cello Concerto (Angel disc COLH-30, now deleted).

MARIA CEBOTARI
(pronounced: cheh-bo-*tah*-ree)

Soprano. Born February 10, 1910, in Kishinev, Bessarabia (then part of Rumania, now part of the Soviet Union). Died June 9, 1949, in Vienna. After vocal study in Berlin, she made her opera debut in Dresden in 1931. From 1936 to 1944 she was a star of the Berlin Opera, and from 1946 to 1949 of the Vienna Opera. During the 1930's she also made eight films, including *The Dream of Butterfly* and *The Life of Verdi* (both made in Italy), which still appear occasionally on U.S. television. She was scheduled to make a much-awaited American debut at the Metropolitan Opera the year she died of cancer at age thirty-nine. Her husband, anti-Nazi actor Gustav Diessl, had died a year before. Their two children were then adopted by British pianist Clifford Curzon.

Recommended recordings: Maria Cebotari (BASF 2-disc set KBF-21483, *mono only*). Maria Cebotari—Opera Arias (Heliodor Historical Series disc 2548-700, *mono only*).

ALDO CECCATO
(pronounced: cheh-*khah*-toe)

Conductor. Born in 1942 in Milan, Italy. He started as a pianist, playing not only classical concerts in his teens but also jazz. While studying at the Giuseppe Verdi Conservatory in Milan, he decided to be a conductor, and went to Berlin to study with Sergiu Celibidache, whose assistant he later became. In the 1960's he conducted Italy's leading orchestras in Rome, Venice, and Florence. His American debut with the Chicago Lyric Opera in 1969 was such a success that he was invited to conduct the Chicago Symphony, the Detroit Symphony, and the New York Philharmonic—and he was promptly hailed as a forceful, virtuoso conductor. In 1973 he became music director of the Detroit Symphony. He is married to the granddaughter of Italian conductor Victor de Sabata.

Recommended recording: Donizetti *Maria Stuarda*, with Sills, Farrell (ABC stereo 3-disc set ATS-20010/3—*complete*).

BORIS CHRISTOFF
(pronounced: *kris*-tauff)

Bass. Born May 18, 1918, in Sofia, Bulgaria. He studied first in Sofia, then in Rome, and made his opera debut in 1946 in Rome. In 1949 he made a much-acclaimed debut at London's Covent Garden in the title role of Mussorgsky's *Boris Godunov*. He became closely identified with that role in the 1950's, scoring successes with it for his debuts in Buenos Aires and San Francisco. Since 1957 he has been a principal bass with the Chicago Lyric Opera and at Europe's major opera houses, much respected for his penetrating, subtle characterizations.

Recommended recording: Mussorgsky *Boris Godunov* (Angel stereo 4-disc set S-3633; highlights only on stereo disc S-36169).

82

Aldo Ceccato

83

Boris Christoff

84

Van Cliburn

85

Sergiu Comissiona

86

Franco Corelli

Régine Crespin

87

88

Colin Davis

89

Alicia de Larrocha

90

Lisa della Casa

91

Victoria de los Angeles

92

Edo de Waart

93

Misha Dichter

94

Dean Dixon

95

Placido Domingo

Antal Dorati

96

97

Jacqueline du Pré

98

Philippe Entremont

99

Christoph Eschenbach

VAN CLIBURN
(pronounced: *kly*-burn)

Pianist. Born July 12, 1934, in Shreveport, Louisiana. He studied with his mother from 1937 to 1950, then at Juilliard in New York with Rosina Lhevinne, graduating in 1954 with highest honors. He made his recital debut at Shreveport in 1940, and his concert debut in 1947 with the Houston Symphony Orchestra. In 1948 he won the National Music Festival Award, then the Leventritt Award in 1954, and the first Tchaikovsky International Competition in Moscow in 1958. The latter, coming at a significant time in changing U.S.-Soviet relations, made him a national hero. He has since remained one of the most popular American pianists of this century, best-known for his elegant, clean-lined performances of the 19th-century Romantics.

Recommended recordings: Rachmaninoff Piano Concerto No. 3 (RCA Red Seal stereo disc LSC-2355; cartridge R8S-5011). Tchaikovsky Piano Concerto No. 1 (RCA Red Seal stereo disc LSC-2252; cassette RK-1002; cartridge R8S-1002 or R8S-5011).

SERGIU COMISSIONA
(pronounced: *koh*-mis-ee-*yoh*-nah)

Conductor. Born June 16, 1928 in Bucharest, Rumania. In the late 1940's he was a violinist in the Bucharest Radio Quartet and the Rumanian State Ensemble, becoming conductor of the latter in 1950. In 1955 he became principal conductor of the Rumanian State Opera, but was dismissed in 1959 after he and his wife (a ballerina) applied for permission to emigrate to Israel. After a year as official "non-persons," they were allowed to leave. He became music director of the Haifa Symphony in Israel, then of the Israel Chamber Orchestra, which he led on a U.S. tour in 1963. Since 1966 he has been music director of the Göteborg (Sweden) Symphony Orchestra, and since 1969 also of the Baltimore Symphony Orchestra.

Recommended recordings: Poulenc Concerto in D minor (London stereo disc CS-6754). Britten *Diversions* and Laderman Concerto for Orchestra (Desto stereo disc DC-7168).

FRANCO CORELLI
(pronounced: koh-*rehl*-lee)

Tenor. Born April 8, 1923, in Ancona, Italy. Primarily self-taught in singing, he made his opera debut in 1952 at Spoleto (Italy). He first appeared at Milan's La Scala the following year, and has since become a leading tenor with that company, as well as with the Metropolitan Opera in New York since 1961. His tall, handsome appearance, coupled with the warmth, vitality, and power of his voice, have made him one of the most popular tenors of recent years—though some fault him for lack of subtlety.

Recommended recordings: Franco Corelli—Operatic Arias (Angel stereo disc S-35918; cassette 4XS-35918). Franco Corelli—Portrait of the Artist (Angel stereo 3-disc set S-3744).

RÉGINE CRESPIN
(pronounced: kres-*pan*)

Soprano. Born March 23, 1927, in Marseilles, France. Following study at the Paris Conservatory, she made her debut at the Paris Opera in 1951, dividing her performances for several years between that house and the Opéra-Comique in Paris. Her American debut took place in 1962 with the Chicago Lyric Opera, and her Metropolitan Opera debut followed that same year. She has since established herself as a leading soprano at most of the world's leading opera houses, much-admired for her sensuous, expressive, always tasteful singing.

Recommended recordings: Berlioz *Nuits d'Été* and Ravel *Shéhérazade* (London stereo disc OS-25821). Régine Crespin—Prima Donna from Paris (London stereo 2-disc set OSA-1292).

COLIN DAVIS

Conductor. Born September 25, 1927, in Weybridge (Sussex), England. From 1957 to 1959 he was conductor of the BBC Scottish Orchestra, and then from 1961 to 1965 music director of the Sadler's Wells Opera Company in London. His international reputation grew during the early 1960's when he shared with Georg Solti the conductorship of the London Symphony Orchestra on several overseas tours. In 1971 he succeeded Solti as music director of London's Royal Opera House at Covent Garden. Since 1972 he has also held the title of principal guest conductor (together with Michael Tilson Thomas) of the Boston Symphony Orchestra.

Recommended recordings: Berlioz *Romeo and Juliet* (Philips stereo 2-disc set 839716/17). Mozart *Requiem* (Philips stereo 2-disc set 802862; cassette PCR4-900-160; cartridge PC8-900-160).

ALICIA DE LARROCHA
(pronounced: de lah-*rohk*-ah)

Pianist. Born May 23, 1923, in Barcelona, Spain. She made her recital debut in 1928 at the age of five. In 1943 she won the Academia Granados Gold Medal for her stylistic excellence in traditional Spanish music. Since 1947 she has performed regularly throughout Europe, and since 1954 throughout the U.S. She ranks as one of the most respected of presentday pianists for her warm, expressive interpretations of a broad range of Classical and Romantic music, but is best-known for her performances of Spanish music (Granados, Turina, Falla, Espla, etc.).

Recommended recordings: Piano Music of Granados (Epic stereo disc LC-3910). Spanish Piano Music of the 20th Century (London stereo disc CS-6677).

LISA DELLA CASA
(pronounced: deh-la *cah*-sah)

Soprano. Born February 2, 1919, in Burgdorf, Switzerland. She began vocal study at the age of fifteen in Switzerland, and made her debut with the Zurich Opera in 1943. After World War II she sang with the Vienna State Opera, the Munich Opera, London's Covent Garden, and Milan's La Scala—and was soon recognized as an uncommonly sensuous-voiced singer, at her best in the "cooler" roles of Mozart and Richard Strauss. She made her Metropolitan Opera debut in 1953, and remained there as a leading soprano for nearly a decade. She became particularly identified in both the U.S. and Europe with the title role of Strauss' *Arabella,* and is one of the few sopranos to have sung all three of the major female roles in Strauss' *Der Rosenkavalier.*

Recommended recordings: Strauss *Arabella* (London/Richmond stereo 3-disc set S-63522). Mozart *The Marriage of Figaro* (London 4-disc set 1402; highlights only on London disc 25045).

VICTORIA DE LOS ANGELES

(pronounced: de los *anh*-kheh-les)

Soprano. Born November 1, 1923, in Barcelona, Spain. Following study at the Liceo Conservatory in Barcelona, she made her opera debut in that city in 1945 (as the Countess in Mozart's *The Marriage of Figaro*). Two years later she won first prize in the International Singing Competition at Geneva. In the 1950's and early 1960's she sang at London's Convent Garden, the Paris Opera, Milan's La Scala, and New York's Metropolitan Opera—and was much admired for her exceptionally clean-lined, lyrical singing and unsentimental interpretations of major operatic roles. In recent years she has confined herself mostly to recital tours, and has become best-known as an exponent of classical Spanish songs.

Recommended recordings: Victoria de los Angeles—Portrait of the Artist (Angel stereo 3-disc set S-3728). Songs of Catalonia (Angel stereo disc S-36682).

EDO DE WAART

(pronounced: de *vahrt*)

Conductor. Born June 1, 1941, in Amsterdam, Holland. At the age of twenty-three he won one of the top prizes in the Mitropoulos International Conducting Competition, serving a year in New York as assistant to Leonard Bernstein as part of the prize. He also spent a year studying with George Szell in Cleveland in 1967. The following year he became conductor of the Netherlands Wind Ensemble, and then of the Rotterdam Philharmonic Orchestra. Since 1970 he has also been a conductor of the Netherlands Opera in Amsterdam. In 1973 he made a much-acclaimed last-minute substitution 'for an ill conductor of the Boston Symphony Orchestra at Tanglewood, and in 1974 became principal guest conductor of the San Francisco Symphony. He is one of the most talented and sensitive conductors of his generation.

Recommended recordings: Mozart Serenades Nos. 3, 8, 9, 12 (Philips stereo disc 6500-002). Rachmaninoff Symphonic Dances and *Caprice Bohème* (Philips stereo disc 6500-362).

MISHA DICHTER

(pronounced: *dick*-ter)

Pianist. Born September 27, 1945, in Shanghai, China, of Polish parents who had left their homeland at the outbreak of World War II. He grew up in Los Angeles, and started studying piano at the age of twelve. In 1966 he won second prize in the Tchaikovsky International Competition at Moscow, but delayed full-time concertizing for several years in order to complete his schooling at Juilliard in New York, where he studied with Rosina Lhevinne. In recent years he has won increasing recognition as an unusually sensitive and probing young pianist.

Recommended recordings: Tchaikovsky Piano Concerto No. 1 (RCA Red Seal stereo disc LSC-2954). Schubert Sonata in A and Beethoven Andante Favori in F (RCA Red Seal stereo disc LSC-3124).

DEAN DIXON

Conductor. Born January 10, 1915, in New York City. He was the first black American conductor to establish an international reputation in this century. During the 1930's he organized his own youth orchestra in New York to help train Negro players, and during the 1940's he was the first black man to conduct the NBC Symphony Orchestra, the Boston Symphony Orchestra, the New York Philharmonic, and the Philadelphia Orchestra. But, as he has put it, "then—nothing." Discouraged, he left the U.S. in 1949 to settle in Europe, conducting mostly in France, Italy, and Sweden. Since 1962 he has been principal conductor of the Hessian State Radio Orchestra in Frankfurt, Germany. Between 1964 and 1967 he was also conductor of the Sydney Symphony in Australia. Since 1970 he has again been active in the U.S. as a guest conductor of major orchestras.

Recommended recordings: Mendelssohn Symphony No. 3, "Scotch" (Nonesuch stereo disc 71254). Thompson Symphony No. 2 and Cowell Symphony No. 5 (Desto stereo disc 6406).

PLACIDO DOMINGO

(pronounced: doh-*ming*-go)

Tenor. Born January 21, 1941, in Madrid, Spain. He was raised and educated in Mexico City, where his parents were *zarzuela* (operetta) singers. He made his opera debut in Mexico City in 1961, and then spent several years with the Tel Aviv Opera in Israel. He became an overnight star at twenty-five when he sang the title role in the premiere of Ginastera's *Don Rodrigo* at the New York City Opera in 1966. He joined the Metropolitan Opera in 1968, substituting at the last minute for Franco Corelli. He has since become one of the most popular tenors in both Europe and the U.S., noted for his ringingly strong, expressive singing in a wide range of roles.

Recommended recordings: Placido Domingo—Italian Operatic Arias (London stereo disc OS-26080). Domingo Sings Caruso (RCA Red Seal stereo disc LSC-3251; cassette RK-1233; cartridge R8S-1233).

ANTAL DORATI

(pronounced: doh-*rah*-tee)

Conductor. Born April 9, 1906, in Budapest, Hungary. He was active as a conductor in Hungary and Germany during the late 1920's, before coming to the U.S. as conductor of the Ballet Russe de Monte Carlo (1933–1941) and then Ballet Theatre (1941–1945). He has been music director of the Dallas Symphony Orchestra (1945–1949), the Minneapolis Symphony Orchestra (1949–1960), the BBC Symphony Orchestra in London (1962–1966), the Stockholm Philharmonic (1966 to the present), and the National Symphony of Washington, D.C. (1969 to the present). The latter became the principal symphonic component of the John F. Kennedy Center for the

Performing Arts in Washington in 1971. He is at his best with dramatic, colorful works of late 19th- and early 20th-century composers.

Recommended recordings: Tchaikovsky *The Nutcracker* (Mercury stereo 2-disc set SR-9013; highlights only on stereo disc 90528). Bartok *The Miraculous Mandarin* (Mercury stereo disc 90531).

JACQUELINE DU PRÉ
(pronounced: du *pray*)

Cellist. Born January 26, 1945, in Oxford, England. She began musical studies at an early age, and made her recital debut at the age of seven. As a teenager she studied in Paris with Paul Tortelier, then in Moscow with Rostropovich. At fifteen she won the Queen's Prize for British Instrumentalists. Her U.S. debut took place in 1965 with the touring BBC Symphony Orchestra under Dorati. She has since won wide acclaim as one of the outstanding cellists of our time, and is particularly noted for her intensity, soaring tone, and big melodic line. In 1973, however, she was forced to withdraw indefinitely from performing because of serious illness. She married pianist-conductor Daniel Barenboim in 1967.

Recommended recordings: Haydn Concerto for Cello and Orchestra in D (Angel stereo disc S-36580; cassette 4XS-36580; cartridge 8XS-36580). Elgar Concerto for Cello and Orchestra (Angel stereo disc S-36338).

PHILIPPE ENTREMONT
(pronounced: *ahn*-tray-mont)

Pianist. Born June 7, 1934, in Rheims, France. He studied at the Paris Conservatory with Marguerite Long and Jean Doyen, and in 1953 won the Marguerite Long-Jacques Thibaud Competition. That same year he made his U.S. debut. His tall, handsome, youthful appearance, combined with his crisply impressive piano technique, have made him something of a "matinee idol" among concert-goers ever since. In 1970 he made his debut as a conductor in London, but indicated he would continue to perform primarily as a pianist.

Recommended recordings: Ravel Piano Concerto for the Left Hand (Columbia stereo disc M-31426; cassette MT-31426). Philippe Entremont Piano Recital (Columbia stereo disc MS-6938).

CHRISTOPH ESCHENBACH
(pronounced: *eh*-shehn-bahkh)

Pianist. Born February 20, 1940, in Breslau, Silesia, then part of Germany. His earliest years were marked by a series of family tragedies and serious illness in the upheavals of World War II. After the war he studied in Hamburg and Cologne, winning prizes in several German and European piano competitions before he was seventeen. In the 1960's he became one of the most acclaimed of the younger generation of European pianists, performing frequently in Europe with Herbert von Karajan and in the U.S. with George Szell. In 1971 he introduced the complex, modern Henze Piano Concerto No. 2, but he has been primarily identified with the music of Mozart and Beethoven, and is noted for his unusually sensitive, deeply poetic interpretations.

Recommended recordings: Beethoven Piano Concerto No. 3 (Deutsche Grammophon stereo disc 2530254). Mozart Complete Piano Sonatas (Deutsche Grammophon stereo 7-disc set 2720031).

EILEEN FARRELL
(pronounced: *faa*-rel)

Soprano. Born February 13, 1920, in Willimantic, Connecticut. During the 1940's, she was a member of the CBS radio chorus in New York, and then had her own weekly half-hour network program, "Eileen Farrell Presents," on which she sang everything from opera to current popular songs. In the 1950's she turned to concert work, appearing frequently with the Bach Aria Group and in concert performances of seldom-performed works (Cherubini's *Medea*, Berg's *Wozzeck*). She also recorded the soundtrack for the 1955 film *Interrupted Melody* (based on the life of soprano Marjorie Lawrence). Although long reluctant to appear on opera stages, she finally made her debuts with the San Francisco and Chicago Operas in the late 1950's, and with the Metropolitan Opera in 1961. Since the late 1960's she has again confined herself to concert appearances. An impressively big-voiced and versatile singer, she is widely regarded as the greatest American dramatic soprano of this century.

Recommended recording: Brünnhilde's Immolation Scene from Wagner's *Götterdämmerung* (Columbia stereo disc MS-6353). Eileen Farrell (Angel disc 35589).

ARTHUR FIEDLER
(pronounced: *feed*-ler)

Conductor. Born December 17, 1894, in Boston, Massachusetts. In the 1920's he first organized the Fiedler Sinfonietta, and then the Boston Esplanade Concerts for free outdoor summer performances. Since 1930 he has been conductor of the Boston Pops Orchestra, made up of all but the first-desk players of the Boston Symphony, playing special spring programs of lighter fare. He has made the Pops a unique American institution, and its recordings, combining popular music with light classics, have been best sellers for many years. Fiedler, noted for his jaunty, spirited performances, frequently guest conducts in San Francisco, Chicago, and other cities. He is also an honorary fire chief in about ninety cities.

Recommended recordings: Offenbach *Gaité Parisienne* (RCA Red Seal stereo disc LSC-2267; cassette RK-1003; cartridge R8S-1003). Gershwin *An American in Paris*, etc. (RCA Red Seal stereo disc LSC-3319; cassette RK-1299; cartridge R8S-1299).

DIETRICH FISCHER-DIESKAU
(pronounced: *fihsh*-er *dees*-kow)

Baritone. Born May 28, 1925, in Berlin. His vocal studies, begun at the age of sixteen in Berlin, were interrupted when he was drafted into the German Army in 1943. A year later he was captured by the Americans on the Italian front, and spent the next two years in a prisoner-of-war camp in Italy. When a copy of Schubert's song cycle *Die Schöne Müllerin* was found in the camp, he studied it and gave his first public recital for his fellow prisoners. In 1948 he became a principal baritone with the Berlin State Opera, and that same year made his debut as a *lieder* singer in Leipzig. His American

102

Dietrich Fischer-Dieskau

100

Eileen Farrell

105

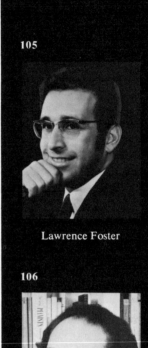

Lawrence Foster

101

Arthur Fiedler

103

Kirsten Flagstad

106

Malcolm Frager

104

Leon Fleischer

debut took place in 1955 with the Cincinnati Symphony. Although he divides his time between opera and concert appearances, and in 1973 made his debut as a conductor he is now regarded primarily as a *lieder* singer—the greatest of our time. He is also probably the most widely recorded singer in history. He is especially noted for his mastery of tone color and phrasing.

Recommended recordings: Fischer-Dieskau—Portrait of the Artist (Angel stereo 3-disc set S-3729). Schubert *Winterreise* (Deutsche Grammophon stereo disc 270728).

KIRSTEN FLAGSTAD
(pronounced: *flahg*-stahd)

Soprano. Born July 12, 1895, in Oslo, Norway. Died December 7, 1962, in Oslo. After studying singing with her mother, an operatic coach, she made her debut at the Oslo Opera in a minor role in 1913. For several years she appeared in operettas and musical comedies in Norway, but after joining the Göteborg Opera she decided to concentrate on opera. In 1929 she retired following her marriage to a wealthy industrialist, but in 1933 she accepted an invitation to sing a minor role at Bayreuth. Her Bayreuth performances led to an audition with the Metropolitan Opera in New York, and she made a sensationally acclaimed debut there in 1935 (as Sieglinde in *Die Walküre*). Over the next few years she repeated her American triumph in London, Paris, Vienna, and Prague, and was widely hailed as the greatest Wagnerian singer of her time. In 1941 she left the U.S. to return to Norway, then occupied by the Nazis, and retired from performing until after World War II. Controversy over her wartime behavior continued for many years, and she made only occasional U.S. appearances after 1949 before her formal retirement in 1955.

Recommended recordings: Wagner *Tristan und Isolde*, highlights (Seraphim 60145, *mono only*). Flagstad—Immortal Performances (RCA Victrola disc VIC-1517, *mono only*).

LEON FLEISCHER
(pronounced: *fly*-sher)

Pianist and conductor. Born July 23, 1928, in San Francisco. He made his recital debut as a pianist at the age of seven in San Francisco, and at ten was accepted as a pupil by Artur Schnabel. In 1952 he won the Queen Elisabeth of Belgium Competition. His busy and successful career was interrupted in the mid-1960's by an ailment affecting his right hand, although he has performed occasionally as soloist in concertos for the left hand alone in recent years. He also began appearing as a conductor in the early 1970's.

Recommended recordings: Beethoven Five Piano Concertos, complete (Columbia stereo 4-disc set M4X-30052). Britten *Diversions for Piano Left Hand* (Desto stereo discs DC-7168).

LAWRENCE FOSTER
(pronounced: *faw*-ster)

Conductor. Born October 23, 1941, in Los Angeles. He made his conducting debut as a teenager with the Young Musicians' Foundation Debut Orchestra in Los Angeles, and in 1960 became its music director for four years. During the 1960's he was also assistant conductor of the Los Angeles Philharmonic and associate conductor of the San Francisco Ballet. In 1969 he became principal guest conductor of the Royal Philharmonic in London (the youngest in its history), and co-conducted (with Rudolf Kempe) its American tour the following year. In 1972 he became music director of the Houston Symphony Orchestra.

Recommended recording: Rachmaninoff–Hoiby: Suite No. 2 (Desto stereo disc DC-6431).

MALCOLM FRAGER
(pronounced: *fray*-gher)

Pianist. Born January 15, 1935, in St. Louis, Missouri. He made his recital debut in St. Louis at the age of six, and appeared as a soloist with the St. Louis Symphony when he was ten. His New York recital debut was in 1952. He attended Columbia University from 1953 to 1957, majoring in languages and graduating Phi Beta Kappa. He won the Geneva International Competition in 1955, the Leventritt Award in 1959, and the Queen Elisabeth of Belgium Competition in 1960. Since then he has performed extensively throughout the United States and Europe, winning increasing recognition as one of the leading pianists of his generation. He is particularly noted for his clean-lined, always tasteful performances of Classical and Neoclassical works.

Recommended recordings: Brahms Piano Sonata No. 1 in C and Variations and Fugue on a Theme by Handel (BASF stereo disc 21393). Mozart Sonata for Two Pianos and Schumann Andante and Variations, with Ashkenazy (London stereo disc CS-6411).

NELSON FREIRE
(pronounced: *fray*-reh)

Pianist. Born November 20, 1944, in Boa Esperança, Brazil. He won the Rio de Janeiro International Music Competition in 1957, the Dinu Lipatti Medal in London in 1964, and the Vienna da Motta First Prize in Lisbon in 1964. His U.S. debut was with the Los Angeles Philharmonic under Boulez in 1969. He has since won increasing international acclaim, with some critics comparing his powerhouse technique to Horowitz's.

Recommended recording: Grieg and Tchaikovsky (No. 1) Piano Concertos (Columbia stereo disc MS-7396).

RAFAEL FRÜHBECK DE BURGOS
(pronounced: *froo*-beck deh *boor*-gohss)

Conductor. Born September 15, 1933, in Burgos, Spain. Of mixed German and Spanish parentage, he added "de Burgos" to his professional name in the 1960's in order to stress his Spanish upbringing. He started as a child prodigy on the violin and changed to conducting while studying at the Madrid Conservatory. After several years of conducting *zarzuelas* (Spanish operettas) in Madrid theatres, he became conductor

107

Nelson Freire

108

Rafael Frühbeck de Burgos

109

Wilhelm Furtwängler

110

Nicolai Gedda

111

Nicolai Ghiaurov

Walter Gieseking

112

113

Emil Gilels

114

Carlo Maria Giulini

115

Tito Gobbi

of the Bilbao Municipal Orchestra in 1959, and of the Orquesta Nacional de España (Spanish National Orchestra) in Madrid in 1962—the youngest conductor in its history. He is noted internationally for his conducting of Spanish music and 20th-century works with a strong rhythmic pulse.

Recommended recordings: Falla *The Three-Cornered Hat* (Angel stereo disc S-36235). Orff *Carmina Burana* (Angel stereo disc S-36333; cassette 4XS-36333; cartridge 8XS-36333).

WILHELM FURTWÄNGLER
(pronounced: *foort*-veng-gler)

Conductor. Born January 25, 1886, in Berlin, Germany. Died November 30, 1954, in Eberstein. After extensive success as a conductor in Berlin, Vienna, and Leipzig, he made a highly-acclaimed U.S. debut with the New York Philharmonic in 1925. In 1936, he was nominated by the Philharmonic to succeed Toscanini as music director; but a public uproar ensued because he was then the head of the leading orchestra in Nazi Germany, and the nomination was withdrawn. He continued as head of the Berlin Philharmonic throughout World War II, despite several confrontations with Nazi officials which forced him into "leaves of absence" on two occasions. In 1947 he was cleared by an Allied investigation of charges of Nazi collaboration, and again became conductor of the Berlin Philharmonic. He and the orchestra were preparing for their first U.S. tour in 1954 when he died. One of the conducting giants of the century, he was a highly individualistic, often profound interpreter of the Classical and Romantic repertory, particularly noted for the unique elasticity of his interpretations.

Recommended recordings: Furtwängler Conducts Wagner (Seraphim 2-disc set 6024, *mono only*). Beethoven Symphony No. 9 (Seraphim 2-disc set 6068).

NICOLAI GEDDA
(pronounced: *gehd*-dah)

Tenor. Born July 11, 1925, in Stockholm, Sweden. Although he received early vocal training from his father, who was choirmaster of the Russian Orthodox Church in Stockholm and for many years a member of the famous Don Cossack Chorus, Gedda started out in the banking business. A casual conversation with a bank customer led him to compete for an award to study for two years at the Royal Conservatory of Music in Stockholm, which he won. He made his opera debut in 1952 with the Stockholm Opera, and a year later appeared at Milan's La Scala. He joined New York's Metropolitan Opera in 1957, and has been one of its leading tenors ever since. He is highly regarded as an uncommonly versatile singer, and noted for his elegant phrasing.

Recommended recordings: "Recondita armonia" (and other arias) (Angel stereo disc S-36623). Berlioz *L'Enfance du Christ* (Angel stereo 2-disc set S-3680).

NICOLAI GHIAUROV
(pronounced: ghee-*ow*-roff)

Bass. Born in 1929 in Velimgrad, Bulgaria. Despite his parents' poverty, he managed to develop his musical interests as a boy, learning to play violin, clarinet, and piano. He won a scholarship to the Moscow Conservatory, graduating with highest honors in 1955. The same year he won the Grand Prix in a singing competition in Paris. He made his operatic debut in Sofia in 1956, and joined the Bolshoi Opera in Moscow in 1958. He soon became one of the Bolshoi's most popular leading basses. He made his U.S. debut with the Chicago Lyric Opera in 1963, and his Metropolitan Opera debut in 1965. A Salzburg Festival production in 1965 in which he had the title role in *Boris Godunov* (led by Karajan) created a sensation, and firmly established his international reputation as one of the foremost basses of our time.

Recommended recordings: Mussorgsky *Boris Godunov* (London stereo 4-disc set OS-1439). French and Russian Arias (London stereo disc OS-25911).

WALTER GIESEKING

(pronounced: *ghee*-zeh-king)

Pianist. Born November 5, 1895, in Lyons, France, of German parents. Died October 26, 1956, in London. He made his recital debut in 1920 in Berlin. His U.S. debut in 1920 was followed by thirteen tours before World War II. In 1945 he was blacklisted by the American Military Government as a wartime Nazi collaborator. In 1947 he was permitted to play for U.S. occupation troops. Later he resumed his concert career in Britain, France, Holland, and (in 1953) the United States. He ranks as one of the century's great masters of the piano's tonal palette; a subtle, elegant, and unusually soft-textured performer, particularly noted for his performances of Debussy, Ravel, and Mozart.

Recommended recordings: The Complete Piano Music of Ravel (Angel 3-disc set 3541-5S, *mono only*). Mozart Piano Concerto No. 23 and Beethoven Piano Concerto No. 4 (Odyssey disc 32160371, *mono only*).

EMIL GILELS

(pronounced: ghil-*els*)

Pianist. Born October 19, 1916, in Odessa, Russia. He won the 1936 Brussels International Piano Competition, and has been a professor at the Moscow Conservatory since 1954. In 1955 he was the first Soviet artist to perform in the U.S. as part of the U.S.-Soviet cultural exchange agreement. Although mostly known as a strong, exuberant performer of Romantic works, he can sometimes also be disarmingly graceful in interpreting Beethoven and others.

Recommended recordings: Tchaikovsky Piano Concerto No. 1 (RCA Victrola stereo disc VICS-1039; cartridge V8S-1001). Beethoven Piano Concerto No. 5, "Emperor" (Angel stereo disc S-36031).

CARLO MARIA GIULINI

(pronounced: joo-*lee*-nee)

Conductor. Born May 9, 1914, in Barletta, Italy. He studied at Rome's Santa Cecilia Academy, and made his debut as a conductor in Rome in 1944. He became a conductor of the Orchestra of Radio Milan in 1951, and principal conductor at Milan's

La Scala Opera in 1953. Following his debut at the Edinburgh Festival (Scotland) in 1955, his international reputation grew rapidly as a sensitive, lyrical conductor of Mozart and the early Romantics. In 1969 he became principal guest conductor of the Chicago Symphony, and in 1973 director of the Vienna Symphony Orchestra.

Recommended recordings: Mozart *Don Giovanni* (Angel stereo 4-disc set S-3605, *complete*; or Angel stereo disc S-35642, *highlights*). Stravinsky *Firebird* and *Petrushka* Suites (Angel stereo disc 36039).

TITO GOBBI

(pronounced: *gaub*-bee)

Baritone. Born October 24, 1915, in Bassano del Grappa, near Venice, Italy. A law student before deciding to become a singer, he studied first in Rome, then in Vienna. In 1938 he won an international competition in Vienna, and made his operatic debut in Rome that same year. In 1942 he joined Milan's La Scala, and soon became its leading baritone. In 1947 Gobbi made his first appearances outside Italy, with the Stockholm Opera. The following year saw his U.S. debut with the San Francisco Opera, and in 1956 he joined the Metropolitan Opera. He has made numerous motion pictures, including screen versions of *Rigoletto, Pagliacci, The Barber of Seville*, and *Tosca.* He ranks as one of the century's outstanding baritones, noted for his rich, lyrical voice, and for the penetrating depth of his interpretations.

Recommended recordings: The Art of Tito Gobbi (Angel stereo 2-disc set SIB-6021). Puccini *Tosca*, in which he sings "Scarpia" (Angel 2-disc set 3508, *mono only*).

GLENN GOULD

(pronounced: *goold*)

Pianist. Born September 25, 1932, in Toronto, Canada. While studying at Toronto's Royal Academy of Music (1943–52), he made his debut in 1947 with the Toronto Symphony. His U.S. recital debut took place in 1955. A year later he won wide acclaim for a recording of Bach's *Goldberg Variations* (Columbia ML-5060, now deleted), and was launched on an international career. In the late 1960's he announced that he would no longer tour, and would restrict his playing primarily to recordings. He is regarded as a highly individualistic, sometimes eccentric, but most frequently a sensitive and rhythmically animated performer.

Recommended recordings: Bach *The Well-Tempered Clavier* (Columbia stereo 3-disc set D3S-733). Liszt piano transcription of Beethoven Symphony No. 5 (Columbia stereo disc MS-7095).

GARY GRAFFMAN

(pronounced: *graf*-man)

Pianist. Born October 14, 1928, in New York City. He studied at the Curtis Institute in Philadelphia (1936–46) and at Columbia University. He won the Rachmaninoff Fund Special Award in 1948 and the Leventritt Award in 1948. In the 1960's he played a major role in organizing prominent concert artists to agree to perform only to nonsegregated audiences in the South. He ranks today as one of the leading "middle generation" pianists, at his best with late Romantics and early 20th-century composers.

Recommended recordings: Tchaikovsky Piano Concertos Nos. 2 and 3 (Columbia stereo disc MS-6755). Prokofiev. Piano Concertos Nos. 1 and 3 (Columbia stereo disc MS-6925)

BERNARD HAITINK
(pronounced: *hy*-tink)

Conductor. Born March 4, 1929, in Amsterdam, the Netherlands. He was originally a violinist, then a conductor of the Netherlands Radio Philharmonic in the 1950's. In 1956 he took over on short notice when Carlo Maria Giulini was unable to conduct a concert of the Amsterdam Concertgebouw Orchestra—and the subsequent acclaim led to many other appearances, culminating in his appointment as the Concertgebouw's music director in 1961. Since 1967 he has also been principal conductor of the London Philharmonic, and is credited with restoring it to the front rank of London's orchestras. He is particularly noted for his performances of Mahler and Bruckner, and is considered one of the finest all-around conductors of Europe's present "middle generation."

Recommended recordings: Mahler Symphony No. 5 (Philips stereo 2-disc set 6700048). Ravel *Ma Mère l'Oye* and *Daphnis et Chloé* Suites (Philips stereo disc 6500311).

JASCHA HEIFETZ
(pronounced: *hy*-fehts)

Violinist. Born February 2, 1901, in Vilna, Russia. He started playing the violin at the age of three, and entered the Royal Music School at Vilna at five, graduating at nine. Later he studied at St. Petersburg with Leopold Auer. His U.S. debut took place in 1917, and he quickly became one of the most widely acclaimed violinists on the concert stage. After the Russian Revolution, he settled permanently in the U.S., becoming an American citizen in 1925. He acted and played in a 1938 Hollywood movie, *They Shall Have Music*, and was a frequent radio performer during the 1940's. He retired from active concertizing in the early 1960's, and now lives and teaches in southern California. One of the century's great violin virtuosos, he is considered by most critics to be the personification of impeccable technique combined with impeccable musical taste.

Recommended recordings: Brahms Violin Concerto (RCA Red Seal stereo disc LSC-1903; cartridge R8S-5042). Sibelius Violin Concerto (RCA Red Seal stereo disc LSC-4010).

LORIN HOLLANDER
(pronounced: *holl*-an-der)

Pianist. Born July 19, 1944, in New York City. The son of a violinist with the New York Philharmonic, he made his New York concert debut in 1956, and was a frequent performer on television shows in the late 1950's. In 1969 he was the first classical artist to give a recital at Fillmore East, then one of the nation's major theatres for rock

118

Bernard Haitink

116

Glenn Gould

121

Marilyn Horne

117

Gary Graffman

119

Jascha Heifetz

122

Vladimir Horowitz

120

Lorin Hollander

concerts, and introduced Baldwin's new electronic grand piano for the occasion. He has also been an active exponent of less formal attire for concert performers, giving concerts in turtleneck sweaters, suede pullovers, and other casual styles. He is best known for his dynamic performances of contemporary music.

Recommended recordings: Dello Joio *Fantasy and Variations* and Ravel Piano Concerto in G (RCA Red Seal disc LSC-2667). Lorin Hollander at the Fillmore East (Angel stereo disc SFO-36025).

MARILYN HORNE
(pronounced: *horn*)

Mezzo-soprano. Born January 16, 1934, in Bradford, Pennsylvania. While studying at the University of Southern California on a voice scholarship, she took part in many Los Angeles radio broadcasts and recorded with Igor Stravinsky, Robert Craft, and the Roger Wagner Chorale, as well as dubbing her voice for Dorothy Dandridge in the title role of the film *Carmen Jones*. In 1957 she went to Europe for further study, returning in 1960 to score a triumph with the San Francisco Opera (as Marie in Berg's *Wozzeck*)—for which the Los Angeles *Times* nominated her as "woman of the year." During the 1960's she became widely admired not only for the sumptuousness of her voice but also for the varied range of her performances—including Baroque, *bel canto*, contemporary serial music, and Wagnerian opera. In 1969 she made her debut at Milan's La Scala, and in 1970 at New York's Metropolitan Opera. She has been married since 1960 to conductor Henry Lewis.

Recommended recordings: Marilyn Horne (London stereo disc OS-25910). Marilyn Horne Sings Rossini (London stereo disc OS-26305).

VLADIMIR HOROWITZ
(pronounced: *hoh*-roh-witz)

Pianist. Born October 1, 1904, in Kiev, Russia. He made his debut in Russia in 1921, then in Europe in 1925, and the U.S. in 1928. He quickly established himself as a pianist of fantastic virtuosity, with a Romantic flair that made him one of the most popular of concert stars during the 1930's and 1940's. In 1953 he gave up public performing, partly for health reasons, though he did continue to make recordings. In 1965 he gave a historic "return" concert at New York's Carnegie Hall, but has performed only occasionally in public since then. One of the giants of the century.

Recommended recordings: Horowitz in Concert (Columbia stereo 2-disc set M2S-757). The Horowitz Collection (RCA Red Seal disc LD-7021, *mono only*).

BYRON JANIS
(pronounced: *jan*-niss)

Pianist. Born March 24, 1928, in McKeesport, Pennsylvania. He studied in the 1940's with Vladimir Horowitz, who had never previously accepted a pupil. He made his debut with the Pittsburgh Symphony in 1944, and his New York recital debut in 1948. In 1960 he made a sensationally-acclaimed tour of the Soviet Union, and in 1962 was the first American pianist to record Russian works with a Russian orchestra and an American engineering team. An intense, virtuoso pianist, he is most noted for his performances of late Romantic and early 20th-century works.

Recommended recordings: Rachmaninoff Piano Concerto No. 1 and Prokofiev Piano Concerto No. 3 (Mercury stereo disc SRI-75019). Rachmaninoff Piano Concerto No. 3 (RCA Victrola stereo disc VICS-1032; cartridge V8S-1038).

DONALD JOHANOS
(pronounced: yoh-*hah*-nohss)

Conductor. Born February 10, 1928, in Cedar Rapids, Iowa. In 1957 he joined the Dallas Symphony as a second violin player, and rose rapidly to assistant conductor, then associate conductor, and in 1962 was named music director—the first native-born musician to "rise through the ranks" to the directorship of a major U.S. orchestra. In 1970 he left Dallas to become associate conductor of the Pittsburgh Symphony under William Steinberg.

Recommended recordings: Ives *Holidays* Symphony (Vox/Turnabout stereo disc 34146). Rachmaninoff Symphonic Dances (Vox/Turnabout stereo disc 34145).

HERBERT VON KARAJAN
(pronounced: *kah*-rah-yahn)

Conductor. Born April 5, 1908, in Salzburg, Austria. He first conducted in Salzburg at the age of twenty, then throughout Germany and Austria in the early 1930's. By 1937 he was director of the Berlin State Opera's symphony concerts. Some say he became a pawn of Nazi Air Marshal Göring in a feud Göring had with Nazi Propaganda Minister Goebbels (a champion of Furtwängler) over who was to control Berlin's cultural life. In 1942 Karajan apparently fell into disfavor when he married a "non-Aryan," and was moved to Vienna. When World War II ended, Allied officials denied him permission to conduct until 1948. In 1954 he became principal conductor of London's Philharmonia Orchestra, and in 1956 director of the Berlin Philharmonic, a post he now holds "for life". He quickly established himself as one of Europe's most popular conductors, noted especially for his vibrant, tonally sleek, rhythmically supple performances of German classics and most Romantics. In the 1960's his many varied activities as leader of musical organizations in virtually every European music capital led to his being nicknamed Europe's *"Herr Generalmusikdirektor"* (Mr. General Music Director).

Recommended recordings: Beethoven Symphony No. 3, "Eroica" (Deutsche Grammophon stereo disc 138802; cassette 923-063; cartridge 88-802). Tchaikovsky Symphony No. 4 (Deutsche Grammophon stereo disc 139017; cartridge M-89-017).

JEAN-RODOLPHE KARS
(pronounced: *kahrz*)

Pianist. Born in 1947 in Calcutta, India, of Austrian-French parents, but raised in France after 1948. He studied at the Paris Conservatory, later with pianist Julius Katchen. He was laureate winner of the 1965 Gabriel Fauré Competition in Paris, and

123

Byron Janis

124

Donald Johanos

125

Herbert von Karajan

126

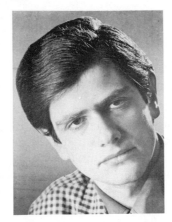

Jean-Rodolphe Kars

127

Julius Katchen

Istvan Kertesz

128

129

Dorothy Kirsten

130

Erich Kleiber

131

Otto Klemperer

winner of the 1968 Messiaen Competition for Contemporary Music at Royan, France. He is one of the most subtly lyrical of today's young pianists.

Recommended recordings: Delius Piano Concerto (London stereo disc CS-6657). Kars Plays Messiaen and Liszt (London stereo disc CS-6604).

JULIUS KATCHEN
(pronounced: *katch*-en)

Pianist. Born August 15, 1926, in Long Branch, New Jersey. Died April 29, 1969, in Paris, France. He made his debut at the age of eleven with Ormandy and the Philadelphia Orchestra. At Haverford College, he was top man in his class, majoring in philosophy and graduating in 1946. He won a French government fellowship for study in Paris in 1947, and remained there permanently, concertizing extensively until cancer struck him in the early 1960's. He was particularly noted for his dynamic, beautifully flowing performances of Brahms.

Recommended recordings: Brahms Piano Trio No. 2, with Suk, Starker (London stereo disc CS-6549). Bartok Piano Concerto No. 3 (London stereo disc CS-6487; cassette M-10196).

ISTVAN KERTESZ
(pronounced: *kayr*-tehsh)

Conductor. Born August 28, 1929, in Hungary. Died April 17, 1973 in Tel Aviv, Israel. After studying in Budapest and Rome, he became a conductor of the Győr Philharmonia in Hungary in 1953, then of the Budapest Opera in 1956. He left Hungary during the 1956 revolution, settling in West Germany. He was conductor of the Augsburg (Germany) Symphony (1958–63) and the London Symphony (1965–68). From 1964 until his death he was also music director of the Cologne Opera in West Germany. He was in Israel to guest-conduct the Israel Philharmonic in 1973 when he drowned while swimming in the Mediterranean. He was most highly regarded for his warmly lyrical performances of Schubert, Dvořák, and most Romantics.

Recommended recordings: Dvořák Symphony No. 8 (old No. 4) (London stereo disc CS-6358). Bartok *Bluebeard's Castle* (London stereo 2-disc set OSA-1158).

DOROTHY KIRSTEN
(pronounced: *keer*-stehn)

Soprano. Born July 6, 1917, in Montclair, New Jersey. To pay her way through the Juilliard School in New York, she worked first as a telephone operator, then as a radio singer. Film star and Metropolitan Opera soprano Grace Moore heard one of her broadcasts, and sponsored further voice studies for her in Italy. She returned to the U.S. to sing with the Chicago Opera, the New York City Opera, and after 1945 the Metropolitan Opera. For the next three decades she remained one of the Met's most popular stars, best known for her warmly expressive Puccini heroines (*Madama Butterfly*, *Tosca*, *Manon Lescaut*, *The Girl of the Golden West*). During the 1950's she made several films (*The Great Caruso* with Mario Lanza, *Mr. Music* with Bing Crosby), and appeared frequently on radio and television. Regrettably—and strangely considering her popularity—she did not make many recordings after the mid-1950's, and no complete operas for a major record company.

Recommended recordings: Dorothy Kirsten—By Popular Demand (Odyssey disc Y-31737, *mono only*). Dorothy Kirsten in Opera and Song (RCA Victrola disc VIC-1552, *mono only*).

ERICH KLEIBER

(pronounced: *kly*-ber)

Conductor. Born August 5, 1890, in Vienna, Austria. Died January 27, 1956, in Berlin. From 1923 to 1935, he was one of Berlin's leading symphony and opera conductors, and spent one year (1930–31) as principal guest conductor of the New York Philharmonic, during which time he conducted its first coast-to-coast radio broadcast. In 1935 he left Germany over differences with the Nazis, settling first in Salzburg, then Milan, then Havana. He frequently appeared as a guest conductor in the U.S. during World War II. After the war he often conducted the Amsterdam Concertgebouw. In 1955 he was named music director of the (East) Berlin State Opera, but resigned later that same year charging government interference. He died suddenly of a heart attack a few months later. He was best known for his exciting and highly dramatic performances of Beethoven, Mozart, and Richard Strauss.

Recommended recordings: Strauss *Der Rosenkavalier* (Richmond 4-disc set 6400, *mono only*). Beethoven Symphony No. 5 (Richmond disc B-19105, *mono only*, now deleted).

OTTO KLEMPERER

(pronounced: *klehm*-per-er)

Conductor. Born May 15, 1885, in Breslau, Germany. Died July 7, 1973, in Zurich, Switzerland. He became a conductor of the Prague Opera in 1907 at Mahler's recommendation. Later he held posts at the Cologne Opera (1917–24), Wiesbaden (1924–27), and the Berlin State Opera (1927–33), resigning the latter when the Nazis took power. For several years in the mid-1930's he was conductor of the Los Angeles Philharmonic, and from 1947 to 1950 he led the Budapest Opera. A series of debilitating accidents and illnesses plagued his life, and he was partially paralyzed after the 1950's. From 1964 until his death he was principal conductor of the New Philharmonia Orchestra of London. He was highly regarded as an eloquent, penetrating interpreter of most Classics and some Romantics, although he leaned toward slow, sometimes ponderous tempos that divided many critics.

Recommended recording: Brahms *A German Requiem*, with Schwarzkopf, Fischer-Dieskau (Angel stereo 2-disc set S-3624).

KIRIL KONDRASHIN

(pronounced: kon-*drahsh*-een)

Conductor. Born May 5, 1914, in Moscow, Russia. During the late 1930's he was an opera conductor in Leningrad, then between 1943 and 1956 principal conductor of the Bolshoi Ballet in Moscow. Since 1956 he has been conductor of the Moscow

134

Serge Koussevitzky

132

Kiril Kondrashin

137

Ruth Laredo

133

André Kostelanetz

135

Josef Krips

138

Jaime Laredo

136

Rafael Kubelik

Philharmonic. In 1958, when Van Cliburn won the first International Tchaikovsky Piano Competition in Moscow, it was Kondrashin who conducted the orchestra and then, at Cliburn's request, conducted the pianist's homecoming concert in New York's Carnegie Hall. Since then, Kondrashin has become the best-known and most popular Soviet conductor in the U.S., most admired for his colorful, dramatic performances of Tchaikovsky, Rachmaninoff, and Shostakovich.

Recommended recordings: Shostakovich Symphony No. 9 and *The Execution of Stepan Razin* (Melodiya/Angel stereo disc S-40000; cassette 4XS-40000). Rachmaninoff Symphonic Dances (Melodiya/Angel stereo disc S-40093).

ANDRÉ KOSTELANETZ
(pronounced: koss-tehl-*ah*-netz)

Conductor. Born December 22, 1901, in Petrograd, Russia. After his graduation from the St. Petersburg Conservatory in 1922, he came to the U.S., where he remained permanently, becoming a U.S. citizen in 1928. During the 1930's he led a popular radio series over the CBS network, specializing in symphonic arrangements of pop music. During the 1930's and 1940's he also appeared in a number of movies, and was a guest conductor of major U.S. orchestras, usually in performances of light classics. Since 1963 he has been music director of the New York Philharmonic's spring "Promenade" series, where he mixes his colorful, lively performances of Romantic classics with lesser-known works by 19th- and 20th-century composers.

Recommended recordings: Light Music of Shostakovich (Columbia stereo disc MS-6867). Great Moments from The Promenades (Columbia stereo 2-disc set MG-31415).

SERGE KOUSSEVITZKY
(pronounced: koo-seh-*vits*-kee)

Conductor. Born July 26, 1874, in Iver, Russia. Died June 4, 1951 in Boston, Massachusetts. He began his career as a double bass player, and for a long time was considered the world's finest. In 1905 he settled in Berlin to study conducting with Nikisch. By 1907 he had his own orchestra in Russia—a wedding present from his bride's father, who was one of Russia's wealthiest merchants. After the Russian Revolution in 1917, his orchestra was disbanded, and he became director of the Russian State Symphony. But in 1920, discouraged by conditions in the Soviet Union, he left and went to Paris, where he directed the Concerts Koussevitzky for several years. From 1924 to 1949 he was conductor of the Boston Symphony Orchestra, rebuilding it into one of the world's great orchestras and founding its summer festival and school at Tanglewood. Through the Koussevitzky Foundation, he also established funds for the commissioning of hundreds of new works. One of the century's great musicians; noted for his taut, dramatic, often electric performances of Russian and French music of the late 19th and early 20th centuries (particularly Tchaikovsky, Shostakovich, Prokofiev, Ravel).

Recommended recordings: Sibelius Symphony No. 2 (RCA Victrola disc VIC-1510, *mono only*). Serge Koussevitzky—Treasury of Immortal Performances (RCA Victor 3-disc set VCM-6174, *mono only*).

JOSEF KRIPS

Conductor. Born April 8, 1902, in Vienna. In the early 1920's he was a conductor at the Vienna Volksoper, and by 1933 had become first conductor at the Vienna State Opera. After the Nazis took over Austria in 1938, Krips—a Catholic, but with Jewish antecedents—was barred from conducting, and spent most of World War II working in a food processing factory. After the war he was a major figure in the reorganization and rebuilding of the Vienna Opera. He has since been conductor of the London Symphony Orchestra (1950–55), the Buffalo Philharmonic (1954–63), and the San Francisco Symphony (1964–1969). He is best known as a straightforward, thoughtful interpreter of the Classical and Romantic German repertory.

Recommended recordings: Beethoven Symphonies Nos. 2 and 4 (Everest stereo disc 3113). Haydn Symphonies Nos. 94 and 99 (London Stereo Treasury disc STS-15085).

RAFAEL KUBELIK

(pronounced: *koo*-beh-lick)

Conductor. Born June 29, 1914, in Bychory, Czechoslovakia. The son of violinist Jan Kubelik, he was accompanist on his father's U.S. tours from 1934 to 1936. In 1936 he became acting conductor of the Czech Philharmonic in Prague, then in 1939 first conductor of the Brno Philharmonic. During World War II he was principal conductor of the Czech Philharmonic, but was in and out of difficulty for his refusal to cooperate with the officials of the Nazi occupation. He left Czechoslovakia when the Communists took over in 1948. He was music director of the Chicago Symphony Orchestra (1950–53), of the Covent Garden Opera in London (1955–58), and since 1961 of the Bavarian Radio Orchestra in Munich, Germany. In 1973 he became music director of the Metropolitan Opera in New York, but he resigned in 1974 after a series of controversies. He is best known for his refined, somewhat restrained performances of the late Romantics, especially Dvořák, Smetana, and Mahler.

Recommended recordings: Smetana *Ma Vlast* (Deutsche Grammophon stereo 2-disc set 2707054; cassette 3581008). Dvořák Symphony No. 7 (old No. 2) (Deutsche Grammophon stereo disc 2530127; cassette 3300224; cartridge 89445).

JAIME LAREDO

(pronounced: lah-*ray*-doh)

Violinist. Born June 7, 1941, in Cochabamba, Bolivia. He started playing the violin at the age of six, and came to the U.S. as a teenager to study in San Francisco, Cleveland, and Philadelphia. He won the 1959 Queen Elisabeth of Belgium competition. In recent years he has been active as a performer in chamber music as well as a soloist—and is widely admired as an especially supple, lyrically expressive violinist in the 18th- and 19th-century repertory. He is probably the only living musician to be honored with an air mail stamp (in Bolivia) bearing his photo and the musical notes La, Re, Do. In 1960 he married pianist Ruth Meckler, now known professionally as Ruth Laredo.

Recommended recording: Mendelssohn Violin Concerto and Bruch Violin Concerto No. 1 (RCA Victrola stereo disc VICS-1033).

RUTH LAREDO

(pronounced: lah-*ray*-doh)

Pianist. Born November 20, 1937, in Detroit, Michigan. She studied with Rudolf Serkin and Mieczyslaw Horszowski at the Curtis Institute. In 1960 she married violinist Jaime Laredo. Both Laredos have been closely associated with the Marlboro Festival in Vermont for many years, and have toured Europe and the Middle East with the "Music from Marlboro" concerts. Mrs. Laredo is a vibrant, clean-lined, subtly detailed pianist, most noted for her interpretations of Ravel and Scriabin.

Recommended recordings: Ravel *Gaspard de la Nuit, Valses Nobles et Sentimentales,* and *La Valse* (Connoisseur Society stereo disc S-2005). Scriabin Sonatas Nos. 3, 4, 6, and 10 (Connoisseur Society stereo disc S-2034).

EVELYN LEAR

Soprano. Born January 18, 1930, in New York City. She studied at Hunter College and at Juilliard, where she met and married baritone Thomas Stewart. After several years of finding opportunities to sing only in churches and nightclubs, she and her husband left the U.S. in 1957 for Germany. Within a year, both were under contract to the West Berlin Deutsche Oper. Over the next decade, she became one of the leading sopranos of the opera houses of Berlin, Vienna, and Munich, and scored a particular triumph in 1962 in the first staged performance of Berg's *Lulu* in his native Vienna. In 1966 she sang in Berg's *Wozzeck* with the Chicago Lyric Opera, and a year later made her Metropolitan Opera debut in the world premiere of Marvin David Levy's *Mourning Becomes Elektra.* She has since sung many leading operatic roles (in *Tosca, Der Rosenkavalier, The Marriage of Figaro,* etc.), as well as establishing herself as one of the finest American singers of German *lieder.*

Recommended recordings: Berg *Lulu* (Deutsche Grammophon stereo 3-disc set 2709029). Ives *American Scenes, American Poets,* with Thomas Stewart (Columbia stereo disc M-30229).

ERICH LEINSDORF

(pronounced: *lynss*-dorf)

Conductor. Born February 4, 1912, in Vienna, Austria. After several seasons as an assistant to Arturo Toscanini and Bruno Walter at Salzburg (1934–37), he came to the U.S. in 1937, settling permanently and becoming a U.S. citizen in 1942. He was chief conductor of Wagnerian opera at the Metropolitan Opera (1937–42), then conductor of the Cleveland Orchestra (1943–44) until he was drafted into the U.S. Army during World War II. After the war he was director of the Rochester Philharmonic (1947–56) and the Boston Symphony (1962–69), as well as conducting at both the New York City Opera and the Metropolitan Opera. He is highly regarded as an intelligent, perceptive, always tasteful but sometimes emotionally restrained conductor, at his best with Wagner, most German classics, and Prokofiev.

Recommended recordings: Prokofiev *Romeo and Juliet* (excerpts) (RCA Red Seal stereo disc LSC-2994). Strauss *Till Eulenspiegel* and Suite from *Die Frau öhne Schatten* (Seraphim stereo disc S-60097).

RAYMOND LEPPARD

(pronounced: leh-*phard*)

Conductor and harpsichordist. Born in 1927 in England. He began his professional career as a harpsichord soloist, then in 1952 formed the Leppard Ensemble, which became famous throughout England for its performances of Baroque music. During the 1960's his research into music by Monteverdi, J. C. Bach, Cavalli, and others resulted in more authentic "performing editions," for which he was highly praised at the annual Glyndebourne Festivals. He has also conducted opera at London's Covent Garden, and composed incidental music for British Shakespearean productions. Since 1970 he has been a principal conductor of the English Chamber Orchestra.

Recommended recordings: Handel *Water Music* (Philips stereo disc 6300047; cartridge 7300060). Haydn Symphonies Nos. 22, 39, and 47 (Philips stereo disc 839796).

JAMES LEVINE

(pronounced: leh-*vine*)

Conductor. Born June 2, 1943, in Cincinnati, Ohio. He made his debut at the age of ten, as a pianist with the Cincinnati Symphony. At Juilliard he studied piano with Rosina Lhevinne and conducting with Jean Morel, completing his undergraduate requirements in an unprecedented one year. The following year (1964) he was chosen for the Ford Foundation's American Conductors Project. Among the judges was George Szell, who invited him to become an assistant conductor of the Cleveland Orchestra. He remained in that post for six years. In 1970 he made a much-praised debut as a conductor with the Metropolitan Opera, and also appeared as a guest conductor of the orchestras of Boston and Philadelphia. In 1972 he was chosen principal conductor of the Met by its new music director, Rafael Kubelik—the first principal conductor in the Met's history.

Recommended recording: Verdi *Giovanna d'Arco* (Joan of Arc) (Angel stereo 3-disc set SCL-3791).

RAYMOND LEWENTHAL

(pronounced: *loo*-en-thahl)

Pianist. Born August 29, 1926, in San Antonio, Texas. He studied at Juilliard, the Siena (Italy) Academia, and with Alfred Cortot, making his debut with the Philadelphia Orchestra in 1948. During the 1960's he was in the forefront of the revival of the long-neglected 19th-century Romantic piano works of Alkan, Henselt, Scharwenka, and others, writing numerous articles about them as well as playing their grandiose, virtuoso pieces in his sweepingly dynamic style.

Recommended recordings: Piano Music of Alkan (RCA Red Seal stereo disc

139

Evelyn Lear

140

Erich Leinsdorf

141

Raymond Leppard

142

James Levine

143

Raymond Lewenthal

144

Henry Lewis

145

Dinu Lipatti

146

George London

147

Pilar Lorengar

LSC-2815). Henselt Piano Concerto in F minor and Liszt *Totentanz* (Columbia stereo disc MS-7252).

HENRY LEWIS

Conductor. Born October 18, 1932 in Los Angeles, California. He became a double bass player in the Los Angeles Philharmonic while studying at the University of Southern California, and later was its associate conductor for three years. While in the U.S. Army in the early 1950's he was conductor of the Seventh Army Orchestra. In 1958 he founded the Los Angeles Chamber Orchestra, and from 1965 to 1968 was music director of the Los Angeles Opera Company. Since 1968 he has been music director of the New Jersey Symphony Orchestra, and one of the first blacks to head a major U.S. orchestra. He has also been active in the U.S. and Europe as an opera conductor. He is married to mezzo-soprano Marilyn Horne.

Recommended recordings: Marilyn Horne Sings Rossini (London stereo disc S-26305). Strauss *Don Juan* (London stereo disc 21054; cassette M-94053).

DINU LIPATTI

(pronounced: lee-*pah*-tee)

Pianist. Born March 19, 1917, in Bucharest, Rumania. Died December 2, 1950, in Geneva, Switzerland. He began giving concerts at the age of five. In 1934, when he won second prize in an international competition at Vienna, the popular French pianist Alfred Cortôt resigned from the jury in protest because Lipatti had not been awarded first prize. World War II interrupted his performing career outside Switzerland. In 1946 he was preparing for a U.S. tour when it was discovered he had leukemia. Igor Stravinsky, Charles Munch, and Yehudi Menuhin contributed large amounts of money for expensive cortisone treatments, but he died in 1950 at age thirty-three. The recordings he made in the late 1940's have confirmed his reputation as one of the century's great pianists—a subtle tone colorist, rhythmically vibrant, and with an unequaled evenness of sound.

Recommended recordings: Chopin Waltzes (Odyssey disc 32160058, *mono only*). Schumann and Grieg Piano Concertos (Odyssey disc 32160141, *mono only*).

GEORGE LONDON

Baritone. Born May 30, 1921, in Montreal, Canada. Although he was born in Canada, his parents were Americans, and he was raised primarily in Los Angeles. During the late 1940's he toured the U.S. with tenor Mario Lanza and soprano Frances Yeend as the Bel Canto Trio. He made his operatic debut in Vienna in 1949, and two years later joined New York's Metropolitan Opera. In 1953 he sang the title role in the first Metropolitan production of the original version of Mussorgsky's *Boris Godunov*, and in 1960 he became the first American to sing the role with the Bolshoi Opera in Moscow. In the late 1960's a throat ailment forced his virtual retirement at the height of his career. He served for a time as music administrator for the John F. Kennedy Center for the Performing Arts in Washington, D.C.

Recommended recordings: Mussorgsky *Boris Godunov* (Columbia stereo 4-disc set

MS-696). Strauss *Arabella* (London stereo 4-disc set 1404, complete; or stereo disc OS-25243, highlights).

PILAR LORENGAR

(pronounced: *loh*-rhen-ghar)

Soprano. Born January 16, 1930, in Zaragosa, Spain. She first sang in the choir of a convent school, and went to Madrid to study voice as a teenager. By 1951 she had won two awards, including the prestigious Bellas Artes Medallion, and was playing leading roles in *zarzuelas* in Madrid. She made her U.S. debut in 1955 in a New York concert performance of Granados' rarely performed opera, *Goyescas*. The following year, she joined the West Berlin Deutsche Oper, and quickly established herself as one of its stars. After marrying a Berlin dental surgeon, she made Berlin her home, but continued to sing occasionally in Paris, Vienna, Milan, Buenos Aires, and other cities. She made her San Francisco Opera debut in 1964, and her Metropolitan Opera debut in 1966. She has since established herself as one of today's most admired sopranos, noted for the distinctively vibrant sheen of her voice and the lyrical beauty of her phrasing in a wide range of styles from Mozart to Puccini.

Recommended recordings: Pilar Lorengar (London stereo disc OS-25995). *Prima Donna in Vienna* (London stereo disc OS-26246).

CHRISTA LUDWIG

(pronounced: *lood*-vihg)

Mezzo-soprano. Born March 16, 1929, in Berlin, Germany. The daughter of tenor Anton Ludwig and contralto Eugenie Ludwig-Besalla of the Vienna State Opera, she began her musical studies with her mother. Her operatic debut took place in 1946 in Frankfurt. In 1955 she joined the Vienna State Opera, where she met and married baritone Walter Berry. Her Metropolitan Opera debut took place in 1959, and she and Berry scored a personal triumph in 1966 in the Met's first production of Strauss' *Die Frau öhne Schätten*. She and Berry were divorced in 1970, but have continued to perform together professionally. An uncommonly versatile, compellingly dramatic singer, she has alternated between mezzo-soprano and soprano roles, including some of the dramatic soprano roles of Wagner.

Recommended recordings: Brahms *Alto Rhapsody* and Wagner *Wesendonck* Songs (Angel stereo disc S-35923). Strauss Scenes from *Die Frau öhne Schätten*, *Elektra*, and *Der Rosenkavalier*, with Berry (RCA Victrola stereo disc VICS-1269).

LORIN MAAZEL

(pronounced: mah-*zehl*)

Conductor. Born March 6, 1930, in Paris, France, of American parents, and raised in the United States. He became a child prodigy on the violin and as a conductor. He conducted at the New York World's Fair in 1939 and then Toscanini's NBC Symphony in 1941. As he approached his teens, he was (in his own words) "dropped flat as soon as I lost my market value as a monstrosity." At fifteen, he joined the Pittsburgh Symphony as a violinist while studying philosophy and languages at the

150

Bruno Maderna

148

Christa Ludwig

151

Zubin Mehta

153

Yehudi Menuhin

149

Lorin Maazel

152

Lauritz Melchior

154

Robert Merrill

University of Pittsburgh. In the 1950's he went to Rome to study, became a radio conductor, and then, in 1960, became the first American ever to conduct at the Bayreuth Festival. From 1964 to 1972 he was music director of both the (West) Berlin Radio Symphony and the Berlin Opera. In 1971 he became principal conductor of the New Philharmonia Orchestra in London, and in 1972 he succeeded George Szell as music director of the Cleveland Orchestra. He is noted for the clarity and balance of orchestral textures in his performances.

Recommended recordings: Prokofiev *Romeo and Juliet*, complete (London stereo 3-disc set CSA-2312). Strauss *Death and Transfiguration* (London stereo disc SPC-21067).

BRUNO MADERNA
(pronounced: mah-*dayr*-nah)

Conductor and composer. Born April 21, 1920, in Venice, Italy. Died November 13, 1973, in Darmstadt, Germany. In the 1950's he was active with avant-garde groups in Milan and Darmstadt. In 1969 he became conductor of the Radio Italiana Orchestra in Milan. In 1971, while teaching at Tanglewood, Massachusetts, he substituted on short notice for an ill conductor of the Boston Symphony, to great acclaim. A few months later he made a similar last-minute substitution with the Philadelphia Orchestra, leading to invitations to conduct in Chicago, New York, and other major cities. His international career as a conductor was just beginning to bloom when he was stricken with cancer. Although he specialized in recording contemporary music, he was also an intense, dramatic, if sometimes provocatively unorthodox interpreter of the traditional repertory, especially Mahler and Brahms.

Recommended recordings: Maderna Serenata No. 2 (Mainstream stereo disc 5004; cassette MS-5004; cartridge M8-5004). Penderecki *Threnody for the Victims of Hiroshima* and Stockhausen *Kontra-Punkte* (RCA Victrola disc VICS-1239).

ZUBIN MEHTA
(pronounced: *may*-tah)

Conductor. Born April 29, 1936, in Bombay, India. At the age of eighteen he went to Vienna to study, and soon after began attracting attention as the first major Indian conductor in Europe. From 1961 to 1967 he was conductor of the Montreal Symphony, and since 1962 has been music director of the Los Angeles Philharmonic. He has also conducted opera at New York's Metropolitan, Milan's La Scala, and the Vienna State Opera. Since 1968 he has also been musical adviser of the Israel Philharmonic. He is most noted for robust, dramatic performances of large-scale late 19th- and early 20th-century works.

Recommended recordings: Respighi *Feste Romane* and Strauss *Don Juan* (RCA Red Seal stereo disc LSC-2816). Strauss *Also Sprach Zarathustra* (London stereo disc CS-6609; cassette M-10209).

LAURITZ MELCHIOR
(pronounced: *mehl*-kee-or)

Tenor. Born March 20, 1890, in Copenhagen, Denmark. Died in Santa Monica, Calif., March 18, 1973. He made his debut with the Royal Danish Opera in 1913 as a baritone, but withdrew the following year in order to retrain his voice as a tenor. He made his tenor debut in Copenhagen in 1918 (in Wagner's *Tannhäuser*). Over the next thirty years, his stirringly sonorous, dramatically expressive voice made him the most famous Wagnerian tenor of his time—and, in the view of some critics, perhaps the greatest *Heldentenor* (heroic tenor) of all time. From 1924 to 1950 he sang primarily at New York's Metropolitan Opera. During the late 1940's he also made a number of popular films, in which he usually played light-hearted supporting roles (in contrast to his operatic image as a *Heldentenor*).

Recommended recordings: Lauritz Melchior/Wagner (RCA Victrola disc VIC-1500, *mono only*). The Lauritz Melchior Album (Seraphim 2-disc set IB-6086, mono only).

YEHUDI MENUHIN
(pronounced: *mehn*-yoo-in)

Violinist and conductor. Born April 22, 1916, in New York City. He started playing the violin at the age of four, and was a soloist with the San Francisco Symphony at seven, then a child prodigy performing throughout the world. He "retired" for several years in the 1930's, studying with Georges Enesco in Paris, then with Adolf Busch in Switzerland, before resuming his career. He has sometimes appeared (and recorded) as a violist. In the 1950's he also turned to conducting, becoming director of the Bath Festival in England (1958–68), and founding the Menuhin Festival Orchestra in Windsor, England, in 1969. As both violinist and conductor, he is noted for his elegant, sensitive, tasteful performances of Classical and Romantic works.

Recommended recordings: Portrait of the Artist—Yehudi Menuhin (Angel stereo 3-disc set S-3727). Walton Violin Concerto and Viola Concerto (Angel stereo disc S-36719).

ROBERT MERRILL
(pronounced: *mehr*-ihl)

Baritone. Born June 4, 1919, in Brooklyn, N.Y. After singing for several years in New York clubs and at Radio City Music Hall, he won the Metropolitan Opera Auditions of the Air in 1945, and made his debut at the Met that year. Since then he has become one of the Met's most popular baritone stars, noted for his vibrant, noble-sounding performances in the standard 19th-century Italian opera repertory. He has also been a popular radio and television performer. In 1952 he was dismissed from the Met by then-manager Rudolf Bing in a disagreement over his appearance in the movie comedy *Aaron Slick from Punkin Crick*, but he was later reinstated. In 1970 he made his musical comedy debut in a production of *Fiddler on the Roof* in Indianapolis.

Recommended recordings: Verdi *La Traviata* (*complete*—RCA Red Seal stereo 3-disc set LSC-6154; *highlights*—stereo disc LSC-2561; cassette RK-1025; cartridge R8S-1025). *Merrill and the Prima Donnas*, with Price, Sutherland, Tebaldi (London stereo disc OS-26183).

JORGE MESTER
(pronounced: *mehss*-ter)

Conductor. Born April 10, 1935, in Mexico City, Mexico, of Hungarian parents. Educated in Mexico and the U.S., he became a ballet conductor in the early 1960's—first for Martha Graham, then the American Ballet Theatre, then the Robert Joffrey Ballet. Since 1967 he has been music director of the Louisville (Kentucky) Orchestra, continuing its unique tradition of performing, commissioning, and recording new works by contemporary composers while also exploring the neglected works of earlier masters.

Recommended recordings: Husa *Music for Prague* and Penderecki *De Natura Sonoris* No. 2 (Louisville stereo disc S-722). Menotti and Copland Piano Concertos, with Earl Wild (Vanguard stereo disc S-2094).

ZINKA MILANOV
(pronounced: *mee*-lah-nawf)

Soprano. Born May 17, 1906, in Zagreb, Yugoslavia. After studying at the Zagreb Conservatory, she made her debut with the Zagreb Opera in 1927 (in Verdi's *Il Trovatore*) under her maiden name, Zinka Kunc; she adopted her husband's name in the 1930's. In 1935 she was invited by Bruno Walter to sing with the Vienna State Opera, and in 1937 by Arturo Toscanini to sing at the Salzburg Festival. Several months later she made her Metropolitan Opera debut, and although most of the critics praised the beauty of her voice, some were openly critical about her pitch control and an inclination toward a *tremolo.* She studied determinedly to correct these problems, and within a few years had become one of the leading and most dependable sopranos at the Met. She is one of the few singers to be honored with two successive opening nights at the Met (1951, 1952). She retired in the late 1960's. Her voice at its prime was a soaringly beautiful, warmly expressive, and dramatically exciting one, capable of spinning out some of the most lovely soprano sounds of any soprano of this age, especially when singing Verdi.

Recommended recordings: The Art of Zinka Milanov (RCA Victrola stereo disc VIC-1336, electronically reprocessed from original mono). Verdi *Aïda* (RCA Victrola 3-disc set VIC-6119, *mono only*).

SHERRILL MILNES
(pronounced: milnz)

Baritone. Born January 10, 1935, in Downers Grove, Illinois. He began singing in church choirs as a boy, and played tuba in the school band at Drake and Northwestern universities. For several seasons he was a member of the Margaret Hillis Choir in Chicago, and then made five national tours with the Boris Goldovsky Opera Company. In 1962 he won a Ford Foundation award which sponsored appearances in opera in Pittsburgh, Houston, Central City, and Cincinnati. In 1964 he made his debut with both Milan's La Scala and the New York City Opera. The following season he joined the Metropolitan Opera (on the same night as Montserrat Caballé), and has since

155

Jorge Mester

158

Anna Moffo

160

Nathan Milstein

156

Zinka Milanov

161

Pierre Monteux

57

Sherrill Milnes

Dimitri Mitropoulos

159

162

Charles Munch

163

Riccardo Muti

164

Birgit Nilsson

165

Garrick Ohlsson

166

David Oistrakh

Eugene Ormandy

167

168

Seiji Ozawa

169

Luciano Pavarotti

170

Itzhak Perlman

become one of its most popular baritone stars, noted for his richly lyrical, compellingly dramatic baritone.

Recommended recordings: Milnes—The Baritone Voice (RCA Red Seal stereo disc LSC-3076). Sherrill Milnes—Operatic Recital (London stereo disc OS-26366).

NATHAN MILSTEIN
(pronounced: *mihl*-styn)

Violinist. Born December 31, 1904, in Odessa, Russia. He studied with Leopold Auer and Eugene Ysaye, and began touring Russia at the age of nineteen, sometimes with Horowitz as his pianist. His U.S. debut took place in 1929. Since then he has been a leading violin soloist throughout the U.S. and Europe, much admired for his warm, lyrical, silken tone, and generally at his best in the Romantic repertory.

Recommended recordings: Dvořák and Glazunov Violin Concertos (Angel stereo disc S-36011). Chausson *Poème* and Saint-Saens Violin Concerto No. 3 (Angel stereo disc S-36005).

DIMITRI MITROPOULOS
(pronounced: mih-*traw*-poo-lohs)

Conductor, pianist, and organist. Born March 1, 1896, in Athens, Greece. Died November 2, 1960 in Milan, Italy. He was a rehearsal conductor with the Berlin Opera in the 1920's, then a conductor in Athens. From 1937 to 1948 he was conductor of the Minneapolis Symphony, and from 1949 to 1958 of the New York Philharmonic. He was also active at La Scala (Milan), the Vienna State Opera, and New York's Metropolitan Opera for most of the late 1950's. Although he was the first conductor to take the New York Philharmonic out of the concert hall—to play an engagement at the Roxy Theatre in New York City in 1952—his tenure with the Philharmonic was controversial because of his dedication to Schoenberg, Berg, and contemporary music generally. He was also noted as a dramatic, intense interpreter of Mahler, Strauss, and other late Romantic composers.

Recommended recordings: Shostakovich Symphony No. 10 (Odyssey disc 32160123, *mono only*). Vaughan Williams Symphony No. 4 (Columbia Special Projects disc CML-5158, *mono only*).

ANNA MOFFO
(pronounced: *mah*-foh)

Soprano. Born June 27, 1934, in Wayne, Pennsylvania. While attending the Curtis Institute in Philadelphia on a four-year scholarship, she won the Philadelphia Orchestra Young Artists Auditions in 1954. Later that same year she was awarded a Fulbright Fellowship to study in Italy. She made her operatic debut in an Italian television production of Puccini's *Madame Butterfly*. She was soon invited to sing at Milan's La Scala, the Vienna State Opera, and the Paris Opera. She made her U.S. opera debut in 1957 with the Chicago Lyric Opera, and two years later joined New York's Metropolitan Opera. One of the most beautiful opera stars of our time, she has been widely praised for her acting ability as well as for her sensuous, warmly expressive singing, especially in the lyrical music of Puccini and Verdi. She has also been the star of a popular Italian television series.

Recommended recordings: Puccini: *La Rondine* (RCA Red Seal 2-disc set LSC-7048, complete; stereo disc LSC-3033, highlights). Villa-Lobos *Bachianas Brasilieras* No. 5 and Canteloube *Songs of the Auvergne* (RCA Red Seal stereo disc LSC-2795).

PIERRE MONTEUX
(pronounced: mawn-*tuh*)

Conductor. Born April 4, 1875, in Paris, France. Died July 1, 1964, in Hancock, Maine. He started as a violinist in the orchestra of the Paris Opéra Comique (1896–1911), then became conductor for the Diaghilev Ballet Russe in the years before World War I. He was music director of the Boston Symphony Orchestra (1919–24), the Orchestre Symphonique of Paris (1930–35), the San Francisco Symphony (1935–52), and the London Symphony (1961–64). In the decade before his death, he was one of the most beloved of all conductors, frequently appearing as a guest conductor in Boston, Amsterdam, Tel Aviv, and other cities, and directing a summer music school at Hancock, Maine. He was best known as a warm, vibrant, always elegant and tasteful conductor of Brahms, Beethoven, most French composers, and most Romantics.

Recommended recordings: Franck Symphony in D minor (RCA Red Seal stereo disc LSC-2514). Stravinsky *Petrushka* (RCA Red Seal stereo disc LSC-2376).

CHARLES MUNCH
(pronounced: moonch)

Conductor. Born September 26, 1891, in Strasbourg, Alsace (then part of Germany). Died November 6, 1968, in Richmond, Virginia. He began his career as a violinist, first in Strasbourg's orchestra, then as concertmaster of the Leipzig Gewandhaus Orchestra under Furtwängler. He was drafted into the German Army in World War I, and was wounded at Verdun. After the war, he turned to conducting. In 1933 he married an heiress of the Nestlé (Swiss chocolate) family, who helped him found his own orchestra, the Paris Philharmonic, in 1935. In 1938 he became conductor of the Paris Conservatory Orchestra, remaining its head throughout World War II (turning over most of his salary to the anti-Nazi Resistance movement, and allowing his house to be used as a secret "underground railway" station). He was conductor of the Boston Symphony Orchestra from 1948 to 1962, retiring after a series of heart attacks. In 1967 he agreed to help launch the new Orchestre de Paris, and was leading it on a U.S. tour when he died. He was best known as an exciting, colorful master of Ravel, Berlioz, and Honegger, and as a conductor who sometimes sacrificed details for overall effect but whose rhythmic and coloristic flair has rarely been equaled in this century.

Recommended recordings: Ravel *Daphnis et Chloé*, complete (RCA Red Seal stereo disc LSC-2568). Berlioz Overtures (RCA Red Seal stereo disc LSC-2438; cartridge R8S-5050).

RICCARDO MUTI
(pronounced: *mooh*-tee)

Conductor. Born July 28, 1941, in Naples, Italy. He won first prize in the Guido Cantelli International Competition in 1967. This led to engagements with the Vienna Philharmonic and Berlin Philharmonic, and then with the major orchestras of London, Amsterdam, and Prague, as well as Milan's La Scala and the Salzburg Festival. In 1972 he made his U.S. debut with the Philadelphia Orchestra, and it was such a success that he was promptly invited back for the two subsequent seasons. In 1973 he conducted the Boston Symphony at Tanglewood and the Chicago Symphony at Ravinia. That same year, as his reputation as an exciting, imaginative young conductor soared, he was named Principal Conductor of the New Philharmonia Orchestra of London, following the death of Klemperer.

Recommended recording: Cherubini Requiem (recorded in England in 1973, and scheduled for release in the U.S. by Angel in 1974).

BIRGIT NILSSON
(pronounced: *neel*-suhn)

Soprano. Born May 17, 1918, in Karup, Sweden. After studying at the Royal Academy of Music in Stockholm, she made her debut with the Stockholm Royal Opera in 1947. The following year she was invited to appear at the Glyndebourne Festival. In 1953 she joined the Vienna State Opera, and in 1954 scored a triumph at Bayreuth (as Elsa in *Lohengrin*). She made her American debut with the San Francisco Opera in 1956 (as Brünnhilde in *Die Walküre*), and joined the Metropolitan Opera three years later. Her powerful, clear soprano has made her the most successful Wagnerian soprano of her generation, but she has continued (unlike her great Wagnerian predecessors, Flagstad and Traubel) to sing non-Wagnerian roles regularly.

Recommended recordings: Final Scenes from *Salome* and *Götterdämmerung* (London stereo disc OS-25991). Wagner *Tristan und Isolde* (Deutsche Grammophon stereo 5-disc set 2713001, complete; stereo disc 136433 or cartridge 922-029, highlights).

GARRICK OHLSSON
(pronounced: *ohl*-son)

Pianist. Born April 3, 1948, in White Plains, New York. He began piano studies at the age of eight, later studying at Juilliard in New York with Rosina Lhevinne. In a four year period between 1967 and 1971 he won three major international piano competitions: Italy's Busoni Prize, Montreal's International Piano Competition, and Warsaw's International Chopin Competition (he was the first American ever to win the latter). Engagements with leading American orchestras soon followed, and he quickly established himself as a deeply lyrical, probingly expressive young pianist.

Recommended recordings: Chopin Etudes, complete (Angel stereo 2-disc set SB-3794). Garrick Ohlsson Plays Chopin (Warsaw prize-winning performances) (Connoisseur Society stereo discs CS-2029/30).

DAVID OISTRAKH
(pronounced: *oy*-strahk)

Violinist. Born in 1908, in Odessa, Russia. He made his first public appearance at the age of twelve. In 1937 he won first prize in the Ysaye Competition at Brussels, and established his international reputation. Since 1947 he has also been a professor at the Tchaikovsky Conservatory at Moscow, and during the 1950's he became an active conductor as well as a violinist. His son Igor (born in 1931) is also a gifted violinist, and they occasionally perform together. He is internationally admired as a warm, vibrant, intensely lyrical violinist with a full, rich sound, and at his best in 19th- and early 20th-century Russian music.

Recommended recordings: Tchaikovsky Violin Concerto (Odyssey stereo disc Y-30312). Shostakovich Violin Concerto (Angel stereo disc S-36964).

EUGENE ORMANDY

(pronounced: *ohr*-man-dee)

Conductor. Born November 18, 1899, in Budapest, Hungary. At five and a half he was the youngest pupil of Budapest's Royal Academy of Music; he graduated at fourteen. He came to the U.S. in 1921 and became a citizen in 1927. First he was a violinist, then concertmaster, then conductor of Broadway's Capitol Theatre orchestra (1922–28). In 1931 he substituted for Arturo Toscanini as conductor of the Philadelphia Orchestra—and his symphonic career was on its way. From 1931 to 1936 he was conductor of the Minneapolis Symphony, and then in 1936 he became music director of the Philadelphia Orchestra, a post he still holds. One of America's most popular conductors, he is highly regarded as a colorful, polished, highly virtuoso conductor, at his best with the music of Rachmaninoff, Sibelius, Strauss, Brahms, and most Romantics.

Recommended recordings: Mahler-Cooke Symphony No. 10 (Columbia stereo disc M2S-735). Glière Symphony No. 3, "Ilya Murometz" (RCA Red Seal stereo disc LSC-3246).

SEIJI OZAWA

(pronounced: *oh*-zah-wah)

Conductor. Born September 1, 1935, in Hoten, Manchuria, of Japanese parents. After study at the Toho School of Music in Tokyo, he won the 1959 International Competition of Orchestra Conductors at Besançon, France. Charles Munch, one of the Besançon judges, invited him to study at Tanglewood. Later he became an assistant to Herbert von Karajan in Europe and to Leonard Bernstein in New York. He rose rapidly to become the first successful Japanese conductor in America. In 1964 he became music director of the Chicago Symphony's Ravinia Park summer concerts, and then of the Toronto Symphony (1964–68). In 1970 he became music director of the San Francisco Symphony and of the Boston Symphony's summer music festival at Tanglewood. In 1973 he became music director of the Boston Symphony, while continuing to hold his San Francisco post. He is highly regarded as one of the most kinetic conductors of his generation, usually at his best in late 19th- and 20th-century works.

Recommended recordings: Orff *Carmina Burana* (RCA Red Seal stereo disc LSC-3161; cartridge R8S-1161). Berlioz *Symphonie Fantastique* (Deutsche Grammophon stereo disc 2530358).

LUCIANO PAVAROTTI

(pronounced: pah-vah-*roht*-tee)

Tenor. Born October 12, 1935, in Modena, Italy. He began taking singing lessons at the age of four. In 1964 he made his debut at Milan's La Scala (as Rodolfo in Puccini's *La Bohème*) under Karajan's direction, and became an international star. Two years later he created a sensation at London's Covent Garden when, in a production of Donizetti's *Daughter of the Regiment* with Joan Sutherland, he became the first tenor in more than a century to sing "Tonio's" famous first-act aria and *cabaletta* in its original key, hitting every one of its string of high C's. In 1968 he made his Metropolitan Opera debut, and has since become one of its most popular stars, much admired for the brilliance and range of his lyric tenor and for the warmth and intelligence of his acting.

Recommended recordings: Puccini *La Bohème* (London stereo 2-disc set OSA-1299, complete). Donizetti *Daughter of the Regiment* (*complete*—London stereo 2-disc set 1273; cassette D-31143; or *highlights*—London stereo disc OS-26204; cassette M-311209).

ITZHAK PERLMAN

(pronounced: *perl*-man)

Violinist. Born August 31, 1945, in Tel Aviv, Israel (then Palestine), the son of Polish refugees who had settled in Palestine in the mid-1930's. He was stricken with polio at the age of four, and still walks with the aid of metal crutches, and plays sitting down. He came to the U.S. in 1958 to study at Juilliard in New York. He won the Leventritt Award in 1964, and has since gone on to become one of the most popular of the younger generation of violinists. He is especially noted for his warm, strong, singing tone.

Recommended recordings: Sibelius Violin Concerto and Prokofiev Violin Concerto No. 2 (RCA Red Seal disc LSC-2962). Wieniawski Violin Concertos Nos. 1 and 2 (Angel stereo disc S-36903).

ANDRÉ PREVIN

(pronounced: *preh*-vihn)

Conductor and pianist. Born April 6, 1929, in Berlin, Germany. After early study in both Berlin and Paris, he came to the U.S. in 1938, later becoming a U.S. citizen. From 1950 to 1959 he worked for the Metro-Goldwyn-Mayer film studios in Hollywood as an arranger and conductor, later free-lancing for other studios. He won several Academy Awards for his film work (*Gigi*, *My Fair Lady*, *Irma la Douce*). During this period he was also active as a jazz pianist, mainly on the West Coast. In 1966 he decided to concentrate on a symphonic career, and became music director of the Houston Symphony. Controversy over his private life led to his resignation. Since 1968 he has been principal conductor of the London Symphony Orchestra. In recent years he has succeeded in playing down his jazz and movie-music image, and is widely respected for his perceptive, restrained, lyrical performances of late Romantic and early 20th-century orchestral works. He is married to film star Mia Farrow.

Recommended recordings: Prokofiev *Romeo and Juliet*, complete (Angel stereo 3-disc set S-3802). Vaughan Williams "Sea" Symphony (RCA Red Seal stereo disc LSC-3170).

LEONTYNE PRICE

Soprano. Born February 10, 1927, in Laurel, Mississippi. Her father was a sawmill worker and carpenter, her mother a midwife (who "delivered more babies than necessary so I could have music lessons"). A wealthy Laurel family, the Alexander Chisholms, helped put her through Juilliard in New York. Virgil Thomson heard her in a student production, and cast her in a Broadway revival of his opera *Four Saints in Three Acts* in 1951. The following year she scored a triumph as Bess in a production of Gershwin's *Porgy and Bess* that toured Europe under U.S. State Department auspices, and later toured the U.S. In 1955 she sang the title role in an NBC-TV production of Puccini's *Tosca*, the first black to perform a major operatic role in a nationwide telecast. Two years later she made her debut with the San Francisco Opera, and appeared with the Vienna State Opera. She joined the Metropolitan Opera in 1961. She has since established herself as one of the most popular and critically praised sopranos of her time, admired for her creamily beautiful, vibrant, rich-sounding voice, and generally at her best in the music of Verdi, Puccini, and Richard Strauss. In 1966 she sang one of the title roles in Barber's *Antony and Cleopatra*, written especially for her, to open the new Metropolitan Opera House in New York's Lincoln Center.

Recommended recordings: Verdi *Aïda* (London stereo 3-disc set 1393; cassette D-31164). *Puccini Heroines* (RCA Red Seal stereo disc LSC-3337).

FRITZ REINER

(pronounced: *rye*-ner)

Conductor. Born December 19, 1888, in Budapest, Hungary. Died November 15, 1963, in Weston, Connecticut. After graduating from Budapest's Royal Academy of Music (where Bartók was one of his teachers), he conducted at the Budapest Opera (1911–14) and the Dresden Opera (1914–1921). He came to the U.S. in 1921, and became a U.S. citizen in 1928. He was conductor of the Cincinnati Symphony (1922–31), the Pittsburgh Symphony (1938–48), and the Chicago Symphony (1953–63), raising each of them to significantly high levels of performance and prestige. For many years during the 1930's and 1940's, he headed the orchestra and opera departments at the Curtis Institute of Music in Philadelphia, and later was a leading conductor at the Metropolitan Opera in New York. He had a reputation as a demanding orchestral taskmaster, noted for his incisive, dramatic performances of a broad repertory from Mozart to Bartók.

Recommended Recordings: Beethoven Symphony No. 6, "Pastoral" (RCA Red Seal stereo disc LSC-2614; cassette RK-1094; cartridge R8S-1094). Strauss *Don Quixote* and *Der Rosenkavalier* Waltzes (RCA Victrola stereo disc VICS-1561).

173

Fritz Reiner

171

André Previn

174

Ruggiero Ricci

176

Artur Rodzinski

172

Leontyne Price

175

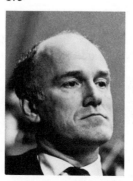

Sviatoslav Richter

177

Mstislav Rostropovich

180

Thomas Schippers

178

Gennady Rozhdestvensky

181

Elisabeth Schwarzkopf

183

Rudolf Serkin

179

Artur Rubinstein

184

Beverly Sills

182

Peter Serkin

RUGGIERO RICCI

(pronounced: *ree*-chee)

Violinist. Born July 24, 1920, in California. He made his recital debut in San Francisco at the age of eight, and has since performed regularly throughout the U.S. and Europe. A dynamic, frequently virtuosoistic performer, he has specialized in recent years in rarely performed early music and in contemporary works.

Recommended recordings: Sarasate *Danzas españolas* and other works (Decca stereo disc 710044). *Virtuoso Showpieces* (London Stereo Treasury disc STS-15049).

SVIATOSLAV RICHTER

(pronounced: *rihkh*-ter)

Pianist. Born in 1915, in Zhitomir, the Ukraine. He started as an assistant conductor with the Odessa Ballet in 1930, and did not begin formal piano training until 1937. Eight years later he won first prize in the U.S.S.R. Competition of Executant Musicians as a pianist. He made his first appearances in Western countries in 1960, although his reputation as Russia's finest pianist had preceded him through recordings. He ranks today as one of the century's greatest pianists—a dynamic, subtle, and lyrically expressive performer, called by one critic "the perfect amalgamation of sound, rhythm, and technique." He is married to singer Nina Doloyak.

Recommended recordings: Mussorgsky *Pictures at an Exhibition* (Odyssey stereo disc Y-32223). Prokofiev Piano Concerto No. 5 and Mozart Piano Concerto No. 20 (Deutsche Grammophon stereo disc 138075; cassette 3300-021).

ARTUR RODZINSKI

(pronounced: rud-*jihn*-skee)

Conductor. Born January 2, 1894, in Spaleto on the Dalmatian coast (now part of Yugoslavia). Died November 27, 1958, in Boston. Under family pressure, he began studying law in Vienna, then switched to music. In the early 1920's he was a conductor at the Warsaw Opera; there he was seen by Leopold Stokowski, who invited him to be his assistant with the Philadelphia Orchestra in 1924. He was later conductor of the Los Angeles Philharmonic (1928–32), the Cleveland Orchestra (1933–43), the New York Philharmonic (1943–46), and the Chicago Symphony (1946–47). He helped organize and train the NBC Symphony for Toscanini in 1937, and was widely regarded as one of the century's master orchestra builders. He spent the final decade of his life conducting in Italy and England, and died just after a sensational return to Chicago conducting *Tristan und Isolde* in 1958.

Recommended recordings: Rimsky-Korsakov Russian Easter Overture, plus works by Glinka, Mussorgsky, Tchaikovsky (Seraphim stereo disc S-60074). Wagner *Die Walküre*, excerpts, with Traubel (Odyssey 2-disc set 32260018, *mono only*).

MSTISLAV ROSTROPOVICH

(pronounced: rah-strah-*poe*-vitch)

Cellist. Born August 12, 1927, in Baku, U.S.S.R. He made his recital debut at the age of eight. Later he studied at the Moscow Conservatory, and has been a member of its faculty since 1953. In the late 1940's he was first cellist in the Moscow Philharmonic, before embarking on a solo career. In the 1960's he was a frequent visitor to the U.S., but in 1971 he was temporarily denied permission to leave the Soviet Union because of his defense of Soviet author Solzhenitsyn and other critics of Soviet artistic controls. He is married to soprano Galina Vishnevskaya.

Recommended recordings: Dvořák Cello Concerto (Deutsche Grammophon stereo disc 139044; cassette 923-098; cartridge 89-044). Shostakovich Cello Concerto (Columbia stereo disc MS-6124).

GENNADY ROZHDESTVENSKY
(pronounced: rohj-*dest*-vyen-skee)

Conductor. Born in 1931 in Moscow. He began studying the piano at the age of eight. He entered the Moscow State Conservatory in 1949, and while there conducted the student orchestra. In 1951 he won a competition to be assistant conductor of the Bolshoi Theatre. The following year he became full conductor, leading performances of both ballet and opera. Beginning in 1952 he also guest-conducted the Leningrad Philharmonic and other orchestras in the Soviet Union and Eastern Europe. During the 1960's he was principal conductor of both the Bolshoi Ballet and the Moscow Radio Symphony Orchestra. He gave up the ballet post in 1970 to concentrate on symphonic conducting. He has conducted in the U.S. on several tours of the Bolshoi Ballet and on the 1962 and 1973 tours of the Leningrad Philharmonic. He ranks today as the foremost Soviet conductor of his generation, and is much admired internationally for the rhythmic suppleness and lyrical qualities of his performances. In 1974 he became conductor of the Stockholm Philharmonic—the first Soviet conductor to be allowed to accept a post in a Western country.

Recommended recordings: Prokofiev *Cinderella* (*complete*—Melodiya/Angel stereo 2-disc set S-4102; *highlights*—Melodiya/Angel stereo disc S-40138; cassette 4XS-40138). Bizet–Shchedrin *Carmen Ballet* (Melodiya/Angel stereo disc S-40067; cassette 4XS-40067; cartridge 8XS-40067).

ARTUR RUBINSTEIN
(pronounced: *roo*-bihn-styn)

Pianist. Born January 28, 1889, in Warsaw, Poland. He studied in Warsaw and Berlin, including study of the violin under Joachim in Berlin. He made his debut as a pianist in Warsaw at the age of six, and performed as a soloist with the Berlin Philharmonic at thirteen. His first U.S. concert was in 1906, with the Philadelphia Orchestra. He has lived in the U.S. since the 1930's, and became a U.S. citizen in the 1940's. Since 1950, he has been probably the most popular and most respected pianist in the U.S., particularly admired for his youthful vigor and remarkably sustained abilities as he entered his 80's. He has remained a performer in the "grand" tradition—a colorful, frequently exciting, powerfully elegant interpreter of the Classical and Romantic standards, particularly Chopin.

Recommended recordings: The World's Favorite Chopin (RCA Red Seal stereo disc

LSC-3322; cassette RK-1302; cartridge R8S-1302). Beethoven Piano Concerto No. 4 (RCA Red Seal stereo disc LSC-2848).

THOMAS SCHIPPERS
(pronounced: *ship*-pers)

Conductor. Born March 9, 1930, in Kalamazoo, Michigan. He won a national contest to conduct the Philadelphia Orchestra in a youth concert in 1947. A year later he was a conductor of the Lemonade Opera in New York, and in 1949 took over as conductor of Menotti's *The Consul* on Broadway when the regular conductor became ill. In the 1950's he conducted other Menotti operas (*Amahl and the Night Visitors* on NBC-TV, *The Saint of Bleeker Street* on Broadway), and became a conductor at the New York City Opera and at La Scala. He was also one of the founders, with Menotti, of the Spoleto Festival in Italy. Since 1970 he has been conductor of the Cincinnati Symphony Orchestra.

Recommended recordings: Prokofiev *Alexander Nevsky* Cantata (Odyssey stereo disc Y-31014). Barber *Medea's Dance of Vengeance* and other works (Columbia stereo disc 32110006).

ELISABETH SCHWARZKOPF
(pronounced: *shvahrts*-kawpf)

Soprano. Born December 9, 1915, in Poznan, Poland, of German parents. As a teenager she lived in England for a year as a League of Nations exchange student. At seventeen she entered the Berlin High School for Music, and made her opera debut the following year with the Berlin State Opera in a minor role (in *Parsifal*). She continued to sing minor roles with the company until 1942, when she joined the Vienna State Opera as a leading singer. She also gave her first *lieder* recital in Vienna in 1942. At the end of World War II, she was barred from performing because of reputedly close associations with some of the former leaders of Nazi Germany. Following her marriage in 1947 to British recording executive Walter Legge, she resumed her career, scoring major triumphs at Milan's La Scala Opera and the Vienna State Opera. She overcame antagonisms resulting from her alleged wartime activities and became increasingly admired for the sheer beauty of her voice and the depth and sensitivity of her interpretations—especially in German opera and *lieder*. In 1953 she made her U.S. debut in a New York *lieder* recital, and in 1955 her U.S. operatic debut with the San Francisco Opera as the Marschallin in *Der Rosenkavalier*. That role was to become her most famous over the next decade, and she filmed it in 1960. In recent years she has concentrated mostly on *lieder* recitals. One of the great singers of this century, as well as a woman of almost classical beauty, she is most admired for her finely spun, patrician, and elegant interpretations of Mozart and Strauss.

Recommended recordings: Strauss *Four Last Songs* and other songs (Angel stereo disc S-36347; cartridge 8XS-36347). Strauss *Der Rosenkavalier* (*complete*—Angel stereo 4-disc set S-3563; *highlights*—Angel stereo disc S-35645).

PETER SERKIN
(pronounced: *sir*-kihn)

Pianist. Born July 24, 1947, in New York City. He is the son of pianist Rudolf Serkin, and studied at the Curtis Institute in Philadelphia (1958–64). As a teenager, he attracted favorable attention for his performances in chamber and solo works at his father's Marlboro Festival in Vermont. He made his New York recital debut in 1959, and since then has concertized extensively in the U.S., Europe, and Japan. During the late 1960's he acquired a reputation as a young maverick because of his "hip" attire and attitudes, but his reputation as a thoughtful and versatile musician has also grown steadily.

Recommended recordings: Mozart Sonata in F and other works (RCA Red Seal stereo 2-disc set LSC-7062). Beethoven Violin Concerto, piano version (RCA Red Seal stereo disc LSC-3152).

RUDOLF SERKIN

(pronounced: *sir*-kihn)

Pianist. Born March 28, 1903, in Eger, Bohemia. He made his debut at the age of twelve with the Vienna State Symphony. Later he studied composition in Vienna with Arnold Schoenberg. He performed throughout Europe in the 1920's and 1930's, making his U.S. debut in 1933. He soon acquired a major reputation as an intense, nervous, powerful interpreter of the Classical and Romantic repertory. In 1936 he married the daughter of violinist Adolph Busch (with whom he had frequently appeared in chamber recitals); their six children include pianist Peter Serkin. For many years he headed the piano department at the Curtis Institute, and he has been the director of the Marlboro Festival in Vermont since the 1960's.

Recommended recordings: Beethoven Piano Concerto No. 5, "Emperor" (Columbia stereo disc M-31807; cassette MT-31807; cartridge MA-31807). Brahms Piano Concerto No. 1 (Columbia stereo disc MS-7143).

BEVERLY SILLS

Soprano. Born May 25, 1929, in Brooklyn, New York. As a child, she started imitating Galli-Curci recordings in her mother's collection, and knew twenty-three arias by heart by the time she was seven. She became a child singing star on radio (known first as Bubbles Silverman, then after age nine as Beverly Sills), and even played a dramatic role in a radio soap opera (*Our Gal Sunday*) for several years. In 1945, after she was graduated from high school, she toured the U.S. in various operettas. In 1953 she became a member of the San Francisco Opera, then in 1955 of the New York City Opera. She has remained with the latter company since then, rising to become its major star. Since 1960 she has also sung at Milan's La Scala, the Vienna State Opera, and London's Covent Garden, where she has been hailed as America's leading *diva*. After having reportedly turned down offers to sing at the Metropolitan Opera for a number of years (partly because of the roles she was offered), she agreed to sing there in 1974 for the first time.

Recommended recordings: Donizetti *Maria Stuarda* (ABC stereo 3-disc set ATS-20010). Handel *Julius Caesar* (RCA Red Seal 3-disc stereo set LSC-6182, *complete*; LSC-3116, *highlights*).

STANISLAW SKROWACZEWSKI
(pronounced: skroh-vah-*chehv*-skee)

Conductor. Born October 3, 1923, in Lwow, Poland. He began composing at the age of seven, and his First Symphony was performed by the Lwow Philharmonic in 1931. Later he became conductor of the Wroclaw Philharmonic (1946–47), the Katowice National Philharmonic (1949–54), the Krakow Philharmonic (1955–56), and the Warsaw Philharmonic (1957–59). He was invited to the U.S. to conduct the Cleveland Orchestra by George Szell in 1959, and the following year became conductor of the Minneapolis Symphony (renamed the Minnesota Orchestra in 1968), a post he still holds. He is best known for his incisive, elegant, rhythmically vibrant performances of Classical and Neoclassical composers.

Recommended recordings: Prokofiev *Romeo and Juliet* Suites (Mercury stereo disc SR-90315). Skrowaczewski Concerto for English Horn and Orchestra (Desto stereo disc 7126).

ALEKSANDER SLOBODYANIK
(pronounced: sloh-boh-*dyah*-nihk)

Pianist. Born 1944 in Kiev, the Ukraine. He entered the Central Music School in Moscow at the age of twelve. When he came in seventh in the Warsaw Competition of 1960 (at age sixteen), he gave up practicing and was expelled from the Moscow Conservatory, but was later readmitted. He has a reputation in the U.S.S.R. as a popular youung maverick. Internationally, he is regarded as a sensitive and highly individualistic pianist of uneven technique, at his best up to now in music of a lyrical nature.

Recommended recording: Chopin Etudes, complete (Angel stereo discs S-40204 and S-40205).

SIR GEORG SOLTI
(pronounced: *shohl*-tee)

Conductor. Born October 21, 1912, in Budapest, Hungary. In the late 1930's, he was a conductor at the Budapest Opera, but after the Nazi takeover of Hungary he escaped to Switzerland. In 1942 he won the Geneva International Piano Competition, and considered pursuing a career as a pianist. Then in 1944 he was invited by Ernest Ansermet to be a guest conductor of the Orchestre de la Suisse Romande, and has since devoted himself exclusively to conducting. He has held several posts as an opera conductor: at Munich (1946–51), Frankfurt (1952–60), and London's Covent Garden (1961–70). During this period his international reputation as both an operatic and symphonic conductor rose impressively, primarily due to recordings. Since 1969 he has been music director of the Chicago Symphony Orchestra, and has led it to new heights of national and international prestige. In 1972 he also became director of the Orchestre de Paris (succeeding Karajan). He ranks today as one of the world's foremost conductors, best known for his dramatic, full-blooded performances of Romantic classics, and especially Wagner.

185

Stanislaw Skrowaczewski

186

Aleksander Slobodyanik

187

Sir Georg Solti

188

Hilde Somer

189

Janos Starker

William Steinberg

190

191

Isaac Stern

192

Thomas Stewart

193

Leopold Stokowski

Recommended recordings: Wagner *Der Ring des Nibelungen* (*highlights*—London stereo 4-disc set OSA-1440; his complete *Ring* is also available in a 19-disc special set). Mahler Symphony No. 8 (London stereo 2-disc set CS-1295; cassette J31211DP).

HILDE SOMER

(pronounced: *soh*-mir)

Pianist. Born February 11, 1930, in Vienna, Austria. She made her debut at the age of ten with the Vienna Symphony, followed by engagements in Prague, Budapest, Milan, and Rome. At the age of twelve she made her U.S. debut, playing four concertos with the New York Philharmonic. Two years later she won a scholarship to study at the Curtis Institute with Rudolf Serkin. A warmly expressive, often robust interpreter of a wide range of 19th- and 20th-century music, she has been an active champion of Latin American composers (notably Ginastera) and has been in the forefront of the recent Scriabin revival—often performing his music with light shows.
Recommended recordings: Ginastera Piano Concerto and Piano Sonata (Desto stereo disc 6402). Corigliano Piano Concerto and Strauss *Paragon* (Mercury stereo disc 90517; cassette MCR4-90517; cartridge MC8-90517).

JANOS STARKER

(pronounced: *shtahr*-ker)

Cellist. Born July 5, 1924, in Budapest, Hungary. He studied at the Franz Liszt Academy in Budapest. In 1948 he came to the U.S., and has been an American citizen since 1953. He was a cellist in the Dallas Symphony (1948), the Metropolitan Opera Orchestra (1949–53), and first cellist of the Chicago Symphony (1953–58), before embarking on a solo career. Since 1961 he has also been a member of the faculty of the University of Indiana. He is highly regarded as a darkly lyrical, penetrating interpreter of a broad repertory from Bach to Bartók.
Recommended recordings: Dvořák Cello Concerto (Mercury stereo disc 90303; cassette MCR4-90303; cartridge MC8-90303). Boccherini Cello Concerto in B flat and Haydn Cello Concerto in D (Angel stereo disc S-35725).

WILLIAM STEINBERG

(pronounced: *styne*-berg)

Conductor. Born August 1, 1899, in Cologne, Germany. In the early 1920's he was a conductor at the Cologne Opera, the Prague Opera, and the Berlin Opera. He left Germany after the Nazi takeover, helping to found the Palestine Symphony (later the Israel Philharmonic). He came to the U.S. in 1938 at the invitation of Arturo Toscanini to be a guest conductor of the NBC Symphony. He has since been conductor of the Buffalo Philharmonic (1945–52), the Pittsburgh Symphony (1952 to date), the Boston Symphony (1968–72); and for several years in the late 1950's he was also principal conductor of the London Philharmonic. He is noted as a solid, forceful conductor of most major 19th-century works.
Recommended recordings: Strauss *Also Sprach Zarathustra* (Deutsche Grammophon

stereo disc 2530160; cassette 3300185; cartridge 890436). Schubert Symphony No. 9 (RCA Red Seal stereo disc LSC-3115; cassette 4XS-36044; cartridge 8XS-36044).

ISAAC STERN

Violinist. Born July 21, 1920, in Kreminiecz, Russia. He came to the U.S. with his parents in 1921, and was raised in San Francisco. He began piano studies at the age of six, then turned to the violin at eight. His debut took place when he was eleven, with the San Francisco Symphony under Monteux. Six years later he made his New York recital debut, and has since concertized extensively throughout the world. He was "ghost fiddler" for actor John Garfield in the 1946 film *Humoresque*, and appeared in the Sol Hurok film biography *Tonight We Sing*. In recent years he has been as active a performer of chamber music (with the Stern-Istomin-Rose Trio) as he has been a soloist. In the early 1960's he was the leader of the group which fought successfully to block the tearing down of New York's Carnegie Hall (at the time of the building of Lincoln Center), and has since served Carnegie Hall as its president. He ranks today as the century's outstanding American-trained violinist, and is best known for his evenness of tone and his warm, vibrant interpretations of Romantic works.

Recommended recordings: Beethoven Violin Concerto (Columbia stereo disc M-31805; cassette MT-31805). Barber Violin Concerto (Columbia stereo disc MS-6713).

THOMAS STEWART

Baritone. Born August 29, 1928, in San Saba, Texas. He originally studied to be an electrical engineer at Baylor University, then switched to music. At Juilliard in New York he met and married soprano Evelyn Lear. After one season with the New York City Opera and appearances opposite Maria Callas in *Lucia di Lammermoor* in Chicago, he sang in a touring nightclub production of *Kiss Me Kate*. Despairing of finding major operatic work in the U.S., he and his wife went to Germany in 1957, where he was promptly signed by the West Berlin Deutsche Oper. He made his debut at Bayreuth in 1960. He returned to the U.S. in 1966 to sing with the Metropolitan Opera, and has since become one of its leading baritones, while continuing to perform in the major opera houses of Europe as well.

Recommended recordings: Wagner *The Flying Dutchman* (*Der fliegende Holländer*) (Deutsche Grammophon 3-disc set 2709040). Ives *American Scenes, American Poets*, with Lear (Columbia stereo disc M-30229).

LEOPOLD STOKOWSKI
(pronounced: stoh-*kawf*-skee)

Conductor. Born April 18, 1882, in London, England. Originally an organist as well as a conductor. He came to the U.S. in the early 1900's, and became a U.S. citizen in 1915. He was conductor of the Cincinnati Symphony (1909–12), the Philadelphia Orchestra (1912–36), the All-American Youth Orchestra (1940–42), the New York City Symphony (1944–45), the Hollywood Bowl Symphony (1945–47), and the American Symphony Orchestra (1962–72). He is most famous for having built the Philadelphia Orchestra into one of the world's greatest orchestras, and for his introduction of much major new music to the U.S.—a record challenged only by Serge Koussevitzky. He conducted the music for Walt Disney's *Fantasia* (1941) and several other films, and has long been active in improving the sound qualities of recordings. He has sometimes been criticized for being perhaps too much of a showman, but is universally recognized as one of the century's great masters of orchestral color and dramatic effect—usually at his best in 19th-century and early 20th-century music, and at his most controversial in his own Romantic transcriptions of Bach and other early composers.

Recommended recordings: Stokowski's Greatest Hits (RCA Red Seal 2-disc set VCS-7077; cassette RK-5072; cartridge R8S-5072). Messiaen *The Ascension* and Ives Orchestral Set No. 2 (London stereo disc SPC-21060).

JOAN SUTHERLAND

Soprano. Born November 7, 1929, in Sydney, Australia. She worked as a secretary to pay her way through the Sydney Conservatory, where she made her operatic debut in 1950 in a Conservatory production of Goossens' *Judith.* In 1952 she joined London's Covent Garden, singing minor roles for several years. In London she married conductor Richard Bonynge, whom she had known in Australia. He coached her in *bel canto* singing, which he believed more appropriate to her voice than the dramatic soprano roles she had been singing. In 1958 she scored a triumph at Covent Garden in Donizetti's *Lucia di Lammermoor* and Handel's *Samson.* Since then she has specialized in the Italian lyric and coloratura repertory. She made her U.S. debut in 1961 in a New York concert performance of Bellini's rarely performed *Beatrice di Tenda,* and joined the Metropolitan Opera several months later. She also sings regularly with the Paris Opera and Milan's La Scala. She ranks as one of the era's most exciting, remarkably agile sopranos, with a more "weighty" sound than the usual coloratura, particularly noted for her performances of what she has called "the demented dames" of the Bellini, Donizetti, and Rossini repertory.

Recommended recordings: Bellini *Norma* (London stereo 3-disc set OSA-1394; cassette D-31168—*complete;* or London stereo disc OS-26168; cassette M-31178—*duets only,* with Horne). Sutherland's Greatest Hits (London stereo disc OS-26348).

GEORGE SZELL

(pronounced: *sehl*)

Conductor. Born June 7, 1897, in Budapest, Hungary. Died July 30, 1970, in Cleveland, Ohio. Originally a pianist, he made his debut playing a Mozart concerto with the Vienna Symphony at the age of ten. At eighteen he was an assistant conductor at the Berlin Opera, then a conductor of the Berlin Broadcasting Symphony (1924–29) and principal conductor of the Prague German Opera (1929–38). Just before World War II, he came to the U.S., spending his first years as a teacher and writing orchestral transcriptions for a publisher. In 1941 he joined the conducting staff of the Metropolitan Opera, and after 1945 was a frequent guest conductor of the New York Philharmonic. From 1946 until his death, he was conductor of the Cleveland Orchestra, building it into one of the world's finest orchestras. He was admired as an exceptionally precise, rhythmically incisive if often unemotional conductor, with an incredible ear for balance, and at his best in the late 18th- and 19th-century repertory.

Recommended recordings: Schubert Symphony No. 9 (Odyssey stereo disc Y-30669). Dvořák Slavonic Dances (Columbia stereo disc MS-7208; cartridge 18-11-0098).

RENATA TEBALDI
(pronounced: teh-*bahl*-dee)

Soprano. Born February 1, 1922, in Pesaro, Italy. She first studied piano at the Pesaro conservatory, then switched to voice at the Boito Conservatory at Parma. She made her opera debut in 1944 in a minor role in Boito's *Mefistofele* at Roviogo. When Toscanini returned to Milan at the end of World War II to prepare for the 1946 reopening of La Scala, he auditioned Tebaldi and chose her for his opening concerts. She remained a principal singer at La Scala until 1954. Her U.S. debut took place in San Francisco in 1950 (as *Aïda*). In 1955 she joined New York's Metropolitan Opera, where she soon became—and has remained—one of its most popular stars. She is most admired for the silken beauty of her voice and for her lyrically elegant interpretations of Verdi and Puccini heroines. In the late 1950's she recorded the soundtrack for a film version of *Aïda* starring Sophia Loren.

Recommended recordings: Puccini *Suor Angelica* (London stereo disc OS-1152). Tebaldi's Greatest Hits (London stereo disc OS-26348).

MICHAEL TILSON THOMAS

Conductor. Born December 21, 1944, in Hollywood, California. He is the son of Hollywood film writer and director Ted Thomas, and a grandson of the Thomashefskys of New York's Yiddish Theatre. He studied at the University of Southern California and at Tanglewood. He was assistant to Pierre Boulez during the 1966 Bayreuth Festival and 1967 Ojai (California) Festival, and for several years led a youth orchestra in Los Angeles. In 1969, a few weeks after he became assistant conductor of the Boston Symphony, he made a dramatic, mid-concert substitution for William Steinberg, who was ill, and conducted more than thirty subsequent concerts in the months before Steinberg's recovery. In 1971 he became music director of the Buffalo Philharmonic, and in 1972 principal guest conductor of the Boston Symphony. In 1972 he also succeeded Leonard Bernstein as director of the New York Philharmonic's popular, televised Young People's Concerts. He is regarded as one of today's most exciting young conductors, most noted for his colorful, emotionally impassioned performances of the late Romantics and his intellectually probing performances of early music and avant-garde works.

Recommended recordings: Tchaikovsky Symphony No. 1, "Winter Dreams" (Deutsche Grammophon stereo disc 2530078; cassette 3300-107; cartridge 89430). Ives *Three Places in New England* and Ruggles *Sun-Treader* (Deutsche Grammophon stereo disc 2530048; cassette 3300-017).

ARTURO TOSCANINI
(pronounced: taw-skah-*nee*-nee)

Conductor. Born March 25, 1867, in Parma, Italy. Died January 16, 1957, in New

196

Renata Tebaldi

194

Joan Sutherland

197

Michael Tilson Thomas

199

Helen Traubel

195

George Szell

200

Richard Tucker

198

Arturo Toscanini

York. A cellist in a touring Italian opera company, Toscanini made a last-minute substitution for an ill conductor in Rio de Janeiro on June 15, 1886—and remained a conductor ever after. Before World War I, he was active at Milan's La Scala and New York's Metropolitan Opera, and from 1928 to 1936 was music director of the New York Philharmonic. In 1937 the NBC Symphony was organized for him, and he remained its conductor until his retirement in 1954. For most of the first half of this century, he was the most famous and most widely respected conductor in the world. His insistence on being faithful to the letter as well as the spirit of a musical score significantly influenced performance standards away from the more individualistic interpretations of previous generations. He was noted for his incisive, penetrating, exciting performances of Classical and Romantic works, especially Beethoven, Brahms, Wagner, Rossini, Verdi, Puccini, and Respighi.

Recommended recordings: Beethoven Symphony No. 9 (RCA Victrola disc VIC-1607, *mono only*). Boito *Mefistofele* Prologue and Berlioz *Romeo and Juliet* excerpts (RCA Victrola VIC-1398, *mono only*).

HELEN TRAUBEL

(pronounced: *trow*-behl)

Soprano. Born June 20, 1903, in St. Louis, Missouri. Died July 31, 1972, in Santa Monica, California. She began voice studies at the age of thirteen, and made her debut at sixteen with the St. Louis Symphony. She turned down a contract from the Metropolitan Opera in 1926, feeling she was not yet ready. She continued her studies, singing regularly on NBC radio and in churches and synagogues. In 1937 she made her Met debut in the premiere performance of Walter Damrosch's *The Man Without a Country.* She sang her first Wagnerian role with the Met in 1939, and was soon acclaimed as the first great American Wagnerian soprano, especially after a series of broadcasts with Toscanini in 1941. She was particularly admired for the warmth and opulence of her voice as well as its power. In 1953 she left the Met following a disagreement with then-manager Rudolf Bing over her performances in nightclubs and on television. She went on to become a popular TV and film performer, and in 1955 starred on Broadway in Rodgers and Hammerstein's *Pipe Dream.* She retired in the 1960's.

Recommended recordings: Wagner *Götterdämmerung*, excerpts, with Toscanini (RCA Victrola disc VIC-1369). *Wagner Die Walküre*, excerpts (Odyssey 2-disc set 32260018, *mono only*).

RICHARD TUCKER

Tenor. Born August 28, 1913, in Brooklyn, New York. He began his career as a cantor at the Brooklyn Jewish Center, and as a radio singer on the Chicago Theatre of the Air. His Metropolitan Opera debut took place in 1945, and he has remained one of the company's leading and most popular tenors ever since—noted for his brilliantly rich-voiced, passionately expressive performances in the operas of Verdi, Puccini, and Mascagni. He has also sung at Milan's La Scala, the Vienna State Opera, and London's Covent Garden with great success.

Recommended recordings: *Celeste Aïda—The World's Favorite Tenor Arias* (Columbia stereo disc MS-6957). Puccini *La Bohème* (RCA Red Seal stereo 2-disc set LSC-6095—*complete;* or RCA Red Seal stereo disc LSC-2655; cassette RK-1077; cartridge R8S-1077—*highlights*).

TAMAS VASARY
(pronounced: vah-*shah*-ree)

Pianist. Born April 11, 1933, in Hungary. He studied at the Franz Liszt Academy in Budapest with Kodály and Hernandi. He was winner of international competitions in Warsaw and Paris in 1955, in Brussels in 1956, and in Rio de Janeiro in 1957. He left Hungary during the 1956 revolution, settling in Switzerland. A series of 1961 concerts in London established his international reputation. He is now regarded as one of the finest pianists of his generation—a dynamic and poetic interpreter of 19th-century Romantic and early 20th-century music.

Recommended recordings: Chopin Etudes (Deutsche Grammophon stereo disc 136454; cassette 922-021). Vasary Plays Debussy (Deutsche Grammophone stereo disc 139458).

BRUNO WALTER
(pronounced: *vahl*-tir)

Conductor. Born September 15, 1876, in Berlin, Germany. Died February 17, 1962, in Los Angeles, California. He started conducting at the age of seventeen in Cologne, and at twenty joined the Berlin Opera's conducting staff (under his real name, Bruno Schlesinger). In 1911 he became director of the Vienna State Opera, and from 1913 to 1922 he was director of the Munich Opera. During the 1920's he was a guest conductor in Berlin, Leipzig, Salzburg, and New York. In 1933 he left Germany after his concerts were banned by the Nazis as "a threat to public order" (because he was Jewish). He spent the World War II years in America, and from 1946 to 1950 was musical adviser to the New York Philharmonic, an orchestra with which he had been long associated as a guest conductor. He was widely admired for his warm, supple, generally introspective, and often profound interpretations of 19th-century Classical and Romantic works—and especially those of Mahler, with whom he had been a close friend and colleague in the first decade of this century.

Recommended recordings: Mahler Symphony No. 9 (Odyssey stereo 2-disc set Y2-30308). Mahler *Das Lied von der Erde* (The Song of the Earth) (London/Richmond disc R-23182, *mono only*).

LEONARD WARREN
Baritone. Born April 21, 1911, in New York City. Died March 4, 1960, in New York. Originally a singer in the chorus at New York's Radio City Music Hall, he won the Metropolitan Opera Auditions of the Air in 1938, and made his Met debut the following year. He quickly rose to become one of the company's leading baritones. In 1953 he made his debut at Milan's La Scala, and in 1958 toured the Soviet Union as part of the cultural exchange program. He died suddenly of a cerebral hemorrhage on

201

Tamas Vasary

202

Bruno Walter

203

Leonard Warren

204

André Watts

205

Alexis Weissenberg

Earl Wild

206

207

Fritz Wunderlich

208

Pinchas Zukerman

209

Paul Zukofsky

the Metropolitan's stage during a performance of Verdi's *La Forza del Destino*. He remains admired as perhaps the greatest American baritone of the century—a rich-voiced, excitingly dramatic yet subtle singer, at his best in the operas of Verdi, and probably the finest Scarpia of his time in *Tosca*.

Recommended recordings: Puccini *Tosca*, with Milanov, Bjoerling (RCA Victrola stereo 2-disc set VICS-6000; cartridge V8S-1022—complete). Verdi *Rigoletto* (RCA Victor 2-disc set LM-6021, *mono only*).

ANDRÉ WATTS

Pianist. Born June 20, 1946, in Nürnberg, Germany. His father was an American G.I. stationed in Germany, his mother a Hungarian living there as a displaced person after World War II. He made his debut in 1955 at a Philadelphia Orchestra children's concert. After further studies, he made a highly acclaimed last-minute substitution for Glenn Gould, who was ill, at a New York Philharmonic concert under Bernstein in 1963. In the following decade, he developed into one of the most popular of today's young pianists—much admired for the extroverted brilliance of his technique and the probing qualities of his interpretations, particularly with Brahms and other 19th-century composers.

Recommended recordings: Brahms Piano Concerto No. 2 (Columbia stereo disc MS-7134). Liszt Piano Concerto No. 1 and Chopin Piano Concerto No. 2 (Columbia stereo disc MS-6955).

ALEXIS WEISSENBERG
(pronounced: *vy*-sehn-berg)

Pianist. Born July 26, 1929, in Sofia, Bulgaria. As a teenager he spent nine months in a concentration camp following the Nazi takeover of Bulgaria, escaping in 1944 to Turkey and then coming to the U.S. He was graduated from the Juilliard School of Music in New York in 1947—the same year he won the Leventritt Award and made a much-acclaimed concert debut with the New York Philharmonic under Szell. During the early 1950's he toured extensively throughout the U.S. and Europe. But then he decided to retire for a number of years, to reassess the direction of his career and to study further. He finally settled in Paris, where he still lives. In 1967 he resumed an active performing career in both the U.S. and Europe, and immediately won high critical praise for a new maturity in his playing. He is now one of the most popular pianists of his generation, widely admired for his electric, broadly perceptive performances, and for an incredibly fast, clean finger stroke that gives him a distinctive sound.

Recommended recordings: Rachmaninoff Piano Concerto No. 3 (RCA Red Seal stereo disc LSC-3040). Stravinsky *Petrushka* Suite (Swedish Odeon stereo disc ALP-C8).

EARL WILD

Pianist. Born November 26, 1918, in Pittsburgh, Pennsylvania. As a teenager, Wild was engaged by Toscanini to play Gershwin's *Rhapsody in Blue* with the NBC

Symphony. For many years in the 1940's he was "house pianist" at NBC in New York, participating in many radio and television shows. In the 1960's he was in the forefront of the revival of Romantic piano music, performing long-neglected works by Liszt, Scharwenka, Paderewski, and others. He has also been a soloist for the premieres of piano concertos by Paul Creston and Marvin David Levy. He is noted as a pianist with a fantastic technique, capable of enormous velocity and virtuosity. He has also composed ballet and orchestral music, and his Easter oratorio, *Revelations*, was presented by the American Broadcasting Company in 1962 and again in 1964.

Recommended recordings: Scharwenka Piano Concerto (RCA Red Seal stereo disc LSC-3080). *The Daemonic Liszt* (Vanguard stereo disc C-10041).

FRITZ WUNDERLICH
(pronounced: *vun*-dir-lihkh)

Tenor. Born September 26, 1930, in Kusel, Germany. Died September 17, 1966, in Heidelberg, Germany. As a teenager he played in a student dance band, occasionally singing operetta or popular songs with the band. He won a scholarship to study at the Freiburg Conservatory, and in 1955 sang Tamino in a student production of Mozart's *The Magic Flute*. Later that same year he was called on to substitute in the same role with the Württemberg State Opera in Stuttgart, with great success. He then sang at Salzburg and at the Bavarian State Opera at Munich. He made his debut at London's Covent Garden in 1965, and was scheduled for his debut at New York's Metropolitan Opera in 1966. Three weeks before the latter date, he was killed in a fall down a staircase in Heidelberg. He had an uncommonly bright, brilliant, lyrically fluid tenor, and was especially noted for his Mozart, Haydn, and Bach performances, and for his many recordings of Viennese and German operettas.

Recommended recordings: *Close-Up: Fritz Wunderlich* (Angel stereo 2-disc set SBB-3751). Fritz Wunderlich Operatic Recital (RCA Victrola stereo disc VICS-1235).

PINCHAS ZUKERMAN
(pronounced: *zoo*-ker-mahn)

Violinist. Born July 16, 1948, in Israel. At the age of twelve, he won a scholarship from the American-Israeli Foundation for special studies. Two years later he came to the U.S., on the recommendation of Pablo Casals and Isaac Stern, to study at Juilliard. He substituted for Stern in a 1968–69 series of concerts in the U.S. and Europe, and has since become one of the most popular young soloists of the younger generation. He is highly regarded as a technically brilliant, interpretively expressive violinist with a natural feeling for the big sweeping line of a composition, especially in Beethoven and 19th-century music.

Recommended recordings: Mendelssohn and Tchaikovsky Violin Concertos (Columbia stereo disc MS-7313; cassette 16-11-0162). Vivaldi *The Four Seasons* (Columbia stereo disc M-31798; cassette MT-31798; cartridge MA-31798).

PAUL ZUKOFSKY
(pronounced: zhoo-*kawf*-skee)

Violinist. Born October 22, 1943, in Brooklyn, N.Y. He started playing violin at the age of five, and made his debut at eight with the New Haven Symphony. He received his Master's degree from Juilliard at twenty, his doctorate at twenty-two. He has won awards in more than half a dozen national and international competitions, including the Albert Spaulding prize and the Jacques Thibaud competition. He is widely admired as an adventurous, technically dexterous violinist who can conquer the most complex and difficult of contemporary scores with seemingly astonishing ease. Several scores have been written for and dedicated to him.

Recommended recordings: Penderecki Capriccio for Violin and Orchestra (Nonesuch stereo disc H-71201). Davidovsky Synchronisms No. 2 (CRI stereo disc S-204).

The Top Orchestras

The United States now has more than half of the world's two thousand professional symphony orchestras—and nearly twice as many as all of Europe's nations combined.

Yet numbers are one thing, quality another. And when a person buys a recording, he usually wants it played by "the best." So the great majority of recordings seem to be made by a few dozen major orchestras in both the U.S. and Europe—as they are the ones the record companies believe will sell.

Which are the greatest orchestras? This is how the author sizes them up:

The Top American Five

Philadelphia Orchestra: Tonally the most splendorous, and self-billed as "the world's greatest orchestra"—with some justification. Its lush string tone, in particular, is unequaled. Since 1912, it has had only two regular conductors: Leopold Stokowski (1912–1936) and Eugene Ormandy (1936 to date).

Boston Symphony Orchestra: At its best the most brilliant-sounding and exciting of U.S. orchestras, particularly noted for its tonal transparency and rhythmic crispness. Under Serge Koussevitzky (1924–49), Charles Munch (1949–62), and Erich Leinsdorf (1962–69), it has achieved an outstanding record for introducing new music, and for its polished way with the classics. Present music director: Seiji Ozawa, who (like Leonard Bernstein) is a graduate of the summer school connected with the BSO's Berkshire Festival at Tanglewood, Massachusetts—the nation's oldest and best-known summer music festival. The **Boston Pops Orchestra**, led since 1930 by Arthur Fiedler, is the unique, spirited Spring edition (May–June) of the BSO, playing both standard classics and pop novelties.

Chicago Symphony Orchestra: An orchestra of great brilliance of sound, solidity, and technical precision—although it has had periods of ups and downs over the years. It reached particularly high peaks under Fritz Reiner (1953–63) and has again been restored firmly to the top ranks by its present music director, Georg Solti, who shares the season with Carlo Maria Giulini as principal guest conductor.

New York Philharmonic: Noted for its uncommonly "weighty" or massive sound, which makes it especially impressive in the Germanic repertory (Mahler, Beethoven, etc.), and for its versatility with contemporary music. Its past conductors have included Gustav Mahler (1909–11), Arturo Toscanini (1926–36), Artur Rodzinski (1943–46), Dimitri Mitropoulos (1949–58), and Leonard Bernstein (1958–69). Bernstein, whose television programs with the Philharmonic are well known, is still associated with the orchestra as Laureate Conductor for life. Since 1971 the orchestra's music director has been Pierre Boulez.

Cleveland Orchestra: Next to the Philadelphia, probably the most consistently polished and technically assured U.S. orchestra. First under Artur Rodzinski (1933–43) and most significantly under George Szell (1946–70), it rose steadily into one of the world's most tightly disciplined, masterful ensembles. Present music director: Lorin Maazel.

The Top European Five

Berlin Philharmonic: Rebuilt since the end of World War II into one of the world's foremost orchestras, first under Wilhelm Furtwängler (also its pre-war director), and then under Herbert von Karajan (1954 to date). Under Karajan it is renowned for its tight discipline, dark-hued tone, and creamily smooth ensemble.

Amsterdam Concertgebouw Orchestra (pronounced, roughly: kawn-*sayrt*-geh-bow, and meaning, in Dutch, "concert house"): Rebuilt since the end of World War II to its former eminence under Eduard van Beinum (1945–59) and Bernard Haitink (1961 to date). An exceptionally mellow-toned, cleanly transparent ensemble, particularly noted for its stylistic tradition in the works of Mahler and Strauss (both former Concertgebouw conductors).

Vienna Philharmonic Orchestra: Long one of Europe's most eminent orchestras, with its members drawn from the two orchestras which play for the Vienna Staatsoper (State Opera) and the Vienna Volksoper (Peoples Opera). Its post-war conductors have included Wilhelm Furtwängler, Karl Böhm, and Herbert von Karajan. Since 1971 its conductor has been Claudio Abbado. Particularly noted for its velvety sound.

London Philharmonic Orchestra: Founded in 1932 by Sir Thomas Beecham, the orchestra has since undergone periods of ups and downs, but entered the 1970's reestablished as one of Europe's best orchestras under principal conductor Bernard Haitink (also conductor of the Amsterdam Concertgebouw). Its former conductors have included Sir Adrian Boult (1950–57) and William Steinberg (1958–60).

London Symphony Orchestra: Like London's Philharmonic, it has had its ups and downs over the years, but in the 1960's and '70's has established itself as one of Europe's most versatile, technically assured ensembles. It is also one of Europe's busiest orchestras, recording background scores for many films. Its former principal conductors have included Pierre Monteux, Istvan Kertesz, and Colin Davis. Present principal conductor: André Previn.

The Runners-Up

The New Philharmonia Orchestra: Reorganized in 1964 after the original Philharmonia Orchestra (founded in 1946) ended its affiliation with EMI, the giant British recording complex for which it served as principal recording orchestra and movie soundtrack orchestra. During the 1950's, the Philharmonia, particularly under Herbert von Karajan, established itself as London's foremost symphony orchestra as well. In the 1960's its principal conductor was Otto Klemperer. Riccardo Muti succeeded him in 1973.

Czech Philharmonic: Once one of Europe's top three or four ensembles, and despite the loss of many members during World War II, and the defection of others after the Communist takeover of Czechoslovakia, it is still a fine orchestra, noted for its stylistic versatility and warm sound. From 1942 to 1948 its conductor was Rafael Kubelik, and then until 1968, Karel Ancerl. Its present conductor is Vaclav Neumann.

Orchestre de Paris: France's newest orchestra, founded in 1968, and heavily subsidized by the French government. It is the first Paris orchestra to give its members year-round contracts (a common U.S. practice), and to demand exclusivity of its members ("orchestra-hopping" and the use of last-minute substitutes has long been a problem plaguing other Parisian orchestras). Its first conductor, Charles Munch, died while leading the orchestra on a U.S. tour in 1969. From 1969 to 1972 its principal conductor was Herbert von Karajan, with Serge Baudo as second conductor. Georg Solti succeeded Karajan in 1972. Daniel Barenboim takes charge in 1975.

Orchestre de la Suisse Romande: Based in Geneva, Switzerland, and dividing its time between radio work and public concerts in French-speaking cantons of Switzerland. Founded in 1918 by Ernest Ansermet, who remained its music director until 1967, the orchestra built an international reputation mainly through Ansermet's recordings. The present principal conductor is Wolfgang Sawallisch.

Israel Philharmonic: Founded as the Palestine Symphony in 1936, its principal conductors over the years have included William Steinberg, Max Goberman, Georg Solti, and Istvan Kertesz. Its first U.S. tour in 1950 was shared by Serge Koussevitzky and Leonard Bernstein. Its present musical adviser is Zubin Mehta.

Pittsburgh Symphony Orchestra: A technically assured, rich-sounding orchestra, first under Fritz Reiner (1940–53) and most recently under its conductor-for-life, William Steinberg (1953 to date).

Minnesota Orchestra: Formerly the Minneapolis Symphony Orchestra, it was renamed in 1968 to acknowledge the broader base of its support and activities. Its technical crispness and mellow tonal qualities have been developed through the years by Eugene Ormandy in the early 1930's, Dimitri Mitropoulos in the 1940's, Antal Dorati in the '50's, and most significantly since 1961 by Stanislaw Skrowaczewski.

Los Angeles Philharmonic: An orchestra that has had its ups and downs over the years (among its former conductors: Otto Klemperer, Artur Rodzinski, Alfred Wallenstein), but has recently moved up strongly under its present music director, Zubin Mehta.

San Francisco Symphony Orchestra: Built into a major ensemble in the 1930's and 1940's by Pierre Monteux, it then foundered for various reasons. Today, under Seiji Ozawa (who took over in 1970) it is moving rapidly to regain its lost stature.

Toronto Symphony Orchestra: Canada's foremost orchestra, for many years (1931–56) led by Sir Ernest Macmillan, and more recently by Seiji Ozawa (1964–68) and Karel Ancerl (1969–73).

There are, of course, many other good orchestras throughout the U.S. which record occasionally. Among them:
American Symphony Orchestra (conductor: Kazuyoshi Akiyama)
Atlanta Symphony Orchestra (conductor: Robert Shaw)
Baltimore Symphony Orchestra (conductor: Sergiu Comissiona)
Buffalo Philharmonic Orchestra (conductor: Michael Tilson Thomas)
Cincinnati Symphony Orchestra (conductor: Thomas Schippers)
Detroit Symphony Orchestra (conductor: Aldo Ceccato)
Houston Symphony Orchestra (conductor: Lawrence Foster)
Indianapolis Symphony Orchestra (conductor: Izler Solomon, retiring 1975)
Louisville Orchestra (conductor: Jorge Mester)
Milwaukee Symphony Orchestra (conductor: Kenneth Schermerhorn)
National Symphony Orchestra of Washington, D.C. (conductor: Antal Dorati)
New Orleans Philharmonic-Symphony (conductor: Werner Torkanowsky)
New Jersey Symphony Orchestra (conductor: Henry Lewis)
Oklahoma City Symphony Orchestra (conductor: Ainslee Cox)
Rochester Philharmonic Orchestra (conductor: David Zinman)
St. Louis Symphony Orchestra (conductor: Georg Semkov)
San Antonio Symphony Orchestra (conductor: Victor Alessandro)
Seattle Symphony Orchestra (conductor: Milton Katims)
Utah Symphony Orchestra (conductor: Maurice Abravanel)

In Europe, there are also a number of major broadcasting orchestras which give public concerts and make recordings. Among them are:
BBC Symphony Orchestra, London (principal conductor: Pierre Boulez)
Berlin Radio Symphony Orchestra (principal conductor: Lorin Maazel)
Bavarian Radio Symphony, Munich (principal conductor: Rafael Kubelik)
SWDR (Sudwest Deutsche Rundfunk) Orchestra, Baden-Baden (conductor: Michael Gielen)
Hessian State Radio Orchestra, Frankfurt (conductor: Dean Dixon)
ORTF Orchestre National, Paris (conductor: Jean Martinon)

Russian orchestras pose a difficult problem in classifying, partly because their names have often been mistranslated on American or Western releases of their recordings, and partly because Soviet recordings made before the 1960's usually were not well-engineered. But on the basis of those orchestras which have toured the U.S. and made good stereo recordings in recent years, the following rank highest:

Leningrad Philharmonic Orchestra (conductor: Yevgeny Mravinsky)
Moscow Philharmonic Orchestra (conductor: Kiril Kondrashin)
Moscow Radio Symphony Orchestra (conductor: Gennady Rozhdestvensky)

About Recording Systems

For the benefit of those starting out collecting records or tapes, a few words are perhaps in order about the various systems by which we can hear recorded music today: discs, cassettes, and cartridges.

Most people know about long-playing records or discs (LP's). These are circular plastic platters, usually 12 inches in diameter, containing tiny grooves (sometimes called microgrooves) into which the musical sounds have been electronically "pressed." Each side of the disc usually holds up to a half hour of music. When the disc revolves on a turntable (usually at $33\frac{1}{3}$ revolutions per minute, although sometimes at 16, 45, or 78 rpm), a sound pick-up device (most commonly called a "needle", but more correctly a "stylus") travels over the record grooves and transmits a sound signal to an amplifier and loudspeaker system.

Today there are three kinds of discs: monaural (mono), stereophonic (stereo), and quadrasonic (sometimes called quadraphonic).

On a mono disc, a single sound signal is printed on the record, to be reproduced through the phonograph system.

On a stereo disc, two sound signals are printed within the channels of the disc, to be reproduced and directed to two different speakers. Stereo discs originated in the mid-1950's. Until that time, all recordings were mono. In recent years, some originally mono recordings have been "doctored" electronically for stereo with varying degrees of success; terms such as "electronically enhanced" or "electronically reprocessed" can usually be found somewhere on the labels. Mono releases began to be phased out in the late 1960's.

In 1972 quadrasonic releases began to be issued by a few companies. On a quadrasonic disc, four sound signals are printed within the channels of the disc, to be reproduced and directed to four different speakers.

Over the years, the sound quality or "fidelity" of commercial disc recordings (first mono, then stereo, now quad) has continued to improve. Sound engineers talk in terms of cycles per second (cps) and frequency range. Whereas the average mono recording of the 1940's could reproduce a frequency range of up to about 10,000 cps, those made in the mid-1950's could reproduce 20,000 or more—going beyond the range of normal human hearing. This was what was meant at that time as high fidelity, or hi-fi.

When stereo appeared in the late 1950's, refinements continued to be made in the frequency-range capacity of discs. But the main advance of stereo engineering was in "spreading" the sound more realistically among the multiple channels, and in reproducing more clearly the sound of individual instruments or voices within the total sound fabric. Thus the listener to a stereo disc could hear the violins of an orchestra coming from the left, the cellos or basses coming from the right, and other instruments from various areas in between, with a realistic approximation of nearness and distance as well. Opera and musical show recordings have particularly benefited from stereo's ability to recreate a feeling of stage movement in sound. Prices of stereo discs have ranged from $2.95 to $6.95.

Whereas a stereo system usually places the speakers to the left and right in front of the listener, a quadrasonic system places speakers both in front and behind the listener, to create a more live, "sound-in-the-round" effect. Prices of quadrasonic discs range from $5.95 to $7.95.

Meanwhile, various tape systems had entered the scene to compete with discs. First, back in the 1950's, there were reel-to-reel tape recordings. Essentially, this involves a 7-inch reel of magnetic tape approximately $\frac{1}{4}$-inch wide, onto which the sounds have been magnetically "printed." To play it, the listener must thread the tape through a playback machine (a tape "deck") onto another reel.

There are various kinds of reel-to-reel tape recordings. Some, for example, are called half-track stereo. This means that the tape contains two channels of recorded sound, each one taking up half the tape's width. Accordingly, the tape may be played in only one direction, and then must be rewound for replaying. Beginning in the late 1950's, quarter-track stereo came into wider use. This involved the use of four channels of recorded sound across the surface of the tape, with each channel taking up a quarter of the tape's width. The playback "head" is so arranged that the sound in channels 1 and 3 goes in one direction, and the sound in channels 2 and 4 in the other. The tape can be played in both directions, merely by turning over the reels, just as one turns over a disc. This, in effect, doubles the playing time of quarter-track tapes as compared with half-track tapes.

The playing time, moreover, depends on the speed at which the tape runs through the playback machine. At first, most commercial tapes were recorded at a speed of $7\frac{1}{2}$ inches per second (ips). But by the mid-1960's, a speed of $3\frac{3}{4}$ ips had become more widely accepted, even though most manufacturers at first admitted that the slower tape speed was likely to reproduce a poorer frequency range. By the early 1970's the frequency range of $3\frac{3}{4}$-ips tapes had been significantly improved by the major recording companies.

Despite claims that tapes offered superior fidelity (especially at $7\frac{1}{2}$ ips) and longer wear than discs, reel-to-reel tape failed to catch on with the public, or to seriously challenge discs among buyers of recorded music. Reel-to-reel tape did, however, become popular among an active minority of music lovers for home-recording of FM broadcasts of concert and opera performances not otherwise available on commercial recordings.

What really did make a dent in disc sales, however, was the introduction of tape cartridges in the early 1960's and tape cassettes in the late 1960's. Both are much easier to handle than reel-to-reel tapes, and lessen the likelihood that the user will become helplessly entangled in yards of loose or broken tape. There is also no complicated threading necessary—the cartridge or cassette just snaps into a playback machine and plays.

The cartridge started out as a system for automobiles, and caught on to such a degree that, by 1966, dashboard-model cartridge players were being offered along with radios as optional equipment on all Detroit-manufactured cars. The cartridge players allowed drivers and their passengers to hear their own choice of music—and the sound output remained constant, without fading in and out the way radios do because of geographic range, atmospheric conditions, interference of bridges, tunnels, etc. As cartridges for automobiles flourished, home cartridge players were also introduced.

The cartridge itself is a plastic container about the size of a paperback book. It contains a continuous coil or loop of tape (approximately $\frac{1}{4}$-inch wide) that automatically starts rolling at a speed of $3\frac{3}{4}$ ips when the cartridge is inserted in the playback slot—and will repeat the program continuously until the cartridge is removed.

There are two kinds of cartridges: 4-track and 8-track, with the latter now much more widely accepted. The basic difference between them is in the arrangement of their sound tracks or channels. The 4-track system has two pairs of stereo tracks on the tape loop. As the tape rolls, the playback "head" first plays that part of the program that is on tracks 1 and 3. Then the playback "head" is shifted (usually automatically) to play the second half of the program on tracks 2 and 4. The 8-track system has four pairs of stereo tracks on its tape loop. The playback "head" first plays tracks 1 and 5, then 2 and 6, and so on. Because of the continuous loop system, the tracks on both 4-track and 8-track tapes are all recorded in the same direction, with 4-track cartridges holding up to about forty minutes of music, 8-track cartridges up to eighty minutes. Cartridges range in price from $2.95 to $9.95, depending on the amount of music contained and the nature of the selection.

One of the drawbacks of the cartridge system is the fact that all the tracks must be the same length. Thus track-shifting often occurs at unnatural places in the music—a throwback to the old 78-rpm days of shellac discs when side "breaks" frequently came in the middle of symphonic movements or any longer selection. Furthermore, cartridge players are not equipped with rewind or fast-forward capabilities (although several manufacturers, including Lear-Jet, report they are working on such a system and hope to have it available by the mid-1970's). Therefore, if you stop a piece of music midway through, you must begin at that same midway spot the next time you play the same cartridge.

Cartridges do not as yet offer as much fidelity as either stereo discs or reel-to-reel tapes. Still, the sound can be genuinely impressive, especially in the relatively confined space of an automobile. Tape hiss can be high, but not intolerably so. Flutter (a wavering of sound) can be a risk, especially on piano recordings, because of the slow speed. With 8-track cartridges there also seems to be a bit more of a problem with "crosstalk" (sounds from one track occasionally leaking into a neighboring track) than with 4-track systems.

The cassette system had already made a big impact in Western Europe (where Philips, the giant Dutch electrical complex developed it) before it started catching on in the U.S. in 1970. The cassette itself is a small plastic box, roughly the size of a pack of cigarettes, which encases two tiny reels through which the tape (about $\frac{1}{7}$-inch wide) is automatically wound, running at a speed of $1\frac{7}{8}$ ips. The cassette's tape tracks run in two directions, like quarter-track reel-to-reel tapes. When the tape comes to the end of a reel, the cassette is removed, flipped over, and reinserted into the playback machine to play the cassette's "second side." Most cassettes can also be fast-wound forward or backward for playback of selected portions of the tape. Cassettes range in price from $2.95 to $7.95, depending on the amount of music and nature of the selection.

As for fidelity, cassettes, like cartridges, cannot yet offer as much as either stereo discs or reel-to-reel tapes. And they are highly subject to high tape hiss and flutter. Yet they are surprisingly impressive, considering their narrow track width. They have a frequency response of about 10,000 cps and are getting better each year. Industry spokesmen eagerly point out that newly developed chromium dioxide tape will roughly double—at any speed—the frequency response of today's standard iron oxide tapes. In other words, by the mid-1970's, the frequency response of cassette tapes should be 20,000 cps, equal to that of the best stereo discs.

Also on the horizon for cassettes: A reject button that would interrupt a selection being played and swiftly advance the tape to the next selection, and a standardized index counter on both the cassette and the playback machine. With this device a listener can know exactly where each new selection begins just as he can now tell by the separate bands on a disc.

The biggest advantage of cassettes is their compactness—four cassettes will fit into one cartridge box. Some recording industry spokesmen predict that, because of this, cassettes may have the same kind of impact on record sales as paperback books have had on book sales—not because the cost is lower, but because they are easier for dealers to stock and for consumers to store at home.

One aspect of the cassette boom has the record industry nervous, however. Some manufacturers of cassette machines have equipped them with recording devices. By simply plugging wires into a radio or phonograph, a listener can record music off-the-air or copy it from records onto a blank cassette tape. This do-it-yourself reproduction, it is feared, could cut into sales of pre-recorded discs or tapes disastrously. Warns RCA executive Norman Racusin: "The very existence of the music industry itself may be in jeopardy. Where will the music come from if those who write, publish, perform, produce, and market it are deprived of their income and royalties from recordings? The consumer's monetary saving would be short-lived indeed."

There are some, however, who believe that any initial enthusiasm for do-it-yourself copying via cassette will decline—just as off-the-air taping of records did in the early days of reel-to-reel tape. Most listeners soon discover that their copy just isn't as good as the commercially manufactured product—unless they have the most expensive equipment, which few do. Furthermore, if the price of commercial cassettes is kept competitive with the price of blank tape, the need to copy becomes pointless.

Meanwhile, thousands and thousands of recordings of great music *are* being made available commercially on discs, cartridges, and cassettes—beckoning for listeners to discover them and enjoy them. No generation of music lovers has ever had it so good.

Glossary

absolute music Usually instrumental music which is free from extramusical implications, in distinction from *program music.*

abstract music Same as absolute music.

a cappella (Italian) Choral music performed without instrumental accompaniment.

accelerando (Italian) A speeding up of the tempo.

accompaniment The musical background, especially for a soloist. For example, a solo singer or instrumentalist may be accompanied by a pianist or orchestra. However, in piano music the left hand often plays chords which provide an accompaniment to the principal melody being played by the right hand.

adagietto (Italian) A tempo slightly faster than *adagio.* Also a brief *adagio.*

adagio (Italian) A slow and easy tempo, between *andante* and *largo.* In most traditional symphonies and sonatas, it is the second movement.

agitato (Italian) Agitated, restless, excited.

air In Baroque music, a song or movement of an essentially melodic character, in contrast to the dancelike style of other movements.

allegretto (Italian) A moderately lively tempo between *allegro* and *andante.*

allegro (Italian) A fast tempo, but not as fast as *presto.*

andante (Italian) Usually considered a moderately slow tempo. Literally, the word means "walking" or "going" at a moderate speed. Some composers (including Brahms) have interpreted the word, however, as meaning considerably faster than *adagio* but not so fast as *allegretto.*

aria (Italian) An elaborate song for voice (usually solo voice). In opera, arias are frequently designed to show off the virtuosity of a singer.

arrangement The adaptation of a piece of music into a form or medium different from the one for which it was originally written. See also *transcription.*

assai (Italian) Very. For example, *allegro assai* means very fast.

atonal Music in which a tonal center or key is purposely avoided. Usually used in connection with a certain type of twentieth-century music originating with Schoenberg, although he objected to the term and preferred to call his music *pan-tonal.*

ballad A narrative song, usually telling of a romantic or adventurous occurence.

ballade (French) An instrumental work based on a specific or implied narrative. As used by Chopin, Brahms, and some others, a dramatic piano piece. Although the word is strictly the French word for *ballad,* the word *ballad* is commonly used in English only for a vocal work whereas *ballade* is used for an instrumental piece of the same type.

band On recorded discs, a section of the record separated from other sections. In popular music an instrumental combo of ten or more players is called a band. An orchestra without strings is also called a band.

baritone (Greek) Literally, low sound. A male voice between *tenor* and *bass.*

Baroque In music, the period from about 1600 to 1750. Usually it is used to describe elegantly controlled yet twistingly fashioned music, with an interplay of formal structure and more spontaneous, virtuoso flights of fancy (as in the free *cadenza* of an aria, or the embellished repeats of an instrumental movement).

bass The lowest male voice. Also the colloquial name for the *double bass,* largest of an orchestra's string instruments.

357

baton (French) The thin, white stick used by a conductor in leading an orchestra or instrumental ensemble.

bel canto (Italian) Literally, beautiful song. An Italian vocal style developed during the eighteenth century, characterized by beauty of sound and the ease and brilliance of performance rather than by dramatic or emotional expression.

bitonal The simultaneous use of two different keys in a musical work.

blues A style of vocal and instrumental jazz, deriving from Negro American work songs and *spirituals* of the early twentieth century. Usually (but not always) slow and basically sad in mood. The name is related to the so-called blue notes of the piece which are either deliberately flatted or played out of tune.

bravo (Italian) A term used to express approval of a musical performance. When the performer is female, the feminine form *brava* is usually used.

bravura (Italian) A florid, brilliant style.

brio (Italian) Spirit, dash.

buffa, buffo (Italian) Comic. Usually used to refer to a comic character (most often sung by a bass) in Italian opera. *Opera buffa* is a comic opera.

cacophony A discordant mixture of different sounds.

cadenza (Italian) A solo vocal or instrumental section of a piece, usually intended to display the soloist's technical mastery. Originally, cadenzas were improvised by the performer. But in the nineteenth century it became customary for the composer to write out the cadenza and make it an integral part of the style of the piece.

cantata (Italian) An extended choral work, with or without solo parts, and usually with orchestral accompaniment. The *Baroque* cantata normally consisted of a number of movements and included *arias, recitatives, duets,* and *choruses.*

cappella See *a cappella.*

capriccio (Italian) A composition of a basically capricious or amusing character.

cavatina (Italian) A simple or short solo song, lacking the elaborate form or development found in an *aria.* Usually found in eighteenth- or nineteenth-century oratorios or operas.

chamber music Instrumental music in which there is usually only one player for each instrumental part, in contrast to orchestral music in which many players play the same instrumental part. A *chamber orchestra* normally consists of about twenty-five members, in contrast to the eighty or more players of a symphony orchestra.

choral Relating to a chorus or choir.

chord The simultaneous sounding of three or more notes or tones.

chorus Usually a large group of singers. Also the colloquial term for the *refrain* of a popular song.

chromatic (from the Greek *chroma,* color) In music, a style identified with some twentieth-century composers, and involving the use of half tones and notes outside the normal degrees of the traditional scale. However, use of the term goes back to *Baroque* music, where it involved the use of altered chords to produce "color modification" in a piece.

classical In everyday usage, the term usually means most music outside the fields of popular music or jazz. Among musicians, however, it is more strictly applied to music written in the eighteenth century, especially by the Viennese "classicists" (Haydn, Mozart, and early Beethoven), and marked by a compactness of form and emotional restraint (in contrast to the Romanticism of the nineteenth century).

clavichord The earliest type of stringed keyboard instrument, originating in the thirteenth century and commonly used until the eighteenth as a solo instrument. The sound of the clavichord was very soft and delicate, in contrast to the sharper sound of the harpsichord and the more brilliant sound of later pianos.

clavier The keyboard of a harpsichord, clavichord, or piano.

coda A section or passage at the end of a composition, usually falling outside the basic structure of the composition, designed to heighten the feeling of finality.

coloratura Usually applied to a light, agile, florid style of singing.

Concertgebouw (Dutch) Literally, concert hall. Most commonly known as the name of an Amsterdam concert hall opened in 1888, and of its world-famous resident orchestra.

concertmaster The first violinist of an orchestra. In England, he is called the *leader*.

concerto Usually a piece for a solo instrument accompanied by an orchestra.

concerto grosso A type of work popular in the seventeenth and eighteenth centuries, usually (but not always) marked by an interplay between a large group of instruments and a smaller group.

counterpoint The combination of two or more melodies sounding simultaneously and in a specific relationship to each other.

countertenor An adult male voice higher than a tenor.

crescendo (Italian) Increasing in loudness.

decibel A unit for measuring the loudness of sounds.

diminuendo (Italian) Diminishing or decreasing in loudness.

divertimento (Italian) A work for a small instrumental group combining features of a suite and symphony, popular in Haydn's and Mozart's time.

dodecaphonic (from the Greek *dodeka,* twelve) The twelve-tone technique of composition.

double bass The largest of the string instruments of the orchestra. Also sometimes called the bass viol.

duet A vocal or instrumental composition for two performers.

exposition The initial presentation of thematic material in a composition, particularly in a *sonata* or *symphony*.

expressionism A term applied to a certain type of musical composition of the early twentieth century, particularly by German and Austrian composers. Like *impressionism,* it took its name from the graphic arts and represented a reaction against the refined impressionistic style. Instead, expressionism was marked by fervent emotionalism and self-expression.

fioritura The embellishment of a melody, particularly in vocal music of the seventeenth and eighteenth centuries.

forte (Italian) Loud.

fortissimo (Italian) Very loud.

fugue (from the Latin *fuga,* flight). A type of composition in which a theme (subject) is stated at the beginning in one voice part, and then is imitated by other voices in close succession according to strict compositional rules.

Gregorian chant The liturgical music (plainsong) of the Roman Catholic Church, named after Pope Gregory I (590–604).

harpsichord The most common type of stringed keyboard instrument of the sixteenth to eighteenth centuries, similar in shape to a piano but less brilliant and varied in sound.

heldentenor (German) A male tenor voice of great strength and brilliance, appropriate for the heroic roles of Wagnerian opera.

impressionism A term applied to a certain type of musical composition of the early twentieth century, represented mainly by French composers (especially Debussy). It took its name from the graphic arts, particularly the paintings of Monet, Manet, and Renoir, and represented a reaction against nineteenth-century Romanticism. Musically, it is a style that hints and implies rather than explicitly describing.

improvisation The spontaneous creation of music while performing, rather than playing a composition already written.

key The classification of the notes of the musical scale. Also, in tonal music, the main note or tonal center of a composition.

largo (Italian) Very slow. Slower than *adagio*. A *larghetto* is slightly faster than largo.

leader In British usage, the equivalent of *concertmaster* of an orchestra.

leitmotiv (German) In Wagnerian opera, a short theme identified with a specific character, place, object, or situation throughout the opera.

libretto (Italian) The text of an opera or oratorio.

lied, lieder (German) A form of German art song, particularly the nineteenth century songs of Schubert, Schumann, Brahms, Strauss, etc.

madrigal A type of vocal composition prevalent in the sixteenth century, of Italian origin but also popular in England, and secular in content.

maestro (Italian) Literally, master. An unofficial name used for the most distinguished and most respected conductors, composers, and music teachers.

major, minor Terms used for the two basic scales of music.

mass The principal service of the Roman Catholic Church. In music, the musical setting of that service.

mazurka A Polish dance of moderate speed.

melody A succession of musical notes forming a line of expressive significance.

meter The basic grouping of beats and accents in a musical composition or section of a composition. Sometimes called *time*. For example, the meter (or time) of a piece may be 3/4, 4/4, 3/8, 6/8, etc., indicating the number of beats in each measure or time signature.

mezzo-soprano (from the Italian *mezzo*, half) A type of female voice halfway between soprano and contralto.

microtone A fractional tone, used by some twentieth-century composers.

minor See *major*.

moderato (Italian) At a moderate speed. For example, *allegro moderato* is somewhat less fast than *allegro*.

modulation The change of *key* within a composition.

monaural Commonly used to describe the type of record or tape in which a single sound signal is printed on the record or tape to be reproduced through the sound system, in contrast to a *stereophonic* or *quadrasonic* recording. Nicknamed *mono*.

monophonic The oldest type of music, basically music of a single melodic line without accompanying chords. In recent years, the term has also been used to describe phonograph systems made before the 1950s, in which a single sound signal reproduces the music (in contrast to a *stereophonic* system).

movement The term for the single pieces which make up a composite musical work such as a *symphony, concerto,* or *sonata*.

mute A device used for softening the sound of a musical instrument.

nationalism In music, the movement of the nineteenth century which emphasized the development of strong national elements (especially folk elements) in composition, or the use of national history or legends in operas, songs, etc.

neoclassical A type of music written in the twentieth century in reaction against Romanticism. It is basically characterized by an emphasis on musical forms derived from the pre-Romantic period, but is frequently more rhythmically and harmonically complex.

nocturne A type of piece of lyrical mood, designed to reflect the feelings of night. First used by Irish composer John Field (1782–1837), but most closely identified with works of that name by Chopin.

nonet A composition for nine instruments or nine voices.

note A musical sound of a specific pitch and duration.

note-cluster A group of adjacent notes played or sounded together, used in some twentieth-century compositions, particularly by Ives.

obbligato (Italian) Literally, a part that is obligatory and cannot be omitted in the performance of a piece. However, the term has somehow come to mean just the opposite in everyday usage—in other words, it usually refers to an optional part, *not* an obligatory one.

octave The range of musical sounds divided into eight (octo in Latin) steps. Notes that are an octave apart from each other have the same letter-names.

octet A composition for eight instruments or eight voices.

ondes martenot (French) An electronic keyboard instrument invented in 1928 by Maurice Martenot, and used in compositions by Messiaen, Honegger, Jolivet, and some other contemporary composers.

opera A type of play or drama in which all or most of the characters sing to the accompaniment of an orchestra.

opus (Latin) A term used to signify the compositional number of a work by a composer. Usually abbreviated *op.*

oratorio A type of musical composition for solo voices, chorus, and orchestra, usually based on a religious text and performed on a concert stage without costumes or scenery.

orchestra A large body of instrumentalists. The modern symphony orchestra consists of 80 to 100 players, divided into four basic sections: strings, winds, brass, and percussion. Chamber orchestras usually consist of about 25 players.

orchestration The writing or scoring of a work for orchestra.

overture Instrumental music composed as an introduction to an opera, oratorio, or other work.

pan-tonal See *atonal.*

paraphrase In music, a free modification or adaptation of a composition, as in Liszt's paraphrases for piano of music from Wagner's operas.

partita A type of *suite,* particularly of the eighteenth century.

passacaglia A type of composition (originally a dance) involving continuous variations of a short theme, particularly in Baroque music.

Passion A musical setting of the story of the Crucifixion as told by St. Matthew, St. Mark, St. Luke, or St. John.

percussion The collective name for those instruments whose sound is made by having a resonating surface struck by the player. Examples: drums, xylophone, triangle, tambourine.

pianissimo (Italian) Very soft.

piano (Italian) Soft. Also commonly used instead of *pianforte,* the correct name for the popular keyboard instrument first built in the early eighteenth century and which eventually displaced the harpsichord.

pizzicato (Italian) The plucking of the strings of an instrument rather than bowing them.

plainchant or **plainsong** A type of early church music consisting of a single vocal line, usually without accompaniment. See also *Gregorian chant.*

poco (Latin) Slightly. For example, *poco adagio* means slightly slow.

polka A dance in quick meter originating in Bohemia (not Poland as commonly misunderstood).

polonaise A stately Polish dance dating from the sixteenth century.

polyphonic Literally, the simultaneous sounding of different notes. Music is considered polyphonic if it consists of two or more parts having individual melodic significance. Accordingly, in general usage, music is considered polyphonic if it has *counterpoint.*

polyrhythm The simultaneous use of different rhythms in a passage or piece.

polytonality The simultaneous sounding of different tonalities or keys in a passage or piece. Where only two keys are used simultaneously, the correct term is *bitonal*; much of the twentieth-century music that is called polytonal is really bitonal.

postlude A piece played at the conclusion of

a church service or program. The opposite of *prelude,* but much less commonly used.

potpourri (French) A loosely strung together collection of pieces with little formal relationship between them. In general usage, it refers to a collection of light, entertaining pieces.

prelude Literally, a piece preceding something—as the prelude (or introduction) to an opera.

presto (Italian) Very fast. A variation, *prestissimo,* means as fast as possible.

prima donna (Italian) Originally, the singer of the leading female role in eighteenth-century Italian opera. In general usage, it also means any leading female opera star.

Prix de Rome (French) A famous prize awarded annually by the French Academy of Fine Arts (of Paris) on the basis of a music competition. The prize entitles the winner to study in Rome. Among the winners have been Berlioz (1830), Bizet (1857), and Debussy (1884).

program music A piece of music interpreting a specific story or extramusical idea. The *program* may be based on literature (example: Liszt's *Faust Symphony*), on history (Tchaikovsky's *1812 Overture*), or the composer's own imagination (Berlioz's *Symphonie Fantastique*).

progressive tonality The beginning of a movement in one key and moving it systematically to an ending in another key, particularly as used by Mahler.

quadrasonic The term used to describe the four-channel system of sound reproduction (in contrast to *monaural* or *stereophonic*) developed in the early 1970s. The system involves the use of four loudspeakers to "stretch" the sound in a 360° relationship around the listener.

quartet A composition for four instruments or four voices.

quasi (Italian) Almost or approximating. For example, *allegro quasi presto* means "allegro almost presto."

quintet A composition for five instruments or five voices.

ragtime A type of early jazz of the late nineteenth and early twentieth century, characterized by the constant syncopation ("ragging") of a tune.

recorder A type of reedless woodwind instrument much used from the sixteenth to eighteenth century.

recital A public performance by a solosit, in contrast to that given by an orchestra or ensemble which is called a concert.

recitative A type of speechlike singing, usually to a simple accompaniment, used for some narrative episodes in operas, oratorios, and cantatas.

refrain The part of a song that recurs at the end of each stanza, usually using the same words as well as the same tune.

Renaissance (French) The period of history roughly from 1400 to 1600, or between the Middle Ages and the Baroque period.

Requiem The mass for the dead in the Roman Catholic Church, which begins with the Latin words "requiem aeternam dona eis, Domine" (Give them eternal rest, O Lord).

rhapsody A musical work freely adapted from or inspired by an existing theme, as in Liszt's *Hungarian Rhapsodies* (freely based on Hungarian gypsy music), or a freely formed, improvisationlike work, as in Gershwin's *Rhapsody in Blue.*

rhythm The time value of a sequence of notes.

ripieno (Italian) In Baroque music, an indication for the full orchestra as distinct from the solo group (marked *concertino*).

ritardando (Italian) A gradual slackening of speed.

Romantic, Romanticism In common usage, the type of music developed in the nineteenth century characterized by the development of more emotional and subjective elements than the preceding *Classical* style.

rondo (Italian) A type of movement in a sonata or symphony, common in the time of

Mozart and Beethoven, in which the principal theme recurs at least three times, with contrasting themes (called episodes) in between.

saraband   A slow, stately dance originating in Spain in the sixteenth century.

scale   A progression or succession of musical notes arranged in ascending or descending order, usually a whole tone or half tone apart.

scherzo   (Italian, literally *joke*) A type of lively movement in a symphony, sonata, string quartet, etc., usually the third movement, sometimes humorous or playful in mood but not necessarily so.

score   The printed manuscript of a musical work.

septet   A composition for seven instruments or seven voices.

serial music   A style of composition used by some twentieth-century composers, originating with Schoenberg, in which the composition is based on a so-called series or tone-row in which the notes are placed in a particular order as the basis of the work, with no note repeated in the row. See also *dodecaphonic*.

sextet   A composition for six instruments or six voices.

signature   In music, a sign placed at the beginning of a piece indicating the *key* (key signature) and the *meter* (time signature).

sinfonietta   A short *symphony*, usually for a chamber orchestra.

solo   A piece or passage performed by one performer (soloist), with or without accompaniment. For example, in a *concerto* a soloist plays the solo part (for piano, violin, or other instrument) while the orchestra plays the accompaniment.

sonata   (Italian) A form of instrumental music, usually in three or four *movements*, following certain conventions of structure (called sonata form), and originating in the *Baroque* period. A *symphony* is a development of the sonata for orchestra.

song cycle   A group of songs connected by one general idea and designed to be performed as a unit.

soprano   (Italian for upper) The highest female voice. Sopranos are usually classified as dramatic, lyric, or *coloratura,* depending on tone quality and range. In children's choruses, a *boy soprano* is one with a high voice approximating the highest female voice.

spiritual   A type of religious folk song among black Americans.

sprechstimme   (German) A vocal line that is half sung, half spoken, particularly as used in some twentieth-century works by Schoenberg, Berg, and others.

suite   A form of instrumental music, originating with the Baroque, involving a number of different movements based on dance rhythms and not written in *sonata* form. In modern usage, suites are most often excerpts from ballets or other stage music arranged for concert performance.

symphonic poem   A term introduced by Liszt to describe an orchestral work in which an extramusical idea (for example, a literary idea) provides the basis for the composition and the form of its development.

symphony   (From the Greek for sounding together) One of the major forms of orchestral music. Essentially a *sonata* for orchestra. Originally, a symphony was an overture to an opera. But since Haydn's time it has indicated a serious orchestral work of substantial length, usually with three or four contrasting movements. A *symphony orchestra* is an orchestra large enough (usually eighty or more members) to play major symphonies.

tempo   (Italian for time) The pace of a piece, or rate of speed at which it is to be played.

theme   A grouping of notes or musical subject which forms an important and often recurring element in a piece of music.

tone poem   A variation of *symphonic poem.*

tone row   See *serial music.*

transcription   Essentially the same as an *ar-*

rangement, but often with extensive changes of the original material.

trio A composition for three instruments or three voices.

tune In common usage, a simple and easily remembered melody. Also a term referring to the singing or playing of a piece in the proper pitch, as "in tune" or "out of tune."

twelve-tone music See *dodecaphonic* and *serial music.*

variations A musical form in which a *theme* is presented and then altered and developed in a series of varied versions (variations).

verismo (Italian) A type of opera developed in Italy in the late nineteenth century, particularly by Puccini and Mascagni, with emphasis on realistic drama from everyday life, rather than on heroic, mythological, or romantic librettos.

vibrato In violin or string playing, the minute, rapid fluctuation of pitch produced by a kind of shaking motion on the part of the player's hand. In singing, the slight wavering of pitch sometimes cultivated by singers for dramatic effect, or sometimes caused by lack of full vocal control (in which case it is often deridingly termed a wobble).

virginal A type of sixteenth-century harpsichord, used mainly in England.

virtuoso Excelling in technical ability (when used with a performer) or in technical demands (when used with a piece of music).

vivace (Italian) Quick, lively.

zarzuela A type of Spanish opera, usually containing spoken dialogue as well as musical *arias.*

Index

References to interviews with people and major discussions of their work, either as a composer or performer, appear in boldface type.

Index • 373

Milnes, Sherrill, 41, 98, 129, 130, 131, 264, **321**

Milstein, Nathan, **324**

Milwaukee Symphony Orchestra, 351

Minneapolis Symphony Orchestra, 105, 293, 324, 327, 336. *See also* Minnesota Orchestra

Minnesota Orchestra, 54, 336, 350

Minton Yvonne, 78, 91, 93, 98, 181, 182, 186, 190, 191, 248, 249

Mitropoulos, Dimitri, 177, 223, 241, **324**, 349, 350

Mitropoulos International Conductors Competition, 292

Moffo, Anna, **43**, 91, 173, 174, 268, **324**, 325

Monteux, Pierre, 133, 134, 141, 143, 185, 218, **325**, 339, 349, 351

Monte Carlo Opera Orchestra, 232, 234

Monteverdi, Claudio, 9, 14, 39, 41, 56, 70, **71–74**, 160, 161, 314

Moog synthesizer, 10, 11, 31, 56, 58, 84

Moore, Grace, 308

Moravec, Ivan, 116

Morel, Jean, 314

Morgenstern, Sheldon, **43–44**

Mormon Tabernacle Choir, 169, 194

Moscow Philharmonic Orchestra, 201, 226, 239, 241, 310, 332, 351

Moscow Radio Symphony Orchestra, 163, 227, 333, 351

Moscow Symphony Orchestra, 146

Mozart, Leopold, 88, 89

Mozart, Wolfgang Amadeus, 3, 5, 6, 7, 8, 9, 11, 17, 18, 19, 20, 21, 24, 25, 26, 28, 29, 31, 36, 38, 39, 41, 43, 44, 46, 48, 50, 51, 54, 59, 61, 64, 86, **88–94**, 96, 106, 114, 144, 150, 227, 276, 278, 279, 283, 291, 292, 294, 298, 301, 302, 309, 317, 329, 332, 334, 335, 340, 347

Mozarteum, Salzburg, 278

Mravinsky, Yevgeny, 351

Munch, Charles, 35, 36, 101, 104, 106, 107, 108, 109, 110, 111, 112, 115, 134, 145, 149, 159, 160, 161, 184, 185, 186, 188, 199, 200, 208, 209, 210, 231, 265, 279, 316, **325**, 327, 348, 350

Munich Bach Orchestra, 81, 83

Munich Opera, 291, 344, 347

Munich Philharmonic Orchestra, 168

Munich Radio Orchestra. *See* Bavarian Radio Orchestra

Mussorgsky, Modest, 3, 62, 106, **151–55**, 162, 211, 217, 259, 260, 287, 301, 316, 332

Muti, Riccardo, **325–26**, 350

Nabokov, Nicholas, 215

Nash, Ogden, 147, 230

National Symphony Orchestra, Washington, D.C., 293, 351

NBC Opera, 263

NBC Symphony Orchestra, 30, 95, 96, 97, 98, 108, 125, 141, 143, 149, 153, 156, 165, 173, 188, 266, 277, 286, 293, 317, 332, 338, 343, 346. *See also* Symphony of the Air

Netherlands Opera, 292

Netherlands Radio Orchestra, 303

Netherlands Wind Ensemble, 292

Neuhaus, Rudolf, 190

Neumann, Vaclav, 136, 225, 245, 350

New England Conservatory, 51, 98, 108, 110, 186, 209, 220

New Haven Symphony Orchestra, 178, 179, 348

New Jersey Symphony Orchestra, 316, 351

Newman, Ernest, 126, 224

New Philharmonia Orchestra, London, 92, 99, 101, 104, 131, 149, 152, 163, 181, 184, 185, 186, 208, 216, 219, 245, 265, 276, 309, 319, 326, **350**

New Symphony Orchestra, London, 82, 115, 280

New York City Ballet, 82, 220, 221, 237

New York City Opera, 44, 79, 223, 293, 308, 313, 321, 334, 335, 339

New York City Symphony Orchestra, 339

New York Philharmonic Orchestra, 8, 19, 20, 25, 32, 56, 60, 75, 85, 86, 95, 96, 97, 99, 100, 104, 108, 109, 111, 112, 118, 121, 126, 134, 142, 143, 145, 146, 149, 150, 155, 159, 161, 162, 165, 166, 169, 177, 179, 180, 182, 184, 189, 190, 200, 205, 206, 207, 208, 213, 214, 217, 218, 219, 225, 227, 228, 229, 230, 234, 235, 236, 237, 239, 240, 241, 244, 246, 247, 255, 259, 262, 273, 278, 282, 283, 287, 293, 300, 303, 309, 311, 324, 332, 338, 340, 341, 343, 344, 346, **349**

Nikisch, Artur, 311

Nilsson, Birgit, 92, 126, 127, 128, 176, 192, 278, **326**